The Sum of the Satisfactions

The
Sum
of the
Satisfactions

Canada in the Age of National Accounting

Duncan McDowall

McGILL-QUEEN'S UNIVERSITY PRESS | Montreal & Kingston · London · Ithaca

© McGill-Queen's University Press 2008

ISBN 978-0-7735-3288-5

Legal deposit third quarter 2008
Bibliothèque nationale du Québec

Printed in Canada on acid-free paper that is 100% ancient forest free
(100% post-consumer recycled), processed chlorine free.

This book is also available in French under the title *La Somme des
satisfactions – Le Canada à l'ère des comptes nationaux*.

McGill-Queen's University Press acknowledges the support of the Canada
Council for the Arts for our publishing program. We also acknowledge
the financial support of the Government of Canada through the Book
Publishing Industry Development Program (BPIDP) for our publishing
activities.

Library and Archives Canada Cataloguing in Publication

McDowall, Duncan, 1949–
The sum of the satisfactions : Canada in the age of national accounting /
Duncan McDowall.

Includes bibliographical references and index.
ISBN 978-0-7735-3288-5

1. National income—Canada—Accounting—History. I. Title.

HC120.I5M32 2007   339.37109   C2007-904502-2

This book was designed and typeset by studio oneonone in Sabon 10/13

For George Luxton, Agatha Chapman,
and all those who followed

Contents

Acknowledgments

I approached this assignment with trepidation. Like many people, I had always regarded statistical matters with considerable apprehension. An "artsie" in university, I gave statistics courses the widest possible berth. My tax returns always came back to me citing, as Revenue Canada politely put it, "an error on my part." Therefore, the notion of writing a book on the concept of national income – a complex statistical *system* – seemed daunting. The entry on national income in *The New Palgrave: A Dictionary of Economics*, perhaps the most authoritative font of economic information for the layman, offered little encouragement. The first sentence of its long entry on *national income* began with the phrase: "Although there are numerous complexities and ambiguities attached to this concept ..." A search of the library revealed that few other historians had tackled the problem. Americans like John Kendrick and Nancy and Richard Ruggles had provided their national perspective, as had André Vanoli in France. But on the whole, national accountants seemed to be a shy lot. "All in all," Vanoli has noted, "national account compilers write little, unlike scholars and researchers whose careers often depend on publications."[1]

That this book came to be written at all is firstly a testament to the convictions of the members of the National Accounts Advisory Committee, a panel of eminent economists drawn from universities, government, and private practice that connects Statistics Canada's national accounting with the society it serves. The committee's belief that Canada's national accountants had hidden their light under a bushel prompted it to seek an outside historian to write a book on Canada in the age of national accounting. Canadians, they believed, needed to be shown how the national accounts had become woven into their economic lives. I was won over by their fervour. Throughout my research and writing, the committee members were supportive in every way as interview subjects, sounding boards, and conscripted audiences. They are Tom Wilson (chair), John Grant, Mike McCracken, Stewart Wells, Agathe Côté, Steven James, Alice Nakamura, Anthony Scott, Richard Lipsey, Doug May, France St-Hilaire, Steven Landefeld, Peter Victor, Mary Webb, Nancy Olewiler, and Robert Parker.

Statistics Canada obliged the instincts of the advisory committee by appointing me a senior research fellow from 2004 to 2006. Philip Smith, the assistant chief statistician for National Accounts and Analytical Studies, facilitated my research in every way and ensured that all doors were open to me in the agency. Philip's quiet professionalism and active interest in the project sustained me throughout. This support was evident everywhere I turned at Statistics Canada. Ivan Fellegi, Canada's chief statistician, lent the valuable perspectives that fifty years of public service have given him. Karen Wilson, director general of Canada's System of National Accounts (SNA), provided a valuable link to the system's day-to-day operation and to its international affiliations. Other Statistics Canada directors and managers always lent their time and expertise to my often naive questions. Among them are Roger Jullion, Pat O'Hagan, Michel Pascal, Jim Tebrake, Chris Jackson, Yusuf Siddiqi, Joe Wilkinson, Hans Messinger, Michel Girard, Robert Smith, Art Ridgeway, Ian Macredie, Leroy Stone, John Baldwin, and Tarek Harchaoui. Philip Cross, the editor of the *Canadian Economic Observer*, gave freely of his worldly and often contrarian view of economics. So many others at Statistics Canada helped me on my way: Bonnie Bercik, Susan Storey, Hasheem Nouroz, Harpreet Kaur Randhawa, Kazi Islam, Frank Chow, Guy Gellatly, Desmond Beckstead, Francine Roy, David Pringle, Erika Young, and Mark Brown. Steve Romer applied his wizardry to my computer. Brenda Etchells and Anita Choquette responded to all my administrative needs with friendliness and efficiency. Jennifer Pagnotta and Volodymyr Rebinczak ministered to my every request in Statistics Canada's superb library. To all and sundry at Statistics Canada, thank you for making me feel at home.

Archival research provided the backbone of my analysis of the early decades of national accounting in Canada. Many hours were spent working through the Dominion Bureau of Statistics and Statistics Canada collection at Library and Archives Canada in Ottawa. As usual, the service there was excellent. Special thanks are due reference archivist extraordinaire Bill Russell. Similar thanks go out to Queen's University Archives (Paul Banfield, in particular), McGill University Archives, University of Toronto Archives, University of British Columbia Archives,

Bank of Canada Archives (especially Jane Boyko), Royal Financial Group Archives, Harvard University Archives, and the Archives of King's College, Cambridge.

Interviews were an indispensable facet of the entire project. I was privileged to meet some of the best and brightest in the fields of Canadian economics and public administration. Interviews give history back its life, and I am most grateful for my enlivening contact with Edward Safarian, Carol Carson, Lucie Laliberté, Rod Dobell, Shaila Nijhowne, Stewart Wells, Simon Reisman, William Hood, Ed Neufeld, Robert Crozier, Harry Postner, Jack Sawyer, Donald Daly, Ian Stewart, Guy Leclerc, Gideon Rosenbluth, Anthony Scott, Richard Lipsey, Thomas Shoyama, Thomas Rymes, Larry Read, Kari Levitt, David Slater, John Randall, Lorne Rowebottom, and Hans Adler. For many years, Bruce Little wrote a wonderful column for the *Globe and Mail* called "Amazing Facts." This column gave me something to aim for: the knack of conveying complex statistical matters in lucid, useful prose. Thank you, Bruce, for your amazing inspiration.

I count myself fortunate that my former dean, Mike Smith, at Carleton University encouraged me to undertake this project and allowed me a leave of absence to do so. My then departmental chair, Peter Fitzgerald, displayed similar support. (When I approached Peter, an economic historian, with my plans, his instant response was to give me a pep talk on the historical importance of input-output tables!)

The challenge of this project has been to write a book that will not appal the practitioners of national accounting yet at the same time will convey something of its essence and importance to that mythical "average intelligent reader" on the streets of Canada. In this respect, I was wonderfully served by a small group of readers who kindly read drafts of chapters as they appeared. At Statistics Canada, Philip Smith, Robert Smith, and Kishori Lal performed this time-consuming task. For the reaction on the street, how lucky I was to enlist the assistance of Sandy Campbell, a women's studies professor at Carleton University, and Charlotte Gray, Canada's most gifted popular biographer. Their deft reading of my text ensured that my message would not be lost in the wilderness.

A book is only as good as the publisher who undertakes to guide it to publication. In this respect, I have been privileged to have worked with McGill-Queen's University Press. Special thanks to Senior Editor Don Akenson and Coordinating Editor Joan McGilvray for their calm authority and to Robert Lewis for his judicious editing.

Any national accountant will tell you that at the end of the day the accounts have to balance. In this respect, I have failed the test. There are two inputs to this project that I can never satisfactorily repay.

Kishori Lal came to Canada's national accounts from the Punjab via McGill University. From 1967 until his retirement in 2003, he lived and breathed national accounting at Tunney's Pasture, where Statistics Canada is headquartered. In later years his reputation as director general of Canada's System of National Accounts spread beyond Canada to wherever national accounting issues are seriously discussed. In retirement, Kishori has been a member of Statistics Canada's Alumni Program and as such has been available to pass on the faith to younger national accountants. I picked Kishori's brain constantly and sat in on his Friday morning SNA seminar. This book reflects his wisdom on every page.

My wife, Sandy Campbell, has been, for thirty years, the most tangible asset on my life's balance sheet. In this book, as in all the others, she has acted as editor, critic, and booster. She made the work better in every respect. When I undertook this project, she insisted that the first book I read be by Marilyn Waring. Now that the work is done, I can truly say that I have a better appreciation of the importance of unpaid labour in our society. She is the sum of my satisfactions.

The Sum of the Satisfactions

When you can measure what you are speaking about, and express it in numbers, you know something about it; when you cannot measure it, when you cannot express it in numbers, your knowledge is of a meager and unsatisfactory kind; it may be the beginning of knowledge, but you have scarcely, in your thoughts, advanced to the stage of science.
~ William Thomson, Lord Kelvin (1824–1907), "Electrical Units of Measurement" (1883)

Briefly, national income is the aggregate of all the incomes received and disposable for consumption and net new investment by all the individual citizens of the country during a specified period of time, usually a year. In its widest and most logical sense this aggregate is *the sum of the satisfactions* made possible by production and the existing stock of wealth. Satisfactions, however, are psychic things and hence cannot be expressed in quantitative terms. Therefore, for practical purposes, the money incomes or the goods and services from which satisfactions are derived are measured rather than the satisfactions themselves.
~ John J. Deutsch, Bank of Canada, "The National Income," *The Canadian Banker* (1941)

Introduction
The Arithmetic of Human Welfare

Statistical thinking will one day be as necessary for efficient
citizenship as the ability to read and write.
~ H.G. Wells, *Mankind in the Making* (1904)

Whenever you can, count.
~ Sir Francis Galton, *Memories of My Life* (1909)

There is no more effective quietus to economic quackery
and misguided "pressures" than statistical fact.
~ R.H. Coats, *Annual Report of the Dominion Statistician*
(1941)

Facts arranged in the right way speak for themselves;
unarranged they are as dead as mutton.
~ J.R. Hicks, A.G. Hart, and J.W. Ford, *The Social
Framework* (1942)

We live in an age of measurement. Citizens of Western democracies like
Canada calibrate their lives with cradle-to-grave statistics. Our births,
marriages, and deaths have long been plotted as so-called vital statistics; every five years the federal census redefines our demographic
parameters. Our political preferences are captured by pollsters. Our
investments are tracked with minute precision by various financial barometers. The bulls and bears of Bay Street move in a statistical herd.
Social trends as diverse as same-sex marriage and obesity are given
legitimacy and urgency by statistics. Always obsessively concerned with
their. weather, Canadians have of late brought statistical precision to
such worrisome phenomena as global warming and ozone depletion.

Even our leisure pastimes are paced by statistics; professional athletes, for instance, ply their trade on gridirons of figures. Writers and performers aspire to "top-ten" status on charts that measure consumption of popular culture. In short, statistics have become the metronome of modern life.

The centrality of statistics to our wellbeing is nowhere more evident than in the economic underpinnings of our daily lives. A morning seldom passes without radio, television, and newspaper headlines conveying to the breakfast tables of the nation some impression of how we are faring on the economic front. In the years since the Second World War, Canadians have equipped themselves with an elaborate lexicon of economic indicators. Terms like gross domestic product (GDP), inflation, and productivity have a long-familiar, if perhaps vaguely understood, ring to Canadian ears. "Retail sales up 1.7% in February, topping $30B for 1st time," the CBC Business News website announces. "Foreign ownership good for Canada: study," the *National Post* tells its readers. "Chicken McNuggets Make the UK Inflation Basket," Reuter's news agency reports from London. Such statistics habitually make grist for the mills of public-policy making: "You say prosperity, I say productivity," sermonizes *Globe and Mail* columnist Jeffrey Simpson. Thus inflation, trade flows, unemployment, and production data have become commonplace in the dialogue of Canadian life. Indeed, when the National Hockey League locked out its players in the fall of 2004, plunging Canadians into a bleak hockeyless winter, the newspapers screamed: "Hockey lockout slashes GDP, economic growth put on ice."[1]

Statisticians have been the handmaidens of this process of national quantification. They have provided the yardsticks of national growth. Their findings and pronouncements carry Delphic significance and consequently heat or cool the national mood. Sir Wilfrid Laurier's hallowed claim that the "twentieth century belongs to Canada" can be seen as a prescient assertion that immigration, agriculture, and industry would soon demonstrate Canada's unbounded destiny in numbers. Indeed, in 1918, before Laurier died, Canada established a centralized national statistical agency – the Dominion Bureau of Statistics. From then on, statistics became an indispensable ingredient in national dialogue. "Jobs! Jobs! Jobs!" Brian Mulroney repeatedly promised in 1984, vowing to increase the employment numbers. Numbers, politicians had come to instinctively know, brought precision to the nation's economic anxieties.

Ironically, statisticians have never enjoyed high national recognition. "Statistics wear a dry-as-dust and repellant look to many," Dominion Statistician Robert Hamilton Coats frankly admitted as early as 1919.[2] In 1947 Herbert Marshall, one of Coats's successors, mused to a radio audience on Ottawa's CKCO that the general public regarded the statistician as a man of "questionable worth ... the first cousin of a doodler ... an idle dreamer sitting at his desk with pencil and paper, figuring out the number of hot-cross buns it would take to reach from Timbuctoo to Zamboango, or the number of snowflakes it would take to cover Pike's Peak." There were, he added, a dismaying number of jokes to the effect that if you placed all the statisticians in the world end to end, "they would never reach a conclusion."[3]

Marshall's ribbing of the public perception of statistics did capture an ambivalence about the role that numbers grew to play in the twentieth-century world. Statistics were broadly accepted as the measuring stick of the regulated economies and welfare states that were unfolding across Europe and North America. Even the command economies of the Soviet bloc constructed statistical benchmarks that measured the "material base" of their economies. In this sense, statistics were empowering and legitimizing. No public policy, it seemed, went forward without a supporting cast of numbers. Statistics were called into service to illuminate many other aspects of human activity. In the early 1950s, for instance, Alfred C. Kinsey, a zoologist-turned-human-behaviourist, electrified American society with his statistical analysis of human sexuality. Kinsey's numbers helped to open the door to the sexual liberation of the 1960s.

On the other hand, there was a growing sense that numbers were not neutral things, that they could be groomed to serve preordained purposes. Dr Kinsey's analysis of what was normal sexual behaviour was, for instance, soon criticized by other experts who suggested that the good doctor had bent his numbers to serve his purpose. In 1954 W.W. Norton in New York caught this mood when it published Darrell Huff's *How to Lie with Statistics*. Huff, an editor with *LOOK* magazine, flippantly claimed that his book was "a sort of a primer in ways to use statistics to deceive ... The secret language of statistics, so appealing in a fact-minded culture, is employed to sensationalize, inflate, confuse, and oversimplify." We all now lived, Huff claimed, in a world of "gee-whiz graphs." The art of "misinforming people by the use of statistical information," he argued, should be called "statisticulation." The book remains a paperback bestseller to this day.[4]

Marshall's lament has echoed down to the present. Sir Claus Moser, Britain's premier statistician of the late twentieth century, bemoaned the statistician's unhappy lot in his 1979 presidential address to the Royal Statistical Society. "We know how people move away from us at parties when they learn of our profession, we know that look of incredulity, amusement and resigned boredom ... At worst, we are regarded as purveyors of lies, at best as boring and cold: I still resent a newspaper comment that 'statisticians are passionless people and Professor Moser is no exception.'"[5]

Despite the superficial cynicism of the "lies, damned lies and statistics" view of their profession, Marshall and Moser never wavered in their faith that statistics provided modern societies with what Marshall called "the arithmetic of human welfare."[6] The point has often been made. Sir Francis Galton, an early-twentieth-century pioneer of English number crunching – and, alas, sometime eugenicist – argued that statistics were "the only tools by which an opening can be cut through the formidable thicket of difficulties that bars the path of those who pursue the Science of Man."[7] A contemporary of Galton's, Arthur Conan Doyle, found a more colloquial way of stressing the importance of empirical observation. "Data! Data! Data!," Sherlock Holmes cries out in *The Adventure of the Copper Beeches*, "I can't make bricks without clay."

Since 1918, Canada's principal statistical brickworks has been Statistics Canada, known until 1972 as the Dominion Bureau of Statistics. If Canada has one abiding claim to statistical fame, it is that the nation has doggedly insisted that the collection and interpretation of its statistics be conducted on a *centralized* basis. Robert Hamilton Coats, our founding national statistician, was fond of portraying his bureau, borrowing the words of the great English economist Arthur Bowley, as a "central thinking office."[8] The bureau was in the business of providing Canadians with as encompassing a profile of their condition as possible. As Coats argued in his first annual report: "There is need for a national 'laboratory' for the observation and interpretation of economic and social phenomena on behalf of the Government and the production of monographs on features thrown from time to time into prominence." Such statistics would furnish the young nation with "an articulated conspectus" (a term that Coats appropriated from Australia's Commonwealth statistician, George Knibbs) of its wellbeing. "The statistics of a nation are, in point of fact, the quantitative expression of the character and activities of the people, and hence are of the most profound significance."[9] There could indeed be passion in the numbers.

Since the harrowing depression of the 1930s and the galvanic shock of the Second World War, the efforts of Ottawa statisticians have taken an increasingly economic bent. While the main timbers of Canada's statistical framework – most conspicuously the census – remain sturdily in place, the economic pulse of the nation has often dominated our attention. The half-century after the war saw Canadians comfortably installed in what came to be loosely called the "Keynesian world," a partnership of private enterprise and state economic management. This was the high noon of macroeconomics, analysis predicated on an empirically driven overview of the economy as a whole with income, output, prices, and employment seen as the crucial levers of performance. For the first time in Western economic history, business and government acquired the skill to look *inside* the national economy – to break apart its structure and flows in order to report on its strengths and weaknesses. Hence concepts like gross national product and productivity as well as processes like deflation were developed to provide a stethoscope for assessing our economic wellbeing. In doing so, statisticians and economists equipped Canadians – citizens and policymakers alike – with a new vocabulary of economic citizenship.

A sea of statistics thus lapped the shores of Keynesianism. Bolstered by carefully collected data, economics was transformed from a *deductive* science built on extrapolation from broad theory into an *inductive* science built on empirical observation and measurement. Previously, we built economic policy on what we *believed* – trust in the working of the "invisible hand," for instance. Since the Second World War, we have come to act on what we *observe*. John Maynard Keynes liked to portray the national economy as a "cake." Statisticians would reveal the recipe of the cake. Economists would decide how big a piece of the cake each segment of society could be served without choking the overall performance of the economy. Without statistics, the distribution could only be capricious. "Every government since the last war has been unscientific and obscurantist," Keynes complained as the war broke over Britain in 1939, "and has regarded the collection of essential facts as a waste of money." Others, like Colin Clark at Cambridge, had predicted the necessity of more incisive statistics in the dark days of the Depression, but it took the panic of war to provoke action. In 1941 Churchill responded to this logic and established the Central Statistical Office. In the wake of these early initiatives, the gathering, massaging, and reporting of economic statistics grew throughout the war and the peace that followed into a vast enterprise that soon stretched through all the Western economies.

The statistical monitoring of national economies acquired the rather ponderous label of the System of National Accounts (SNA). It is a term that very few citizens recognize. Many recognize and trust the outcomes of the system – GDP estimates, current account balances, productivity indices – but few understand the architecture of the overall system. Upon hearing the term System of National Accounts, most people lapse into the state of mystification and incredulity that Claus Moser so often encountered at social events. But for all the bureaucratic stuffiness of its name, the SNA has dutifully read the pulse of Western economic performance for over a half-century. However much we may debate the ideological underpinnings of our economic arrangements, there can be no denying that not just Western democracies but indeed the entire United Nations community have been equipped for an intelligent discussion of their economic prospects by the labours of national accountants across the world.

Over its long and restless evolution, national accounting has thus furnished the tools by which policymakers and average citizens comprehend their economic circumstances and plot rational responses. In the words of American economist Paul Samuelson, national accounting was a "great invention of the twentieth century – without [which] macroeconomics would be adrift in a sea of unorganized data."[11] Canadian-born John Kenneth Galbraith, who first detected the critical importance of national accounts when writing for *Fortune* magazine in 1944, was more forthright: "No history of Keynesian economics should ever be written without giving nearly equal credit to the scholars who took Keynes out of the realm of theory and into the real world. The numbers in the National Accounts made it impossible for the practical man to deny the validity of Keynesian thinking."[12] The Nobel Prize for economics has been awarded only since 1969, but in this span four economists – Richard Stone, Wassily Leontief, Simon Kuznets, and John Hicks – have won the award for their work in building national accounting theory and practice. Many other laureates – for example, Lawrence Klein the econometrician and James Meade the theorist of international trade – rooted their early creativity and later achievement in the availability of national accounts data.[13]

Today, the accumulated wisdom of national accounting resides in a hulking paperback volume solemnly titled *System of National Accounts 1993*. It resembles the Manhattan phonebook in size. This is perhaps an appropriate metaphor, especially given that since 1947 the United Nations in New York has overseen the definition and implementation of national accounting as it has unfolded globally. Earlier, in 1953 and

1968, much leaner iterations of the "system" appeared. *SNA 1993* is a document that is expected to provide a framework of national accounting to all members of the United Nations community. It is thus a truly universal document. The cover of the volume accordingly bears not just the imprimatur of the United Nations but also those of the World Bank, International Monetary Fund, Commission of the European Communities, and Organisation for Economic Co-operation and Development (OECD). *SNA 1993* is a reflection of multilateral deliberation, and its definitions and implementation are today overseen by an awkwardly titled body called the Inter-Secretariat Working Group on National Accounts. *SNA 1993* is also designed to accommodate the marked variations in economic advancement across the face of the earth. Standards of national accounts implementation are set out for "developed," "transition," and "developing" economies.

At 711 pages, *System of National Accounts 1993* is an intimidating publication. It is packed with densely worded descriptions of process, finely pared definitions of economic transactions, and, worst of all for the layman, inscrutable economic jargon. What in the world is a "chain Fisher index"? Nonetheless, the book's official publisher, the United Nations' Statistical Division, boasts that *SNA 1993* is a "bestseller" at both the UN and OECD publications centres.[14] Such success reflects two realities: (1) *SNA 1993* projects a charter belief held by all UN member nations that "official statistics provide an indispensable element in the information system of a democratic society, serving the Government, the economy and the public with data about the economic, demographic, social and environmental situation"[15]; and (2) despite its unavoidable technicalities, the system exists to ensure that trustworthy, transparent, and comparable statistics are made available to citizens and policymakers of the world.

On a more practical level, well-thumbed copies of *SNA 1993* can be found on the bookshelves of finance ministries and statistical agencies the world over. This is the bible of national accounting, where economists and statisticians habitually turn to unravel the mysteries of economic exchange and production. It is the operator's handbook in the glove box of the global economy. Without reliable and internationally comparable statistics of economic performance, national economies are left to the uncorrectable whims of fortune. As the renowned American columnist Walter Lippman told the United Nations General Assembly in 1965: "we have at last begun·to learn how local and national economies can ... be brought under human control ... The art of managing the economy is perhaps the youngest of all the arts. But as it is perfected, it is one of the most promising revolutions in the human condition. For the successful management of the developed economies should produce a rate of growth in the production of wealth which can wipe out the material causes of social conflict."[16]

Nobody has ever claimed that the national accounts system is perfect. Born out of the agonies of depression and war, its abiding purpose was to act as a handmaiden of economic policy that would promote economic stability and growth in the postwar years. Many have suggested that its Achilles' heel has been its dedication to *monetized* economic activity. It measures only those things that bear a price tag. In this hard statistical sense, only money talks. In their scramble to bolster postwar economic recovery, early national accountants focused almost exclusively on those things that they could readily measure – things that could be readily quantified, like wages, industrial production, and taxation. "Free goods" like water, air, and the unpaid labour of housewives did not fit easily into this economic universe. In recent decades the national accounts system has had vocal and effective critics. Feminist Gloria Steinem has argued that the system supports "traditional, one-eyed, inaccurate economics" that fail to take account of women's role in economic production. New Zealand activist Marilyn Waring has castigated the system for "its dismissal of the environment" and "the severe invisibility of women and women's work" in its analyses. "The national accounts," she writes, "just record a pattern of economic activity. But from the outset, the figures are rigged."[17]

Over the past few decades, even some of those within "traditional" economics have suggested that national accountants have acted as cheerleaders for unrestrained growth and consumption. "Is Growth Obsolete?" American economists William Nordhaus and James Tobin wondered aloud to their profession in the early 1970s when they sensed that the major growth-oriented goals of the postwar era had seemingly been achieved.[18] Another distinguished economist, Kenneth Boulding, suggested that national accounting was an accomplice in the reckless promotion of a "cowboy economy," one in which "consumption is regarded as a good thing and production likewise; and the success of the economy is measured by the amount of the throughput from the 'factors of production,' a part of which, at any rate, is extracted from the reservoirs of raw materials and non-economic objects, and another part of which is output into the reservoirs of pollution." The years since the 1980s have therefore seen national accounting slowly and often controversially trying to adjust its ways to what Boulding described as "the coming spaceship earth," a global economy "without unlimited reservoirs of anything ... capable of continuous reproduction of material."[19]

As the twentieth century ended, the iconic stature of national accounts, a stature rooted in the Western world's escape from the Great Depression and the triumph of the Second World War, thus came under pressure. The half-century veneration of GDP as the all-sufficient yardstick of economic performance was increasingly questioned by demands that the national accounts system be stretched to accommodate new demands from society. These demands – driven by legitimate concerns about the environment and social equality – were usually political, not methodological, in origin. They therefore placed statisticians in an awkward bind. Market price calibration had worked well for the "old" national accounts system because it had an unequivocal common denominator: the price that society had put on a good or service. The challenge now placed before statisticians was to include new sensibilities in the national accounts system, sensibilities that could not be neatly calibrated by price.

The quandary was devilish – a methodological response to a political demand. As early as 1963 Richard Lipsey, an up-and-coming Canadian economist at the London School of Economics, sensed the delicacy of the situation. "We must be aware of the essentialist fallacy of believing that there is one true national income and it is our task to discover it," he wrote in his bestselling economics text, *An Introduction to Positive Economics*. "There are various concepts and measures of national income, each appropriate for a particular purpose. Questions are often raised, such as: *Should the services of housewives be included in national income?* The answer is that it all depends what we are interested in. If we want national income to measure national welfare, so that the higher the income the 'better-off' is a country, then we shall have very great difficulties since the concept of a *country* being 'better off' is a very vague one and, since it is uncertain what we means by the concept, it will be difficult to decide how to measure it." National accountants must therefore be *nominalists*; a term or concept like "national income" can mean only what we choose it to mean. Forty years later, Lipsey still warns of the danger of bending GDP at market prices to ends for which it was not designed. The system was designed to calibrate economic performance, not to reshape society. Therefore, it should not be "polluted" with other incompatible observations. For these ends, appropriate yardsticks suitable to their ends should be devised. But the two should not be mingled.[20]

Nonetheless, a week seldom passes in which national accountants do not gather at some international forum to discuss the remaking or modification of their art. Under the aegis of the United Nations Statistical Commission, "working groups" of experts try to fine-tune national accountancy to new exigencies. How can the environment be calibrated for economic measurement? Can national accounting take into consideration the *negative* impacts of economic activity like the drawing-down of natural resources? Does smog have economic weight? How do you take economic account of volunteerism, altruistic activity that does not create wages but still carries economic weight? What economic weight should be given to the explosion of employee stock options, a startling economic outcome of the high-tech revolution of the 1990s? In short, the national accounts system is constantly being tinkered with and stretched – too slowly for some; recklessly for others.

Indisputable is that the national accounts system has never been static. National accounting is today being prodded to adapt its ways, just as the traumas of depression and war initially spurred it into existence a half-century ago. It has always been alive to the economic world that it serves. As coteries of national accounting experts around the world push toward the next iteration of the national accounts system in 2008, the United Nations Statistical Commission's website provides daily access to their deliberations and differences.[21] "Our advice to statisticians?" the *Economist* has pontificated: "Keep revising yourselves as often as your numbers."[22]

To find Canada's national accountants you have to leave the inner sanctum of the federal capital in downtown Ottawa and head west along the picturesque Ottawa River Parkway to Tunney's Pasture, a sprawling civil service campus set in riverside green space. Dominating Tunney's Pasture are the twin towers of Statistics Canada. Nestled between these 1970s edifices is the much lower 1950s home of the Dominion Bureau of Statistics. Dominion Statistician Herbert Marshall loved to call this attractive Art Deco building his "facts factory." Nothing speaks more clearly to Canada's late-twentieth-century embrace of statistics than the dramatic dwarfing of Marshall's little enterprise by these towers. Nearly 5,000 Statistics Canada employees fill the Tunney's Pasture complex today, a vast majority of whom dedicate their daily energy to the sorts of things that most Canadians readily identify with the agency: the census and wide-ranging surveys of social and economic behaviour.

In fact, Statistics Canada's National Accounts and Analytical Studies group at Tunney's is a distinct minority of the Statistics Canada labour force – just under 350 people. Perhaps what most differentiates them from the rest of their confreres is that they do not generally *collect* data. While they do directly gather their own data on balance of payments and public institutions, national accountants more often take data from other frontline statisticians. They then pull it apart and reassemble it into the framework of national accounting that reveals all the flows and nature of transactions within Canada's national and regional economies. It is esoteric work. National accountants must adeptly juggle mathematics, economics, and plain logic; their work is never straightforward counting and summation. Their analysis of the state of the Canadian economy depends as much on hard economic understanding as it does on acquired intuitions about how economic transactions take place in a modern society. A cynic might say that they engage in well-informed "guestimation." They are members of what Statistics Canada microeconomist John Baldwin calls "the priestly profession."[23] They deliberate over the body and soul of the economy.

Spread over several floors high up in the R.H. Coats Building, Canada's national accountants have a spectacular view up the Ottawa River as it disappears over the horizon into the northland. Metaphorically, it is a fitting vista. Just as the Ottawa River was once one of the main arteries of Canada's emerging national economy, the publications of today's national accounts furnish Canadians with intimate statistical analysis of the arteries of Canada's modern economy. In the eyes of most observers, they do a world-class job. In the early 1980s the eminent Yale economist Richard Ruggles came to Ottawa to review Canada's System of National Accounts and found it "of a very high order." "From an international point of view," he concluded, "it is one of the most highly developed and integrated systems of information available."[24] In the early 1990s the *Economist* pronounced from London that Statistics Canada had placed first in its "good statistics guide" for "trustworthy" economic statistics.[25] Early in the twenty-first century the Swedish national statistical agency, Statistiska centralbyrån, joined the chorus. Eager to compare their efforts with other models of national accounting, the Swedes noted that the centralized Canadian system, while labour intensive, was one that delivered accuracy and quality for money spent. "Canada is also the country," they concluded, "which appears to value official statistics the most."[26]

In the world of national accounting, Canada has never led a derivative existence. From the dawn of international cooperation in setting national accounting standards in the dying months of the Second World War, Canada has always been at the table as a senior, contributing member. Our closest collaborators have been the British and the Americans. Canadians have therefore never been fawning imitators in the realm of national accounting. Yes, much has been adopted from British and American theorizing. Where indeed would the whole enterprise be without the brilliant intuitions of a Simon Kuznets, Richard Stone, or John Maynard Keynes? But Canada has at the same time fed its own ideas onto the international scene. The phrase "Canadian model" has punctuated documents of the United Nations and of national accounts systems since the 1960s. Canadian innovation in areas of national accounting – like rectangular input-output tables that break the economy down into its most detailed production outputs and inputs and the tourism "satellite" account that gives statistical expression to the burgeoning global travel industry – has set benchmarks for excellence. Canadians have thus been instrumental in participating in one of the great intellectual adventures of the last century, in producing a system of economic measurement that Philip Smith, the assistant chief statistician who oversees Canada's System of National Accounts, notes is now "deeply embedded in the workings of western society."[27]

Closer to home, national accounting has provided an initial stepping stone in the careers of many policy mandarins and academic economists. To know the national accounts is to understand the economic rhythms of the nation. Former deputy minister of finance Simon Reisman has typically portrayed national accounts as "a boon to economists and policy makers."[28] Every federal and provincial budget delivered in Canada is rooted in our System of National Accounts. The system has supplied the arithmetic for programs at the heart of Canadian federalism – most notably equalization. When, for instance, Ontario Premier Dalton McGuinty launched his "$23 billion gap campaign" in 2005, it was in the national accounts that he found authority for his claim that Ontarians paid more into Confederation than they took out.

And all this from a nation that went to war in 1939 with little practical inkling of what was going on inside its national economy. Before national accounting, public and business policies were set on the basis of hunches and blind faith in economic nostrums. When times proved good, we were glad to reap the harvest, but when times turned bad, we were largely powerless to alter our fate. In the Dirty Thirties we lacked the statistics to diagnose the ravages of a fearful depression. The following half-century of developing national accounting was rooted in the determination never to return to such dark days.

How did we get here from there? The easy answer might be that necessity was the mother of invention. Confronted with the rubble of an economic system that suffered structural collapse in the 1930s and the imperative need to defeat fascism, Canadians applied their fabled pragmatism to the challenge of reconnecting their economy to the constructive needs of their society. Economists in the late 1940s embraced national accounting not simply because they liked numbers but because they believed that numbers could change society. The evolution of national accounting in Canada and elsewhere was nonetheless a tough intellectual journey, one that drew on the talents of some of the best postwar minds, a fact that the Nobel Prize juries would later recognize. What made the journey so arduous was that national accounting had to be a *system*, not just a random collection of economic tools and templates. The system had to explain the *whole economy* – or at least all its monetized inputs and outputs – and, like good bookkeeping, had to balance at the end of the day. It is a breathtaking endeavour that tries to capture economic activity ranging from the purchase of a sidewalk ice cream to the manufacture of an airliner.

There would be only a handful of master theoreticians like Keynes and meticulous methodologists like Kuznets who brilliantly grasped the entire architecture of the structure. In the final analysis, it took a legion of hard-thinking economists and statisticians to slowly and cautiously perfect a new conceptualization of how Western society conceives of its economic circumstances. It is not always a riveting story; the theory is often esoteric, the detail intricate. But the result of these labours has been deeply significant for how we have come to measure and govern our economic lives. The excitement of this story thus lies in the bold initial intuitions of strategic thinkers *and* in the meticulous working-out of myriad details that ultimately shaped big ideas into a working system. Nobel Prize winner Paul Samuelson has put his finger on the achievement: national accounting *is* one of the great "inventions" of the twentieth century because it offers philosophical integrity, a means of contemplating the whole in an otherwise fragmented world. American economist Carol Carson has put it more colourfully: national accounting brings rhyme and reason to all the "confetti" that flutters through our economic lives.[29] In an age characterized by many as one of secular materialism, national accounting explains the economic cosmos around us and thereby has made life more predictable and more comfortable. Thus we have come to live in an age of measurement.

For the historian today, any attempt to chronicle the evolution of national accounting poses much the same challenge: being sure that the central principles are grasped in an intelligent and accessible way and then presenting the day-to-day outcomes in a practicable light. It is a daunting assignment: the theory is intricate, the detail thick, and the outcomes important. Many years ago in England, Sir Francis Galton sensed this same challenge: "I have a great subject [statistics] to write upon, but I feel keenly my literary incapacity to make it easily intelligible without sacrificing accuracy and thoroughness."[30]

1 A Mere Counting House

Accounting and statistics may seem dull and pedestrian proposals, but they are the only keys that will unlock the first barriers to better conditions.
~ *Report of the Royal Commission on Price Spreads* (1935)

Where a people thrive, there the income is greater than the expense.
~ Sir William Petty, *Political Arithmetic* (1690)

No one knew what was happening. The data available then were neither fish nor flesh nor even red herring.
~ Simon Kuznets (1960s), cited in *Current Biography* (1972)

[There was] no cat in the bag, no rabbits in the hat, no brains in the head ... an obstinate adherence to ancient rules of thumb.
~ John Maynard Keynes after the 1933 World Economic Conference, cited in Louis W. Pauly, *The League of Nations and the Foreshadowing of the International Monetary Fund* (1996)

Sir George Eulas Foster had something on his mind. It was July 1915 and the war that had gripped Canada since 1914 showed no signs of abating. The naive early predictions that the conflict with Germany would be gloriously concluded by Christmas had been dashed. Now, a year into the fray, Canadians faced the grim reality that this was to be a war of attrition. As the minister of trade and commerce in Robert Borden's wartime government, Foster sensed that victory depended not just on the military frontline but also on the strength of the home economy.

This was "total war" that stretched from the wheat fields of Sask-atchewan and the munitions plants of Montreal to the trenches of the western salient. Did Canada have the economic muscle, Foster won-dered, to endure the fray?

Foster was a political veteran. A Tory now in his late sixties, he had left his post as a professor of classics at the University of New Bruns-wick to enter politics in 1882. He had been Sir John A. Macdonald's last finance minister and now, as war engulfed the nation, again found himself in a crucial economic portfolio. Foster epitomized Anglo-nationalism. War was about "duty." He was, for instance, a fanatic tee-totaller – no nation should "waste" precious resources on drink in wartime. But in the summer of 1915 his mind was fixated on gaining some sense of what strain Canada's economy could actually bear in the conflict. What was our national wealth? How deep were our national pockets? During his years in politics Foster had seen Canada's econo-my finally realize its potential as immigrants flooded the West, new railways stretched from coast to coast, and "Made in Canada" was stamped on an increasing range of goods. But just how strong had the economy become?

Foster knew that other nations allied against Germany were ponder-ing the same question. In the wake of the bloody Gallipoli campaign, the Australian government had initiated a "war census" aimed at ascer-taining the depth of manpower *and* material resources available to bol-ster its war effort.[1] To do this, Australia obliged every citizen over the age of eighteen to report all details of their "wealth" – property, in-come, and investments. When 2.2 million Australians declared net assets of £1.65 billion, the nation felt confident enough to commit another 50,000 men to the European conflict. In Britain, Josiah Stamp, the bright young assistant secretary of the Department of Inland Revenue, reported to the Royal Statistical Society on the "wealth and income of the chief powers." Such estimates, he argued, provided a "test of pro-gress" and "relative prosperity" and consequently an indication of staying power in war. To do this, Stamp employed what he called an "inventory" method. This entailed toting up the implied capital value of physical assets as disparate as livestock in the field, mineral resources in the ground, and machinery in the factories and combining it with the financial value of imports and exports, investment abroad, and so on to arrive at a gross valuation of a nation's wealth.[2] Aware of these efforts, Foster wanted to know what resources were at Canada's disposal. For the answer, he knew that he needed a man who was good with num-bers. National wealth was all about methodical counting. Robert

Hamilton Coats, Ottawa's newly appointed Dominion statistician and commissioner of the census, was the obvious candidate.

Coats and Foster shared a number of passions. Each had begun his journey into public life with study of the classics. Throughout his career Coats would liberally sprinkle his speeches with Latin phrases and classical allusions. More important, Foster and Coats shared the firm belief that modern problems required modern facts. After graduating from the University of Toronto, Coats had worked for the *Toronto Globe*, where his eyes were opened to the sorry effects of industrialization and urbanization on working-class Canadians. For all its exuberant growth, the Laurier boom seemed to be penalizing many Canadians, who struggled to make ends meet as prices climbed. Market liberalism reigned; the market would propose and dispose according to its own instincts. Furthermore, nobody could really get inside the workings of the economy. Coats would later write that "our best production figures were 'spotty' in the extreme. They hung together, what there were of them, not at all. They told us nothing of the agencies of production."[3]

In 1902 Coats was called to Ottawa by his old university classmate William Lyon Mackenzie King, another earnest young man engaged by the problems of the new century. King was deputy minister of the newly created federal Ministry of Labour and fervently believed in the power of investigation and publicity to right wrong. Coats would act as the assistant editor of the *Labour Gazette*, applying facts to the solution of conflict in the workplace. Coats's focus quickly shifted from journalism to data collection. Statistics, he later reflected, shed light on "the doings of mankind in society."[4] Believing this, he helped the Ministry of Labour to develop a system of wholesale prices, using a "weighting" method that gave statistical prominence to those commodities central to home consumption. The "cost of living" – a new term that entered the national vocabulary – could now be crudely plotted, a fact reflected in Coats's authorship of a 1910 study of wholesale prices in Canada since 1890. The data were intended, Coats said, to throw "a partial light" on a social problem confronting Canadians: prosperity-induced inflation.[5] "This is the economic impulse underlying what is popularly called the Discovery of the Last Best West. Around this hinges the general scheme of economic progress during the last twelve years."[6]

Sensing that the economic structure of Canada was undergoing seismic change, George Foster flexed his authority as trade and commerce minister in the newly elected Conservative government of Robert Borden. In 1912 he appointed a commission to provide a blueprint for a "comprehensive system of general statistics adequate to the necessities of the Country."[7] Prominent in its membership were Coats and Adam Shortt, a Queen's University political economist addicted to empirical investigation. The commissioners were blunt in their assessment. Although Confederation in 1867 had given Ottawa statistical preeminence in the young nation, "little or no statistical information exists in a form suitable for practical application." Canadians were in the dark about what "phenomena in Canada" required scientific measurement "if national development is not to proceed blindly or at a disadvantage."[8] Vigorous centralization of statistics, the commission concluded, should be the unbending order of the day. What Canada needed was "a central thinking office" for statistical affairs.

Armed with such unequivocal advice, Foster acted. On 1 July 1915 he appointed Coats Dominion statistician and commissioner of the census; a strongly centralized agency would follow. Six days later the minister buttonholed his new chief statistician: "I have however been anxious that we should be in a position to know the yearly production and broad lines of dispersal of the principal striking industries of Canada."[9] Coats went to work, but there was not much to work with. The Australian approach of conducting a census was out of the question – too time consuming and cumbersome to administer. Extrapolating wealth from tax data or probate records involved arbitrary assumptions being made from distinctly thin evidence. An "inventory" approach promised the quickest result. For it, there was already the boilerplate of the 1911 national census, to which could be added industrial data from such sources as the annual *Census of the Manufactures of Canada*. Thus Coats assembled a kind of running total of Canadian wealth: the value of farms added to the capital invested in the fishery, plus the value of the canals, railways, manufacturing machinery, inventories of commodities, and even household furnishings. And so on.[10]

By December, Coats had an answer for his minister. "The Office, I find," he cautioned, "never systematically attacked this problem, and the following is only a very rough review of the figures immediately at hand … We are expecting to be able to handle the subject better in the near future." His caveats made, Coats unveiled the result: Canada's national wealth in 1915 was $16,293,500,000.[11] The figure had two evident outcomes. It confirmed Foster's esteem for Coats and accelerated Canada's trajectory toward the 1918 creation of the Dominion Bureau of Statistics, an agency that would be empowered "to collect, abstract, compile and publish statistical information relative to the commercial, industrial, social, economic and general activities and conditions of the people." By the time Foster left Canadian politics in 1921 he felt confident that he had "placed statistics in Canada on a footing not inferior to that of any other country."[12] On another less tangible plane, knowledge of what Canada was "worth" fed Canada's coming-of-age in the First World War. Despite the figure's vague utility, it did seem to flatter the notion that Canada was a nation on the move and worthy of respect on the world stage. For many Anglo-Canadians, statistical evidence that Canada carried economic weight in the world justified the call to conscription later in the war. The nation could, they believed, afford the fullest possible participation in the fray. That the calculation did nothing to measure the impact of wartime inflation – or the uneven regional impact of the war – escaped mention.

The 1915 national wealth estimate proved a godsend for Robert Hamilton Coats. It was just the kind of figure that journalists wanted in order to buttress their treatment of Canada. Coats subsequently worked the estimate up into an article that was snapped up by the *Monetary Times*, the nation's leading financial sheet, and by the august *Journal of the Canadian Bankers' Association*. In 1919 the *Sun* in New York published the estimate – "Canada's National Riches Set at 17 Billion Dollars."[15] A Spanish-language version appeared in the *Inter-American Magazine*. Thus national wealth figures became a mainstay of newspaper editorials and a talisman of nationalism throughout the 1920s, held up as evidence of Canada's budding potential among nations.[16] The estimate was installed in a regular Dominion Bureau of Statistics publication, *Report on the National Wealth of Canada and Its Provinces*. By 1929 Coats was reporting that Canada had burgeoned to a net worth of $30.8 billion. In the midst of all this attention, Coats was quick to demur: "It must be understood that statistics of this character are suggestive and indicative rather than strictly accurate; the concept of wealth is distinctly intangible and there are numerous elements of uncertainty in a calculation of this nature."[17]

The "guestimation" of national wealth may have been a novelty for Canadians, but it was a calculation with a long pedigree in Europe. Since the Middle Ages war and taxation had provoked European nations to produce crude estimates of their fiscal strength. As early as the reign of King Henry I in the twelfth century, English monarchs convened a Court of Exchequer at which taxes owed to the king and a record of their actual payment were calculated. A large chequered cloth was spread before the king's treasurer and the sheriffs who were charged with collecting regal entitlement in the counties. Each square on the cloth represented a monetary value – pounds, shillings, and pence – and tally sticks were deployed to indicate what had been paid

Robert Hamilton Coats (1874–1960), Dominion statistician from 1915 to his retirement in 1942. First appointed as a statistician in the Ministry of Labour in 1902, Coats oversaw the construction of Canada's modern statistical system. He likened the Dominion Bureau of Statistics to "a national 'laboratory' for the observation and interpretation of economic and social phenomena."[13] Winnipeg journalist Grant Dexter called him "Canada's recording angel."[14] Courtesy of Library and Archives Canada, PA-805647.

and what remained owing. By the end of the session, the monarch had a good sense of the worth of his realm. The name of the court stuck, and to this day Britain's fiscal affairs have remained in the hands of its chancellor of the Exchequer. One early royal treasurer, Richard Fitz Nigel, clearly understood the linkage between fiscal strength and worldly power. "For indeed abundance of means, or lack of them, exalts or humbles the power of princes," he wrote in his *Dialogue Concerning the Exchequer* of 1179. "For those who lack them will be prey to their enemies, to those who have them their enemies will fall prey."[18]

The seventeenth century precipitated more interest in national wealth. The pressure exerted by military ambition and by taxes increased; wars and territorial expansion obliged states to measure their economic reach. When, for instance, English forces under republican Oliver Cromwell invaded and subjugated Ireland in the 1650s, the question arose of just how much the conquest had augmented England's wealth and how it might be apportioned. But beyond such mercenary considerations, deeper influences were at work on European society. The profit motive was on the rise. This was an age of mercantilism in which nations conceived of wealth as a fixed entity, the product of a global zero-sum game by which one nation grew at the expense of another. Capture trade, and you expanded your national prowess. The idea was to treat your economy as a vast warehouse into which you tipped the commodities of the world as well as to deny other nations access to such trade. It is far from a coincidence that Canada's oldest company, the Hudson's Bay Company, received its royal charter at just this juncture in 1670 and then set forth in monopolistic pursuit of profit on the beaver ponds of the western plain. Such nascent capitalism required calibration; both double-entry bookkeeping and calculation of credit and profit now mattered.

Profit-mindedness dovetailed with the sixteenth- and seventeenth-century passion for empirical investigation.[19] The "modern fact" was born, the fact based on observation and measurement, not intuition. Western man began to abandon what Francis Bacon labelled his "pernicious and inveterate habit of dwelling on abstractions" and increasingly began to base his actions on empirical investigation.[20] As Thomas Hobbes wrote in *The Leviathan*, "all ratiocination is ... addition and subtraction."[21] This was the age of Newton and gravity, Mercator and maps, and Galileo and planetary systems. Science thus established its role as the lodestar of statistics: as one commentator has put it, "to the modern scientist, random events are not simply wild, unexpected, and unpredictable. They have a structure that can be described mathematically."[22] In 1662 the Royal Society was founded in England to allow such observers of the world to share their discoveries. Not surprisingly, men in this curious time soon also turned their attention to the economic nexus.[23]

Profit and scientific observation found a ready partner in the expanding fiscal needs of the seventeenth-century state. Armies and fleets were needed to support mercantilist pretensions abroad; at home, governments began to equip themselves with the apparatus of centralized administration. Such growing states could no longer rely on revenues rooted in feudal obligation. National revenue had to be regularized and made to reflect the broad wealth of the society that it served. The English Civil War of the 1640s epitomized this dramatic shift. Cromwell's triumphant Commonwealth (note the name) imposed a crude income tax on items of common consumption. From hereon, whenever war with the Dutch, Spanish, or French loomed, England girded itself with taxes.

The science of figuring out the dynamic relation of wealth, consumption, and income acquired the label of "political arithmetic." The phrase was coined by an English doctor, William Petty, who attached himself to Cromwell's army of occupation in Ireland. Once in Ireland, Petty ministered to more than military aches and pains. How were the English to capitalize on the forfeited Irish estates that they now possessed? Soldiers had to be paid, English immigrants settled, and creditors satisfied. Petty proposed a massive survey of Ireland's people and land, a survey that would facilitate the English remaking of Ireland. He promised to base his work solely on the "visible Foundations in Nature" and to express himself only "in terms of *Number, Weight or Measure*."[24] Out of these calculations, Petty mustered a remarkable string of publications – most notably his *Political Arithmetic*, an eight-volume treatise culminating in 1690 – out of which emerged the first embryonic model of how an economy worked.

Petty's model moved beyond the static mercantilist view. An economy worked, his medical instincts told him, like the human body. To understand its operation, one had to get at its inner structure and the flows that sustained it. Money was a surrogate of the ability of an economy to transact business and store wealth. "Money," he wrote, "is but the Fat of the Body-politick, whereof too much doth as often hinder its Agility, as too little makes it sick."[25] Like a healthy person, a healthy economy enjoyed good circulation; the faster and the greater the volume of transactions – of rents, taxes, wages – the stronger the economy. Petty thus revealed that national wealth was not just the product of accumulated mercantilist booty but also a reflection of dynamic patterns of labour and consumption. And in order to trace all these actions, political arithmetic depended on objective, statistical measurement to reach its conclusions. Facts mattered. Petty, for instance, calculated that the average Englishman needed 4½ pence a day to cover the necessities of life. Thanks to Petty, the king was better positioned to calculate just how much he could remove from his subjects' pockets.

Political arithmetic flourished in the late seventeenth century. A one-time sundial maker and bookkeeper named Gregory King fashioned population and family income data into a "Scheme of the Income and Expence of the Several Families of England Calculated for the Year 1688." By isolating those in society who increased national wealth and then deducting the impact of those who decreased the wealth of the nation, King grandly announced that England's total wealth in 1688 was £1,825,100. Others followed. When war with the French broke out shortly thereafter, Charles Davenant published his *Essay on Ways and Means of Supplying the War* in 1695 to assist regal fiscal calculations. In the 1750s Malachy Postlethwayt used political arithmetic to demonstrate that foreign trade, even in slaves, stimulated national income. The influence of such political arithmetic spread. During the American Revolutionary War, for instance, Alexander Hamilton, soldier and future nation builder, would carry a copy of Postlethwayt's *Universal Dictionary of Trade and Commerce* in his saddlebag. As America's first treasury secretary, Hamilton was converted to the belief that the republic must build its wealth through trade.

Political arithmetic was not an exclusive birthright of the English. Stimulated by the Enlightenment's emphasis on reason and systematic knowledge, French thinkers began to probe the nature of economic activity. Led by François Quesnay, the Physiocrats concluded that agriculture was the mainstay of the economy and that all other sectors of the economy lived off and fed into this central engine of the economy. In the 1760s Quesnay worked out a series of *tableaux économiques* that plotted the relationship between French landlords, farmers, and artisans working in agriculture. The *tableaux* demonstrated how the production of agricultural commodities was dictated by the ongoing interaction of capital, rents, and prices. Quesnay even devised a crude matrix in which commodity production by landowners and farmers was traced in a reciprocal zig-zag fashion right down to the final product. Each step in effect multiplied the impact of the step preceding it. Quesnay understood that economic activity reflected money in circulation and that dynamic economies generated surpluses. In the spirit of the Enlightenment, the Physiocrats argued that judicious reform of rents, the imposition of fair prices – a *bon prix* – and equitable taxes would stimulate the overall economy and drive France forward. Some saw the Physiocratic prescription as an assault on aristocratic privilege, but others saw it as a shrewd analysis of the power of laissez-faire economics.

The Physiocrats' insistence on agriculture as the linchpin of national wealth echoed into England. Arthur Young, an early proponent of "scientific" agriculture, spent a lifetime cataloguing the agricultural endowments of England, Ireland, and France. Young's *Political Arithmetic* of 1774 argued that by improving its agriculture a nation improved its national wealth. In Scotland, Sir John Sinclair produced his twenty-one volume *Statistical Account of Scotland* between 1791 and 1799. At the heart of Sinclair's statistical labour was a 166-item questionnaire that he administered to every one of Scotland's 938 parishes. Better information, Sinclair believed, would lead to better agriculture and better social conditions. Indeed, Sinclair is usually credited with bringing the word "statistics" into popular currency. In many cases across Europe, political arithmetic became indentured to the narrow notion that agriculture was the exclusive fountainhead of national wealth.

Adam Smith begged to differ, suggesting in his famous 1776 treatise on economics, *The Wealth of Nations*, that a society did not build enduring wealth by agriculture alone. Manufacturing, transportation, and trade also enhanced national wealth. While Smith thus accelerated the evolution of laissez-faire economics, he steadfastly insisted that labour expended in society's service functions – servants, doctors, teachers – had no lasting economic worth. Such production disappeared with the sweat that produced it; it had no lasting economic effect. Like the Physiocrats, Smith clung to a notion that national wealth was essentially anchored by material goods. Thus the activities of government and the payment of rent on dwellings had no lasting economic impact. Nonetheless, Smith and the Physiocrats had moved the concept of national wealth from a static, mercantilist construction to one that was dynamic and amenable to human engineering. And they had both invoked the power of systematically gathered evidence – statistics – to elucidate the workings and reform of the national economy.

Colonial Canada proved fertile ground for such calculations. Land and man's activity on it were at the heart of the colonial economy. Immigrants crossed the Atlantic in search of land and what it might produce. Early Canadian economic thought, one historian has noted, was dominated by "constructing an economic rationale for land disposal and settlement." In the hard-scrabble environment of the imperial outback, colonists had no time to ponder the finer points of economic theory. Instead, "the application of borrowed theory to the formulation of domestic policy" became the norm in British North America.[27] Typical of this pattern was a young Scot, Robert Gourlay, who arrived in Upper Canada in 1817. Born into a landholding family in Fifeshire, Gourlay had helped Arthur Young to compile his agricultural survey of England. He then studied farming at the University of Edinburgh just as John Sinclair released the results of his survey of land use in Scotland. Such statistics fanned a growing sympathy in Gourlay for the plight of the rural poor and their treatment at the hands of rapacious landlords and antiquated poor laws.

In 1817, facing debts and political opprobrium in England, Gourlay emigrated to Upper Canada. His expectation of colonial prosperity fuelled by ample land and hard-working immigrants was soon shattered. A Tory clique, he concluded, was hoarding land and exacting crippling rents from beleaguered tenants. To substantiate his case, Gourlay fell back on the methods of Sinclair and Young. He devised a thirty-one-item questionnaire designed to furnish a "statistical account" of the young colony and mailed it to 700 township officials throughout Upper Canada. Many of the questions were rhetorically loaded. What, farmers were asked, had most "retarded" the development of the colony? At the same time, Gourlay issued a series of "addresses" to the people of Upper Canada in which he alleged that economic progress was being choked by the misdistribution of land and faltering immigration. Gourlay's penchant for vituperative politics easily outstripped his skill as a statistician. He assailed the entrenched Tory clique as "the vile, loathsome and lazy vermin of Little York." Progress was being stunted by "a system of paltry patronage and ruinous favouritism." Predictably, Gourlay paid a price for his obstreperousness: he was tried for libel and sedition and banished from the colony in 1819. Three years later, his *Statistical Account of Upper Canada*, a useful but flawed compendium of detail garnered from the fifty-seven townships that did reply to his inquiry, appeared in London.[28]

Others began to plot British North America's statistical emergence in more even-handed ways. The surveyor general of Lower Canada, Joseph Bouchette, painstakingly surveyed his native Quebec and then extended his scope into the rest of British North America. In 1815 he began publishing his "topographical description" of the colonies, providing colonists for the first time with an objective inventory of their natural wealth. While Gourlay's statistical extremism faded, nineteenth-century economic statistics in Canada usually remained harnessed to some cause – land reform, free trade, and the promotion of immigration being perennial hobbyhorses.

In the mid-nineteenth century a crude statistical enterprise emerged in Canada. "Canadians" had taken censuses as far back as the administration of Jean Talon in New France, but they were episodic, imperfect surveys. The nineteenth century brought modern methods. In 1847 a Bureau of Agriculture was established in central Canada to collect "useful" statistics that tended to "promote improvements within the province."[29] In 1851 the first systematic census was administered in colonial Canada; its updating every ten years would provide the young nation with demographic benchmarks. In 1867 the Fathers of Confederation had no hesitation in assigning "census and statistics" to the new federal government.[30] Ottawa immediately began publishing a *Year Book and Almanac of Canada*, a compendium of facts and useful information about the young nation. Throughout all this, the old Physiocratic association of agriculture and national wealth persisted. As Liberal finance minister, Richard Cartwright noted in an 1870s speech: "there are but three great sources of wealth in Canada – our farms, our forests, our fisheries and our ships ... in regulating the policy of this country we must look first and foremost to see how any policy will affect the welfare of the men who are actually engaged in adding to the real and substantial wealth of the country."[31]

When not counting wheat sheaves, Canada made fitful attempts to measure its industrial might. Enumerators in the 1891 census were instructed to capture information on the numbers of "industrial establishments" in Canada. By collecting data on the capital, wages, raw materials, and employees of Canadian mechanical and manufacturing establishments, the Canadian public would be able "to see at once in what directions our industrial development was taking place."[32] This calculation required a good deal of cajoling on the part of the enumerators, who were then obliged to sort the data into five groupings according to the value of each establishment's production. The result, published in 1895 as a "special report," indicated that Canadian manufacturing had grown a sturdy 53.7%[33] in the decade from 1881 to 1891. The manufacturing census was readministered in 1906, this time by means of a questionnaire mailed to 15,796 establishments. The results showed that Canada's industrial take-off was in full flight: since 1900 industrial capital invested in Canada had increased 86%.[34]

Such industrial statistics had only a narrow utility. Their completeness was dubious; the 1895 report admitted that the enumerators had "raked and scraped" together the data for small establishments employing fewer than five people.[35] Much more debilitating was the omission of service functions in the economy from this crude calculation of national production. Thus services as varied as cold storage and doctoring were not captured in these early attempts to probe Canada's modern economy. Crude estimates of services were attempted to fatten the national total. "We might add therefore one-half to the present total as a rough estimate of the total productive activity of the Canadian people," a survey of production suggested as late as 1923, "according to the economist's definition of production, which approximates to the concept of national income."[36]

With slippery figures such as these at his disposal, it is not surprising that Robert Hamilton Coats told his minister in 1915 that statisticians had "never systematically attacked this problem" of measuring Canada's national wealth in terms that straddled *both* its agricultural and industrial fullness.[37] The failure was rooted in other broad cultural tendencies in the nineteenth-century Canadian mind. Most pervasive was the belief in classical economics – the notion that economies were self-regulating organisms. Economic progress was the product of the mysterious workings of the "invisible hand." The economics profession embraced this notion with unshakable, deductive fervour. The tendency was to look to the theory and deduce the outcomes in real life – to draw down from principle to practice. Having succumbed to this deterministic logic, economists could muster little enthusiasm for prying the economy apart with statistics. Why compile intimate data on something you cannot control? Consequently, economics was largely a descriptive, not an analytical, science. When pushed, early Canadian economists studied agriculture, the much-acclaimed workhorse of the economy. At Canada's few universities, economics was clumped together with political science and labelled "political economy," the implication being that the external hand of political policy was more explicable than the hidden magic of the invisible hand.

The handful of intrepid economists who did establish themselves on Canadian university campuses tended to research economic history and institutional growth. When Adam Shortt, for instance, donned his robes as a political economist at Queen's University in the 1890s, he embarked on a laborious study of the evolution of Canadian banking and currency. In the classroom, professors' trust in classical economics gave the discipline a moralistic tone. The individual's role was to conform to the natural rhythms of the economy. Well into the 1930s most Canadian universities used Duncan Alexander MacGibbon's *An Introduction to Economics* to coach young Canadians on the nature of their economy.

"During the period of depression," MacGibbon intoned, "the consumption of goods is at a low ebb. Almost everyone feels the pinch and endeavours to save as much as possible."[38] The invisible hand was, it seemed, capable of pinching the economy, but few economists could say why.

But, as Coats himself had sensed in his work on the cost of living in the "new" Canada, urbanization and industrialization were pushing economists and statisticians toward a more intrusive and dynamic reading of their national economies. As the new century unfolded, there was broad recognition of the need for what the great Austrian economist Joseph Schumpeter would later call "aggregative analysis," the treatment of national economies in a holistic rather than fragmentary fashion. Alfred Marshall, the godfather of modern English economics, echoed the ambition: "Everything that is produced in the course of a year, every service rendered, every fresh utility brought about is a part of the national income."[39] The drift was toward what the Norwegian economist Ragnar Frisch would soon label "macroanalysis" and away from theoretical, fragmentary, nonstatistical economics. *Macroeconomics* was in the process of being born; only by establishing the aggregate performance of an economy could one begin to determine its dynamic functioning, as opposed to its static condition. Alfred Marshall's 1923 aphorism "The many in one, the one in the many"[40] captured this interplay.

The creation of the Dominion Bureau of Statistics (DBS) in 1918 reflected this trend. The Statistics Act predictably stipulated that Coats's new agency was to perpetuate the census and the collection of agricultural statistics. But it was also to intensify the investigation of trade, transportation, and industry. Centralization of all these data was now paramount. "Not only must statistics be available on the main subjects of national interest," Coats emphatically wrote in 1921, "but they must be properly 'articulated' with each other, so as to form a single conspectus."[41] The twenties saw some progress toward this goal. In 1917 the *Census of Manufacturing* was made an annual survey. In 1923 the *Survey of Production in Canada* appeared with its rough estimate of national income derived from combining commodity production with service-producing industry. And throughout the decade, Coats kept updating his 1915 estimate on national wealth.

On the theoretical front, there were small methodological advances. In calculating industrial output, for instance, the danger of overlapping was ever present. A brick or a tile might first be counted as part of national mineral production and then be recounted as an outcome of manufacturing. Rigorous classification of products had to be observed. More attention was given to identifying trends in production. In 1926 index numbers were applied to the figures appearing in the Dominion Bureau's *Monthly Review of Canadian Business Statistics*. This entailed a monthly average that reflected the seasonal rhythms of the Canadian economy – fall was, for instance, the shipping season. Each index was "weighted" to reflect its traditional relative strength in the economy. With the application of 1926 as the base year in the system, users of the monthly index could henceforth identify the trends evident in the Canadian economy. At the same time, industrial censuses began to differentiate between "gross" and "net" production. Net production deducted the value of materials consumed in the manufacturing process and avoided the double counting of gross production, which simply aggregated all facets of one productive chain. For instance, the value of raw iron used in making railway wheels would be subtracted from the final value of the wheel. One last ingredient in the calculation of national production was supplied in 1918 when the calculation of Canada's trade abroad was brought over to the young bureau from the Ministry of Trade and Commerce. Slowly, the jigsaw of national production was coming together.

Coats reinforced this momentum by recruiting some new faces in the 1920s. A bright Oxford-trained economist, Sedley Cudmore, was brought in from the University of Toronto to head the bureau's General Statistics Branch. Herbert Marshall soon followed Cudmore from the University of Toronto and began collecting trade and investment statistics. Finally, Sydney Smith, an industrial census specialist, joined Cudmore's branch as the assistant on business statistics. Smith edited the *Monthly Review of Canadian Business Statistics*, thereby becoming the resident expert on "barometric" indices. For the first time, Canada had a team of statisticians dedicated to assembling some semblance of the nation's overall economic performance. To accommodate these and other expanding functions, the bureau moved to new premises in 1928 – a converted lumber mill on Green Island just off Sussex Drive. It was a miserable place, frigid in the winter and a steam bath in the summer. To control the rats that wandered freely in the building, Coats found funds in his budget to "employ" several cats.[42]

Despite Coats's boast to Prime Minister King that his agency provided a "bird's eye view of progress" in Canada,[43] Canada's economic statistics in the 1920s offered little real insight into the workings of the national economy. Yes, there was a flattering estimate of national wealth and some "barometric" indicators of production trends, together with

The Dominion Bureau of Statistics' office on Ottawa's Green Island in 1940. An old lumber mill converted into an office building, the structure was inadequate in every respect. Cold in winter, stiflingly hot in summer, its over-crowded offices were home to Canada's first, halting attempts to produce a set of national economic accounts in the 1930s and 1940s. The burgeoning demand for postwar demographic and economic statistics finally prompted the government to give the DBS a new home in the early 1950s at Tunney's Pasture, farther west along the Ottawa River. Courtesy of Library and Archives Canada, PA-151669

some rather loosely researched surveys of production. The underlying principle in all this calculation was a straightforward process of aggre-gation – calculating the value added by each stage of a product or com-modity's production to arrive at a grand, single column total. Beyond these aggregates, it was impossible to tell what was happening *inside* the economy. Which social groups and regions were bolstering nation-al growth and which ones were languishing? Who spent how much on what? Where did wages and profits actually go in the economy? In prosperous times, like the late 1920s, such insight was perhaps not much in demand, but when the economy faltered the statistics offered little guidance. When, some years later, a Montreal advertising re-searcher wrote to Coats asking for insight into Canada's "total realized income by type" – by wages, business profits, dividends – Coats was obliged to glumly answer: "I do not know of any study of the national income of the kind you mention, though we propose working on this subject in the Bureau of Statistics during the next few months."[44]

Throughout the 1920s Canadians therefore clung to their old economic attitudes. They watched the stock market and tracked the performance of certain "barometric" stocks like those of Canadian Pacific, which were generally believed to act as a telltale of overall economic performance. They listened to bank presidents, who delivered hortatory pronouncements on the country's economic health. "Almost all indices of Canadian production," Sir Herbert Holt assured Royal Bank shareholders in 1929, "have shown a spectacular rise during the past four years."[45] To clinch the point, the bank adorned its calendar with iconic images of wheat being harvested, mines being excavated, and railways carrying exports to tidewater. Business magazines like *Canadian Business*, founded in 1928, extolled the efficiency of the invisible hand. Universities started offering bachelor of commerce degrees to budding young practitioners of market liberalism.

Many construed these practices as the "science" of understanding business fortunes and those of the wider economy. A young political economist at Queen's University, Clifford Clark, could confidently write in 1923, "Now certain statistical facts are symptomatic of business change. It is, therefore, possible to build up a barometer or a series of barometers that will be highly susceptible to changes in business and financial weather and which can therefore be used as a guide by those business and financial men who direct and control industrial activity."[46] Imbued with such confidence, Clark himself soon left academe to become a banker in Chicago. The bullishness of the Roaring Twenties tended to disguise that in the absence of credible macroeconomic insights, quackery could easily be dressed up as sage advice. Subscribers to *Babson's Composite Plot*, perhaps the most popular wind vane of the economy in the decade, soon made this discovery.

Despite its abiding trust in the verities of classical economics, the business community after the First World War sensed a need for more incisive economic intelligence. To know was to anticipate, to plan. This urge was particularly evident in the United States, where "big business" felt increasingly ill at ease with the whims of the invisible hand. In 1916 an electrical engineer, Magnus Alexander, convinced a group of company presidents that the credibility of American business depended on objectively researched data that would guide businessmen to decisions that were both profitable and socially responsible. The National Industrial Conference Board (NICB) was born and immediately began to study the cost of living and labour conditions from its Park Avenue offices in New York. Although the NICB styled itself as a bastion of economic liberty against "statism," it soon moved into the area of detailed statistical analysis of the economy. Around the corner in New York, the National Bureau of Economic Research (NBER) was established in 1920. A quasi-academic research body, the NBER was dedicated to impartial, quantitative, and scientific analysis of the economy. Directed by a Columbia University economist, Wesley Mitchell, the bureau promised "to meet a growing demand for a scientific determination of the distribution of national income among individuals and families" in relation to taxation, legislation, and industrial readjustment.

The NBER drew on the work of economists such as Willford King, who in 1915 had published *The Wealth and Income of the People of the United States*, a study that constructed its total from production

---

Babson's Composite Plot

Roger W. Babson (1875–1967) was a Massachusetts businessman-turned-business-guru. He devised a theory of how the economy worked by drawing the notion from the physical sciences that for every action there is an equal reaction. Babson proceeded to combine a gallimaufry of unrelated business statistics – bank clearings, immigration arrivals, business failures, foreign exchange rates – into a composite index that he then plotted on a graph. He then contrasted the current position of the index with what ought to be its "normal" trajectory, thereby indicating the economy's relation to the business cycle. Companies subscribed to *Babson's Composite Plot*, and Babson was soon a millionaire. He reinforced his success by writing "how to" books such as *Fundamentals of Prosperity* (1920). In 1929 he confidently predicted that Herbert Hoover's arrival in the White House would mean unbounded prosperity. When the economy tanked later that year, so did Babson's credibility. He fell back on moralistic platitudes: "When we are flat on our backs, there is no way to look but up."* During the Depression, Babson hired immigrant stone masons to carve inspirational inscriptions into boulders near his Massachusetts home – "Keep out of debt," "Help mother," and "Be on time/study."

*www3.babson.edu/archives

data in a traditional value-added fashion. By 1922 the bureau had produced its own national income estimate, one that focused on income received by individuals, businesses, and even governments. Whereas King tended to use census data, the NBER preferred to study income tax data. There were still many bones of contention (e.g., how to account for capital gains), but, overall, American research in the 1920s made national income a dynamic mechanism, the product of continuous flows of production and income through the economy.[47] Canada produced no equivalents to either the NICB or the NBER in the 1920s.

The Great Depression changed everything, although not immediately. The comfort of hindsight has allowed historians to demarcate the 1930s as a watershed decade during which Western economies dramatically altered their socio-economic values. Sensationalistic images of Black Thursday and Wall Street suicides aside, the Depression had jagged beginnings. In Canada the onset of persistent drought in the West in 1928 began the slow strangulation of the wheat staple, the lifeblood of Canada's export trade. By 1929 other commodities began to falter, the result of overcapacity and sputtering consumer demand for everyday commodities like paper. By October the financial markets picked up on the anxiety. The Roaring Twenties had sparked a bout of irrational exuberance on the stock market; stock watering, margin buying, and merger mania had driven prices higher and higher. Now they fell.

But even as stock prices plunged and exports contracted in the autumn of 1929, Canadians did not jettison their faith in established economic verities. Canada's "hewer of wood, drawer of water" economy had seen downturns before and had always bounced back. Most Canadians accepted the notion that they were at the mercy of a powerful business cycle – a kind of undulating pattern of investment and consumption – that usually stimulated their nation's resource-driven economy but could, when world commodity prices dropped, cloud the economic sky. When such clouds did appear, government, business, and the citizen at large had to mimic the economy at large by reducing demand and retrenching – "tightening their belts," as the famous cliché suggested. The economy was a self-correcting mechanism and would rebound of its own accord. In this spirit, Prime Minister Mackenzie King assured Canadians in late 1929 that the nation was experiencing a familiar "seasonal adjustment" and that long-term gain would surely follow short-term pain. The minister of finance, Charles Dunning, followed suit, bringing in a federal budget that tinkered with the sales tax, juggled tariffs, and smugly reported a small surplus. Canada, he implied, had its economic affairs in order.

Throughout 1930 the downturn showed no sign of abating, and Canadians grew apprehensive. Mackenzie King's stand-patishness brought disaster upon the Liberal party in the federal election that October. The electorate wanted activism, and they got it in the new Conservative prime minister, R.B. Bennett. But Bennett's activism proved old-style activism. Tariffs were jacked up to daunting levels, government expenditure was mercilessly cut back, and only modest, one-time grants were made to provincial governments, which found themselves on the frontline of the "relief," or unemployment, problem. Canada, Bennett promised, would "blast" its way back into world trade by negotiating protectionist roll-backs from its erstwhile trading partners. In the interim, the nation would live out the downturn on as self-sufficient a basis as possible.

The private sector shadowed this approach to tough times. If income – sales, profits, and wages – was down, then expenditure – consumption – must also be curtailed as well. Consequently, the banks reined in borrowing; loans were called and credit mangers told to become stingy. Everywhere, Canadians looked for some telltale of an upturn – a wheat sale here, a pick-up in machinery sales there. This ambition was, however, more an act of hope than an outcome of incisive examination of the economy. Sitting in his office at the Dominion Bureau of Statistics, Robert Coats was only marginally better positioned to divine the economic condition of the nation than the average citizen. When the governor general wrote early in 1931 asking for some economic prescience, Coats could reply only that Canada was in "the trough of a major depression" and that the "dark spot is wheat." "The immediate future is, of course, obscure," Coats unhelpfully concluded.[48]

The view from the prime minister's office was equally obscure. Having promised to blast his way into foreign markets and thereby stimulate employment at home, Bennett naturally wondered just how bad unemployment was in Canada. There were no official figures. Desperate to plumb the depths of the problem, the prime minister wrote to the mayors of every Canadian town and city asking them to report unemployment in their bailiwick. Some, embarrassed by their predicament, low-balled their tally. Others, eager for a larger relief payment from Ottawa, exaggerated their plight. Rural Canada was not canvassed at all. In the end, Bennett was no closer to measuring the social disaster that had put him in office but was now destroying his credibility.[49] The situation at the White House in Washington was little different. President Hoover saw his economic woes as a "bankers' depression." His secretary of the Treasury, Andrew Mellon, took a moralistic line on the slump. "It will purge the rottenness out of the system," he told Hoover. "High costs of living and high living will come down. People will work harder, live a moral life. Values will be adjusted, and enterprising people will pick up the wrecks from less competent people."[50] When Franklin D. Roosevelt offered Americans a "New Deal" in 1932, voters showed their enterprise by dumping Hoover.

As unemployment, bankruptcy, and social unrest began to stalk the land, the perception grew that Canada was facing not just a cyclical recession but a major structural collapse of its economy. There was, in the first place, a crisis of underconsumption. The country lacked sufficient income to support its productive capacity: the constriction of exports, bank credit, government spending, and wages all combined to place a huge damper on demand. Classical economics had suggested that prices and wages were codeterminants and that depressed wages would soon bring an adjustment in prices that would prompt the economy back to full employment. Supply and demand would thus magically realign, and prosperity would return. Coats reflected this faith in the self-correcting virtue of a free economy; the phrase "gradually righting itself" frequently occurred in his correspondence.[51]

But in this recession there seemed to be disquieting evidence that the self-righting mechanism was malfunctioning. Global overindulgence in protectionism had, for instance, etherized international trade. At home the contracted domestic market had delivered power into the hands of the large producer and retailer, who were placed in a position to subvert the free adjustment of prices. What classical economics suggested should have been an atomistic readjustment was instead subverted by oligopolies and monopolies that used their economies of scale to drive the "little guy" out of business. Canadians labelled this phenomenon "price spreads," and by 1934 the damage that they were perceived to be inflicting on the economy provoked a now-beleaguered Prime Minister Bennett to convene a royal commission on the subject. Headed by Bennett's outspoken minister of trade and commerce, Harry Stevens, the commission quickly found fault with classical economics: "It is, furthermore, a tragic delusion," the commission reported in 1935, "that the solution for those economic problems can be left to automatic forces, because conditions which once permitted the easy and equitable operation of such forces have ceased to exist ... Nor can we assume any longer that this monopolistic tendency is a merely incidental intrusion into a system predominantly and naturally competitive."[52]

The Depression revealed other destabilizing inequalities in the national economy. Like prices and wages, there seemed no natural equilibrium among regions in Canada. Provinces like Saskatchewan that rested their economies on external markets staggered through the Depression. Central Canada, with its more-rounded economic base, weathered the storm on a more even keel. And the Maritimes? "I do believe," the commissioner of the Saint John Board of Trade confided to Coats, "that we are growing poorer all the time … [that we are] the least developed section of the Dominion. Our money goes to Central Canada, but how little of it ever returns in the form of some new economic activity financed with some of our own money that passes into Central Canada."[53] Coats could reply only that "the inadequacy of interprovincial trade statistics is a problem we have discussed many times." When a Winnipeg grain merchant complained to the Dominion statistician that Manitoba had become a "poverty-stricken" region, Coats replied that "accurate statistics of wealth and income of Manitoba would dispel a good deal of confusion and possible wrong thinking" but that the agency had made only a "stab" at such analysis. "I fear we have not accomplished very much."[54]

By 1935 both Bennett and Coats seemed to reach their road to Damascus. Laissez-faire capitalism seemed to have lost its instinct for self-correction. Coats began writing about capitalism being an "evolving" institution of humanity. For his part, Bennett announced the creation of an Economic Council of Canada for which the DBS would undertake "special statistical investigation" into Canadian social and economic policy. Coats personally undertook to write Bennett's speech justifying the council. Quoting English social scientist Sir William Beveridge, Coats had the prime minister declare that "most countries of the world" were no longer "leaving the machine to right itself." The key now lay in intelligent intervention in the economic system, in learning how to restore "purchasing power." And here, Coats wrote, understanding national income – "We know something about its aggregate amount, but little about its distribution" – was all-important. Better statistics were the key. Like most of Bennett's last-minute conversions, the Economic Council came to naught.[55]

Canada's Depression malaise of underconsumption and regional disparity was reinforced by constitutional rigidity. While Ottawa controlled the main levers of the national economy, such as trade policy, agriculture, and industrial development, the provinces oversaw social development. And the Depression delivered a crippling blow to the provinces' ability to administer unemployment relief, education, and basic social services. Yet just as Canadians clung to now unworkable economic notions, so too did they cling to the notion that there was a sacred division of federal and provincial authority in Canada. The handiwork of the Fathers of Confederation was not to be tampered with. Prime Minister Bennett discovered this in 1935 when he promised Canadians a "New Deal" in which the federal government would assume interventionist powers over the marketplace and begin to provide social assistance to the victims of hard times. Many provinces screamed "trespass." The courts intervened.

Opposition leader Mackenzie King deftly fanned such anxieties when he offered the electorate "King or Chaos" in the federal election of October 1935. Back in power, King proved cautious. Canada's intransigent economic and constitutional problems needed study by experts before any restructuring could be broached. Satirists would come to ridicule King's penchant for gradualism – "The height of his ambition / Was to pile a Parliamentary Committee on a Royal Commission," poet Frank Scott would later write – but there was quintessential Canadian wisdom in his method. Gather the facts, review the options, then act.

In the summer of 1937 King appointed the Royal Commission on Dominion-Provincial Relations to study the tattered fabric of Canada's Constitution and its social and economic underpinnings. The commission was soon labelled the Rowell-Sirois Commission, after its two leading lights, Ontario's Newton Wesley Rowell and Quebec's Joseph Sirois. A massive research effort followed. Lawyers, academics, and journalists were deployed to unravel the national experience. One of the commission's guiding principles was the conviction that a society was fuelled in its ambitions by its national income. "We are fully alive," the commissioners reported to the nation three years later, "to the importance of maintaining, and expanding as rapidly as possible, the national income which is woefully inadequate for the standards of well-being which Canadians have come to adopt." Indeed, "this need for a large national income," the commissioners claimed, had pervaded their deliberations. The "unequal distribution of the national income" between different regions and income groups was endangering national unity. This state of affairs required "bold departures from former practices."[56]

But bold departures required accurate information, and here the outlook was distinctly gloomy. The royal commissioners soon discovered what others already knew: Canada had some sense of its national *wealth* but little sense of how its national *income* was generated. The 1935 Price Spreads Royal Commission had complained that "all the problems presented to this Commission have been complicated by a general lack of economic facts of critical significance. The Commission has had to spend much of its own time and much money on the unearthing of facts which should have been readily available." More data on the economic rhythms of society – wages, earnings, cost of living – were needed. The Dominion Bureau of Statistics needed to be "considerably extended." "Accounting and statistics may seem dull and pedestrian proposals, but they are the only keys that will unlock the first barriers to better conditions."[57]

The Dominion-Provincial Commission heard the same message. Witnesses appearing before it uniformly cited the thinness of Canadian economic statistics. Even Tim Buck, the head of the Communist Party of Canada, bemoaned the fact; it was hard to fault the capitalist system if the numbers were not there to demonstrate the point. The party had been forced to base its "arguments upon estimates. This, I think, everyone will agree, is not our fault, but is rather our misfortune and the misfortune of the people of Canada."[58] Robert Coats could do little in his own testimony before the commission to disguise that the statistical structure of the national economy was very poorly understood. "Well," he sheepishly admitted, "we have statistics of national wealth by province compiled by the so-called inventory method. It is not a bad figure, but it is not a very good one either." Better insights into the economy, Coats suggested, would come only if business and federal tax officials were more forthcoming with raw data on wages, profits, and taxes.[59]

If the statistics were poor, this was largely because economic theory had not called them forth. Just as the Depression crushed the credibility of laissez-faire capitalism, so too did it reveal the futility of deductive economics. The Depression confounded simple trust in the theory of classical economics. Markets were not in fact "righting" themselves. Falling wages were not redefining the labour market and creating new jobs. Protectionism was not prompting fruitful renegotiation of world trade. The bareness of the cupboard of economic theory became all too apparent as attempt after attempt to reinvigorate trade and state policy failed. After the collapse of the 1933 World Economic Conference, John Maynard Keynes, a Cambridge economist with a contrarian mind, lampooned this bankruptcy. World leaders, he wrote, had "no cat in the bag, no rabbits in the hat, no brains in the head." They were all victims of "an obstinate adherence to ancient rules of thumb."[60] "Every government since the last war has been unscientific and obscurantist," he would later write, "and has regarded the collection of essential facts as a waste of money."[61] Across the Atlantic opinion was equally pointed.

Simon Kuznets, a young Russian émigré economist working at the NBER, dismissed American efforts to map the economy statistically: "No one knew what was happening. The data available then were neither fish nor flesh nor even red herring."[62] Another Russian economist, Wassily Leontief, haughtily announced in the *Review of Economic Statistics* that anyone interested in the problems of production, consumption, and distribution would find "the proverbial boxes of theoretical assumptions ... as empty as ever."[63]

The Russians Are Coming

The pioneering of national accounting in North America involved a remarkable Russian contribution. Three men born in Czarist Russia left an indelible mark on the conceptualization and implementation of national accounting. Simon Kuznets (1901–85) was the son of a fur trader in the Ukraine, where he studied to be an apprentice economist through the tumultuous years of the Revolution. Coming to the United States in 1922, Kuznets earned a doctorate by 1926 and then joined the National Bureau of Economic Research. Kuznets, who believed that economics was not a matter of abstract theory but a science of precise measurement, dedicated much of his career to reconstructing America's national accounts back to 1919. Wassily Leontief (1906–99), the son of a St Petersburg economist, earned a doctorate in Berlin after studying economics in early Soviet Russia. After advising the Chinese on railway policy, he came to the United States, to the NBER and Harvard, where he devised the input-output table as a key tool of national accounting. Kuznets and Leontief became Nobel laureates. Paul Studenski (1887–1961) was never an architect of national accounting, but his 1958 history of national accounting, *The Income of Nations*, remains a benchmark. After studying law in Russia and medicine in Paris, Studenski came to America as a stunt pilot, forsaking barnstorming for economics (thereby belying any suggestion that economics was for dull people). Studenski taught at New York University until 1955.

Why the Russian penchant for national accounting? Perhaps it is a reflection of the strong mathematical emphasis in Russian education. Perhaps it arises from exposure to Marxism's insistence that material conditions are the only basis for understanding the operation of society. Perhaps it bespeaks a legacy of observing the Soviet command economy's heady early years.

Slowly the ethos of economics began to shift. It was recognized that perhaps inductive analysis – driven by the gathering and observation of fact – should underlie the discipline. Out of the right facts might come the right theory and the right public policy. History has conceded the commanding heights in this transformation of economic thought to John Maynard Keynes, whose *General Theory of Employment, Interest and Money* appeared in 1936. At the time, however, Keynes joined a chorus of theorists wrestling with the problem of correcting unemployment and underconsumption. (In the provincial election of 1935 Albertans had, for instance, embraced Social Credit, the doctrine of an English engineer, C.H. Douglas, who preached that the state should pump additional purchasing power – "funny money" the critics said – into the economy.)

Keynes built his case around the problem of aggregate demand. He discarded the notion of automatic economic adjustment and argued that the state must take an activist role in stimulating the economy. By advocating that the state use its own purchasing power to cyclically off-set the boom and bust cycle of capitalism, Keynes was suggesting that overall economic performance could be stabilized and consumption bolstered. The money supply should also be managed; cheap money promoted capital investment and thereby fuelled income growth, which in turn fed back into the healthy maintenance of consumption. Keynes's prescription also held out the prospect that such intervention in the economy could be used to tackle economic rigidities – like regional inequalities within a nation.[64]

Keynes's prescription for prosperity immediately became, and has remained, a bone of vigorous contention. Whatever theoretical or ideological perspective one brought to Keynes, there was no denying that he focused attention on the centrality of *national income* to economic wellbeing. And if the national income had to be managed, then it first had to be understood. "How can economists be expected to produce a clear and unanimous diagnosis," he wrote to the *Times* of London, "when the facts they have to go upon are so obscure and imperfectly known?"[65] There needed to be a system of national accounts that would act as the bedrock of any endeavour to manage the economy, a system that allowed policymakers to look inside the economy and identify its rhythms of production and consumption.

Keynes was not alone in this intuition. His colleague at Cambridge, Colin Clark, had been busy since the early 1930s trying to trace the patterns of production, distribution, and income within the British economy. This he called his "scaffolding."[66] Clark sensed that once an economy had been broken down into its component transactions, it could be rebuilt in its aggregate form in a way that showed the respective contribution of each activity. Clark is generally credited with popularizing the term "gross national product" as a figure that conveyed the value of all final goods and services produced in an economy over a set period. For their part, disciples of Keynes began using the equation c (consumption) + I (investment) + G (government spending) to reveal final demand in any economy. Economists were beginning to equip themselves with the jargon of a new conceptualization of the economy's workings.

Across the Atlantic, other economists were tending in the same direction. As the Depression broke over America, Wesley Mitchell at the NBER determined to compile a more incisive set of national accounts using the fresh results from the 1930 census. To this end, he hired a bright, newly minted doctoral graduate in economics from Columbia University. Simon Kuznets had grown up in Czarist Russia, where he had become an apprentice economist before fleeing the chaos of the Russian Revolution. Kuznets instinctively rejected economics by theory alone; he was an empiricist who believed that "economics is the basis of all social problems."[67]

Two things propelled Kuznets to the forefront of American national accounting. First, in June 1932 the United States Senate passed the LaFollette Resolution, which called on the secretary of commerce to compile "estimates of total national income of the United States" for the traumatic years 1929–31.[68] The estimates were to show how American income was generated by all sectors of the economy and how it was distributed in wages, rents, royalties, profits, and other payments. The NBER got the job. Under Mitchell, it had acquired a powerful reputation for getting its numbers right; it was less inclined to abstract theory and fixated on hard numbers, which were conspicuously absent in the crisis of the Depression. Second, almost simultaneously, Kuznets was commissioned to write the entry on national income for the prestigious *International Encyclopedia of the Social Sciences*. In a decade when economists were scrambling for new concepts and tools, Kuznets's nineteen-page essay on the subject quickly became the template for national accounting. Kuznets opted for a "production-driven" model – a model that would measure the value of goods and services for final demand – a critical measure for a nation locked in depression. Using tax data, special surveys, and census returns, Kuznets was able to assemble a detailed dissection of the American economy, which he delivered to the Senate in early 1934. America's national income had plunged from

$89 billion in 1929 to $49 billion by 1932. The data was flexible and could be broken down to reveal the role of individual industries, regions, and types of business organization. Kuznets's tables also revealed how the share of each of these components changed over time. How, for instance, had the auto industry fared in the grim downturn after 1929? Which groups within society shouldered the greatest tax burden?[69]

In Canada, Kuznets's approach was only vaguely understood. In 1934 the DBS produced its own first attempt at a comprehensive statement of national income. *The National Income of Canada* was produced by Sedley Cudmore and focused on income produced – but only in a crude fashion. Unlike Kuznets, Cudmore had no tax data on which to draw and instead built his estimate on existing surveys of production figures, special surveys of retail purchases, and census-derived estimates of wages. But since the production figures captured only "five-eighths of gainfully occupied Canadians," Cudmore had to base his estimate on the dubious assumption that the other three-eighths of working Canadians were "quite as productive as the other five-eighths." Cudmore was obliged to admit that the estimate contained "a considerable margin of error."[70]

Impatient with such rough estimation, the Bank of Nova Scotia commissioned Professor Donald MacGregor of the University of Toronto to construct another estimate that did not make the easy assumption that employees who produced goods and those in the service industry were comparable in their productivity. The bank's estimate, for instance, drew directly on actual payroll records of railways to calculate service industry incomes. MacGregor also tried to weed out some of the duplications in the DBS – double counting of materials, for instance.[71] But the result was largely the same: Canada was left in the middle of the Depression with only the haziest estimation of its national income. This realization was immediately arrived at by the commissioners appointed to the Royal Commission on Dominion-Provincial Relations. With a mandate to repair the disequilibrium of Canadian federalism, the commissioners had to be able to break apart the national economy on a province-by-province basis to demonstrate who produced what and who consumed what. A "fresh approach to the problem" was needed.[72]

This fresh approach was evident in the appointment of four economists to the task of preparing a study on national income for the commission. Donald MacGregor came to Ottawa from Toronto, where he joined J.B. Rutherford, head of the DBS's agriculture branch, and John J. Deutsch, a young researcher at the recently created Bank of Canada. George Britnell rounded out the team, arriving from the University of

American economist Simon Kuznets (right) receives his Nobel Prize for economics in Stockholm in 1971. A Russian émigré to the United States, Kuznets pioneered the calculation of national income estimates in response to a mandate from the Senate for figures that would allow Americans to track the inner workings of their depression-ravaged economy. In his famous 1933 entry in *The Encyclopedia of the Social Sciences*, Kuznets described national income as "the net total of desirable events enjoyed" by a society. Since its inception in 1969 the Nobel Prize for economics has been awarded four times for work on the understanding of national accounting. Courtesy of Corbis, U1724238.

Saskatchewan, where his specialty was agricultural economics. The commission's research director, Alex Skelton, was emphatic in telling MacGregor what the commission wanted. His team was to "revise" the DBS estimates of national income to arrive at "a summary of income produced, by provinces and by industries, and by income paid out, by provinces, from the earliest year for which approximate estimates are available to the present."[73] Since the commission's overriding mandate was to investigate the social and regional strains exerted on Confederation by the Depression and modern urban-industrial society, a cataloguing of income *produced* by industry would not do. A constructive dissection of Canada's problems seemed likely only if national income could be traced on the basis of income *received* or *paid out* by province and by income category. Furthermore, the new team was to tackle something that Kuznets's income-produced method had conspicuously skirted: the contribution of government to the generation of national income.

Almost immediately, the Rowell-Sirois economists were overwhelmed by the magnitude of the task before them. If they were to pinpoint national income by industry and region, then the DBS's income-*produced* approach based on census data was of little use. The problems of identifying income at the point at which it was *received* were immense. Could it be assumed, for instance, that a corporation with a Toronto head office paid wages only to Ontario workers? Obviously not, but how could those paycheques be traced, province-by-province, into the households of the nation? Paycheques had dollar signs on them, but if a farmer ate his own produce, was this income? And what about investment income – rent, interest, and dividends? Did government services rendered to citizens represent actual income or were they simply a neutral transfer of resources between one sector and another?

Faced with these daunting questions, MacGregor and his colleagues realized that they were being asked to completely reconceptualize how Canadian policymakers understood the economy. Rowell-Sirois wanted answers quickly; the Depression had seemed to ease in 1937 but had come back with a vengeance the next year. If the commission was to recommend ways to alleviate regional and social stress in Canada, it needed not only evidence of the problem's complex national dimensions but also a means of tracing the impact of the remedies – taxes, subsidies, investment – that might subsequently be applied. This was to be an exercise in *applied* economics. The data would dictate both the analysis and the outcomes of public policy.[74]

It seemed natural that the statisticians at Green Island would act as first cousins of the royal commission researchers. Officially, the MacGregor group made polite noises about "the generous co-operation of the Dominion Bureau of Statistics," but behind the scenes they found the bureau too set in its ways to help them penetrate the inner workings of the economy. "It has not been possible to devise a method of correcting the Bureau's estimate of 'income produced' on the basis of year-to-year data," MacGregor told Skelton.[75] The bureau's figures were full of unwarranted assumptions. What evidence was there that goods workers and service workers had "equal productivity"? The bureau's figures were full of duplication. The only deductions in agricultural production were for fuel and feed; no allowances were made for machinery costs, fertilizer, and capital depreciation. The bureau's 1934 estimate of national income was therefore "too high."[76] More worrisome was the bureau's continuing inclination to employ a production approach to the whole issue of calculating national income. This was hardly surprising. The bureau had always taken a census approach to economic statistics, which focused on production, not on income consumption. Its chief business statistician, Sydney Smith, was clearly more happy counting pig iron production than engaging in the meticulous tracing of income as it percolated through the economy.

MacGregor privately seethed at the impoverished state of statistics in Canada. He was by nature a man of blunt opinions and little regard for others' sensibilities. A member of the Department of Political Economy at the University of Toronto since 1930, MacGregor had done well by carrying his economic skills into the world of public policy. Economics was now less a matter of pontificating about abstract theory in the classroom; it was about hard, cold research and policy prescription. Thus students had to be equipped with proper statistical training, which was, MacGregor wrote in a submission to a 1939 committee on promoting better academic engagement in the social sciences, woefully inadequate in Canada. Canadian universities showed little interest in teaching statistics. The "influence of deductive and literary or philosophical traditions in Canadian economics" had bred parochialism in the discipline. On Canadian campuses, "one can easily count on two hands the number of academic men who have a good working knowledge and some critical understanding of the main primary [statistical] sources" that might promote a more inductive, empirically driven approach to economic policy.[77]

MacGregor was equally withering in his assessment of Ottawa's statisticians. After a noble start, Robert Coats's quest for an efficient, centralized statistical agency had become bogged down in political and bureaucratic intrigue. The agency, he argued, had been reduced to "a tail end of the Department of Trade and Commerce" where "low standards" and "the vice of secrecy" prevailed. Long-term economic problems were "given less attention than the work of providing schoolboys and the daily press with statistics without tears." Thus the federal government had been "caught with its pants down" in the Depression, unable to supply "the new political arithmetic of economic nationalism, social security, monetary control and other forms of intervention." MacGregor's cruel evaluation of the bureau conveniently overlooked its stellar success as a census taker and national demographer. But he had put his finger squarely on its failure – both intellectually and methodologically – to equip the nation with a more incisive way of understanding the workings of its economy. "This," his indictment concluded, "provides good justification for those who call the Bureau a mere counting house and who doubt its capacity to assume greater responsibilities for the conduct of economic research."[78]

Not surprisingly, the Rowell-Sirois team adopted a "go-it-alone" attitude to their research. They constructed an *income-received* template of the economy, which aimed to do three things: first, it would estimate all salaries and wages paid out by employers, including government, to individuals in each province; second, to this it would add a calculation of investment income ranging from bond coupons to rental income received by landlords in each province; and third, it would estimate the income of all unincorporated businesses – farmers, fishermen, retailers, small businessmen, and so on – by province. MacGregor himself set to work analyzing wages and salaries, doggedly pursuing tax data, corporate payrolls, and provincial records to pinpoint who received what in each province. He produced twenty-seven tables demonstrating wages and salaries in sectors as diverse as forestry and municipal education. In another set of tables, MacGregor traced investment income to its recipients, even calculating dividends paid into Canada by foreign corporations. He fine-tuned his income estimate in innovative ways. A surrogate figure was developed to impute the invisible income from owner-occupied homes. MacGregor also broke new ground by including in national income those wages and salaries paid by government. He did not include social benefits, like pensions, arguing that they were in fact only transfers from one part of society to another. If government borrowed to fund its services, the cost of such borrowing should be included because it became income for another sector of society. Professor George Britnell from the University of Saskatchewan and J.B. Rutherford, on secondment from the bureau, turned their attention to Canada's all-important agricultural sector. What receipts were generated by the sale of grain, cattle, and Canada's other harvests? What income "in kind" could be imputed for farm produce eaten by farm families? John J. Deutsch from Queen's University, himself a Saskatchewan farm boy, compiled data to estimate farm operating expenses that had to be deducted from income.

Finally, in January 1939, their work was done. The royal commission researchers presented an entirely new definition of national income: "The national income, which is the aggregate of all incomes earned in the production of goods and services, is the most comprehensive measure of the economic welfare of the nation," their report began.[79] MacGregor and his colleagues had indeed produced a "fresh approach to the problem" of understanding the mechanics of an econ-

The commissioners and research staff of the Royal Commission on Federal-Provincial Relations, c. 1939. Commissioners Henry Angus, John W. Dafoe, Joseph Sirois, and Robert MacKay sit (left to right) in front of the researchers and administrators who supported their investigation. John J. Deutsch (second from right at rear) and academics such as Donald MacGregor from Toronto were tasked by the commissioners to make an estimate of Canada's national income along the lines suggested by Simon Kuznets (far right) in the United States. In their report the commissioners described this work as a "fresh approach to the problem" of understanding the inner dynamics of a national economy. Courtesy of Queen's University Archives.

omy locked in the grip of a dreadful depression. It was an approach that showed the regional complexity of Canada and acknowledged the more active role of government in society. For the very first time, Canadians were presented with a province-by-province breakdown of the salaries and wages paid to them, together with their investment income. The income of "individual enterprisers,"[80] farm income, and federal transfers to provinces for pensions and relief were also calculated. In Depression-flattened Saskatchewan, for instance, salaries and wages had plunged from $157 million in 1928 to a mere $78 million in 1934, while relief payments had soared from $2.5 million to $24 million in the same period.

But MacGregor's work was only a study for a royal commission that had yet to report. When Rowell-Sirois did finally report in 1940, its findings would endorse the approach taken by MacGregor. The commissioners argued that "a large national income" could be realized in Canada only if the right statistics were at hand. Ottawa must commit itself to the "continuation and improvement of the economic and financial statistics which we have gathered, and for the refinement and development of technique in measuring the relative financial positions of governments and making equitable inter-governmental adjustments in the future." To achieve this, a "small, but highly competent, permanent research staff and secretariat" must be established to act as a "clearing house" for national income data.[81] But in the still-dark days of 1939, MacGregor's work was just a projection of what *might* be, not official government policy or even accepted statistical practice in Canada.

As a courtesy, Alex Skelton sent along a copy of the commission study to Robert Coats. Coats was defensive. The study, he admitted, was "an elaborate and interesting one, based on competent investigation, in a very important and hitherto partially-covered field." The bureau had "envisaged" such work but had "never been able to give it the attention it deserved." That said, Coats reiterated the bureau's commitment to a production-based approach to national income calculation. Coats quibbled with MacGregor's figures – they were "on the low side" – and with the report's reluctance to treat government social services as a neutral activity. But Coats did acknowledge that the study's ability to demonstrate the provincial distribution of income was "an outstanding contribution." Then, in a flash of prescience, Coats suggested that any "final treatment" of national income should include "both these approaches" – income and production. But this was a daunting prescription: "The truth is that the subject is so large and many-sided that we have never been able in the Bureau to pursue either method of approach in detail."[82]

Back at Green Island, not much changed. To begin with, the bureau's national income staff was small, overworked, and out of touch with the powerful currents of opinion in Depression economics. Its budget had been pinched by Depression austerity. The bureau's chief business statistician, Sydney Smith, had but one statistician to assist him, Ray Bangs, and he was an engineer whose expertise lay in transportation statistics. A handful of clerks handled the data and rounded out the team. But the real obstacle lay in the Dominion statistician's office. Robert Coats was not an economist, and as much as he might tip his hat to the many-sidedness of the national income problem, he had little intuition of the intricacies of modern economics. His brilliant success as the architect of the modern Canadian census inclined Coats to methods that hinged on straightforward aggregation, not the subtle breaking-down and isolation of economic flows within the aggregate. A few years later Robert Bryce, a brilliant economist in the Ministry of Finance, caught the problem. Coats, he learned after a tearful interview with the overworked and underappreciated Bangs, had "not taken very much interest in the national income work and, in fact, did not understand very much about it."[83] That Coats felt insecure in the changing world of Depression economics was further illustrated in 1940 when Harold Innis, Canada's premier economic historian, wrote to tell the Dominion statistician that the Department of Political Economy at the University of Toronto was about to adorn its walls with his portrait. "I will certainly be in bad company," Coats replied, "if 'hung' among the economists."[84]

One senses that Coats's inaction was also rooted in bureaucratic intransigence. He had committed his agency to Kuznets's production approach to national income calculation, and retreating from this decision might be construed as a defeat. No doubt he also feared the possibility that national income work might be snatched away from his office and delivered into the hands of another government agency. In many other countries, the central bank already oversaw monitoring of national income. The Bank of Canada, for instance, had established its own research department. The cocky and at times acerbic opinions of out-of-town academics like Donald MacGregor no doubt heightened Coats's refusal to budge.

Throughout the summer of 1939 the most that Coats was prepared to do was allow Sydney Smith to prepare a confidential review of the growing debate on the calculation of national income.[85] Smith reviewed the "scope of inquiry and method of approach" to the national income question in an even-handed fashion, but the bureau's bias toward a production approach still shone through. Perhaps, Smith conceded, if better income tax data were available, Canada might embrace the income-received method more heartily. But in North America the focus was on production. This had been good enough for Simon Kuznets and the National Bureau of Economic Research. "We do not think that, in the present state of the studies on the subject," the assistant Dominion statistician, Sedley Cudmore, informed the Ministry of Finance, "we have made any mistake by following the latest United States methods."[86] Thus legitimized, Smith and his staff were instructed to prepare a new set of national income figures stretching back to 1919 that would employ what obviously appealed to Coats as the tried-and-true method of calculating national income.

By 1939 statistics had not solved the problems of the Depression. Yet economists and statisticians had at least opened new windows on the economy. As Coats and MacGregor had sadly and somewhat acrimoniously discovered, the windows did not always agree in their perspectives. Experts might now deploy the term gross national product to describe the grand goal of their labours, but few could actually settle on a figure to attach to it. In 1934, for instance, the bureau employed its production-driven method to suggest that Canada's national income in 1930 was $5,150 million. "Too high," MacGregor said. Five years later, MacGregor and his team measured income paid out to Canadians and came up with a total for 1930 of $4,167.6 million. "Too low," Coats said. Who was right? How were policymakers, businessmen, and even citizens to make plans with figures that were so disparate? Could income and consumption within an economy ever be segregated and then reconciled? In the interim, Canadians waited on their royal commissions and held onto the faint hope that the invisible hand might once again revive national prosperity.

And then, in September, war came again. For academics and those old enough to remember, the economic wounds of the Great War quickly came to mind – inflation, debt, and regional disparity. From his desk at the Bank of Canada, John J. Deutsch hastily put together a salutary survey of Canada's economic experience in the previous war. This war would have to be fought with "detailed planning, a high degree of centralized direction, and effective co-ordination." This war would have to be managed from the outset. "The problems of war finance," he warned, "under this situation cannot be solved simply by the laissez-faire expedient of inflation."[87] Across the Atlantic, Keynes took pen in hand and lectured the readers of the *Times* on "how to pay for the war." The era of the "brave guess" in economic matters was over. The times now demanded "an open mind to untried ideas."[88]

Back in Ottawa, Coats undoubtedly waited for his phone to ring. Sir George Foster was long in his grave, but that minister's 1915 query to the then newly appointed Dominion statistician must have reacquired its urgency. Give us the numbers to fight this war, the wartime politicians would soon be demanding.

2 Rough Stabs

This hodge-podge is both meaningless and misleading ...
Everything is vague and difficult to interpret.
~ John J. Deutsch, Bank of Canada, memo in Bank of
Canada Archives, 1941

The arrangement of national income breakdowns and
related statistics into economically significant flow tables
can be a powerful aid to fiscal analysis and to the framing
of fiscal policies ... the time is not far off either in Canada
or the United States, when we can attempt rough stabs
at aggregative current figures.
~ George Luxton, Bank of Canada, memo in Bank of
Canada Archives, 1942

If Canada, U.S. and U.K. can agree on common lines of
development, there will be a good chance of making the
post-war very much better than the pre-war world.
~ J.M. Keynes to R.B. Bryce, 1942, LAC, RG 19, vol. 3444

One good reason for expecting prosperity after the war is
the fact that we can lay down its specifications.
~ John Kenneth Galbraith, Fortune, 1944

Canada's modern System of National Accounts was born on a cold
evening in April 1942. April 9 had been cool and showery, one of those
Ottawa days when winter continued to cheat spring. The weather
matched the mood of the national capital. The war was not going well.
Just months earlier, Pearl Harbor had jolted the nation into a two-front
war. The previous day, news had reached Canada that Japanese aircraft

had sunk a British aircraft carrier and two cruisers in the Indian Ocean. On the home front, the war was rapidly overheating the economy. The Depression had been vanquished but at a cost. Annual inflation in 1941 had jumped to 7%. The minister of munitions and supply, C.D. Howe, was squeezing every ounce of capacity out of the nation's industrial plant. Rationing governed every aspect of consumer spending; the national speed limit had just been reduced to 40 mph to conserve gasoline.

Politically, the nation was locked in a referendum over conscription. The opinion polls were showing that English and French Canadians did not see eye-to-eye on whether Canadians should be forced to fight for their country. Prime Minister Mackenzie King fretted that he had let loose the boogeyman of ethnic division and that the nation might soon fall to fighting itself rather than battling the Axis. That April evening, King conformed to his engrained bachelor routine. In his comfortable Sandy Hill home, he had dinner, took a nap, listened to the radio, and then dictated his daily entry in his diary. "The war news are very bad," he wrote. There were rumours, he noted, that Howe's own son was on one of the doomed British cruisers. The unstoppable Japanese frightened the prime minister: "There is a danger of everything but the heart of the Empire being destroyed."[1]

As King wrapped up his day, an unusual meeting was convening not far away at 295 Manor Avenue, a quiet, tree-lined street in Rockcliffe Village, the enclave favoured by Ottawa's business, bureaucratic, and diplomatic elite. This address was the home of Clifford Clark, a former Queen's University political economist who since 1932 had been Canada's deputy minister of finance. Harvard-trained and with experience in American banking, Clark stood at the central intersection of the war economy. Every crucial decision concerning wartime economic policy crossed Clark's desk before it was passed to an equally stressed James Ilsley, the minister of finance. Throughout all this, Clark contended with chronic arthritic pain. "These men," the prime minister would confide to his diary, "have far too much on their shoulders."[2]

It had taken two weeks to find a niche in Clark's crammed schedule for this meeting, and even at that only an evening meeting was possible. Not that his guests were any less harried. The cars pulling into Clark's driveway bore the best and brightest of Ottawa's wartime bureaucracy, men who would soon acquire the sobriquet of "mandarin" as the architects of Canada's transformation into a modern, managed state.[3] There was Graham Towers, the brilliant young governor of the Bank of Canada, who presided over the country's monetary policy. With Towers came John J. Deutsch, another Queen's University academic who had joined the bank's research department, where he laboured trying to dissect the wartime economy's operation. Clark had also invited his own right-hand man, Robert Bryce, who not only oversaw the Ministry of Finance's research efforts but also sat as the secretary to the all-powerful Economic Advisory Committee, a blue-ribbon group of civil servants created in September 1939 to coordinate Cabinet decision making on war finance and supply. Bryce had studied at Cambridge and Harvard and was still in frequent contact with his mentor, John Maynard Keynes. The deputy minister of trade and commerce, Dana Wilgress, a seasoned expert in Canadian trade, arrived with his first lieutenant, Oliver Master. Rounding out the arrivals that evening were Fraser Elliott, the lawyer who oversaw the Ministry of National Revenue's income tax division, and Sedley Cudmore, the man who had just taken on Robert Coats's mantle as Dominion statistician. Thus, for a few hours on that Thursday evening, Clifford Clark had ensured that he had the undivided attention of the mandarins who mattered most when it came to the national economy.

There was a note of exasperation in Clark's opening remarks to this living room gathering. In the two and a half years since the war began, Canada had made great progress in harnessing its economy to the needs of war. Foreign exchange control and rationing of every conceivable aspect of consumer spending had been introduced. Prices were controlled, war loans initiated, and Crown corporations created to fill production gaps in the private economy. A huge super-ministry – Munitions and Supply – coordinated the production of materiel ranging from screws to tanks under the vigorous orchestration of C.D. Howe, Ottawa's "minister of everything." Expediency had been the abiding order of the day; the mandarins had shown a tremendous capacity for managing on the run. But such pragmatism had its limits. Beyond the challenge of defeating the Axis laid shaping the peace and ensuring that the Dirty Thirties were a thing of the past. To do this, Clark and his inner circle knew that they needed better statistics if they were to dissect, intervene in, and track the national economy. "Figures of the national income are now recognized," Bryce had briefed his deputy minister the day before the meeting, "as the most comprehensive measure of the economic activities of a country and of its capacity for taxation, war expenditures, etc." Aggregate totals were "of relatively little use unless one can break them down into various components."[4]

Bryce believed that the initial phase of the war effort had been a wasted opportunity in terms of improving Canada's national accounts. There had been bureaucratic turf protecting and intellectual confusion of the worst order. The Dominion Bureau of Statistics, the Bank of Canada, and the Ministry of Finance had all adopted a dog-in-the-manger attitude to the problem of furnishing the mandarins with a statistical portrait of the national economy. The Ministry of National Revenue would not, for instance, release crucial income tax data that would get statisticians much closer to understanding exactly where income flowed in the economy. There had been little attempt to settle methodological differences. Would Canada cling to Kuznets or embrace the Keynes-inspired model of Britain's newly created Central Statistical Office? Clark had seen enough. The time had come for a "radical improvement."[5]

The deputy minister first put the pressure on Elliott of National Revenue. He quickly extracted a promise that more precise and more workable tax data would be released to compilers of national income. The ice began to break: "The others present were much encouraged by Mr. Elliott's suggestions and very keen desire to cooperate." A decision to establish "some sort of interdepartmental advisory committee to assist in working out the proposals" followed.[6] It would break the logjam over method. The "experts" would decide.

Clark finally turned to Cudmore, the Dominion statistician. Would the DBS be prepared "to set up a special unit ... to organize and carry out this national income work." Cudmore hemmed and hawed. He still regarded the bureau's Kuznets-based work as effort well spent. He needed more data, better salaries. But he too was willing to join the common pull. Clark immediately stated that it would be imperative to find "a very highly qualified man" to take charge of the new effort. Everyone agreed but there was a strong sentiment that such talent was in thin supply in wartime Ottawa. Clark then rounded out the new consensus by assuring Cudmore that better inventory and "man-hour" figures would soon be coming his way. By the time the mandarins' autos pulled out of the Clark driveway late that evening, they had an "understanding" to "develop new estimates of national income" at the Dominion Bureau of Statistics.[7]

Four days later Clark informed his minister of the decision. He reminded Ilsley of the "very embarrassing situation which exists in the field of national accounts." Canada would continue to be seriously handicapped without "sound and adequate statistics relating to the total national income, its origin by industries and regions, and its disposition in the form of wages, salaries, rents, interest, dividends, etc." Clark warned that "nearly every major problem in the field of fiscal and borrowing policy and economic policy generally could not be solved intelligently without adequate figures of this type." Quick action was needed; Clark feared that without better national income data there would be administrative problems and, worse, "public criticism." Appointing a man of "absolutely first class caliber" at a good salary would pay "the country handsome dividends." Clark proposed John J. Deutsch for the post.[8]

The rosy afterglow of that April evening quickly wore off. It would be two more years before Canada's "special unit" for national accounting actually opened its doors. In the interim, expediency and experimentation continued to prevail. But the die was at least cast that evening. New men and new methods were the order of the future. A "system" of national accounts was in the making, its necessity undeniable, its shape still evolving.

When war came in the fall of 1939, there had been immediate recognition that the experiences of the First World War – inflation, regional inequality, and social dislocation – could not be repeated. Academics quickly supplied a report card on Canada's fiscal and monetary policies in the previous war, and their bottom line was that laissez-faire was out and control should now be the order of the day. Deutsch reminded a joint meeting of Canadian political scientists and historians that the first war had "required, in large part, only an intensification and slight adaptation of normal peace-time activity." This may have provided the boots and rifles, but it also triggered inflation and woeful problems of production. This war, Deutsch believed, would require "detailed planning, a high degree of centralized direction of economic forces, and effective co-ordination."[9] Taxation and voluntary reduction in consumption, not the free play of a laissez-faire market, would pay the bills in this war, he concluded.

Few in Ottawa disagreed, and the Liberal government of Mackenzie King quickly began erecting the framework of a controlled national economy throughout the fall of 1939.[10] Foreign exchange was placed under the Foreign Exchange Control Board. Consumer prices and consumption were placed under the draconian control of the Wartime Prices and Trade Board (WPTB). Canadian purses and wallets were soon full of ration coupons for everything from sugar to gasoline. The end of the "phoney war" in the spring of 1940 prompted similar control on the production side. Crown corporations were created to expedite the manufacture of war equipment, deemed beyond the abilities of the private sector. Ottawa was soon in the business of making things as varied as heavy bombers and synthetic rubber. With the creation of the Ministry of Munitions and Supply that spring, the engineer-politician C.D. Howe quickly acquired the reputation of an economic "czar" whose "controllers" had the power to dictate production in every crucial sector of the industrial economy. Behind this frontline of tight economic management was the Economic Advisory Committee (EAC), formed to coordinate the financial and economic policies bolstering the overall war effort. And here the Dominion Bureau of Statistics found its first foothold in the war effort. The EAC membership drew together the highest echelons of decision making in the federal government: the Bank of Canada, Finance, Trade and Commerce, Customs, Mines and Resources, Agriculture, External Affairs, and the WPTB. Robert Coats joined them as Dominion statistician; from the outset the policymakers realized that they would need numbers to frame and monitor their policies.

To gratify Ottawa's growing appetite for statistics, Coats established the Committee on National Income Statistics back at Green Island. To this committee he appointed the bureau's old stalwarts in compiling national income: Sydney Smith and Ray Bangs. They were joined by Jack Rutherford, the bureau's leading agricultural economist and a one-time member of the Rowell-Sirois team on national income; Herbert Marshall, the bureau's expert on balance of payments; and A.L. Neal, the chief of social statistics. Sedley Cudmore, Coat's deputy, rounded out the bureau's team. To connect the committee with the burgeoning wartime bureaucracy, Coats invited John J. Deutsch and Robert Bryce to join the group. Adding academic luster to the committee was the outspoken Donald MacGregor, now back at the University of Toronto after his Rowell-Sirois work.

The committee first met on 14 November 1939. Ottawa was feverishly gearing its bureaucracy to the new demands of war. Significantly, Deutsch skipped the meeting, probably a reflection of the Bank of Canada's crucial involvement in adjusting the nation to its dramatically altered monetary circumstances. Smith had prepared a briefing document for the committee on the scope and method of national income calculation, in which he once again revealed his preference for the Kuznets approach to the problem. Cudmore reinforced this predisposition, noting that for two decades the bureau had been collecting economic statistics, "the apex or ne plus ultra of which is the approximation of the 'gross national product' and the 'national income' according to the terms of Kuznets." Both Marshall and MacGregor cautioned against too great a reliance on the Kuznets approach, citing the narrowness of the American data. The committee nonetheless endorsed Smith's report, allowing Smith and Bangs to return to their engrained habits. Their energies would now be devoted to producing estimates of Canada's national income since 1919, which would serve as the benchmark for the nation's wartime economy.[11] Their only concession was a commitment to pay closer attention to the *expenditure* side of the economic equation and to try to acknowledge a more dynamic role for government as an active component of national income. This reflected concessions made by Kuznets in the United States, but it still left the bureau committed to a national income approach that emphasized production and minimized government's increasingly active role in Western economies. The committee's approval of Smith's past and prospective work may have saved face for Coats, but it was putting the bureau's research fatally out of touch with the government-centric thrust of Canada's wartime effort.

The years 1940 and 1941 in effect thus became national accounting's phoney war in Canada. A false sense of progress prevailed at the bureau and, at least temporarily, lulled the mandarins downtown into thinking that useful information was on the way. The Committee on National Income met sporadically and indecisively. Coats and Cudmore continued to extol the virtues of a Canadian variant of Kuznets. Then, early in 1941, Smith unveiled the fruit of his labours: *The National Income of Canada: 1919–1938*. The 149-page document was long on wandering discussion and very short on method and reliable data. It acknowledged that national income could be approached from both the income and expenditure perspectives but did little to elaborate the relationship of the two or the role of government as a generator of income itself. The report often slipped into economic moralizing about the "wastage" of the Depression. It sought to disarm its critics by pointing to its inability to gain access to Canadian tax data. The report was nonetheless quick to praise itself as "an advance beyond earlier Canadian work."[12] Few, however, agreed.

The report was circulated confidentially to the members of Coats's hand-picked committee. Even bureau insiders were quick to find fault. Social statistician A.L. Neal castigated his colleague's failure to provide a lucid explanation of the intellectual underpinnings of his conception of the national economy. Free-floating estimates left the user wondering about their credibility. The report, Neal concluded, was little more than a loosely jointed skeleton of suppositions and numbers.[13] Such friendly fire was soon overpowered when the report arrived on John J. Deutsch's desk at the Bank of Canada's research department. The bank was by 1941 still struggling to divine Canada's wartime fiscal and monetary position. Foreign exchange, savings, taxation, and inflation all demanded careful analysis. Such analysis made sense only if it could be fitted into the larger, interactive picture of the national economy. This perspective Smith's report failed to provide or did so in such a slipshod way that there could be no trust in the results. Now, no doubt regretting his earlier failure to take a more active role in Coats's committee, Deutsch took pen in hand on 28 April and eviscerated Smith's 1919–38 report.

Deutsch had little time for niceties. Smith's attempt to apply Kuznets's method to Canada simply transmitted the originator's "faulty methods" into this country and revealed the "difficulty of trying to fit Canadian data into a system designed to meet the circumstances of another country." The report's attempt to calculate income produced by government was naive in the extreme – a simple calculation of all taxes collected less government purchases. This outcome made no allowance for government borrowing to finance its expenditures on goods and services, which Deutsch pointed out was in wartime "an increasing proportion of the national income." Government borrowing was in fact a form of income generation and therefore belonged in national income. At the same time, Smith had included in national income government payment of relief, pensions, public welfare services, and interest on unproductive debt, payments that did not arise out of the production of goods and services but were simply transfers from one group to another. Such payments were therefore being double-counted by Smith and should be excluded. Smith's report contained no reliable way of determining how income was distributed among the provinces or how it flowed between the provinces. "This hodge-podge is both meaningless and misleading," Deutsch cruelly concluded. Like Neal, Deutsch decried the absence of "descriptive material" in the report. "Everything is vague and difficult to interpret." Without such explication, much of the data seemed suspect. How could one take on faith, Deutsch wondered, the claim that the income of stock and bond dealers in 1938 was only 16% less than in 1929? Or that Canada's gross capital formation in Canada was higher in 1937 than 1929. The intuition of anyone who had lived through the Depression suggested otherwise. "Incredible!" Deutsch exclaimed.[14]

Deutsch thus wrote the obituary of the DBS's attempt since the mid-1930s to provide a workable national income model for Canada. "The national income is the most comprehensive measure of economic activity and of the economic welfare of the nation," he pointed out. On such figures depended "the formulation of intelligent, effective and equitable social policies." Not to mention the whole effort to defeat the Nazis. The bureau's "hodge-podge" failed to do this. "The outlook is barren." A whole new start was necessary. "The matter should be placed on a sound and permanent footing as soon as possible" under the control of a "thoroughly competent person." Smith was not that person. And, possibly, the DBS was not the place for such work. If better estimates of national income were to be produced, perhaps the work should be done in the Ministry of National Revenue, where data on income existed in abundance? Or, he seemed to hint, at the Bank of Canada.[15]

Bryce and MacGregor completed the demolition. Bryce took exception to Smith's rather stingy and arbitrary treatment of government activity as income. A soldier being paid out of tax revenues should not be treated as part of national income, but if his pay was financed by loans, as was the case in this war, then that pay was an addition to the national income. Bryce had "a great deal of respect for Dr. Kuznet's statistical work," but its translation into the Canadian context seemed to miss out on the snowballing impact of government on the national economy. Bryce persistently faulted Smith for the lack of "clarity in definition" in his work.[16] MacGregor, never good at holding his tongue, was blunter. Smith's "extremely dangerous fallacy" lay in his fixation on production and neglect of income received. "The Bureau does a very doubtful service to itself, to the Government and to the country," he wrote, "when it relies on unskilled hands to deal with some of the most difficult problems of modern economics."[17]

Throughout the rest of 1941 the DBS continued to fiddle with a system that had no credibility with the wartime mandarins. Smith sent a shirty letter to Bryce saying that he might be able to produce better national income data if better data were forthcoming from other government ministries like National Revenue. The Committee on National Income Statistics discussed small technicalities but avoided the big theoretical road block. It did, however, advise the DBS *not* to make the 1919–38 estimates public. But Coats clearly gave up on the problem. His agency had done sterling work early in the war; census officials had, for instance, turned their talents to the challenge of compiling a register of all able-bodied manpower in the country. But on the theoretically demanding issue of reconceptualizing the national accounts, Coats was out of his depth. After over four decades of daily labour in taking the nation's statistical pulse, Coats was also bone-tired and ready to retire. "But the truth is," he wrote to economist Harold Innis that fall, "I have shot my bolt here, and should now let some new hand draw the bow. This job needs energy and keenness, and I am getting rapidly to the point where I have to pump these up."[18] On the day before he finally stepped down as Dominion statistician in January 1942, Coats wrote to Deputy Minister of Finance Clifford Clark and declared that the national income question was "Cudmore's baby now." Clark quickly learned that the new Dominion statistician was no boat rocker. Cudmore trotted out the now familiar DBS line that there were "so many different points of view on the question of national income that it seems impossible for a single presentation to be satisfactory to every one concerned." Cudmore liked Smith's "application of Kuznet's method to Canadian conditions" and believed that, with a little tweaking, it could serve as the "definitive presentation" of national income in Canada.[19]

The *coup de grâce* for the DBS came in March 1942. Cudmore had asked Bryce to see Ray Bangs, Smith's lieutenant, to review how government income was recorded in the accounts. The discussion initially took a predictable turn: Bryce said that the Kuznets method produced "anomalous" results, and Bangs affirmed his preference for production-based accounts. Bryce admitted that he believed the DBS economists were "greatly overworked." This prompted Bangs to unburden himself of all his frustrations. The crux of the problem was Smith. He was "a very poor organizer" whose research was not "properly recorded or summarized." His methods were not "written down" and were therefore unverifiable. Smith was bitter that all the work he had done on the 1919–38 estimates had yet to be published. He begrudged the advice given him by Coats to make his report "more or less of a popular and general character." Neither Bangs nor Smith thought that Coats understood much about economics. Bryce nudged Bangs into further revelations. "I got the impression that a good deal of the Bureau of Statistics work, in his opinion, is of poor quality ... an audit would show up many errors and deficiencies ... the morale of the staff down there is pretty low. There is a good deal of bickering, jealousy and knifing of one another." What most consternated Bryce was the news that Smith was so overwhelmed by his work that he was taking data home with him and having his family attempt tabulations of the national income. It did not take much to get the now overwrought Bangs to agree that a "new man" was needed to head Canada's System of National Accounts.[20]

Bryce needed no more convincing that the wrong men with the wrong ideas were in charge of Canada's attempt to build a set of national accounts applicable to its wartime circumstance. The problem was much deeper than differences in methodology. Coats and Smith had been working in an intellectual vacuum. They were oblivious to the revolution in economic thinking that had been conceived in the Depression and hatched in the frenzied outbreak of war. The DBS's fixation with production was rooted in an old-fashioned notion of what use statistics played in Canadian economic thinking. The old barometer of growth rationale, popular in the 1920s, still prevailed at the DBS. Statistics were about benchmarking national growth, not about diagnosis of its internal structure. For the DBS, Bryce concluded, the "main purposes were to inform business men and the public what was happening in particular fields, to provide evidence of Canada's development, and to provide certain standard statistics of population, agriculture and business – not very much interrelated or integrated. This was somewhat modified and patched up in the 1930s, with some new figures added, but not fundamentally altered."[21]

While the DBS tinkered with production figures, the focus of economics had shifted from the productive outcomes of capitalism to its *structural* and *distributive* dynamics. The Depression experience had indelibly impressed the role of income – who got what, where, and when – on the minds of economic observers. It was a question not just of where money was generated in the economy but also of where it went. An economic monitoring system should be able to trace these flows, to see where there had been breakdowns on the production side, and to identify the pattern of distribution on the income side. This challenge gained importance when depression or war obliged the state – the "government" in all those memos generated by Bryce, Deutsch, and MacGregor – to intervene to stimulate production or restrain consumption or redistribute income.

Britain led the way. Its longstanding predisposition to political arithmetic was reawakened by depression and war. Throughout the 1930s the British had increasingly fretted about the inadequacy of their national economic statistics. In 1930 Labour prime minister Ramsay MacDonald established the Economic Advisory Committee and turned to distinguished economist Sir Josiah Stamp to lead its deliberations on economic information. Stamp's focus was on the effect of taxation on income and industrial profit and, given the Labour government's predilection for social intervention, how government policy might be better informed by economic statistics.[22]

British universities also took up the challenge of connecting statistics and policy. At Cambridge a young economist, Colin Clark, engaged in a little "plain speaking" about "the disgraceful condition of British official statistics" before going on to construct an estimate of national income rooted in "an analysis of how it is *produced, distributed* and *spent*." Clark's calculations sought to produce an estimate of "gross national income produced" by measuring and then balancing national aggregates for incomes received (drawing on tax data) and for production à la Kuznets.[23] Very simply, Clark wanted a statistical account of the national economy that showed what was generated at one end and what was consumed at the other. The two functions ought to balance at the end of the day. A nation's accounts should mimic how a company kept its books; balanced, double-entry bookkeeping made for clarity and stability. Policymakers could thereby be shown how money moved through the veins of the economy. Clark departed for Australia in 1937 but left behind some young acolytes at Cambridge, most notably two Cambridge graduates of 1935: Richard Stone and David Champerdowne. Not surprisingly, the term "applied economics" came into vogue as these men sought to supply the statistical grist for the mills of economic theoreticians like Keynes, whose *General Theory* called in 1936 for better national income statistics to allow the state to anticipate and manage demand in the economy.

The advent of war in 1939 therefore found Britain predisposed to embrace new statistical ways. Although Sir John Simon's first war budget in September 1939 reflected an orthodox mix of tax increases and borrowing to pay for the conflict, there was a parallel recognition that new means would have to be devised to keep wartime inflation at bay and to pay wartime bills. Keynes was among the first to realize that the Depression bugbear of excess production and depressed demand had almost instantly been eclipsed by a problem of excess demand and overstretched production as the war economy sprang to life and began pumping wages and profits into British pockets. The central economic dilemma was now how to manage the twin pressures of civilian and war consumption and thereby keep the tiger of inflation in its cage.

Ever prepared to carry economic ideas into the public realm, Keynes took it upon himself to instruct the chancellor of the Exchequer on how the fiscal war might be waged. In a series of letters to the *Times* of London – later appearing in book form under the catchy title *How to Pay for the War* – Keynes set out the necessity of managing what he called the "inflationary gap," the gap between the level of aggregate demand for goods and services in an economy and the quantity of goods and services actually available for consumption. If the gap was too wide, inflation would occur. Keynes warned that the traditional nostrums of rationing and taxing profits were "pseudo-remedies." The war was rapidly banishing the Depression and filling workers' pockets with cash; rationing could not completely contain this surge, nor would taxing the profits of the rich suppress working-class spending. The solution, Keynes argued, was to persuade wage earners to defer their consumption for

John Maynard Keynes and his wife, Lydia Lopokova, in 1940. The outgoing Lopokova, a one-time dancer with the Russian Imperial Ballet, provided a flamboyant contrast to the austere and cerebral Keynes. As an economist, Keynes provided the hinge whereon economic thinking swung from adherence to classical economics to new attitudes about maintaining economic equilibrium, thereby inspiring national accountants. "The difficulty lies," Keynes once wrote, "not in the new ideas, but in escaping the old ones, which ramify, for those brought up as most of us have been, into every corner of our minds."[24] Courtesy of Corbis, HU006789.

the duration of the war and thereby allow the war machine to be adequately fuelled and inflation corralled. "In peace time," he wrote, "the size of the cake depends on the amount of work done. But on war time the size of the cake is fixed. If we work harder, we can fight better. But we must not consume more."[25] The war would thus become a vast exercise in the control of demand by fiscal means. Conserve now to win the war and then release pent-up consumer demand, stored in various savings instruments, into the peace to bolster the economy. In the autumn of 1940 Keynes became a government advisor.

The Keynes Plan was an academic prescription for a practical problem. Many called it politically naive – an infringement of workers' economic freedom, a denial of the volunteerism said to be at the heart of the war effort.[26] But others shared Keynes's perspective, and the gist of his program began to seep into British war policy. The venerable Josiah Stamp, now Lord Stamp, advised the Cabinet that demand management was the only feasible way for Britain to meet its war goals. One of the first outcomes of the Stamp Survey was the creation in early 1941 of the Central Statistical Office, with a companion Central Economic Information Service, as the coordinator of the economic data. Keynes had contended in *How to Pay for the War* that "lucidity" was the first ingredient in effective control of wartime demand and consumption. Better statistics would allow the judicious design of controls on consumption and production. Significantly, the Central Statistical Office was attached to the War Cabinet Secretariat. On Churchill's instruction, the office was to prepare a set of national accounts as "an agreed corpus, not subject to departmental argument, but accepted and used without question."[27]

The problem was to get the numbers right, to produce a plausible estimate of the inflationary gap in the wartime economy. London began to recruit good economic minds. James Meade, an Oxford economist who had edited the League of Nations' *World Economic Survey* (1939) in Geneva, returned to England, where he tried to elaborate Clark's system of balancing tables. He was soon joined by Richard Stone, who came over from the Ministry of Economic Warfare. Working in London throughout the Blitz, they produced Britain's first credible estimate of national income – *National Income, Saving and Consumption* – in January 1941. (Anecdotes abound about the tall, dapper, and sociable Stone. One recounts how he arrived at work one morning, his homburg covered in dust from a bomb explosion: "Really, James," he announced, "they have gone too far this time.")[28] Three months later, Chancellor of the Exchequer Kingsley Wood presented Britain's first Keynesian budget, one that had appended to it the Stone-Meade national income calculations as a white paper. The inflationary gap was estimated at £500 million (out of total government spending of £4,207 million), one that would be closed by extra taxation that would be returned to citizens as a tax credit after the war.[29] Conscious that they were pioneering a new method of economic analysis, Stone and Meade began feeding detailed explanations of their method into academic periodicals, an exercise that culminated in 1944 with the publication by Oxford University Press of a thin volume entitled *National Income and Expenditure*.[30] The book would remain in print in updated versions for decades. And each year the British budget would continue to be accompanied by a companion volume of national income and expenditure estimates. The era of the "brave guess" in economics was over.

Washington was not far behind London in mustering its national accounts for war. Throughout the 1930s researchers at the Department of Commerce had acted on the mandate given them by Congress in 1932 to produce national accounts that revealed a more incisive picture of the American economy. Although heavily influenced by Kuznets, who joined its staff in 1933, the department inched toward a more income-driven approach to national accounts as the Depression persisted. By 1939 it was able to publish, in its house journal *The Survey of Current Business*, monthly estimates of income payments and state-by-state income estimates. In 1939 the department created a National Income Division (NID). With the appointment of Milton Gilbert, the editor of the *Survey*, as its head in 1940, the NID moved further away from Kuznets and began focusing its research on commodity flows within the economy and on how income was distributed throughout the economy. Gilbert represented "a sharp break in the national accounts work of the Department of Commerce," a break made evident in his 1942 *Survey* article "War Expenditures and National Production." There, Gilbert applied the Keynesian formula of GNP (gross national product) = C (consumption) + I (investment) + G (government spending) to analyze the relationship between all-important defence expenditure and total economic output. Like Stone and Meade in England, Gilbert gave his government a fiscal plan for paying for the war. His figures revealed that "the full economic potential of the Nation has not yet been reached." Adroit management of labour and investment in production could wring more out of the economy. On the consumption side, Gilbert argued that suppressing private consumption of durables and drawing down inventories would allow America to finance its war without suffocating the civilian economy.[31] Within a year the NID was openly dedicating itself to two methods of national income: "the final products method" (expenditure) and "the method of distributive shares" (income).

Marching off to War

The arts of war have had a long relationship with the statistical arts. With the advent of technological, total war in the twentieth century, this relationship intensified as numbers were increasingly seen as the best diagnostic of strength in the factory and on the frontline. While Keynesian economists were incubating a new system of national accounts during the Second World War, other economists were deploying very similar methodologies and theories to fine-tune the engines of war. The two endeavours often engaged the same minds. After obtaining a doctorate in economics from Harvard in 1942, Richard Ruggles joined the London office of America's wartime think tank, the Office of Strategic Studies. There, he pored over photographs of German military tanks, trucks, and planes captured or destroyed in battle. He meticulously assembled serial numbers from this equipment, sorted them into systematic runs, and thereby was able to estimate the breadth of the production run behind each piece of equipment. Economist James Tobin later celebrated this arcane talent in a piece of doggerel – "The Legend of Dick Ruggles: The Econometric Detective and the Enemy Serial Numbers." "An armchair theory's for the birds," Tobin rhymed, "That lesson, kids, is very clear. It's guided Dick his whole career."* At the end of the war, Ruggles joined John Kenneth Galbraith in picking apart the estimates behind the Allies' saturation bombing campaign against Germany. The Strategic Bombing Survey revealed that the merciless bombing of German industrial cities had been based on faulty statistical analysis and had done little to cripple the German industrial effort. After the war, statistical analysis became a standard instrument of Cold War analysis, employed by such agencies as the RAND Corporation and the Strategic Air Command. Ruggles went on to become the doyen of American national accountants.

*Review of Income and Wealth 47, no. 3 (2001) 409.

Ironically, it was a young Canadian-born economist-turned-journalist who drew popular America's attention to the power of the new statistics at their disposal. John Kenneth Galbraith, an Ontario farm boy who earned a doctorate from Berkeley in agricultural economics in 1932, began the war working for the Office of Price Administration in Washington. But in 1943 he joined the editorial board of *Fortune*, America's blue-ribbon business magazine. He determined that the first piece he would write for the magazine would be on America's new national accounting system. "One good reason for expecting prosperity after the war," he wrote in the lead article in a series entitled "The Job before Us," "is the fact that we can lay down its specifications. For this we can thank a little-observed but spectacular improvement in the statistical measures on the current output of the U.S. plant."[32] Galbraith would subsequently argue that Germany lost the war because it was "badly run," meaning that its war machine never devised a statistical system by which to measure income and expenditure.[33] A good set of balanced national accounts, he liked to quip, was worth "a division of fighting men."[34]

A winterized Robert Bryce of the Ministry of Finance in Ottawa in the late 1940s. Bryce studied economics at Cambridge in the mid-1930s before joining Finance in 1938. He carried Keynesian ideas back to Canada and became their champion as Canadians grappled with the economic challenge of overcoming the Depression and winning the war. Keynes's 1946 obituary in the *Times* of London described him as "a lavish and unwearying helper of young men of promise." Robert Bryce became one of Keynes's great apostles and an intellectual font of the Canadian welfare state. Courtesy of the Bryce Family Collection, Ottawa.

It did not take *Fortune* to carry the message of income-expenditure national accounting from the Potomac to the Ottawa. Throughout the 1930s Canadians returning from studies abroad had been bringing an inkling of Keynes home in their intellectual baggage. Robert Bryce had been the most astute of these intellectual travellers. In 1932 he had graduated from the University of Toronto with an engineering degree and little desire to be an engineer. Instead, he was fascinated by the fractured structure of the economy and by the woeful state of the society that it was supposed to support. This was what needed fixing. Bryce audaciously applied to study economics at Cambridge. Good grades and references got him in. He spent the summer of 1932 at his family cottage on Georgian Bay, sitting on the rocks reading books like Keynes's *Treatise on Money*. Bryce was not the only Canadian lad in Cambridge. Toronto-born Lorie Tarshis had gone to Cambridge for a commerce degree and, like Bryce, had quickly fallen under Keynes's spell. Keynes was a notoriously bad lecturer; spinning an idea out one day, modifying it the next, and then rejecting it on the third. Perceptive students like Bryce and Tarshis quickly recognized that Keynes was wrestling with the central problems of liquidity, employment, and aggregate demand in a depressed economy. As a student in Keynes's seminar, Bryce revealed a particular talent for unravelling the twists and turns of Keynes's thinking-on-the-run. He kept copious notes of Keynes at the podium and in action at his famous Monday evening Keynes Club, where ideas were floated, picked apart, and polished. In 1935, before Keynes had in fact finalized his own thinking, Bryce fashioned a paper out of his notes – "An Introduction to a Monetary Theory of Employment" – which he took to London and presented at the London School of Economics. For many listeners, Bryce offered a lucid distillation of Keynes's thinking. For his part, Tarshis began work on a doctoral thesis on the distribution of labour income. When *The General Theory* was finished in 1936, Keynes asked Tarshis to critique the manuscript before he sent it to the publisher.[35]

Tarshis and Bryce carried Keynes home in the mid-1930s. Tarshis went to Tufts University, from which he applied pressure on "New Deal" Washington that culminated in a manifesto-like pamphlet – *An Economic Program for American Democracy* – that he and other academic economists published in 1938. Bryce headed to Harvard as a Commonwealth Fund Fellow. There, he found that classical economic theory still held sway, which prompted him to reverse the role of student and professor. Bryce proselytized the Harvard faculty on the virtues of Keynes's prescription for a return to prosperity. His thesis supervisor, the famed Austrian economist Joseph Schumpeter, quipped that if Keynes was Allah, then Bryce was his prophet. Keynes appealed not only because his macroeconomic analysis seemed to address the dysfunction of the Depression but also because his insistence on better economic statistics and quantitative analysis promised to equip the economist with tools, not just arid theory, that could be applied to real-life problems. Bryce, the engineer who had once found economics "fuzzy," now felt qualified for a career in applied economics. After a brief stint as an investment analyst at Sun Life Assurance in Montreal, Bryce arrived in Ottawa in 1938 to join Clifford Clark's staff in the Ministry of Finance.

When war came a year later, Bryce concluded that there was little time to worry about economic theory. If the exigencies of war precluded the seminar-like discussion of theory, they did not preclude Bryce reaching into the economic tool kit that Keynes had suggested was now available to policymakers. A set of balanced national accounts seemed like one of the most versatile tools in the kit, especially if they allowed war bureaucrats to dissect the flows of income and expenditure inside an economy. Keynes, Meade, and Stone had said as much in England, and Bryce expected the same in Canada. Despite the gruelling demands of daily life in the wartime Ministry of Finance, Bryce kept in touch with his academic friends. He kept up with the academic journals, occasionally even contributing articles. He read *How to Pay for the War*. He traded ideas by letter. He kept an eye open for bright young economists to pull into the service of their country. The war was for Bryce, like others, a nasty diversion, but it did not deflect him from the purpose that had sent him to Cambridge a decade earlier: to equip modern society with the means of managing a stable, equitable, and growing economy. Just two days after the fateful April 1942 meeting at Clifford Clark's home, Keynes reminded his Ottawa prophet what the end game was: "If Canada, U.S. and U.K. can agree on common lines of development, there will be a good chance of making the post-war world very much better than the pre-war world."[36]

Keynes found other conduits into Canada. Wartime pressure on inflation and foreign exchange obliged the Bank of Canada to intensify its research activities. In 1940 Graham Towers, the bank's cerebral governor, had taken a young London School of Economics-trained economist, Louis Rasminsky, on staff. Rasminsky, after work with the League of Nations in Geneva, returned to Canada as an expert on international trade and finance. Late in 1942 he returned to London to represent Canada at an Allied conference on the promotion of postwar multilateral trade. The conference agreed that a "clearing union" to break the grip of Depression protectionism by facilitating the international flow of trade and credit was necessary and that, for this, consistent statistics were indispensable. This included better national income statistics. Rasminsky reported back to Ottawa that "Keynes said the national income statistics had had a great influence on budgetary policy in the UK and he thought it would be of great value if similar estimates, framed as far as possible on a comparable basis, could be prepared by other Empire Governments."[37]

Towers's knack for picking talented young economists was also evident in the person of John J. Deutsch. Born into a family of nineteen on a hard-scrabble Saskatchewan farm, Deutsch had clawed his way to a Depression-era education. He taught high school in rural Saskatchewan as the Dirty Thirties enveloped his neighbours. In 1933 he entered Queen's University but was obliged to finance his education by teaching at a Kingston vocational college. The road to Cambridge or the London School of Economics never seemed open to Deutsch. With a bachelor's degree in commerce in hand, he joined the research staff of the newly created Bank of Canada in 1936 and immediately showed a precocious ability in applied research. Seconded to the national income team at the Rowell-Sirois Royal Commission, Deutsch quickly realized that Canada was a laggard in reading its national economic pulse. He undertook the dissection of farm operating expenses for the commission and authored the report's crucial introductory statement on national income with its frosty analysis of the DBS's work in the field.

War found Deutsch back at the Bank of Canada and a ready proponent of reform in Canada's national accounting. Exasperated by the DBS's adherence to what he considered outmoded ways, Deutsch went on the offensive. In April 1941 his "hodge-podge" memo had destroyed the credibility of the bureau's 1919–38 estimates. Deutsch then went public, carrying the message of the "new" national accounting to a broader public. In a July 1941 article in the influential *Canadian Banker*, he argued that the "urgencies and cataclysmic effects of depression and war" could be overcome only if policymakers had an intimate statistical portrait of how income and expenditure flowed in the economy. The measurement of war production, regional and social disparities, and the impact of government activity all hinged on such figures. In plain and simple language, Deutsch contended that national income was the "aggregate of all the incomes received and disposable for consumption and net new investment by all the individual citizens of the country during a specified period of time." It was "the sum of the satisfactions made possible by production and the existing stock of wealth." By

John J. Deutsch at his desk in Ottawa in the late 1940s. No wartime advisor understood the necessity of a workable set of national accounts better than Deutsch. His April 1941 attack on the Dominion Bureau of Statistics' slow and imprecise attempts to calculate national income – "faulty methods," "a hodge-podge"[38] – jolted Ottawa into a concerted effort to build national accounts that would guide the country into the postwar period. Deutsch himself would go on to a distinguished career as a mandarin, professor, policy consultant, and university president. Courtesy of Queen's University Archives.

tracking income and expenditure in the "sphere of the exchange economy, the sphere of the household and the sphere of the government," Deutsch assured his readers, Canada could win the war and build a depression-proof postwar society.[39] Little wonder that Clifford Clark told Minister of Finance Ilsley that Deutsch was the man to take charge of national accounting in Canada once the April 1942 decision was made to remove Sydney Smith from the position.

By 1942 the Keynesian view of the economic world was becoming evident elsewhere in Canada. That year a feisty woman economist at the University of Saskatchewan published the first academic monograph on Keynes in Canada. Mabel Timlin's *Keynesian Economics* was hardly a bestseller, but for those who pondered such questions, Timlin left no doubt that Canadian society had reached a junction at which new economic *mores* had to be devised to curb chronic unemployment and unequal distribution of income. Timlin subsequently won a Guggenheim Fellowship and took her message of Keynes in North America to the academic lecture halls of New York.[40] There, she would have been following in the footsteps of Donald MacGregor, whose Guggenheim Fellowship had allowed him to research the national accounts implications of manufacturing expenses and public finance.[41] In the minds of Robert Bryce, John J. Deutsch, Mabel Timlin, and Donald MacGregor, the time had arrived in Canada for national accounting in a Keynesian framework.

The necessity of better national accounting was also the outcome of particular Canadian pressures that would, over time, serve to impart a unique indigenous dimension to a system that had an otherwise distinct resemblance to its British and American cousins. In 1940 the Rowell-Sirois Royal Commission on Dominion-Provincial Relations had finally reported. In a sense, war had already solved the problems of the Depression. The conflict had stoked the fires of the economy. Consumption and tax revenues were reviving. But, the royal commissioners reminded Canadians, there were *systemic* problems with their federation. The old 1867 balance of constitutional and taxation powers had not weathered the twentieth century well. New social responsibilities had landed heavily on the provinces; traditional taxation sources had withered. Provinces with diversified economies were better positioned to adjust; those tied to rural, agricultural bases struggled to maintain standards. The Depression had thrown this imbalance into stark relief. Care of the unemployed fell to the provinces, and the problem quickly overwhelmed many provinces' tumbling taxation revenue. Throughout the 1930s a spectre of provincial bankruptcy haunted the land. The federation was being eroded by a destructive inequality in the power and privileges of Canadians in individual provinces. Rowell-Sirois dared not tamper with the fundamental federal-provincial balance of Canadian federalism. But, the commissioners suggested, some realignment of responsibilities and taxation might reinvigorate the federation.

The commissioners talked about the necessity of ensuring an "average Canadian standard of services" and at the same time ensuring that all Canadians paid taxes of "normal severity." The federation must be equalized; floors and ceilings must be put in place to guarantee that Canadians enjoyed the same coast-to-coast quality of citizenship. To do this, Rowell-Sirois proposed a system of "national adjustment grants" that would see the provinces surrender some responsibility, especially in the area of unemployment, and some taxation in return for a guaranteed annual subvention from the federal government. Each province's entitlement to an adjustment grant would be calculated based on its socio-economic circumstances. There would inevitably be "haves" and "have-nots," but the end result would be a "healthy federal system." To achieve all this, "yardsticks" were necessary – statistics "scientifically and objectively" arrived at that allowed for the equitable calculation of the national adjustment grants. The system would be flexible as the condition of the nation changed; every five years the grants would be recalibrated to a new statistical benchmark.[42]

The Rowell-Sirois Report went nowhere. Prime Minister King felt obliged to lay its recommendations before the provinces at a special 1941 Dominion-Provincial Conference. But King's political instincts told him that the report asked too much of Canada's provinces and did so too quickly. This prescience was borne out by the categorical rejection of Rowell-Sirois by demagogic premiers like Ontario's "Mitch" Hepburn, British Columbia's "Duff" Pattullo, and Alberta's William "Bible Bill" Aberhart. Ottawa immediately fell back on arguments of expediency. The war demanded extraordinary expenditures by Ottawa, monies that would in large measure have to be raised from a patchwork of personal, corporate, and succession taxes administered by the provinces. Citing the *force majeur* of the war, the federal minister of finance, James Ilsley, imposed a "tax rental" agreement on the provinces in 1941. The provinces agreed to temporarily surrender, or "rent," their taxation rights to personal, corporate, and succession taxes to Ottawa in return for a guaranteed annual payment from the federal government. The base year in terms of each province's population and revenues would be 1941.

This back-door renovation of federalism was billed as a temporary measure that would tide the nation over the war, but it introduced a striking new element to the nature of Canadian federalism: equalization. The nineteenth-century focus of the federation on growth had been supplemented by a mid-twentieth-century emphasis on the shared equality of citizenship. And such sharing could not proceed without numbers – numbers that were competently researched and credibly received by politicians and citizens alike. A dynamic national accounts system was thus a prerequisite for such a rejigging of Confederation. Numbers were becoming a necessary ingredient of nationhood, a means of ensuring balance in a coast-to-coast nation that had a vigorous sense of region.

Other legacies of the Depression echoed throughout the war. In 1941 Ottawa introduced Canada's first unemployment insurance system. Mindful of the deep social damage of the unemployment of the 1930s, Ottawa again sought to build some stability into the social fabric of the nation. A contributory scheme of insurance would serve to tide workers over during periods of unemployment. Benefits under the 1941 Act were meager, but the principle was established. In true Keynesian logic, war seemed like a good time to introduce such a scheme; with the economy booming, contributions would far outstrip premiums, and if depression returned with the peace, Canada would have a rainy-day fund to ease the misery. Similar, if still tentative, thinking underlay Ottawa's plans for a postwar welfare state. Early in the war, long before victory seemed even thinkable, the Economic Advisory Committee set academics and social workers the task of studying the possible contours of a state that put socio-economic floors below the feet of its citizens. By 1942–43 these deliberations were suggesting that Canadian mothers might be paid monthly allowances, that businessmen might have their start-up loans guaranteed, and that even health care might be subsidized. Again, Mackenzie King's political antennae twitched; these were bold initiatives that could not be hurried. But, all observers agreed, such social reform could be implemented only with credible statistics to identify the problem and to monitor the outcomes of such interventions. Numbers would pave the path to change.

And by 1942 the Canadian people were demanding such numbers. Public opinion polling had been brought to life by the war; the Canadian Institute for Public Opinion informed Canadians on their preferences from conscription to social reform. Throughout the fracas over the 1919-38 estimates produced by the DBS, the mandarins had lived in fear that the general public might lose faith in the accuracy of Canada's wartime statistical effort. Clifford Clark had warned Minister of Finance Ilsley that "public criticism" of the woeful state of the national accounts might "spread to Parliament."[43] A year later the prediction came true. "Canada's Unsolved Problem – How Big Is Our National Income?" read a *Financial Post* headline. "In a land flowing with statistics and statistical experts, our failure to agree on a procedure for estimating the national income stands as our unforgivable statistical sin of omission."[44]

And so the search began for a new man to head a new unit. Cudmore at the DBS had promised to establish the "new unit," but a man had to be found to lead it. The model of Britain's Central Statistical Office indicated that a balanced System of National Accounts required the best and the brightest minds – men like Richard Stone and James Meade. As in England, the universities seemed the obvious place to look. Why not Donald MacGregor? Nobody in Canada had as much exposure to the problem of national income. Bryce demurred. MacGregor was too acerbic: "he has not the type of temperament to meet these particular difficulties." Bryce accordingly cast his net wider and contacted Vincent Bladen, head of the University of Toronto's Department of Political Economy. "We need a man with a clear head for theoretical matters, some knowledge of Canadian statistics and conditions," he wrote, "and with good general ability to organize a large statistical project and direct the work." Mindful of the egos already bruised by the tussle over national accounting, Bryce concluded that the person put in charge of the unit would have to "be careful and tactful in reorganizing the contacts for this work and persuading others to provide him with the proper information."[45] Neither Bladen nor any of the other academics whom Bryce contacted were encouraging. Graduate studies in economics and statistics were in their infancy in Canada. Toronto's Department of Political Economy was the pinnacle of Canadian economics, but even its undergraduate program in economics was small.[46] Many of the professors remained skeptical of Keynes and the vogue for macroeconomics. While outlying universities advised their promising students to go to Toronto for graduate training, Toronto urged its best students to go the United States or Britain. Tarshis and Bryce himself typified this choice. So Bryce began making inquiries at prominent American universities like Chicago, Harvard, and Berkeley. Were there any promising Canadian economists, he asked, in the graduate common room? There were a few. Most, as John Galbraith had done, were studying agricultural economics, a seemingly sensible field for a would-be Canadian economist but ill-suited to the broad challenge of national accounting. Throughout the summer of 1942 contact was made with a handful of Canadians in American graduate programs. None took the bait. Most had an eye on academic employment. The Ottawa job might not be permanent. The pay seemed low. The Civil Service Commission had approved a $4,200 per annum salary for Canada's chief national accounts statistician, but potential candidates said this was too low.

As the search wore on, the tone became urgent. In September a dejected Clifford Clark decried that "the number of men with any training in the field is so small" to Donald Gordon, the head of the Wartime Prices and Trade Board. "I need not tell you how fundamental the work on national income statistics is to what we all are trying to do now and also to what we have to do in the post-war years."[47] In desperation, attention turned to prying a suitable person out of the existing wartime bureaucracy. Deutsch seemed the obvious man, but Graham Towers at the Bank of Canada was emphatic that he could not be spared. Doug Blyth, a young balance of payments whiz at the Foreign Exchange Control Board (FECB), was approached, but Towers was again adamant that he would not have his bank staff raided. Walter Duffett at the FECB had a master's degree in science from the London School of Economics and experience in the insurance industry, but he too stayed put.

Historian Jack Granatstein has made the point that the mandarins were a group of nimble generalists, men (and a few women) who brought a broad mind and a quick wit to a rolling agenda of war problems. Canada's welfare state was fashioned by their dexterity.[48] National accounting demanded a different type of mandarin: a *specialist* who could deploy complex theory and methods to the understanding of the national economy. This was a job that required the meticulous manipulation of data coupled with a clear head for their broader implications for public policy. Only a handful of such experts existed in London and Washington, so Canada, lacking vibrant graduate programs in economics, was unlikely to have a reservoir of fledgling Keynesians seeking Ottawa employment. Posterity has come to talk of the "Keynesian revolution" as though it were a dramatic, thorough conversion. It was, instead, a creeping kind of transition in which Canadians tinkered their way toward a new comprehension of how their economy worked. In 1942 Mabel Timlin had just published her book on Keynesianism. Bryce had seen the light, as had a few Canadian expatriates like Galbraith. But there was no Colin Clark or Richard Stone ready to step into the national accounts breach in Ottawa.

Or perhaps there was. In his exasperation with the DBS's glacial transition to a balanced form of national accounting, Graham Towers at the Bank of Canada had surreptitiously allowed some of his research staff to experiment with innovative ways of formulating national income. After all, the bank oversaw the monetary condition of the nation, and this necessitated insight into the national economy. Crucial questions confronted the governor, and he had concluded that the DBS could not provide the answers. Which groups and regions suffered most from inflation? What effect were government programs having on income? How much could civilian demand be held in check? In hopes of some guidance on such issues, Towers gave Alex Skelton, head of the bank's small research department, considerable latitude to undertake national income experiments. Skelton had directed the research of the Rowell-Sirois Royal Commission and was instrumental in attracting Deutsch to the bank's research team. While Deutsch battered the DBS's approach to economic statistics in memos to the mandarins, other re-

George Luxton in Quebec's Eastern Townships in the late 1930s. Victoria-born, Luxton relocated to Montreal, where student activism, statistical work at the Sun Life Assurance Company, and a master's degree from McGill aroused his interest in economic analysis. Graduate work at Harvard tilted him toward Keynes. As a wartime economist seconded to the Dominion Bureau of Statistics from the Bank of Canada, Luxton brilliantly sketched the architecture of Canada's modern System of National Accounts. Luxton never enjoyed strong health and died suddenly in early 1945 at age thirty. Tragically, Canada lost one of the best minds the war had produced. Courtesy of Jean Cooper, Ottawa.

searchers at the bank were quietly testing alternative approaches to national income. And here a young economist named George Luxton began to shine.

At twenty-eight years of age, Luxton was intellectually adventurous and hardworking. In photographs he appears lanky, often rather pallid, but always intense. His round tortoiseshell glasses and worsted suits gave him the bookish appearance of an Oxford don. A Victoria boy who had taken a commerce degree at the University of British Columbia, Luxton had headed east to Montreal in the depth of the Depression. There, he took a master's degree in economics at McGill, where he impressed Stephen Leacock, perhaps Canada's best-known political economist, to the point that Leacock assured Luxton that he would do his "very utmost" to get him a job in statistics.[49] But, like Bryce, Luxton went to work for Sun Life as an investment analyst – a solid job in a terrible depression. There were other echoes of Bryce in Luxton. In 1939 he won a scholarship to do further graduate work at Harvard, where he attended the public-policy seminar of Alvin Hansen. Hansen was one of only a handful of established economists in America to readily convert to Keynes's ideas. Hansen argued that fiscal policy and statistical analysis went hand-in-glove. Unfit for military service (tuberculosis lurked in his family), Luxton cast about for an academic job. Bryce backed his applications, telling potential employers that "his general ability is so good that I am sure that he would do a first rate job for you if he were interested."[50] But Luxton's ambition lay in Ottawa, where he arrived in the summer of 1940 and immediately set to work assisting with taking a massive registration of wartime labour. Skelton then recruited him to the bank's research staff, where he began manipulating national income data.

Luxton instinctively understood that to be useful to the mandarins in winning the war and shaping the peace, the national accounts had to be *balanced*, that the income and expenditure flows in them had to be reconciled like any company's books. They also had to be pliable enough to segregate the particular contributions of government, business, and individuals to the overall economy. He read Stone, Meade, and Gilbert to comprehend what the Allies were doing. Early in 1942 he began to proselytize his findings to his superiors. "The arrangement of national income breakdowns and related statistics into economically significant flow tables can be a powerful aid to fiscal analysis and to the framing of fiscal policies." The British had a head start, he wrote, but "the time is not far off either in Canada or the United States, when we can attempt rough stabs at aggregative current figures for these tables." Such tables, he concluded, would "breathe far more realism into the search for the 'inflationary gap.'"[51]

The Bank of Canada Archives still hold the originals of Luxton's national income worksheets. They are stamped "secret." They are crude, messy documents, covered with penciled-in corrections and always flagged with cautionary statements that they were "subject to further revision" and (in unflattering reference to the DBS) "built on weak supporting data." But through the messiness, one can detect the emerging architecture of a modern set of national accounts. Luxton stretched his figures from 1938 into the middle of the war. On one side of the equation was gross national expenditure broken down into figures for government spending on goods and services, foreign investment inflows, private home investment, and consumption by individuals of goods and services. On the other side of the ledger, income was broken down. First was income paid to individuals: wages, salaries, investment income, and agricultural and business earnings. To this was added military pay. Adjustments were then made for inventories, undistributed profits, subsidies from government, taxes paid, and depreciation. The result equaled "gross national product at market prices."[52]

Amid the figures, impressive trends could be easily identified. Luxton noted that between 1938 and 1941–42 there had been a 50% increase in national income paid out and that three-fifths of this was attributable to a surge in wages and salaries. Another one-fifth came from ballooning military pay and a final one-fifth from the rebound of the agricultural sector. Similarly, gross national product had grown a stunning 25%, or $1,570 million between the end of 1940 and the end of 1941. Inside this, Luxton could show that gross private expenditure had fallen by $160 million. Rationing was working: inventories had been dramatically reduced; the economy had little to no productive fat left in it.[53] The enlarged role of government as a creator of income and a buyer of goods and services was evident everywhere in Luxton's tables.

Whenever he could, Luxton pumped out memos extolling the virtue of "balancing" tables. "If we can make independent estimates of all relevant items," he wrote in a research paper, "we can use the measurements to check each other since we know, for example, that income should be equal to outlay."[54] This in-out capability of balanced national accounts statements had an immediate appeal to planners who were now, by mid-war, beginning to speculate about how the postwar economy might be managed by judicious injections of social and economic subsidies. Money given to mothers for family allowance might, for instance, be traced through to farms, dairies, and grocer stores. The mandarins began to talk of "Luxton's estimates" and to employ them in their briefings. Mindful of Luxton's warnings of the tentativeness of his work, they were always quick to add "the strongest sort of qualifications and reservations."[55]

Luxton had whetted the mandarins' appetite for national accounts statistics. Memos in late 1943 began referring to the "thinking staff" working on national accounts. Luxton exuded the magnetism of a man working his way through an intellectual problem, and somewhat like Keynes in England, he soon attracted a small circle of fellow researchers who understood the drift of his inquiry and joined him in prodding the new national accounts system into existence in Canada. Two old chums from Luxton's McGill days in the Depression joined him. Eric Adams had graduated in engineering but had been pulled toward economics by the Depression. Adams took a master's degree in business at Harvard, worked for the Canadian Pacific Railway as an economist, and wrote for the *Financial Post* before joining the wartime bureaucracy as a foreign exchange expert. Agatha Chapman was another McGill chum. With a master's degree in economics from the University of Toronto, Chapman had worked with Luxton at Sun Life and had shown a talent for dissecting wage and salary data.

Other promising young economists drifted into Luxton's orbit. Walter Duffett had been to the London School of Economics and had also passed through Sun Life before lending his talents to the Wartime Prices and Trade Board and to the Bank of Canada research department. Last, there was Malcolm "Mac" Urquhart, a young Albertan economist fresh from the University of Chicago and the Massachusetts Institute of Technology who had joined the research staff of the federal Ministry of Finance. Throughout late 1943 and early 1944 the research department of the Bank of Canada thus became the focal point of an effort to erect a workable scaffold for Canadian national accounts. The hours were long but the camaraderie strong. Percolating up through their work was the language of the new Keynesian world – "aggregate money supply," "full-employment conditions," "size of the labour force" – language that increasingly framed Canadians' perception of the looming peace.[56]

Sedley Cudmore at the DBS was impressed and saw in Luxton's work the kernel of the elusive "new unit" that had failed to emerge since April 1942. Throughout the winter of 1943-44 he launched a campaign to bring Luxton and his work under the bureau's umbrella. "The problem is now one of quality more than quantity of statistics. In the post-war world it is only with some improvement in our organization that the Bureau can hope to maintain the high place it has won in the past." The bureau, he argued to the mandarins and their political masters, was entering the "second stage in our evolution and that stage is one of improving the quality of our statistics and filling in the gaps." Cudmore was clearly worried that the bureau was in danger of being scooped by the bank or by the Ministry of Trade and Commerce. He played the only trump card left to him: that the bureau was Canada's grand master at gathering and sorting numbers. He offered three things. First, the DBS would establish a "central research and development staff" to oversee national accounts work. Cudmore deftly described this as "some strengthening of its thinking staff." Second, the bureau would bolster its methodology efforts to ensure that the best quality data were available in the postwar period. Last, he advocated that an interdepartmental committee on statistics be established to coordinate the needs of users and producers of economic statistics.[57]

The powerful Economic Advisory Committee bought Cudmore's argument and duly established the interdepartmental advisory committee with Cudmore as its helm and with the bureau's balance of payments expert, Herbert Marshall, as its secretary. The big users of economic statistics – Agriculture, Trade and Commerce, Labour, and Finance – all appointed senior officials. Predictably, Robert Bryce carried the flag for the Ministry of Finance; he had presided over every phase of Canada's conversion to a Keynesian model of national accounting, and now, as the system's godfather, he would continue to keep a watchful eye on its adolescence. "It now begins to look as though arrangements at this end for the production of national income statistics are going to be substantially improved," Bryce triumphantly wrote to Guggenheim scholar Donald MacGregor in New York. "There is nothing very definite yet but I would hope that within a month or two changes will have been which will augur very well for the future."[58]

The first really "definite" news in the spring of 1944 was the appointment of twenty-nine-year-old George Luxton as chief of the DBS's fledgling Research and Development Staff. Sometime late in April 1944 Luxton packed up his data-crammed files – many of them stamped "secret" – left the Bank of Canada's lovely new head office on Wellington Street, and headed across town to the DBS. Agatha Chapman rounded out the deployment, arriving at the DBS on loan from the bank. At age thirty-seven, Chapman brought the average age of the two-"man" staff of the new unit up to thirty-three.

The search that had begun two years earlier in a Rockcliffe living room thus ended not far away in the overcrowded and decrepit offices of the Dominion Bureau of Statistics on Green Island. Canada had finally entered the age of modern national accounts. If geography suggested that this had been a short journey, ideas suggested that it had been long and contentious. George Luxton had found the promising "statistical job" that Stephen Leacock had prophesied for him almost ten years before at McGill, but it was a statistical job that nobody would have recognized in 1935. Now the work began in earnest.

3 New Yardsticks

"New Yardsticks of Canada's National Output Clears
Way for Reconstruction Planning"
~ *Financial Post*, headline, 1 December 1945

I went through it over the weekend and thought the
publication represents an admirable putting together of
the many bits and pieces of the cross-word puzzle of
the national accounts, with a lucid and effective analysis.
I congratulate you on the new evidence of the fine work
of the Bureau.
~ W.C. Clark to Herbert Marshall, 27 December 1948,
Library and Archives Canada

[A] sharp spur to human inquiry.
~ Simon Kuznets, *Suggestions for an Inquiry into the
Economic Growth of Nations* (1949)

And you had to *think* – it was all new, it had never been
done before.
~ Robert Crozier to Gordon Betcherman, editor, *Canadian
Business Economics*, 18 November 1997

Early in September 1944 George Luxton welcomed a visitor to his
modest offices. An important visitor. Richard Stone, who in 1941 had
been anointed by Keynes to develop Britain's national accounts at the
new Central Statistical Office, had made the risky trip across the Atlantic to confer with his North American confreres. These were momentous times. A month earlier Keynes himself had ventured across the
war-torn Atlantic. At a conference of forty-four nations at Bretton
Woods in New Hampshire's scenic White Mountains, he took a leading

role in laying the economic foundation of the postwar international financial system. Exchange rates that were fixed on gold values and adjustable only in rare circumstances would stabilize and regularize world trade, while agencies like the International Monetary Fund and the International Bank for Reconstruction and Development would police and stimulate the world economy. Exhausted by these labours – his heart problems were by now chronic – Keynes headed north to Ottawa, where he installed himself and Lydia Lopokova, his flamboyant ballerina wife, in a nine-room suite in the Chateau Laurier. There, he invited a select group of mandarins, including Graham Towers of the Bank of Canada, Donald Gordon of the Wartime Prices and Trade Board as well as Robert Bryce (Keynes's former star pupil), and Clifford Clark of the Ministry of Finance, to a private dinner. In the days after this "sentimental and friendly" affair, Keynes applied pressure on the Canadians to enhance their war aid to cash-strapped Britain.[1]

Stone too came to Ottawa with international matters on his mind. Keynes had never been a details man; his genius was more expansive. Since 1941 it had fallen to Stone at the Central Statistical Office and James Meade at the Economic Information Service in London to furnish the numbers that would make Keynes's economic model come to life. Here, they excelled. Their estimates of Britain's national income and expenditure were now appended to the annual budget as "blue books." In 1944 Oxford University Press had published their slim volume *National Income and Expenditure* with its exhortation that the "citizen who wishes to understand the central problems of the war-time or of the post-war economy must have some knowledge of these figures."[2] Stone was now speculating that national income and expenditure figures might be broken down into what he called "social accounting," figures that identified income and expenditure flows in and out of the four principal reciprocating sectors of the economy: the household, the public sector, business, and what Stone, with Anglo-centric aplomb, called "the rest of the world."[3] But in the fall of 1944 Stone had a more immediate task at hand. In the spirit of Bretton Woods, he would spearhead the effort to standardize the international production of national accounts. The new world economic order had to sit on a common set of national accounting practices. His first stop in this quest was Ottawa, from where he and Luxton boarded a train and headed for Washington, where Milton Gilbert awaited them at the National Income Unit of the Department of Commerce.

The so-called Tripartite Discussions of National Income Measurement in Washington were characterized by "persuasion" and "compromise."[4] The consultation was perhaps most remarkable for the youthfulness of its protagonists: Gilbert was thirty-five, Stone was thirty-one, and Luxton was a mere thirty. Years later, when he received the Nobel Prize in economics for his work in national accounting, Stone recalled that the meetings were "very friendly and the results extremely satisfactory, so that my first taste of international cooperation could not have been more encouraging."[5] A consensus quickly emerged that "no sudden innovation" was necessary, only a "refinement and formalization" of the work "experimentally" undertaken in the war. The centre piece of the postwar accounts would be the gross national product and income account. This would reflect the all-important Keynesian impulse of aggregate demand in the economy, thereby giving government a lodestar in its efforts to stabilize the economy. Around gross national product (GNP) would be a cluster of accounts breaking income and expenditure flows down into their private, business, and government components. Ancillary accounts would measure savings and balance of payments inputs into the economy. Together, these accounts would furnish "a most important tool in the formation of national policy."[6]

After Washington, Stone returned to England, where he was soon appointed director of the newly created Department of Applied Economics at Cambridge. There, he quickly trumpeted his purpose: "The ultimate aim of applied economics is to increase human welfare by the investigation and analysis of economic problems of the real world."[7] Back in Washington, Milton Gilbert and his staff at the National Income Division of the Department of Commerce set to work turning the tripartite accord into America's first fully coordinated set of national accounts. Their work was given added velocity by Congress's enactment of the Employment Act of 1946, which openly dedicated the federal government to a managed economy. The control room of this new economy would be the president's Council of Economic Advisers, a panel that made it clear that macroeconomic statistics were their first order of the day. In July 1947 Gilbert delivered the goods.[8]

The Washington accord set the course of postwar national accounting. It was primarily the handiwork of Stone and Gilbert, but there was no denying that Canada was the third charter member of the group. The minutes of the meeting noted that the final draft of the accord was to be submitted to Luxton "for comment." Nor was it a case of Canada slipstreaming in the wake of its senior Allied partners. In preparation for the tripartite talks, Luxton and his small crew had put together a survey of British, American, and Canadian national income and expenditure practices. In some instances, they were quite prepared to conform to British or American practice, but in other areas they boldly put forth a Canadian alternative.⁹ Not only did Luxton bring intellectual weight to the discussions, but his presence also reflected that Canada's economy was now an indispensable element of the transatlantic economy. From the outset, Canada was thus never destined to play a derivative role in the unfolding of global national accounting. If its national accounts had been a "hodge-podge" just three years before, Canada now possessed the kernel of a modern system of national accounts that could, with much work, be applied to its postwar ambition of economic stability and social welfare. And this all rested on the shoulders of young George Luxton and his small staff back at Green Island.

The Dominion Bureau of Statistics' (DBS) national income effort on Green Island was modest by any measure. There were the old-school business statistics types like Sydney Smith and Ray Bangs, but their utility was largely limited to collating data. Bright young economists from other government departments and agencies drifted in and out of the team. Malcolm Urquhart brought his experience at the University of Chicago and the Massachusetts Institute of Technology over from the Ministry of Finance. Walter Duffett, with his training at the London School of Economics, lent his talent from the Bank of Canada. Eric Adams, the engineer with a master's degree in business administration from Harvard, contributed from the Foreign Exchange Board and more latterly from the Industrial Development Bank. But the indisputable core of the team was the duo of George Luxton and Agatha Chapman. Only Luxton was in fact a full DBS employee; Chapman was only seconded from the Bank of Canada. George and "Aggie," as everybody called her, had seen eye-to-eye on the problems of the Canadian economy long before they darkened the DBS's doors.

Luxton and Chapman had remarkably similar British Columbia roots. Chapman, born in England in 1907, was a child immigrant to Canada. Her Canadian mother had married an English lawyer who had spent years on the High Court of India. (Interestingly, Richard Stone's father had also served as a judge in India.) Aggie's maternal links to Canada were impeccable: her great-grandfather, Sir Charles Tupper, had been a Father of Confederation and one-time prime minister. Her uncle had served as lieutenant governor of Manitoba. In 1918 her family had brought her to Vernon in the British Columbia interior. Chapman's education began at the patrician Cheltenham Ladies College in England and culminated in a master's degree in economics from the University of Toronto in 1932. En route, she projected the impression of a young woman on the rise. The University of Toronto awarded her a prestigious Maurice Cody Fellowship. She served as president of the

University College Women's Literary Society, extolling her love of Walt Whitman's poetry to its members.[10] Chapman's academic prowess served her well as the Depression broke over Canada; her master's degree opened the way to a job as an economist in the investment department of Sun Life Assurance in Montreal. Life had been good to the accomplished young woman from Vernon. In photographs, with her hair pulled tightly into a bun, her wire-rimmed glasses, and her smart floral dresses, Chapman appeared every bit the "new woman." And she was good, very good, with numbers.

George Luxton followed much the same path in life. His parents were English immigrants who had done well in the "colonies." George's father, Arthur, had risen to legal prominence in Victoria before tuberculosis claimed him in 1924. Private school education led George to the University of British Columbia, where he secured a bachelor of arts in 1933 and a bachelor of commerce a year later. In his graduation photograph, Luxton looks mature beyond his years – serious, well-groomed, and focused. A Royal Bank scholarship then carried him to McGill University in Montreal, where he was exposed to some of Canada's most distinguished political economists. With a master's degree in hand in 1935, Luxton succumbed to the same pull as Chapman; in a depression, people who were good with numbers were still in demand. A remarkable number of Canada's future national accountants first found work as accountants and actuaries during the Depression; the work was steady and respectable. Thus, like Chapman and Robert Bryce, Luxton found himself in the employ of Sun Life and later of the International Bond and Share Corporation.

But a steady paycheque and social respectability could not allay deeper anxieties in Chapman and Luxton. On any day, Chapman would, for instance, have witnessed the human cost of the Depression on her walk from her Mansfield Street apartment to her office on Dominion Square. Unemployment and bankruptcy were everywhere in evidence. Monopoly capitalists like Sir Herbert Holt seemed to control every aspect of Montreal's economy, from its streetcars to its banking system. Municipal welfare was overwhelmed and underfunded. The comfortable lecture halls of McGill provided few answers for Canadians' economic woes. Stephen Leacock might pose the question "what is left of Adam Smith?" and warn that "We are on the deck of a ship driving towards the breakers that mean death," but he had no alternatives, no solutions beyond extolling "individual self-interest."[11]

It was in these years that Luxton's and Chapman's paths first crossed, perhaps in the lunchroom at Sun Life but undoubtedly at the

George Luxton as a McGill University graduate student in the mid-1930s. Luxton and his future wife, Mildred Ball (beside him), became deeply involved in the social activism of the Student Christian Movement on campus. Members of Montreal's plutocracy complained of their "radicalism." For Luxton, agitation against the established order heightened his resolve to change the economic structure of society and ultimately led him to Keynes and national accounting. Courtesy of Jean Cooper, Ottawa.

evening meetings of the McGill chapter of the Student Christian Movement (SCM). Founded in 1921, the Student Christian Movement strove to apply Christian activism to the social and economic ills of the urban-industrial world. The SCM's motto – "The Bible in one hand, the newspaper in the other" – conveyed a sense of this engagement. "To introduce positive and appreciative intellectual inquiry into one's religion," the SCM haughtily reported in 1932, "is to eliminate sham, bigotry and sentimentalism. These have no place in the religion of an educated man."[12] Egged on by a handful of reform-minded professors like labour economist Eugene Forsey and constitutional lawyer Frank Scott, the movement focused its attention on poverty, disarmament, fascism, and the "experiment" in the Soviet Union. The movement's campus tearoom, "The Pit," became a focal point for heated debate about the woes of depression-ridden Canada. In the evenings SCM study groups continued the "intellectual search for the highest truth we can find about the situations which face us in the modern world."[13]

At times the SCM's moral vigour spilled into the streets. In 1936 SCM students heckled a Black Watch military parade as it passed their campus office. They arranged a boycott of Japanese goods to protest that country's invasion of China. They visited members of the working class. Not surprisingly, Montreal's establishment was not amused. Why, wrote sugar mogul J.W. McConnell to McGill's principal, were such "radicals" allowed to attack the sacred fabric of Canadian society? "One swallow does not make a summer," the principal replied.[14] As the Depression bit deeper, some SCM members did indeed drift into atheism and communism, but on the whole the SCM remained an incubator of discussion and agitation focused on the wobbly structure of Canadian society. Impatient and inquisitive, yes; but enemies of society, no.[15]

George Luxton found in the SCM answers to questions that his formal education in economics would not address. He plunged into the life of the SCM, offering study groups on topics ranging from the life of Jesus to the "world situation." He read widely, sampling ideas as varied as those espoused by Marxism and Social Credit. Reading led to socializing. Luxton grew attracted to the manager of the SCM tearoom, Mildred Ball, a 1932 bachelor of arts graduate from McGill. In 1939 they would marry. Their daughter from that marriage would later describe her parents' Depression years in Montreal as a "brief flaming time" full of social activism and personal discovery.[16] Other economists in Luxton's orbit travelled much the same road in these years. Eric Adams returned from Harvard with his master's degree in business administration and joined the advertising firm of Cockfield Brown. Dissatisfied with capitalism's inability to cure itself, he boldly toured the Soviet Union in 1934 and reported his findings to the *Financial Post*.[17] A young Manitoba economist, Claude Isbister, arrived at Sun Life in 1935 and was soon following Luxton up to the McGill campus to offer study groups. Throughout all this, Agatha Chapman continued her own exploration of "radical" ideas. She would later remember reading everything from Marx to *Mein Kampf*. Late in the Depression, Chapman left Sun Life – some said because she was fired for her increasingly heretical views.[18]

George's "brief flaming time" was being replicated on campuses, in tearooms, and on streets across the Western world. Richard Stone would later tell an interviewer that he spent much of his time as a Cambridge student in the Depression reading Marx, Lenin, Freud, and others.[19] In Vancouver a young Japanese Canadian graduate of the University of British Columbia wrestled with the same crisis of confidence as Luxton, Isbister, and Adams. Thomas Shoyama had a bachelor's degree in commerce in his pocket, but his race and the Depression denied him useful employment. Instead, he worked with the homeless on Powell Street and edited a civil rights newspaper, the *New Canadian*.[20] The Depression saw Robert Crozier from Saskatchewan earn a bachelor's degree in commerce from Queen's University, but it also saw the family home repossessed and his dentist father commit suicide. "Governments stood by helplessly and watched it all happen," Crozier would later recall. "At the depth of the Depression in 1933, we still didn't know how far the national income had fallen, or how high the unemployment rate had risen. We didn't know how to deal with it, we had no mechanism to protect its victims, and we couldn't even measure its basic dimensions with any degree of precision."[21]

History tends to fixate on the grand tendency, on Keynes's working out a "general theory" or Franklin D. Roosevelt's unveiling a "New Deal" for Americans. But beneath these powerful currents usually lies a constant agitation of less well-known minds – minds that ultimately coalesce and find new meaning and direction in life along the lines of the general tendency. Just as Keynes pointed to the relevance of macroeconomics to policymaking, many young would-be economists were coming alive to the potential of *applied* economics in the Depression and its relevance to their own personal circumstances. The revolution in national accounting that would unfold during and after the Second World War was thus rooted not just in lofty theory but also in the conviction of a generation of economists who were determined to make numbers matter to society. Numbers would cease to be an inert record of bygone performance and would be an active ingredient in plotting a better future. Richard Stone later recalled that "youthful inexperience and innate optimism combined to make me think that if there were more economists the world would be a better place."[22] Not far away at the London School of Economics, Gideon Rosenbluth, a refugee from Hitler's Germany on his way to an eventual career in Canadian economics, devoured courses in statistics and economics in the ardent belief that such knowledge seemed the best way "to improve the world."[23]

Luxton found his own road to Damascus in the autumn of 1939 just as the war broke. The previous spring, he had won a scholarship to Harvard and prepared to follow in the footsteps of his Sun Life colleague Robert Bryce, who had left Sun Life for Ottawa the year before. That same spring Luxton had married his sweetheart, Mildred, before spending an idyllic summer in a rented cottage on Lac St Louis outside Montreal. At Harvard, Luxton enrolled in Professor Alvin Hansen's fiscal policy seminar. A mid-westerner who had landed the prestigious Littauer Professorship of Political Economy in 1937, Hansen used his seminar as a gangplank by which Keynesianism could land in America. Hansen battered the precepts of classical economics, lectured Washington politicians on the necessity of giving Americans a new economic deal, and turned his seminar into a cockpit of debate. On Mondays students presented papers. On Friday afternoons Hansen invited speakers to provoke the students into debate that usually tumbled over into dinner and an evening of contention. Hansen was like an intellectual card dealer, an image enhanced by his famous habit of wearing an eye-shade. James Tobin, a student in the 1938 seminar, later proclaimed that "no American economist was more important for the historic redirection of United States macroeconomic policy from 1935 to 1965." John Kenneth Galbraith described Hansen as "a man for whom economic ideas had no standing apart from their use."[24] Luxton was galvanized. Here was proof that economics could be an activist profession, that numbers were the substructure that supported theory and policy.

The war pulled Luxton back to Canada in the spring of 1940. He would never finish his Harvard doctorate. A frail constitution precluded military service, and after a brief quest for an academic post, Luxton arrived in wartime Ottawa. Strongly recommended by Bryce in the Ministry of Finance, he quickly established himself as a numbers man in the research branches of the Bank of Canada and the Ministry of Labour before accepting the call to the DBS in the spring of 1944. One can only speculate, but Richard Stone and George Luxton must have found much in common as they got to know each other on that train to Washington in September 1944. This was not the first journey they had shared.

George Luxton never lost his SCM fervour. Throughout the war he and Mildred found time to attend evening reading groups where wartime bureaucrats discussed their reactions to current ideas and books. Agatha Chapman's Somerset Street apartment became a favourite meeting place. Luxton and Eric Adams began drawing up plans to write an economic history of Canada, one that would reveal the economic substructure of the nation's development and divert students' attention from traditional constitutional lines of development.[25] Luxton became an active member of the Canadian Youth Commission, a YMCA-inspired research group dedicated to the needs of youth in the postwar period. His speeches on behalf of the commission were punctuated with Keynesian terminology – full employment, aggregate demand, and national income. Indeed, amid all the pressure of gearing up Canada's national ac-

counts after the Washington accord, Luxton could still find time to promote the welfare state – the state that his daytime job was busy making possible. On Friday, 15 December 1944, he spoke in Ottawa to the
Youth Commission on the theme of "Wanted: Jobs after the War."
"The achievement of full employment in Canada after the war," he told
them, "will demand from us even greater resources of imagination."[26]
But then, Luxton was never short of imagination.

Three weeks later, George Luxton was dead. At Christmas, the tuberculosis that had haunted the Luxton family caught up with him.
Four years of war work had worn him down, and just as the new year
broke, Luxton was taken to Ottawa's Civic Hospital. Queen's University economist Frank Knox, an early Canadian convert to Keynesianism,
sadly recorded in his diary: "Geo Luxton dyg w tubercular meningitis."
An old SCM friend and nurse, Mary Issenman, rushed from Montreal
to provide constant bedside care. But on 5 January 1945 Luxton lost
his battle. "Death rportd Sat paper," Knox penciled into his diary.[27]
Luxton's funeral was widely attended by his colleagues at the DBS, with
the Dominion statistician, Sedley Cudmore, leading the contingent. But
the congregation also contained mourners who embodied Luxton's
wider relevance in the Canadian community – filmmaker Budge Craw-
ley, poet Jesse Ketchum, architect Hazen Sise, and economists Mitchell
Sharp and Malcolm Urquhart. Friends started a fund to assist in the education of Luxton's two daughters. Mildred was devastated; in many
ways, she would never recover from the shock. Luxton's body was
taken home to Victoria and buried beside the sea in Ross Bay Cemetery.

Tributes for Luxton emerged out of the initial stunned silence. Alex
Skelton at the Bank of Canada noted that Luxton possessed "a growth
which would have gone on indefinitely." He had "imbued statistics
with a human spark."[28] But perhaps the most telling evidence of Luxton's legacy to humanity came on 9 January when Professor Knox jot-
ted in his diary: "Urquhart at Commerce Club biology lecture room
National Accounts." Urquhart, the Chicago-trained economist who
had spent the war doing research in the Ministry of Finance and was
soon to join Queen's University's Department of Economics, was carrying the message of national accounting to the first batch of postwar
economists. What George Luxton had fought for and worked to bring
into practice was entering the mainstream of Canadian economic thinking. The lecture halls that had been silent a decade before on the causes
of depression now echoed to the strains of activist economics.

Sedley Cudmore returned from Luxton's funeral with an obvious
and momentous problem on his hands – finding a replacement head for

the fledgling national accounts team. Allied advances in Europe indicated that peace was in the offing, and policy pronouncements in Ottawa indicated that the Liberal government of Mackenzie King was determined to "depression proof" the nation. Numbers were thus the national order of the day. To meet this challenge, the DBS had grown dramatically in stature during the war: a staff of 600 in 1939 had almost doubled by 1945. While small in actual staff numbers, the Research and Development Staff was of crucial strategic importance to the process of informing Canada's postwar direction. From a Keynesian perspective, its members were the pathfinders – highly trained and one step removed from the bureau's familiar role of gathering statistics and aggregating them. "The Central [Research and Development] Staff will," an early 1946 memo noted, "therefore, be advisory, interpretative, analytical. Its members are economists first and statisticians second."[29] Forceful leadership was thus imperative. Methodologies had to be worked up, an eye had to be kept on practices evolving in Britain and the United States, and reporting vehicles had to be developed for Canadian consumers. The loss of George Luxton could not have come at a more crucial moment.

There were two possibilities. Agatha Chapman had worked at Luxton's elbow for two years. She had helped Luxton to worry through the first crude national accounts spread sheets at the Bank of Canada and had gone on to refine a Canadian approach to balanced income and expenditure national accounting. "There is no one in the Bureau," its chief administrative officer wrote, "elsewhere in the Government Service, in the universities, or in private industry, who could be obtained with anything like the qualifications equivalent to those possessed by her. Experience coupled with ability have developed her for this particular job. If a competition were set up it would have to prescribe qualifications which no outsider would be able to meet."[30]

Chapman had two strikes against her in the eyes of contemporaries. In a field that was rapidly rising in acclaim, she had only a master's degree in economics. She had never done doctoral work. A more surreptitious barrier to her advancement in this era was that she was a woman in a male-dominated field. Although the economics profession was by no means hermetically sealed to women, female economists were rare. Joan Robinson, a scholar interested in facets of economics ranging from imperfect competition to the dynamics of growth, had been a lecturer at Cambridge since 1937. Closer to home, Mabel Timlin had broken the glass ceiling at the University of Saskatchewan by obtaining an American doctorate that allowed her to forsake the usual lot of women on campus – administrative work. But, by and large, economics and the senior civil service were male domains.[31] Men were men and women were "girls." Thus, however brilliant she may have seemed to her colleagues, Chapman seemed to lack the royal jelly of leadership, given the academic and gender biases of the day.

Claude Isbister was, on the other hand, both brilliant *and* male. There was much of George Luxton in him. As a boy in Winnipeg, Isbister had contracted a debilitating disease from drinking unpasteurized milk and would go through life with one leg bowed and shorter than the other. Many felt that this explained his immense drive to succeed: he would live his life as though he had no disability. Eager to escape Depression-era Manitoba, Isbister took up actuarial studies in Montreal and joined Sun Life. Together with his wife, Ruth, he became involved with the McGill SCM and was soon a friend of both Luxton and Chapman. Like them, Isbister wanted answers to Canada's economic problems. Bored by actuarial work, he left for the University of Toronto, where he took a master's degree under Vincent Bladen before heading for Harvard, where he too soaked up the eminence of Alvin Hansen, Joseph Schumpeter, and Wassily Leontief. "Just had a long chat with Leontief," Isbister breathlessly wrote to Luxton in 1942. "He is very enthusiastic about my working on input-output relations for Canada … It will illuminate the structure of the Canadian economy from a new point of view."[32] In the end, Isbister wrote a thesis on consumer demand. In 1945 he passed up a professorship at the University of Toronto to join the DBS and, with Luxton's sudden death, was appointed chief economist in charge of the entire Research and Development Staff. Passed over for the senior job, Chapman was instead placed in charge of the actual national accounts preparation, reporting to Isbister. The friendship survived, and within months the two had coauthored a paper for the *Canadian Banker* on how well-balanced income and expenditure accounts prepared the nation for peace.[33]

The year 1945 saw a great creative burst of national accounting in Canada. Isbister had a staff of nine specialists under his national accounts umbrella. Together they pulled in an amazing net of price and labour data, industry and merchandising surveys, import and export trade figures, balance of payments flows, business statistics, and even housing data. A sampling expert watched over the methodological integrity of the whole operation. In the *Canadian Banker* Isbister and Chapman noted that these figures were "designed ultimately to portray the functioning of the national economy in all its phases, of production, transportation, distribution and merchandising through to final consumption and external trade." The accounts were "nothing better than careful approximations," but they were undeniably the statistical life-blood of the unfolding postwar Canadian state.[34]

In April 1945 the federal government climaxed its reconstruction planning with a "white paper" declaring that Ottawa's "primary goal" in the postwar period would be "a high and stable level of employment and income." The white paper was delivered in straightforward, layman's language. Although it flowed largely from the academic pen of W.A. Macintosh in the Ministry of Finance, it was in fact the culmination of a careful grooming of Canadians' public sensibilities by the federal Liberal government and the mandarins. Ottawa would "break new ground" to prevent any return to prewar depression. In 1943 an Ottawa-sponsored report, prepared by Leonard Marsh of McGill University, had advocated that the Canadian state maintain "social minimums" for all of its citizens, in effect assuring them cradle-to-grave social security. Macintosh now addressed the economic implications of such a goal. The state would in future have to take an active presence in the economy, using its powers to boost exports, to induce private investment, and to stimulate private consumption and public investment. Historians have come to affix the simplistic label of "mixed" Keynesian economy – a delicate balance of state stimulus and private initiative – to this formula. The white paper talked of a "number of compatible policies," but the abiding goal would be economic stability. And these policies would require numbers, national account numbers, to enable policymakers to look *inside* the national economy in order to identify problems and opportunities and then to track solutions. "The ultimate aim of all reconstruction is the extension of opportunity, welfare and security among the Canadian people."[35] To Isbister and Chapman, such rhetoric must have seemed familiar. They had first heard its strains at countless SCM meetings, in Alvin Hansen's seminar, and in academic journals. Now their personal sympathies had been attached to their professional skills.

At the heart of the emerging Canadian welfare state was the principle of equalization. Canadians were to have statistical floors placed beneath their feet so that, coast-to-coast, certain minimal standards of wellbeing could be maintained. This meant devising a means of smoothing the unevenness of Canada's regional endowment. The tax rental agreements introduced by fiat early in the war had moved in this direction; they were intended not only to help pay for the conflict but also to rebalance the regional disparities of the country identified by the Rowell-

Sirois Royal Commission. But they were *temporary* agreements slated to expire with the end of hostilities.

In August 1945 Prime Minister King convened a Dominion-Provincial Conference on reconstruction in the hope of converting the wartime agreements into a permanent shift in Canada's fiscal arrangements. "We in Canada," he told the conference in avuncular tones, "simply cannot afford in this age to be divided or confused by domestic difficulties. To do so might well imperil the existence of thousands of our people and, indeed, the existence of the nation itself."[36] To this end, Ottawa presented a thick dossier of proposals that shifted fiscal powers from the provinces to the federal government. With these new revenues in hand, Ottawa proposed to embark on a wide-ranging program of public expenditure and enhanced pension, health, and unemployment benefits. To compensate the provinces for their abandonment of corporate, personal, and succession taxes, Ottawa offered an annual subsidy geared to gross national product on a province-by-province basis, a subsidy that was pegged to a 1942 base and that never fell below $12 per capita.[37] Contrary to the prime minister's expectation, the offer was not sweetly received. Those provinces most battered by the Depression were inclined to negotiate, but the more prosperous central provinces proved obdurate. This was a tax grab, they alleged, that would destroy the federal balance of the nation. Quebec's premier, Maurice Duplessis, threatened to take the train home, and Ontario's premier, George Drew, denounced the King government as an autocracy-in-the-making.

Mackenzie King was not prepared to fold his tent and, after a five-day stalemate, convinced the premiers to reconstitute themselves into a "coordinating" committee that would review the proposals in a less pressured fashion. Having got the premiers back to the table, Ottawa realized that it was imperative that authoritative national income figures be readied so that the actual dimensions of the proposed new formulae could be fully understood. Throughout the early fall of 1945 Isbister's staff went into high gear. An interdepartmental committee was comprised of representatives from the DBS and the Bank of Canada, and the Ministries of Reconstruction, Finance, and National Revenue provided guidance. But it was Isbister – now Dr Isbister – and Chapman who put in the long hours building the accounts. Crucial to their labour was the need to build tables that spanned the momentous years from the late Depression through the war so that any equalization formula could reflect the relative prosperity of all the provinces over that whole period. Thus the duo assembled estimates of gross national product for 1938 to 1944 that showed the composition of national *income* in terms of wages and salaries, military pay, investment income, and the earnings of small businessmen and farmers.

On the other side of the equation, they calculated gross national *expenditure*, comprising government spending, private investment, and personal spending, plus the net value of exports of goods and services as well as net investment income from abroad. They then validated this operation by ensuring that the income and expenditure sides balanced. The result showed what modern war could do to an economy: Canada's GNP leapt from $5,060 million in 1938 to an astonishing $11,727 million by 1944. Government expenditure had soared. So had personal expenditure on goods and services. Finally, and crucially for the negotiations on rebalancing Canada's fiscal arrangements, Isbister and Chapman used their national income figures to break down salaries, wages, and other income on a province-by-province basis. The "haves" and the "have-nots" immediately became apparent. Ontario personal income had, for instance, grown from $1,036 million in 1938 to $2,017 million by 1944. In Saskatchewan, by contrast, it had grown more modestly from $98 million to $149 million in the same years.

By the time the first ministers reconvened in November, Canada's first modern set of national accounts was ready. They were hurriedly mimeographed on wartime austerity paper and sent uptown to the conference. An appendix explained the terms and concepts that drove the calculation. "They are put forward in the belief," Isbister wrote, "that they compare not too unfavorably in quality with similar estimates in other countries."[38] The accounts did nothing, however, to break the political logjam. Quebec and Ontario remained intransigent. Ottawa therefore fell back on a "second-best" strategy. The federal budget of June 1946 offered to perpetuate the wartime tax rental agreements – provincial tax surrender in exchange for a guaranteed minimum annual payment. Seven provinces subsequently rented their corporate tax, income tax, and succession duties to Ottawa for the next five years. Formulae that were based on a 1942 population base and on wartime provincial tax revenues would be employed to calculate the ratios behind the payout. Each year, as the postwar economy grew, the payout would be recalibrated to reflect current performance across the nation. DBS census and national accounts data would fuel this annual recalculation of the provincial subsidy. Every year in September the Dominion statistician would issue a certified copy of the national income and expenditure accounts to the federal finance minister and the provincial treasurers to provide the arithmetic of equalization. The new five-year agreement came into operation on 1 April 1947. Ontario and Quebec opted to retain control of their corporate income and succession taxes.

Remarkable throughout all this delicate negotiation was that nobody doubted the validity of the numbers placed before them by the DBS. There were vituperative exchanges about policy outcomes, but the numbers themselves were universally trusted. As one provincial treasurer noted, he may have had some reservations about the agreements, but "those differences do not prevent me from supporting the principle that uniformity of accounting treatment is a desirable objective."[39] From the very outset, therefore, Canada's national accounts demonstrated their ability to play an apolitical role in the highly politicized arena of Canadian federalism. Perhaps the highest praise came from Clifford Clark, who still presided over the Ministry of Finance: "I went through it over the weekend and the publication represented an admirable putting together of the many bits and pieces of the cross-word puzzle of the national accounts, with lucid and effective analysis," Clark wrote to the Dominion statistician in 1948. "I congratulate you on this new evidence of the work of the Bureau."[40]

Throughout this spurt of activity back at Green Island, the fledgling national accounts team had the support of a key new ally. In October 1945 Sedley Cudmore, another victim of wartime overwork, suddenly died of a heart attack and was replaced as Dominion statistician by Herbert Marshall. Marshall was an economist's economist. Recruited from the University of Toronto in the 1920s, he had done pioneering work in the 1930s on Canada's balance of payments and had strong ties with the academic community. Unlike Coats and Cudmore, he felt at ease in the unfolding world of Keynesian macroeconomics. Marshall was acutely aware that the new Canadian welfare state would have an almost insatiable appetite for statistics and that the DBS must anticipate this demand. As he told a 1946 gathering of business newspaper editors, "it would be madness to try to go it blindly. There must be an abundance of reliable statistical information as a guide to policy in the case of business as well as government, for a large share of the responsibility of maintaining high employment is on the shoulders of business."[41] He liked to joke that he was the manager of a "facts factory." Indeed, Marshall projected the image of the statistician as modern mandarin. An avid skier and inveterate cigar smoker, Marshall was portrayed by the *Ottawa Evening Citizen* as "the statistics czar with the cigar." Marshall reciprocated with a healthy wit. "There is nothing an economist should fear so much as applause," he once said.[42] Beyond the banter, Marshall was determined to build up the bureau's intellectual foundation. And in this respect national accounting was his favoured child. Here was a field of economics that was defining itself on the run. The national accounts were not cut-and-dried statistics; they were the outcome of slippery concepts and constant fine-tuning.

To this end, Marshall instituted a National Income Study Group that assembled once a week after work in his office. Isbister, Chapman, and a growing crew of young economists – Clarence Barber, Larry Read, Gideon Rosenbluth – would pull up a chair around Marshall's desk and spend an hour reviewing the latest article by Stone, Gilbert, or Kuznets. The critique was always rigorous. When discussion turned to crude early attempts to measure labour productivity, one economist pounced: "It is an example of the oversimplification of economic problems which results in popular catchwords like full employment, and there is a real danger that the use of definitions such as this will obscure or ignore the analysis which has been worked out in respectable economic theory."[43] With Herbert Marshall at the helm, there was no doubt where national accounts ranked in the bureau's priorities. They were, he often said, "the keystone of the statistical arch."[44]

Beyond the corridors of power, neatly printed copies of the national accounts became available to the general public in April 1946, for 50 cents a copy. Canadians now had a report card on their national economy. Terms like gross national product began to enter the national dialogue. The financial press began adopting the terminology. The *Financial Post* regarded the national accounts as "one of the most important sets of figures" ever issued by the bureau. The accounts put "the country's figures on pretty much the same basis used by a business firm to find out who are its customers, and where its sales dollar goes." They furnished "new yardsticks" of national prosperity.[45] Some years later Senator Norman Lambert remarked to the *Ottawa Evening Citizen* that "we have become almost blasé in the use of such terms as 'gross national production,' and 'net national income.'" This new political arithmetic, he said, acted as a "reliable and trustworthy barometer reflecting trends and portents in Canada's life."[46]

Early in 1946 the national accounts acquired a first cousin when the first *Labour Force Bulletin* was issued by the bureau. Ottawa's new devotion to stable economic growth necessitated tracking unemployment. The great shadow of Depression-era unemployment still haunted the nation, and while the macroeconomic focus of the national accounts may have conveyed aggregate totals, some indicator of the distribution of prosperity throughout the labour force was also imperative. Once again, the DBS showed its verve for innovation. The Labour Force Survey applied sophisticated sampling techniques to a select group of Canadian households. The sample reflected the demographic diversity of the nation and enabled DBS surveyors to undertake doorstep interviews with about 25,000 Canadian families. The interviews targeted each family's employment status during a designated week every quarter; in 1952 the survey became monthly. Once the results were compiled, Canadians could learn the size of the national labour force, its disposition by region and industry, its gender balance, whether people were waged or worked for themselves, and most crucially, how many Canadians were unemployed. Thus, for less than a dollar – 25 cents for the quarterly *Labour Force Bulletin* and 50 cents for the annual edition of the national accounts – Canadians could have a diagnostic reading of their economy and its principal social outcome. In 1948 a magazine-style publication, the *Canadian Statistical Review*, appeared that gave a monthly synopsis of the bureau's latest assessment of economic trends.

Canadians quickly became fluent in the language of GNP and unemployment statistics. Throughout the late 1940s Herbert Marshall maintained a thick file of correspondence reflecting the expanding usership of the accounts. Corporations now had a new means of measuring their markets and labour force. The Steel Company of Canada pulled wage and salary figures for the years 1939–45 out of the accounts to guide its postwar labour projections. RCA Victor of Canada used national provincial accounts to calculate consumer spending on nondurables and to establish an industry benchmark for inventories of the same goods. *Canadian Home Journal* extracted provincial income distribution from the tables to guide its subscription campaigns and advertising rates. Argus Corporation of Toronto employed the national accounts to shape its aggressive expansion as a conglomerate. For a corporation like Argus in the throes of buying control of tractor maker Massey-Harris, figures on western farm income were illuminating. Advertising agencies like Cockfield, Brown & Co. and A.C. Nielsen could now establish historical patterns of spending for their clients.

However, there was not universal satisfaction. Users complained that the accounts came out too long after the fact. As Simpson's department store wrote: "it is questionable how valuable statistics for 1946 are when received toward the end of 1947." Marshall replied that collecting data, collating them, and then working them into historical time series took time, particularly when many businesses took their own time responding to the bureau's questionnaires. Others complained that the annual accounts were too frequently revised after their initial release. Isbister would reply that the Americans did release their estimates quicker but revised them even more dramatically. Canada, he said, took a more cautious approach and thereby limited the range of its revisions.[47]

Beyond the boardrooms and marketing departments, the national accounts began to enter the national economic consciousness. Here too they became yardsticks by which Canadians measured their circumstances. Isbister's staff found themselves answering an ever larger volume of inquiries. John Diefenbaker, a Tory member of Parliament from Saskatchewan, requested data on personal income by province. The Canadian ambassador in Moscow wanted data on the percentage of national income devoted to military expenditure. Jacques Parizeau, a London School of Economics-trained economic journalist with the magazine *L'Actualité Economique*, wondered whether "constant dollar" figures on the national economy were available. Edward Neufeld, an honours student at the University of Saskatchewan, wrote to request data on wartime prices for his honours thesis.[48]

As the national accounts continued to gel in practice and public use, Isbister picked up where George Luxton had left off in the international forum. The postwar embrace of multilateralism included statistics. At San Francisco in 1945 the signatories of the United Nations Charter set up an Economic and Social Council dedicated to the improvement of social and economic conditions around the world. The council, in turn, established a Statistical Commission that would serve as the focal point of international harmonization of national accounting. Good, commonly agreed upon statistics would make a better world. "It is a mark of real progress in statesmanship," Herbert Marshall observed, "that international bargaining today, cold and merciless though it often is, substitutes impartial statistics for preconception and bluff."[49] The new United Nations agency took under its wing the old League of Nations committee of statistical experts, whose work on defining international standards of national accounting had been interrupted by the war. In December 1945, in Princeton, New Jersey, the experts regathered under the chairmanship of Richard Stone. American, Australian, Swiss, Norwegian, Mexican, and Dutch economists followed Stone's British leadership. Claude Isbister and Agatha Chapman carried the Canadian colours.

The four-day meeting bore the unmistakable imprimatur of Richard Stone, a trait that would persist at international get-togethers on national accounting into the 1990s. Stone used the Princeton session to work out the details of his notion of "social accounting" – that is, breaking down the national accounts into income and expenditure flows between the key groups in society: business, government, the household, and the financial sectors of the economy. From a Keynesian point of view, this segregation of the economy into its fundamental private and public sectors offered great insight into the operation of public policy. In the wake of the meeting, the United Nations published a nonbinding summation of the proceedings.[50] In effect, an international "club" had convened to coordinate domestic and international practices in national accounting. It was to be an exclusive club, stocked by fully fledged national accountants backed by their respective governments. Although her name was added as an "addition" to these professionals, Richard Stone quietly made it known to Isbister that he had been mightily impressed by "Miss Agatha Chapman."

Back in Ottawa, however, events were conspiring against Miss Chapman. Within blocks of her apartment at 282 Somerset Street West lived Igor Gouzenko, a Russian cipher clerk attached to the office of the Soviet military attaché to Canada. It would be the cruellest coincidence of Chapman's life that the man who would do so much to inalterably damage her existence lived just down the street. The Soviets had been Canada's wartime allies, and there was nothing unusual in one of their diplomats taking up residence at 511 Somerset West. Diplomats, like bureaucrats, valued walking-distance proximity to the city's downtown in a gas-starved wartime economy. And on 5 September 1945 Igor Gouzenko went on an unusual walk. In mid-afternoon he packed 109 secret documents into a valise and left the Soviet Embassy. The documents contained code names and reports suggesting that Moscow had cultivated a circle of Canadian and British sympathizers in Ottawa who had dutifully fed wartime intelligence to the office of the Soviet military attaché. Gouzenko's job had been to encode these communications. Now he had decided to defect, mostly for personal reasons, although he would later invoke ideological motives.[51] Few in Ottawa were initially inclined to believe the Russian clerk with his broken English and agitated manner. First, the RCMP turned him away, and then the night editor of the Ottawa Journal brushed him off. After a night in hiding, Gouzenko was finally taken in by the RCMP and his documents scrutinized.

Gouzenko's evidence seemed convincing. Most worrying was the hint that information concerning the Allies' atomic weapons program had seeped to the Soviets. But the warm glow of wartime friendship with the Soviets made the Mackenzie King government reluctant to unmask Soviet perfidy. Gouzenko was sequestered at Camp X, a secret wartime training base outside Whitby, and interrogated. Washington was informed, but nothing overt was done. Only when an American syndicated columnist, Drew Pearson, began leaking rumours of Gouzenko's revelations in early February 1946 was Prime Minister King provoked into open action. Two days later, a royal commission headed by judges Robert Taschereau and Robert Kellock was appointed to "investigate the facts" of how officials in "positions of trust" had allegedly given "secret and confidential information" to a "foreign power."[52] The Gouzenko revelations have been installed by historians as a crucial precipitator of the Cold War. Within weeks of Drew Pearson's columns, Winston Churchill, for instance, delivered his famous cautionary oration at a small college in Fulton, Missouri: "an iron curtain," he warned, "has descended across the Continent" of Europe.[53]

In the early hours of Friday, 15 February, the RCMP went to work. Armed with warrants issued by the royal commissioner, the police rounded up thirteen suspect "spies," who were immediately taken to an RCMP barracks in Rockcliffe, held incommunicado, and subjected to intense interrogation. The *Globe and Mail* headline the next day screamed: "Atom Secret Leaks to Soviet – Civil Servants Held for Ottawa Probe." The group contained no prominent names. Instead, the detainees were middle-rank civil servants, scientists, an official at the British High Commission, and some military men. It also contained the name of Eric Adams, a one-time employee of the Wartime Requirements Board, a researcher at the Bank of Canada, and now an official with the federal Industrial Development Bank. At 6:00 that morning the RCMP had arrived at Adams's front door. They found only his wife, Jo, at home. Adams was out of town on a business trip to Saskatchewan. The RCMP instead took Adams's bank books and various notebooks. When one of his children asked who the uniformed men were, Jo calmly answered that they worked for "the same government that Daddy worked for."[54]

Later that same day Adams was arrested at the airport in Prince Albert, flown back to Ottawa, and taken to the Rockcliffe barracks. He later complained that his interrogators grilled him under naked lamps and deprived him of sleep. A tough-nosed interrogator asked him whether he was a communist. The police said that they knew Adams had been a "parlour pink" in college and that he had visited Russia. Now, it seemed, his name had appeared in Gouzenko's files under the code name "Ernst." Adams replied that he had "no political ideas whatever in college" and that he considered himself nothing more than "a middle class intellectual." This response proved of little avail. Adams remained incarcerated until 29 March, when he was finally released on bail after being charged under the criminal code with conspiring to violate Canada's Official Secrets Act.[55]

News of the raids must have brought a cold, sharp pang to Chapman's heart. Two of the detainees were acquaintances of hers. Adams she knew from their close collaboration over national accounts at the Bank of Canada. And there was also Kathleen Mary Willsher, the assistant registrar at the British High Commission. Since 1943 Adams and Willsher had been participants in the study group discussions that had taken place in Chapman's Somerset Street apartment. Other detainees had drifted in and out of these get-togethers: Chapman would later admit to knowing twelve of the thirteen detainees. Even George Luxton's name was dragged into the limelight. When Kathleen Willsher was pushed by the commission's relentless counsel to recall exactly who frequented the study groups, she at times strained to recall details. "I am trying to remember the name. It was Luxton … Who? … Luxton … Do you know his first name? … He has died now … You say he is dead? … Yes, a year ago." Luxton's name never resurfaced in the inquiry.[56]

The royal commission worked with expedition and often without due process. Witnesses were called to appear before the two commissioners and grilled by the commission's counsels. Despite Mr Justice Kellock's claim that "we are a fact finding body," the commission quickly adopted an accusatory style, hectoring witnesses and projecting the sense that their guilt was assumed. Witnesses were initially denied legal counsel. This rush to judgment produced three interim reports and a final report on 27 June 1946. En route, Agatha Chapman was called to give evidence. The questioning left little doubt about the commission's suspicions about the young economist: she was an active communist – a member of the Labour-Progressive Party – who had abetted ideological dissidence while the country was at war and who had facilitated the passing of wartime secrets to the Soviets.

Throughout the spring and summer of 1946 Chapman did her best to defend herself. In what one observer described as her "dreamy, vague, patrician style,"[57] Chapman asserted her loyalty to Canada and her right to free thought. The study groups that she hosted were "not to study definitely what you call communism, but to discuss, as I understand it, current affairs, political ideas in general, or different viewpoints." Surely, the commission's inquisitorial counsel insisted, the purpose was to study Marxism. "Sometimes," Chapman answered, yes, but more usually the group's attention ranged freely over "current affairs." Its interest was in "progressive" ideas. The commission's counsel persisted in his

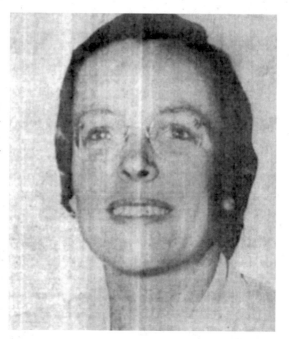

Agatha Chapman in 1946. "The record of responsible citizenship in my family goes back a long way," she told the newspapers during her interrogation by the royal commission investigating the Gouzenko affair. "My great grandfather, Sir Charles Tupper, was one of the Fathers of Confederation ... My work in the Government has been undertaken out of the conviction that this was the best way to make a contribution to my country." Courtesy of *Ottawa Evening Citizen*.

hunt for sedition. Had not Chapman's group collected money for the Canadian-Soviet Friendship Council and for the striking workers at Ford in Windsor? This was true, Chapman admitted – but were not the Soviets our wartime allies? (Moreover, she failed to point out, prominent Canadians like John David Eaton were also members of the Friendship Council.) Did the study group also not read "communistic" periodicals, the counsel demanded? Some would call them communistic, Chapman acknowledged. Without the aid of legal counsel, Chapman's candour seemed to confirm her complicity in treasonous activity. Perhaps most damning was the allegation that Chapman had orchestrated street corner meetings between Adams and Willsher at which "confidential information" from the British High Commission was passed to Adams. Chapman (who had belatedly retained counsel) said that she could not remember arranging such meetings.

Despite this denial, in their June final report the commissioners contended that Chapman was in fact a "cell leader" who had knowingly acted as a go-between for Willsher and Adams. She was not, they concluded, an innocent dupe and should therefore be regarded as having contravened the Official Secrets Act. Chapman's actions were "prejudicial to the safety or interests of the State." The commissioners also reported that they found Chapman's combative style of defending herself incriminating. They did not like "the way her mind works." In their view, she played with words in a way that seemed to reveal sinister motives.[58] Was the word "progressive," she had asked, a seditious word? (Today, scholars would argue that Chapman had failed to conform to the gender roles of the time. As a woman, she had been assertive and intellectually resistant rather than submissive and compliant.) Chapman told the *Toronto Star* that she was "shocked" by the commission's vilification. She protested that she had "always believed in the British traditions of civil rights and fair play."[59] But as the initial shock of the Gouzenko defection quickly turned into Cold War hysteria in the summer of 1946, there was not much "fair play" to be had in Canada.

The Kellock-Taschereau findings hung like a sword of Damocles over Chapman's head throughout the summer of 1946. By day, she worked at the DBS with Isbister readying the first truly comprehensive set of national accounts. In February she and Isbister had published a synopsis of their progress in the *Canadian Banker*, an establishment publication if ever there was one. But her personal life became a nightmare of anxiety. The royal commission had delivered a judgment that was in effect a legal sentence, a sentence that publicly stigmatized her as a "spy." Yet no actual charges had been laid. Nonetheless, with the commission report now public, the bureau told her not to report for work, and the Bank of Canada (still her de facto employer) "put me on leave with pay pending clarification of my position."[60]

Many of Chapman's colleagues were appalled by the treatment being meted out to her. Gideon Rosenbluth, who had just joined the DBS's Labour and Prices Division and had been working closely with Chapman, was "outraged." A young economist imbued at the University of Toronto with Keynesianism, Rosenbluth found himself on a creative "adventure" at the bureau. Chapman, he recalled, was "very dedicated to her work" – "imaginative." Everybody knew that Chapman had a progressive mind, that she projected a "radical" impatience with the existing order. The notion that she was a spy was "absolutely preposterous." But Chapman's fellow economists were themselves soon feeling the inquisitional reverberations of the Gouzenko revelations. As was the Ottawa custom, Chapman, Rosenbluth, and a number of friends had rented a cottage for the summer in the nearby Gatineau hills. Driving there after work each day, Rosenbluth began to notice that a dark sedan seemed to be on his tail every evening. The RCMP, he concluded, was watching him.[61]

In July, Chapman went on the offensive. In the wake of the commission's report, more charges of spying had been laid. Fred Rose, a Labour-Progressive member of Parliament from Montreal and Canada's first federally elected "communist," who the commission said was "schooled in Moscow," was charged with conspiring to subvert the Official Secrets Act. An ugly momentum was clearly growing, and Chapman found herself in the limbo of being uncharged yet perceived as guilty in the public mind. She began talking to the press. She told them that she was a proud Canadian, the descendant of a prime minister. The study groups that she attended were "not communistic but were open to many points of view. They were," she told the Montreal Star, "for the purpose of discussion and study, and had no program of action." She had always taken a keen interest in "political social points of view," something that enhanced her work as a national accountant.[62] (What Chapman and others caught in the Gouzenko net failed to point out was that the study group habit was pervasive in the higher echelons of the Ottawa bureaucracy. Mandarins like Bryce, Macintosh, Rasminsky, and Towers all saw value in evenings spent discussing ideas contained in books. Indeed, Dominion Statistician Herbert Marshall saw a weekly study group on national accounting as a natural way to marry ideas and practice.) Chapman also told the press that she was "bewildered" by Willsher's allegation that she had coordinated clandestine meetings on Ottawa street corners.[63]

Early in August, Chapman wrote to the federal justice minister, Louis St. Laurent, demanding that she be exonerated or that she be put on trial so that she could clear her name. The "stigma" associated with her name was "prejudicial to my employment and seriously embarrassing to my reputation."[64] She was, after all, the great-granddaughter of a Canadian prime minister. "The record of responsible citizenship in my family goes back a long way," she told the Montreal Star.[65] How could her reputation be so recklessly impugned? An editorial in the Globe and Mail took up Chapman's cause: "to leave the situation where it is is either injustice to those over whom the commission has cast a shadow, or evasion of the duty to punish threats to the national safety."[66] The pressure worked. On 19 September, Chapman – "neatly attired in a light blue dress with black hat and purse" – surrendered herself into custody and was charged with conspiring to transmit confidential information to a foreign power. The papers reported that she "fidgeted nervously" before the judge. Chapman elected trial by jury and was released on $2,000 bail. She had become the eighteenth person charged in the Gouzenko affair.

Chapman was by now hardened to the realities of the nascent Cold War. She retained the services of a seasoned Ottawa lawyer, A. Warwick Beament, to face the feisty Crown counsel, John J. Robinette. The trial opened on Tuesday, 26 November, before Ottawa county judge A.G. McDougall. In the public gallery Chapman's friends, including Rosenbluth and a contingent of fellow economists from the DBS, lent moral support. Robinette called three witnesses. It helped that the first, Eric Adams, had already been acquitted in his own trial. What helped more was Igor Gouzenko's testimony that he could not recall ever seeing Chapman's name in the messages he encoded to Moscow. Neither could he recognize her in person. Robinette's principal contention was that Chapman had orchestrated a meeting between Willsher and Adams on Ottawa's Bank Street at which documents and money changed hands. Beament repeatedly challenged Robinette to produce direct evidence of this contention. He had little. After two and a half hours of prosecution presentation, the court recessed. After only two more hours of Crown evidence the next morning, Judge McDougall announced that in his mind the Crown had failed to produce any persuasive evidence that Chapman was a Soviet agent or even a Soviet dupe. "No case has been made out and as far as this trial is concerned the accused is dismissed." The defence, therefore, never presented its case; Chapman got her day in court and carried the day without ever opening her mouth. She left the courtroom "smiling" and surrounded by friends, and she told the press that she was "very, very glad that my name has been cleared." She noted that in her opinion the Bank of Canada had "treated me very fairly" and that she now looked forward to returning to work.[67] Hers had been the shortest Gouzenko trial to date. Many of those closest to her, notably Adams, had also been acquitted. Eleven others, including Willsher and Rose, were convicted and went to jail. There had indeed been fire elsewhere beneath the smoke, but Agatha Chapman had been vindicated as a loyal Canadian.

Despite her innocence, life would never return to normal for Chapman. In August, as the legal tempest surged around her, the Civil Service Commission posted a job competition for a statistician grade 7 at the DBS. The job was essentially a confirmation of the job that Chapman had been doing since being lent by the bank to the DBS in the fall of 1944 – "to organize, develop, and take charge of national income statistics."[68] Chapman applied. Just before her trial in November, she was informed that she was qualified for the job and that she had been selected for "further consideration."[69] The day after her acquittal Chapman was told by the bank to take a month's holiday and thereby await the outcome of the competition. On 6 January 1947 she and two other candidates – both male – were interviewed for the position. Late in January the Civil Service Commission informed Chapman that the position had gone to Angus Sinclair Abell, who had a master's degree and had been a student of Harold Innis at the University of Toronto. Abell was affable but unenergetic – one junior economist in the group at the time described him as "hopeless" – with little intellectual tuning to Keynesian macroeconomics.[70] Chapman was furious and asked for clarification of her own status. None was forthcoming. All she encountered was a bureaucratic chill that left her feeling like she was *persona non grata* at both the bank and the bureau. Early in March the bank informed her that it would not reinstate her in her research post. Unemployed, Chapman was on her own.[71]

A cone of silence descended around the ostracized economist, a silence that extends to this day. Chapman's tarring with the Gouzenko affair is not mentioned in the official DBS history. There are virtually no mentions of her predicament in the organization's archives. Her fate was undoubtedly decided in whispers, nods, and unspoken understandings. Chapman became a nonperson. One lonely exception came from the desk of Claude Isbister in a letter to Richard Stone at Cambridge just after it became public that Chapman had no future at the DBS. In light of the fact, he wrote on 15 February, that Agatha had been acquitted in court "with a clean sheet," it was "unfortunate she is not to be allowed to return to the government service. My own views on the ethics of this situation are strong although I hesitate to commit them to paper. She is now in search of a job and if you know of any position in which her very considerable talents could be used I am sure that she would be pleased to hear from you."[72] Stone knew talent when he saw it and within days had convinced the Committee of Management in Cambridge's Department of Applied Economics to make Chapman a research associate.[73] Late in March, Chapman sailed for England. "I have enjoyed living in Canada and have no bitterness whatever in my mind," she told the *Toronto Star*.[74]

Chapman spent three productive years at Cambridge. She found herself at the academic epicentre of postwar national accounting. With the death of Keynes in 1946, Stone had dedicated himself to the union of macroeconomics and national accounting. Chapman thrived in this atmosphere, and in 1953 the Cambridge University Press published the results of her work on British wages and salaries in the interwar years.[75] Early in the 1950s she returned to Canada and formed a research consultancy with Eric Adams and others in Montreal. Research Associates

Sir Richard Stone at his desk in 1984, the year he won the Nobel Prize in economics for his service in developing an international system of national accounts. In front of him lies a copy of the "blue book," the annual accounting of Britain's national income and expenditure. Appointed to the Central Statistical Office on the advice of Keynes in 1941, Stone went on to advise the United Nations and the OECD on the development of what would become a worldwide System of National Accounts from his postwar Cambridge University posting. His book *National Income and Expenditure*, first published in 1944, was updated into the 1960s and became indispensable reading for undergraduates in economics. Courtesy of Corbis, U841307.

Inc. was dedicated to applying the insights provided by national income to the needs of unions and the labouring man in Canada. It was never a lucrative concern, but it allowed Chapman and Adams to live out their ideals. "Aggie" stayed in touch with some of her erstwhile DBS colleagues; letters from her requesting statistics or suggesting some fine-tuning of the quarterly GNP estimates punctuate the 1950s. But the reality was that Agatha Chapman was condemned to live out her life on the margins. In that she was serving the interests of labour in Canada, she was pleased to be there. But on a more existential level one can also sense that Chapman never recovered from the trauma of the Gouzenko affair. In the 1950s she married Richard Edsall, an American who had fled the intolerance of the McCarthy years. There were no children.

Chapman's income dwindled, and the arthritis that had always plagued her worsened, turning her days into a constant physical misery. On 17 October 1963 she climbed to the top of the stairwell in her Bishop Street apartment building and jumped to her death. The newspapers failed to remark on the event. Her husband requested donations for the Arthritis and Rheumatism Society.[76]

The sudden death of George Luxton and Agatha Chapman's ordeal and exile may have cast a pall over the early years of Canada's effort at national accounting, but ultimately these events did nothing to check Canada's embrace of national accounting. The decade from 1945 to 1955 witnessed a sustained spurt of creativity in bringing the national accounts to the point of broad acceptance and applicability. By 1955 Canadians had come to frame their material existence in macroeconomic terms, which were given statistical substance by quarterly and annual pronouncements from the DBS's Research and Development Staff. The vision of the 1945 white paper – "a high and stable level of employment and income" – had become the new Canadian norm. It was not all smooth economic sailing – poor crops and a winding-down of defence expenditure after the Korean War provoked a shallow recession in 1953-54 – but the nation now seemed adeptly able to combine numbers and policies to prevent any return to the slough of the 1930s. Two facets of this march to economic stability stand out: the exuberant culture of those who built the national accounts and the increasing perfection of the work that they did.

In 1949 the American pioneer of national accounting, Simon Kuznets, praised the dynamic behind the building-up of national accounts: their working-out acted "as a sharp spur to human inquiry and a powerful magnet that attracts effort in one direction rather than another."[77] Such was the mystique of national accounting in these galvanic years. The career of Robert Crozier captures the culture of dedication. When Crozier graduated from Queen's University in 1940, he liked to joke that the bachelor of arts (BA) he now possessed stood for "bugger all." Growing up in Depression-era Saskatchewan had stripped him of the optimism of adolescence. But by the time he left the army in August 1946, Crozier was determined to be an economist, to apply knowledge to the problems of society. His thesis supervisor at Queen's, Bill Macintosh, had by then gone to Ottawa, where he had been the architect of the 1945 white paper. The tide had turned. "In the post-war years," Crozier recalled, "governments hired economists by the car-load, appropriated money for their research, backed up their recommendations ... I was as dedicated and committed as anyone could be to preventing a repetition of that catastrophic experience," the Depression.[78] The era of applied economics had dawned; economists found perches – throughout the growing postwar bureaucracy – in the Ministry of Trade and Commerce, in the Ministry of Finance, in the Bank of Canada, and with the DBS's Research and Development Staff. Crozier was first hired by the bureau to do morbidity studies. He hated it and lobbied to get into national accounts. His wife complained that their grocery money was diverted to buying books by James Meade and Richard Stone. He studied at home every Saturday morning. [He had to entirely relearn his economics; he had been taught *deductive* economics at Queen's, drawing down from general theory to practical circumstance. Now he immersed himself in *inductive* economics, drawing patterns out of empirical observations. And it paid off.] Herbert Marshall spotted him and pulled him into the national accounts team. The challenge was immense, and the hours were long. Years later Crozier chided the editor of *Canadian Business Economics* for overlooking the formative dynamic of national accounting: "We started literally at ground zero. And you had to *think* – it was all new, it had never been done before."[79]

deductive vs. inductive

Crozier had plenty of company in his enthusiasm. The Research and Development Staff became a crossroads for young economists in Canada. Some were hired. Others left their academic posts to undertake summer research projects. Others came from government offices downtown to discuss the new Canadian welfare state's appetite for economic statistics. A young economics professor at Queen's, David Slater, began a long relationship with the national accounts office in these years. The place, he recalled, was "a veritable beehive of industry."[80] Just about the time Slater headed off to Chicago to do a doctorate, young Thomas Rymes was learning from Professor Clarence Barber at the University of Manitoba that national accounting was providing a new roadmap of the national economy. Barber had worked for Isbister before joining academe. Now Rymes headed for Ottawa, where he too encountered the "sense of drama, taking part in something that was really significant."[81] Hans Adler arrived in 1949 with a master's degree from Chicago and teaching experience in Saskatchewan, believing that the DBS was the "basic training ground" for anyone who wanted to understand the new geography of Canadian public policy.[82]

One recruit stood out in this youthful crowd: Simon Goldberg. In Ottawa's postwar scramble to attract promising young talent, the DBS had an unspoken advantage. It had no qualms about hiring Jews. Pioneering the national accounts and the Labour Force Survey perforce placed a premium on brains, not ethnicity or religious background. Gideon

Rosenbluth and Hans Adler are cases in point. Each had fled Hitler's Germany in the 1930s only to find themselves trapped in Britain as "friendly enemy aliens."[83] They joined a handful of fortunate Jews – many others were turned away – who became sponsored wartime immigrants to Canada. Ottawa department store mogul A.J. Freiman posted a bond for Rosenbluth that allowed him to attend the University of Toronto, where he discovered economics. He became convinced that Keynes had the answers, even reviewing Mabel Timlin's book on Keynes in the *Commerce Journal*. Adler first encountered Keynes while interned in a refugee camp in Trois Rivières; Jewish students in the camp told him of the powerful ideas of a professor whom they had studied under at Cambridge. Adler went on to the University of Manitoba. With the peace, Rosenbluth and Adler opted to stay in Canada and began looking for work in economics. Research at the Bank of Canada seemed a natural opportunity. Louis Rasminsky, a brilliant young economist who had worked at the League of Nations and had been at Bretton Woods, worked at the bank. But Rosenbluth and Adler soon learned that as a Jewish employee Rasminsky was the exception, not the rule.[84] The Bank did not even respond to Rosenbluth's application. Herbert Marshall and Claude Isbister had no such biases. As early as 1932 the DBS had hired Nathan Keyfitz, a stellar mathematician who had developed much of the methodological expertise behind the Labour Force Survey. Now the bureau hired Rosenbluth and Adler with alacrity and set them to work on fine-tuning the national accounts and labour force analysis.[85]

Simon Goldberg arrived in Canada from Poland as a child immigrant in 1927. He spent his youth in Canada's largest Jewish community, Montreal, where he graduated from McGill in 1939. Master's degrees in economics, first at McGill and then at Harvard, followed before Goldberg enlisted in the air force. With peace in 1945, he joined the Research and Development Staff and very quickly exhibited a genius for understanding both the internal detail and the broad architecture of national accounting. There was an intensity about his work, an obliviousness to everything but the statistical matter at hand. He wandered about the office incessantly, quizzing and encouraging his colleagues. He bit his nails to the quick. He thought nothing of phoning colleagues at home late in the evening with some latest thought on a problem and offering no apology other than his evident excitement. The combination of his "steely-blue eyes" and the "sheer power of his intellect" proved irresistible.[86] Bob Crozier quickly came to regard Goldberg as the "flywheel" of the whole enterprise. Many found him abrupt and superior, but there was never any doubt of his devotion to constructing the national accounts system.

And this was the key to his genius: Goldberg always regarded the national accounts as a *system*, not a fragmented collection of economic indicators. The system's utility lay in serving as an integrating point for all information on national economic performance and, as a result of centralizing all these data, in providing methodological verification of their quality. The picture of the national economy presented in the income and expenditure accounts would command public credibility only if the data employed in the calculation balanced. "Its major asset lies in the fact that it represents a powerful unifying force in our work," Goldberg remarked in the *Canadian Journal of Economics and Political Science*. "By emphasizing the interrelationships among all economic statistics and the need for over-all consistency in definitions and classifications, it helps to increase the return for each 'statistical dollar' and 'statistical man-hour.'"[87] The national accounts system, in short, must be a self-cleansing and self-justifying exercise.

In 1949 Goldberg took a year away from Ottawa to begin a doctorate at Harvard (a degree that he would complete in 1954). Claude Isbister's decision to become deputy minister of trade and commerce cleared the way for Goldberg to become director of the Research and Development Staff on his return from Harvard in 1950. Goldberg's passion to make national accounting the integrating engine of the entire national statistical system would stay on the intellectual backburner for the time being. There were more pressing operational goals to be achieved in making the accounts useful to the public and methodologically workable. But integration remained Goldberg's abiding statistical vision for Canada – the goal of melding the collection and analysis of economic statistics into one integrated whole.

Progress was quick. In 1946 Larry Read, a graduate student from the University of Toronto, came to Ottawa to work on his thesis at the Ministry of Finance. He used the national accounts to construct a profile of income distribution in Canada. Knowing how national income was spread around the country and how it trickled through the class structure was crucial to monitoring postwar taxation and the impact of new social programs like the mothers' allowance. Read was, for instance, able to show that 44.9% of Canadians in nonagricultural occupations earned less than $1,000 annually in 1942. Canada now had a baseline against which to measure the success of its new social programs.[88] Read's work was perpetuated by Jenny Podoluk, a talented young economist who quickly showed that women continued to play a key professional role after the sad loss of Chapman. Subsequent income break-downs of the national accounts revealed the income pattern of Canadian doctors, dentists, and lawyers. Podoluk showed, for instance, that British Columbia lawyers in private practice were the best paid in the country.[89]

Another enhancement in the national accounts came in the form of "constant dollar" calculation of the gross national product. Early income and expenditure reporting had been done in current dollars, so the gradual erosion of the purchasing power of the currency was not being reflected, thereby robbing the accounts of their "deflated" (i.e., corrected for inflation) year-to-year comparability. Nobody, therefore, could calculate the "real output" of the economy over time.[In 1950 the Research and Development Staff began "deflating" the gross national expenditure by the amount of the year's inflation. The same methodology was used to recreate a time series of national expenditure figures back to 1926. The release of these figures in 1952 gave Canada a long yardstick by which to gauge its economic performance over time. Deflation was also applied on an industry-by-industry basis to demonstrate the relative performance of specific industries within the economy.[90]]

The national accounts were then "seasonally adjusted." Canadians did not have to be told that their country was a big, sometimes hot, and sometimes cold place with dramatic swings in economic performance throughout the seasons. Total production in the country could change in volume from the slow season in January to the peak of agricultural and industrial production in the fall by as much as one-third. Such wide seasonal swings, the DBS realized, could "often obscure underlying trends and baffle the analyst who seeks to study cyclical behaviour or to interpret the significance of current economic developments." In the early 1950s Canadian economists therefore pioneered a method by which normal, repetitive swings in the economy could be factored into the reporting of economic time series. In short, they learned how to "smooth out" seasonal swings in the economy and started issuing a twelve-month "adjusted" moving average of economic performance. A companion "unadjusted" year-to-year average allowed Canadians to compare performance from, say, one January to the next.[91]

Canadians were given a quarterly update on their economic condition, one that factored in the time of the year and the erosion of inflation. The bureau's quarterly estimate of GNP would become the most familiar weathervane in the increasingly comfortable world of the welfare

Number Crunching, the Old-Fashioned Way

The rise of applied economics after the Second World War took place in a world of manual calculation. There were no computers. Since economics was now less based on speculative deduction and more reliant on induction from actual observation, processing data became a central facet of an economist's work. Since the 1890s census takers had eased the labour of toting up their numbers by employing Hollerith tabulating machines. American Herman Hollerith had devised a machine that allowed data to be punched onto cards and the card then electrically "read" – electrical current would pass through the card wherever a hole had been created by the extraction of a "chad," thereby registering a result. Hollerith machines greatly reduced the time needed to compile census numbers but had no analytical capacity. A Hollerith employee, Thomas Watson, would extend the business data frontier when he founded International Business Machines (IBM) in the 1920s.

National accounting by its very nature necessitated a huge exercise in totaling and manipulating data. Vast amounts of raw statistics on manufacturing, investment, government expenditure, and so forth poured onto the desks of the Research and Development Staff and had to be aggregated and groomed to provide flows of income and expenditure. Huge ledger books were employed to record the data, a painstaking process of manual entry by each economist. The actual tallying of these numbers was then done by female clerks who laboured over Frieden Mechanical 'Automatic' Calculators. The Frieden was an electrically assisted adding machine. It was a massive 20 kilogram contraption with a 10 x 10 digit keyboard. The Frieden could perform basic mathematical functions – slowly. It could add two ten-digit figures in about a second and multiply them in about a minute. For the fifteen years after the war, the Frieden was the calculating workhorse of the Western world. It facilitated the mathematical work that lay behind everything from inventing the A-bomb to running General Motors.

Two things stand out about the Frieden's application to national accounting. The machines filled offices with a constant clatter as they quite literally crunched their numbers. They were machines, not circuit boards. When deadlines approached for the quarterly GNP estimates, the machines were run around the clock. And since triple verification was required for all totals, extra Frieden teams were employed to speed the process, thereby increasing the din. The Friedens also drew a very distinct gender line through the Research and Development workplace. Male economists orchestrated the data, and female clerks actually crunched the numbers.

The Frieden soon became a dinosaur. The postwar world demanded speed and volume in calculation. Mechanical calculation could never keep pace. Electronics were the answer. In 1946 the American-built Electronic Numerical Integrator and Computer (ENIAC) pointed the way – slowly. It weighed 30 tons and contained 19,000 vacuum tubes. It would take another fifteen years before the first really practicable computers, like the IBM 360, came to economists' rescue and transformed the way that national accounts were compiled.

Sixty years on: Dr Thomas Rymes (left) and Dr Larry Read, 2007. Rymes and Read epitomized the breed of bright, young economists drawn to national accounting as the postwar Keynesian world unfolded. Numbers – put in the right context and order – would make the world a better place. After doing research at the Dominion Bureau of Statistics, Rymes and Read went onto brilliant careers as academics at Ottawa's Carleton University. Here, they pose in front of a plaque commemorating Simon Goldberg's contribution to Canadian statistics. Courtesy of Statistics Canada.

state. It was always at the top of the news and quickly installed itself as a prime indicator of national wellbeing. Canada's success at seasonal and constant dollar adjustment reflected a sophistication in national accounting methodology that put it in the very forefront of world national accounting; most countries were still able only to report their accounts in current dollars and raw, seasonally unadjusted terms. Indeed, when the United Nations Statistical Commission released its first set of guidelines for the international standardization on national accounting in 1953, there was a tentativeness about the document. "The actual construction of such a comprehensive accounting system is hardly possible at the present time," Richard Stone and his experts admitted.[92] Most nations were still scrambling to reconstruct their war-torn economies. Few had more than the most rudimentary national accounting capacity. The report, for instance, eschewed any attempt at constant currency calculation; current accounting remained the orthodoxy. The 1953 System of National Accounts was instead a visionary blueprint for most nations, a pattern of standards to be aspired to and slowly adopted. Canada had already traversed that territory and was already in the vanguard of international national accounting. There was nothing hollow in Herbert Marshall's boast to the minister of trade and commerce, C.D. Howe, that Canada's national accountants "now rank with the best in the world."[93] Simon Goldberg was typically more assertive: "We have, therefore, buckled on our swords and are prepared to meet whatever challenge comes our way. The challenge is simply that it is up to us to produce the best possible data at whatever time it is required."[94]

The mid-1950s ebullience surrounding these national accounting efforts reflected a broader lustre at the Dominion Bureau of Statistics. The agency had expanded with the times. Like a carpenter's tape, it had nimbly extended itself to measure the many new timbers of the welfare state. Numbers were now an integral ingredient in the making of Canadian consciousness. The mandarins downtown acknowledged the bureau's indispensable role by allowing Herbert Marshall – "the statistics czar" – to commission a new building in the early 1950s for his expanding staff. The building was to be the lead project in an attempt to spread the federal civil service out of Ottawa's inner precinct. Tunney's Pasture on the edge of the Ottawa River was designed as a civil service campus – planned, modernistic, and symbolic of the new Canadian state. The new building would replace the decrepit lumber mill that had served the DBS so poorly for so long.

When it opened in 1952, the Art Deco building was the envy of the civil service. And for the first time the forty-nine members of the Research and Development Staff had offices designed for their needs. Despite the kudos that they were attracting across the nation and at the United Nations, Canada's national accountants tended to be regarded as "eggheads" by their confreres at the bureau. They did not themselves collect data; they aggregated other peoples' data and did so in very esoteric ways well beyond the grasp of ordinary mortals. When a new employee newsletter, the punning *Pasture-ized News*, appeared in 1953, the Research and Development Staff at Tunney's Pasture seized the opportunity to explain themselves to their fellow statisticians. "The main objective of this Unit," the article explained, "is to measure the current Canadian production of goods and services … The nation is looked at as a big family and the work of the unit is to calculate the budget of this big family … Finally, one interesting thing about the accounts is that after a period of depression or prosperity has occurred, they can give a very good description of what hit the economy!"[95] How well this attempt to humanize the work of the eggheads in national accounting worked can only be speculated. Certainly, Lorne Rowebottom, a rising economist in the bureau's Labour and Prices Division, regarded them as "an enclave of brains trusters." He recalled an incident one Christmas Eve in the mid-1950s. Ottawa was still a rather buttoned-down place, but after lunch on the 24 December staff members began slipping boxes of Christmas cookies and bottles of rye out of their desks. Before long a mood of conviviality spread throughout the building. Late that afternoon, Rowebottom happened to pass a conference room. Hearing solemn voices, he pushed the door open to find Goldberg and about fifteen economists thrashing out some problem of national accounting. Not even Santa could distract the national accountants.[96]

4   In Useful Directions

There is gold in them thar DBS reports. It's not all lying
on the surface in the form of shiny nuggets, to be sure.
You have to pan for it ... patiently and assiduously.
~ Scott Feggans, vice president, Dominion Stores, 1961
letter to Dominion Bureau of Statistics

It has been said that politics is the art of the possible.
One may claim the same for statistics.
~ Simon Goldberg, "The Function of Integration in a
Statistical Office" (1962)

The thrust now is towards improving the quality of the
estimates, elaborating the basic income and product accounts in useful directions, and integrating the various
types of accounts into a comprehensive system.
~ John Kendrick, *Economic Accounts and Their Uses* (1972)

[A] statistical toolkit.
~ Kari Levitt, *Input-Output Study of the Atlantic Provinces*
(1975)

Times were good. When Minister of Finance Walter Harris rose to deliver his budget in April 1955, the country could look back on a decade
of solid economic performance. Government policy dedicated to "the
encouragement of enterprise, investment and employment," Harris
boasted, had paid handsome dividends. The Depression had not returned. Canada had found the economic wherewithal to fight a war in
Korea and to put the first timbers of the welfare state in place. Tax

rental agreements between Ottawa and the provinces – soon to be renamed "equalization" – spread the national wealth, providing a "unique and interesting experience in intergovernmental cooperation." True, 1954 had seen growth falter slightly. Reduced defence spending, a below-average grain crop, and hesitant business investment and consumer spending had cooled the economy. But Harris remained confident: "The healthy expansion of the Canadian economy is everybody's business."[1] His budget prescription was structured around the national accounts and their tracing of the flows of money through the economy. What had government spent? What had business invested? What was our trade position? How had households fared?

By now, the language of Richard Stone's social accounting – with its emphasis on the economic relations of households, government, and business – had become the national fiscal language. The new mechanics of the federal budget had become familiar to Canadians; fiscal levers – taxes and federal spending – were carefully pushed up a notch or relaxed to stimulate or cool the economy. The next year's national accounts would capture the outcomes. To certify the whole process, the DBS's national accounts were now annually appended to the budget.[2] In university classrooms, professors used the DBS's published versions of the accounts – dubbed the "brown book" in honour of its sober brown cover – to explain the new Keynesian mechanics of the nation to students.

Harris concluded with a bold announcement that smacked of Canada's newfound economic confidence. There would be a royal commission to study Canada's "economic prospects." The country could no longer plot its economic course on the basis of rosy "after-dinner speeches." The time had come "to spend a little time, thought and money on carefully documenting the reality" of Canada's economic structure. Harris's announcement was full of activist language – "sharpen," "focus," "promote and stimulate." The commission would be asked "to look ahead" twenty-five years and to examine Canada's economic opportunities and challenges.[3] It was an extraordinary mandate. Never before had Canada systematically explored its economic *future*. Indeed, the idea of foretelling the nation's economic future would have struck previous generations of Canadians as utopian and preposterous. A mere twenty years before, Canadians, unable to fathom the depression that engulfed them, would have been dumbfounded by the idea of looking twenty-five *days* into their economic future. But now the tools and the confidence seemed to exist to support such an attempt to map the future.

To spearhead the commission, Harris chose Walter Gordon – Toronto accountant, staunch Liberal, and one-time wartime mandarin.[4] Gordon set a brisk pace and over the next eighteen months oversaw preparation of thirty-three background studies, the taking of coast-to-coast testimony, and the writing of a report. His royal commission became a factory of applied research. Academics dissected the economy in all its facets: by sector, by industry, by region, and by activity. Anthony Scott, a University of British Columbia economist who had just completed a doctorate on the theory of natural resource conservation at the London School of Economics, combined forces with William Hood, a University of Toronto economist, to produce a prognosis of the main drivers of the Canadian economy – output, labour, and capital – down to 1980. Using the growth theory of American economist Robert Solow, their analysis suggested that the next twenty-five years would "not represent a sharp break with the past," as continued reliance on mainstays like resources would push Canadian living standards up.[5] In a similar vein, David Slater, a Queen's University economist finishing his doctorate at the University of Chicago, undertook a study of consumption in Canada. "The picture is one of a rich people becoming richer," Slater concluded. "It is a picture of an acquisitive society, the members of which are prepared to work for but expect substantially higher levels of material living."[6]

En route to its late 1957 final report, the Gordon Commission furnished Canadians with evidence of powerful undertows in their economy – the shrinking importance of agriculture, surging inflows of foreign direct investment, the growth of service industries. Gordon left Canadians with an encouraging picture of their economic future. By 1980 their gross national product would, he estimated, increase 3 to 3½ times. Employment in business, government, and community services would surge; farm employment would retreat. On the whole, Gordon concluded, the "promise of the economic future as we foresee it is one to command enthusiasm."[7]

Gordon's optimism provided further evidence of the incoming tide of postwar macroeconomics – the belief that aggregate demand in the economy could be measured, redirected, and now predicted. Keynesianism, Anthony Scott recalls, had become "the line."[8] In his report Gordon at times slipped into the jargon of the new economic creed: Canada's economy had "now become a more complex and sophisticated mechanism than it was, with a large variety of reciprocating movements and with complex interactions that owe something to the multiplicity of its parts but also something to social and institutional arrangements." Gordon could, however, just as easily slip into the vernacular to get his point across: "Money gets rubbed off on a great many fingers."[9]

If Gordon drew his vocabulary from the world of national accounting and macroeconomics, his researchers drew their facts from the Tunney's Pasture offices of Simon Goldberg and his national accounts team. Virtually every study undertaken for the royal commission gave pride of place to the DBS's Research and Development Staff in its acknowledgments. "Their kindness and co-operation have not only facilitated, but indeed made possible, much of the work which we have undertaken," Gordon summarily wrote. It was not just that the numbers were available but also that the numbers seemed reliable. In ten quick years the

The Phillips Machine

Humans have always been inclined to describe systems in metaphorical terms. Classical economists adopted anatomical analogies to describe the operation of an economy that functioned according to its own whims. Adam Smith's "invisible hand" worked its magic. When they did attempt to convey some sense of what went on within the economy, many classical economists employed the metaphor of the circulation of the blood throughout the body. The twentieth century, with its inclination to manage the economy, witnessed the advent of more mechanical metaphors to describe the economic system. The Physiocrats of the eighteenth century had talked of *tableau économique* – a dynamic zigzag of economic exchange. The Keynesian revolution's emphasis on management of supply and demand and on national accounting's dedication to measuring flows within the economy made mechanical explanation more appealing. Although economists generally wince at the term, Keynesian economics is probably best known by the image of "pump priming." In 1950 the New Zealand economist Alban Phillips (who began his career as an electrical engineer) built a hydraulic machine that depicted flows within the economy. A plexiglass window allowed the observer to see the dynamic working of the economy as income and expenditure. Levers could be manipulated to alter the controlling influences on the economy — exports, taxes, savings, and so forth. Phillips even supplied an extra bottle of water labelled "Bank of England" to enable the user to "top up" the machine. The Phillips Machine was sold as an aid to teaching in universities and public lecturing. Not everybody understood such economic plumbing. *Punch*, England's famous humour magazine, ran a cartoon in 1953 parodying the Phillips Machine, wherein the teapot of income will be tipped by the rising balloon of consumer spending.

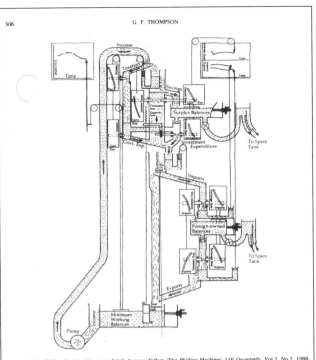

Fig. 10. The 'Phillips Machine' in more detail. Source: N.Barr 'The Phillips Machine' *LSE Quarterly*, Vol.2, No.2, 1988. (Figure 2, p.324)

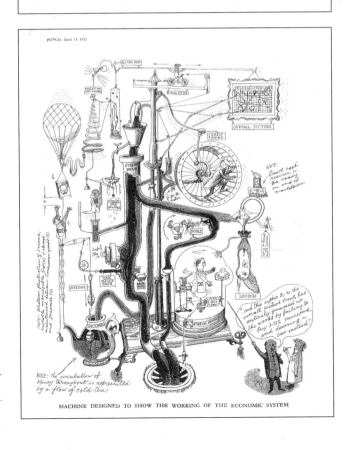

MACHINE DESIGNED TO SHOW THE WORKING OF THE ECONOMIC SYSTEM

Top:
The Phillips Machine
Source: N Barr, "The Phillips Machine," *LSE Quarterly* 2, no. 2 (1988): 324.

Bottom:
Punch, 15 April 1953

DBS had established itself as the unquestioned font of economic statistics in Canada. Goldberg liked to refer to his operation as "our gigantic factory."[10]

Further proof of these kudos came in the spring of 1960, when the Diefenbaker Conservatives, now in power, presented their budget. The national economy had hit a bump. Unemployment was up. Inflation was edging up. And Ottawa was facing its first postwar deficit situation. The easy Keynesian juggling of unemployment and inflation was proving harder to effect. In the House of Commons the Tory minister of finance, Donald Fleming, and the leader of the Opposition, Lester Pearson, locked political horns over an appropriate response to the malaise. The rhetoric turned nasty. Figures were hurled across the Commons floor with accusatory abandon. But neither side questioned the reliability of the DBS calculations. Back at Tunney's, Frank Leacy, one of Goldberg's senior national accountants, heaved a sigh of relief when he realized that the politicians were not debating the *quality* of the nation's economic data, simply its application by the politicians. "In general," Leacy wrote, the "DBS was referred to as a fact-finding agency and its figures considered to be authoritative ... There has been much more attention to statistics recently and greater accuracy is being demanded of us."[11]

Thus Canada's postwar honeymoon with Keynesianism began to fade as Canadians encountered the first strains of maintaining domestic economic bliss. "During the 1950s," economist Doug Hartle wrote in 1960, "Canadians were eager to tell envious European nations of Canada's leaping GNP. But in 1960 disgruntled Canadians were asking themselves how West Germany was now able to show a surplus on its international balance of payments and maintain full employment, when Canada at the end of fifteen years of growth found herself in the doldrums."[12] One of the central assumptions of the Keynesian prescription had been that the private sector was chronically unstable, that it surged and retreated in the face of demand. This instability could be offset by judicious government interventions – in expenditure and taxation. Such actions would trigger "multipliers" that would ripple through the economy, enlivening growth. But Canada's was a remarkably *open* economy, subject to forces beyond its control, and the multipliers could not always be relied upon to behave according to the policy script.

Heavy reliance on exports and inflows of foreign investment best revealed this vulnerability. And in the late 1950s flagging exports and a declining Canadian dollar began to erode Canada's prosperity. Unemployment rose and government attempts to bolster the economy – "Why wait for spring, do it now!" – seemed unable to arrest the slide. The *Canadian Statistical Review* reported "a leveling-off in the aggregate,"[13] and by 1960 the quarterly estimates of the national accounts revealed that Canada was in a recession – two consecutive quarters of negative GNP growth. Politics quickly reflected the malaise; the Diefenbaker government found itself embroiled in a test of wills with the governor of the Bank of Canada, James Coyne, over the setting of the bank rate. Fleming, as minister of finance, wanted lower interest rates and stimulation, while Coyne stood his ground for higher rates and vigilance against inflation. Coyne was eventually forced out. Still the economy faltered. The Liberal Opposition played upon the nation's economic anxiety by printing "Diefenbucks," play money worth 92½ cents on the American dollar. In the 1962 federal election, the Diefenbaker government was reduced to minority status, largely as a result of the country's economic lassitude.

Despite these jitters, there was no questioning of the abiding goals of postwar economic policy – the credo of "a high and stable level of employment and income," the phrase made famous by the 1945 white paper on income and employment. The challenge was instead one of adapting economic attitudes and policies to the complexities of the Canadian situation. As John J. Deutsch at Queen's University admitted, "the problems of social and economic policy have proved to be much more complex than was thought during the first flush of the Keynesian revolution after the war. It has now been shown that the Keynesian doctrine has provided only a partial answer to the question of policy in the present-day world."[14] The 1960s in Canada were therefore dedicated to a fuller working out of the initial impulses of the Keynesian mixed economy. Equalization donned the cloak of regional economic expansion. The welfare state was enlarged to provide universal health care. Governments extended their regulatory arm and intervened in the private sector by means of subsidies and taxation policy, sometimes even succumbing to direct investment when private enterprise was tardy or timid. Global economic conditions obliged, and the Canadian economy consequently enjoyed a decade of boisterous good health.

National accountants in Ottawa responded to these developments first by *broadening* and then by *deepening* their measurement of the flows at the heart of the national economy. Their energies slowly began to shift from monitoring the aggregate performance of the economy to exploring its complexity – to *disaggregating* the national economy into its regional and sectoral components. This shift reflected the wider interest in the phenomenon of growth. The term *productivity* began to enter the national policy debate. Such dissection, much like a medical diagnosis, would allow better understanding of the internal mysteries of the economy and might better equip economists and policymakers to address the macroeconomic needs of the nation.

The 1960s would consequently see Canada move to the forefront of international national accounting. Canadians' engrained pragmatism and their instinct for finding the middle seemed ideally suited to the task of matching numbers and economic performance in a mature welfare state. Canadians were never rigid theorists in these matters. Hans Adler, assistant director of the National Accounts Division, caught this proclivity in a 1967 report on a statisticians' meeting in Geneva. English-speaking countries, he observed, had "a somewhat different approach to national accounts ... more pragmatic, more flexible and sometimes more illogical but on the other hand, in many instances analytically more useful." European national statisticians, he suggested, were more hidebound in their adherence to "highly logical, polished and elaborate" systems. Canadian economists were masters of these "pragmatic solutions and shortcuts," which led to wariness regarding acceptance of certain conventions as "gospel truth."[15] The most telling example of this inventiveness would be the rectangular input-output (I/O) table, an intricate tool of economic analysis made feasible by the advent of the computer. The I/O table allowed economists to delve into the heart of economic transactions and would soon earn the sobriquet of "the Canadian model" in national accounting circles around the world. During the 1960s Canadian national accountants were therefore striving to get it right at home and pushing the boundaries of their art internationally. "It has been said that politics is the art of the possible," Simon Goldberg observed in 1962. "One may claim the same for statistics."[16]

By the early 1960s Canada's national accounts were beginning to take on an established look. The system had inevitably acquired a bureaucratic structure. This became evident in 1961 when the title Central Research and Development Staff, with its overtones of being in the vanguard, was dropped in favour of the more normative National Accounts Division. This shift toward a more established status was powerfully shaped by two men. In 1957 Herbert Marshall had stepped down as Dominion statistician and was replaced by Walter Duffett. Like so many of his confreres, Duffett's trajectory in life had been shaped by the Depression. A master's degree from the London School of Economics, a stint of applied research at Sun Life Assurance, and

Canada's national accountants on a spring day in 1958 on the lawn of the new Dominion Bureau of Statistics building at Tunney's Pasture in Ottawa. The picture conveys a vivid sense of the gender division that ran through the bureau's national accounts team. The men – young war veterans with university degrees and a devotion to the political arithmetic of the welfare state – exude the confidence of Ottawa's burgeoning bureaucracy. The women were largely the administrative foundation of the national accounts effort – clerks who punched numbers into Freiden calculating machines. Very few women broke through this glass ceiling. Two here – Jenny Podoluk and Barbara Clift – would rise to prominence as economic analysts. Courtesy of Robert Crozier, Ottawa.

wartime work at the Wartime Prices and Trade Board had made an applied economist of Duffett. In 1944 he had been considered for the job at the DBS of heading Canada's first sortie into national accounting, a position eventually given to George Luxton. Postwar research work at the Bank of Canada and the Ministry of Labour had honed Duffett's talent for linking research and policy, a bridge often built of DBS data. In 1957 he became the first outsider appointed as Dominion statistician. Throughout the 1960s Duffett was thus well equipped to connect the bureau's data gathering with the needs of uptown policymakers. Statistics were becoming an active ingredient in shaping Canada's managed economy and the welfare state that it was expected to support. Duffett proved adept at building the bureaucratic alliances that kept the DBS in its coveted role as national fact-finder. A good Dominion statistician was a man who could divine what the nation wanted and could link it with what the statisticians could supply.

Back at Tunney's Pasture, Simon Goldberg became the bureau's de facto operational chief. In 1954 Marshall had promoted Goldberg, with his newly minted Harvard doctorate, to assistant Dominion statistician. While Goldberg surrendered direct control over the national accounts work first to Frank Leacy and then to Robert Crozier, national accounting remained his preeminent concern at the DBS. In his new job Goldberg was charged with the task of "integration," of making the myriad statistics produced at the bureau relate to each other. Canada's managed economy and welfare state needed much more than lonely columns of figures; interconnection and standard classification of raw data were now the order of the day. In this spirit, Goldberg dedicated himself to making the national accounts "strongly utilitarian and practical." This meant ensuring that they operated as "a single and harmonious system" that emphasized "the interrelationships among all economic statistics." The accounts had to continue to be balanced – what went in on one side of any equation must be seen to emerge on the other side. But at the same time, the "cracks and gaps" in the accounts, as Goldberg called them, must be filled in and the whole made consistent.[17] What, for instance, went on in the economy between the bald outcomes of income and expenditure? What *intermediate* transactions took place in the production chain? How was the economy financed? What was the ratio of costs to output in the Canadian economy? In short, the system had to be made broader and deeper.

A very conspicuous broadening-out of the national accounts came in 1961 when the calculation of Canada's balance of payments was folded into the national accounts. It was a marriage of two mature entities. In a country historically dependent on trade and the inflow of investment, knowledge of Canada's international financial performance was vitally important. Each year the *current* account revealed how Canadian exporters and importers had fared, whether they had sold more than they had bought in the world marketplace. With a kind of crude mercantilist logic, the public tended to believe that countries that sold more than they bought were strong. Those with a negative balance of trade were weak and vulnerable. (Economists begged to differ from the public's economic literalism, arguing that gains from trade depended on the *volume* of trade, not its balance.) Similarly, a country's *capital* account revealed how much investment it either exported or imported. Britain was, for instance, a perennial lender to the world. Canada, conversely, was a habitual borrower. As early as the turn of the twentieth century, Canadians had tried to calibrate their place in the world of international trade and finance. Robert Coats's pioneering investigation into the cost of living in Canada had shown that prices in Canada were crucially influenced by the country's exposure to international markets. In 1924 Montreal-born economist Jacob Viner published a study of Canada's international indebtedness and went on to make his reputation as America's foremost theorist of international trade at Chicago and Princeton.[18]

The Dominion Bureau of Statistics began collecting data on balance of payments in the 1920s. An ironically named Internal Trade Branch began to monitor current and capital flows across the border. Such data, at first just crudely estimated, were crucial to understanding Canada's trade, exchange rate, and financial standing in the eyes of foreign lenders. Trade negotiations needed such data to determine advantage and vulnerability. The emerging tourism industry had to be measured. As one DBS publication noted, "it would be like taking a leap in the dark to formulate policy, without the aid of these statistics."[19] In many ways, balance of payments estimates in the interwar years were the most sophisticated of the DBS's economic calculations. In the early 1920s, for instance, Herbert Marshall had been hired out of the University of Toronto to construct balance of payments estimates for the DBS. In 1936 Marshall joined forces with academics Ken Taylor and Frank Southard to publish a groundbreaking study of the effects of Canada's heavy dependence on foreign investment.[20] *Canadian-American Industry* was in large part made possible by the DBS's adoption of a system of direct reporting by individual companies of their receipt or transmission of monies across the border. The book's painstaking collation of these figures conveyed the alarming message that Canada was becoming heavily dependent on American direct investment. Some industries, like petroleum, were as much as 80% American-owned. (Once again, some economists begged to differ, arguing that foreign direct investment fostered rapid economic growth and technology transfer. Canadian economist Harry Johnson would later argue that curtailing foreign investment flows was dysfunctional and reflected a "small-town pettiness of outlook.")[21] In 1939 Marshall capped his early spurt of balance of payments activity with the publication of the so-called "red book," a thorough DBS study of the method and outcomes of Canada's balance of payments. The same year, Marshall was awarded the Professional Institute of the Civil Service's gold medal for his innovative balance of payments research.

The war intensified Canadian interest in balance of payments flows. In a tight wartime economy, every drop of foreign exchange, especially American dollars, had to be monitored and regulated. Almost the first wartime regulation imposed by Ottawa in 1939 was foreign exchange control. The Foreign Exchange Control Board (FECB) was placed under the Bank of Canada's umbrella but largely manned by DBS personnel. Marshall's lieutenant, Doug Blyth, was seconded to the bank, where new recruits like McGill-trained Edward Bower Carty soon joined him. Every nickel of foreign exchange – covering everything from the purchase of destroyers for the navy to money spent on tourist junkets to the United States – passed through FECB screening. Blyth and Carty acquired a fine-tuned intuition for every financial transaction that crossed the Canadian border. After the war Blyth was made a Member of the British Empire for his wartime vigilance over Canada's balance of payments.

Peace brought little change. Foreign exchange control was maintained by the Bank of Canada to conserve scarce American dollars. As Canadian trade recuperated, it became more and more tied into the American economy. At the same time, foreign investment surged into Canada. Dividends and corporate financing mimicked the transborder pattern. As Carty told the American Statistical Association in 1952, "the prevailing currents of atmosphere on the New York Stock Exchange can sweep up to Canadian markets even more rapidly than those well-known Canadian cold fronts invade the weather in the cities of the United States."[22] In this environment Blyth and Carty worked hard to monitor balance of payments flows. Sampling techniques were fine-tuned. The coding of transactions was honed. New talent was brought in. Edward Safarian, a bright young University of Toronto graduate now doing doctoral work at Berkeley, was hired to sort out the burgeoning flow of data, thereby giving him an intimate knowledge of Canada's trade and investment underpinnings. When the Gordon Royal Commission set about its research in 1955, its attention automatically turned to the growing importance of the Canadian-American economic relationship. Simon Reisman and Irving Brecher, charged by Gordon with preparing a study of the relationship, called in Safarian, now at the University of Saskatchewan, to spearhead their research on foreign investment.[23] Canada's postwar exposure to the "giantism" of the American economy, their study would conclude in 1957, was provoking "revolutionary changes" in the direction and composition of Canada's trade and investment. Drawing on this analysis, Walter Gordon warned Canadians that foreign investment had a "snowballing" effect in the economy and that some mild measures of restriction should be considered. Other economists demurred. Harry Johnson, an acerbically brilliant Canadian teaching economics at the University of Chicago, suggested that measures designed to crimp foreign investment flows would lead Canada into a "narrow and garbage-cluttered cul-de-sac."[24]

The realization that flows of foreign investment and trade were a powerful determinant of Canada's economic prowess drew attention to the fact that Canada's balance of payments was not an official part of its national accounts. In 1951, with the dollar finally holding its own against its US counterpart, Liberal minister of finance Douglas Abbott ended the "regrettable necessity" of foreign exchange control.[25] In many nations, balance of payments oversight remained with the central bank, but in 1952 the Bank of Canada relinquished its control in favour of the nation's statisticians. The FECB shut its doors, and Blyth, Carty, and Safarian frantically loaded their ledgers into taxis and drove over to the DBS, where the nature of their business dictated that they be up and running as quickly as possible. At Tunney's, they were installed in the International Trade Division, a kind of first cousin to National Accounts. By August 1953 the division began publication of a quarterly estimate of Canada's international balance of payments along with synoptic statistics for the tumultuous years since 1946.[26]

In 1961 the union became complete when the Balance of Payments Division formally moved under National Accounts umbrella. In some ways, Balance of Payments was the oldest aspect of Canada's national economic accounts. It was four decades old and conceptually mature. But in other ways, it remained a world apart. Postwar national accounting's addiction to economic aggregation was in stark contrast to Balance of Payments' focus on the fine dissection of individual transactions. [The work involved a lot of handcrafting of the data, carefully allocating it company-by-company and by financial instrument. It was work for "people who liked to muck with the data."[27] And when Doug Blyth moved on to higher management in 1967, Balance of Payments increasingly became the fiefdom of Bower Carty, an enclave within National Accounts that powerfully expanded the accounts' ability to chart Canada's place in the world.] Carty pushed the group to international excellence, especially in the realm of Canada's capital account.

[Throughout the 1960s and 1970s, as Canadians expressed increasing concern over the implications of their reliance on foreign investment and trade with the United States, Carty and his team were there with the numbers.] When, for instance, Canada and the US signed a 1964 treaty for the mutual use of the hydro-electric potential of the Columbia River, Carty devised a formula to accommodate the shock on Canada's balance of payments of the huge one-time lump sum payment that Washington made to Ottawa for lost river capacity. In 1981 Carty summarized his life's work in a magnum opus study of the sources and methods underlying Canada's balance of payments system, a study that economist Thomas Rymes maintains is "one of the finest studies ever produced at Statistics Canada."[28]

The nesting of the balance of payments function within the national accounts paralleled other expansions. The movement of capital across borders, for instance, begged the question of how money moved around *within* the national economy and how it related to production in the economy. Where did saving and investment come from in an economy? Keynes's famous equation c (consumption) + i (investment) + g (government spending) as the key to understanding final demand in the economy had hitherto commanded national accountants' attention, mainly in terms of consumption and what government spent in part to stimulate and stabilize the economy. The income and expenditure accounts clearly revealed how savings were generated within the economy for individuals and businesses. The problem was that there was only imperfect knowledge of how money worked its way through the economy – the disposition of assets and liabilities throughout the economy. Data collecting for these financial flows through the economy was similarly fragmented. The Ministry of Agriculture, for instance, watched farm credit, and the Bank of Canada consolidated data on the financial activities of the banks, but there was no one overall compendium of financial flows in Canada. When the Gordon Commission asked economist William Hood to investigate the "financing of economic activity in Canada," he reported that the Canadian capital market seemed impenetrable. He "yearned for a method of knitting together the flows of funds and flows of goods in a common framework."[29]

Early in the 1950s an American economist, Morris Copeland, had begun to supply some answers. Copeland's seminal *A Study of Money Flows in the United States* suggested that financial transactions within an economy could be established in parallel with the already established system of social accounting: a financial reflection of all the transactions that took place between households, business, government, and nonresidents could be mirrored in the financial flows accounts. Thus the financial implications of, say, the purchase of a car could be broken down into the purchase loan issued by the manufacturer, the government's slice of sales tax, and all the other financial ripples created by a consumer purchase. Whose assets grew, and whose liabilities grew? Sector-by-sector the pattern of expenditure, saving, and investment would therefore be revealed, as would the channels through which these funds flowed.

Hood's work for the Gordon Commission applied Copeland's method to Canada. Assembling a small team of Bank of Canada and DBS economists – Larry Read, Steve Handfield-Jones, and Frank Emmerson – Hood constructed national transactions accounts for the years 1946-54 that addressed such practical questions as how capital investment was financed in Canada.[30] Everybody agreed that the data behind these estimates were spotty. Realizing this, Simon Goldberg oversaw the 1959 creation of an Interdepartmental Committee on Financial Statistics, which brought the Bank of Canada, the Ministry of Finance, the Central Housing and Mortgage Corporation, and the Ministry of Trade and Commerce together with the DBS in an effort to design a better depiction of financial flows within the Canadian economy. This proved a tall order. New questionnaires had to be designed and new sample bases built up to allow the DBS to extract information on corporate profits, government financial operations, and the activities of financial intermediaries.

Throughout the 1960s the fruits of this labour slowly appeared. Quarterly estimates of profits for nonfinancial corporations, for selected financial institutions, and for aspects of government financial operations began to appear. This evolution was given an added lift when in 1962 the Diefenbaker government, eager to learn more about the geography of corporate ownership in Canada, enacted the Corporations and Labour Unions Returns Act (CALURA). Data collection for CALURA was administered by the bureau and brought in a good deal of information about corporate structure and profits. Nonetheless, by the end of the decade knowledge of the financial dimension of the national accounts was still very much a patchwork. Much statistical legwork remained before a complete picture of what Bower Carty called "this lusty infant" could stand confidently on its own feet. But at least the tributaries of financial flows could now be perceived behind the mainstream of income and expenditure in the national accounts.[31]

Financial flows analysis was rooted in a broader curiosity about how growth took place in an economy. One obvious answer was that growth was a function of the capital investment in the economy. In a sense, this echoed the age-old interest in national wealth. What was the accumulated stock of assets – all the bricks and mortar, investments, and so on – in the national economy? What was its relationship to the productive output of the national economy? Once again, the ubiquitous

Gordon Commission had bookmarked the issue. In an attempt to demonstrate the interrelationship of labour, capital, and output as drivers of national growth, economists Anthony Scott and William Hood had laboriously built up a series of industry-by-industry estimates of fixed capital formation – total accumulated investment in machinery and real estate – in Canada. From this, they were able to suggest the capital-to-output ratio in the Canadian economy, a key indicator of growth. From this platform, they went on to forecast that Canada's GNP growth over the next twenty-five years would remain upwardly steady. Scott, however, cautioned that such projections, given the thinness of the data, were "tentative in the extreme."[32] Goldberg at the DBS was quick to pick up on this and in 1959 initiated the Fixed Capital Stock Project.[33]

To build a portrait of fixed capital formation in Canada, Goldberg turned to another of the bright young men who had been attracted to postwar macroeconomics. Thomas Rymes had first encountered the national accounts as an undergraduate in economics at the University of Manitoba in the early 1950s. There, Professor Clarence Barber, who had worked at the DBS in the heady start-up years of national accounting, had inducted Rymes into the world of the national accounts. They were, Rymes recalls, "an exciting new tool." A master's degree in economics at McGill University followed, then a year at Oxford under the tutelage of John R. Hicks. Hicks's emphasis on the social utility of economics nicely reinforced the bent of McGill's Department of Economics, where professors like Jack Weldon and Tom Asimakopulos instilled students with the belief that economics was about changing the world. By the time Rymes signed onto Goldberg's team in 1958, he was imbued with a "sense of drama, of taking part in something that was really significant."[34]

Rymes set to work with a passion. He adopted an inventory approach to building up the fixed capital base of particular Canadian industries. The DBS had published a quarterly capital investment estimate since 1949. Rymes now reworked these figures, pushing them back over a rolling or "perpetual" inventory that covered a period of twenty years. Each year, new capital goods acquired by an industry were added to the gross capital stock of that industry, and the bottom slice of twenty-year-old assets was removed. It was a devilish calculation. It took years for capital expenditure figures in categories like machinery and equipment to be fully registered. Yet, however tentative Rymes's work was, it allowed the national accounts to take one step closer to undertaking calculations of the efficiency over time with which economies as a whole and particular industries utilized their productive resources.

moving forward towards accomplishment

Calculating the economic return on invested capital was but one indicator of a much broader interest in growth that pervaded Western societies in the 1960s. Fifteen years of postwar growth had nurtured a sense of economic security and control. Understanding the dynamics of growth became an obsession in the 1960s. This preoccupation with growth had many dimensions. It was about ideology, about outstripping the Russians in the Cold War. North America's postwar economic supremacy was being challenged in the era of Sputnik and First Secretary Khruschev's boast that the Soviet Union would "bury" the West. Learning the "secrets" of growth was therefore about global supremacy. "Not long ago the subject of economic growth in the United States consisted largely of description and measurement by a few specialists," the American economist Edward Denison wrote in his 1962 prescription for American economic dominance, *The Sources of Economic Growth in the United States*. Now Americans wanted alternative paths to growth placed before them. They wanted, Denison concluded, a "'menu' of possible ways to affect the rate of growth that stated, in quantitative terms, the probable effect of each alternative on economic growth, and its price tag."[35] Canadians, in predictably less hawkish language, shared the sentiment. In 1963 the federal government established the Economic Council of Canada to provide arm's-length advice on the medium- to long-term prospects of the Canadian economy. "It has recently been suggested that 'growthmania' has been the economic psychosis of the post-war years," council economist Dorothy Walters soon noted. But, she added, Canadians were "still trying to learn the 'how' and the 'why' of post-war economic growth in the expectation that answers to some of these questions will provide guidelines to future growth."[36]

From the Canadian point of view, dissecting growth was not just about trumping the Russians. The lessons of growth could be applied to aiding what was then called the "third world." If the genesis of growth in the developed world could be determined, then the formula could be applied to the developing world. What blend of aid, economic stimulants, and investment would spark the fire of development? In 1968 one-time Canadian prime minister Lester Pearson chaired a World Bank task force that examined just this proposition. The *Partners in Development* report that flowed from these consultations turned to the national accounts for its benchmark: to prime the pump of development, developed nations should dedicate themselves to annual foreign official aid equal to 0.7% of GNP.[37]

Closer to home, there were more immediate applications for the statistical patterns of growth. The ethos of economic equalization implicit in postwar Canadian federalism became more assertive in the 1960s. Now that the big macroeconomic policies of the peace were supporting what seemed like a sturdy national economy, attention started to refocus on the economic dynamics of Canada's regions and their economic inequality. In 1969 Ottawa established the Ministry of Regional Economic Expansion to promote economic development. In the words of Tom Kent, the new ministry's first deputy minister, Ottawa took the view that "it is not enough to manage the economy solely through broad macroeconomic and fiscal measures. To facilitate more balanced regional growth, it is now recognized as essential that specific regional policies and programs be formulated and implemented."[38] To do this, "small area statistics" would be needed to isolate regional strengths and deficiencies.

The prospect of using statistics to determine the dynamics of regional economies paralleled the need for more incisive statistics to fine-tune the maturing welfare state in Canada. Simon Goldberg's antennae were quick to detect this shift. The 1960s had seen a "broadening of economic and social goals" in Canadian society. The adoption of universal medical care, the creation of new federal ministries overseeing manpower, consumer affairs, immigration, and industry, and the Trudeauesque push toward a "just society" all heightened the demand for statistics. "In short," Goldberg concluded in 1967, "contemporary Canadian society has set far more exacting standards for the performance of the economy than in the recent past."[39] With his mandate to encourage statistical integration, Goldberg was determined to be a first mover in stretching the national accounts to encompass more economic phenomena. "Policy makers and social scientists alike," he told a Senate committee in 1968, "are interested in the intersections and interrelationships between a variety of economic and social phenomena all acting upon one another, often simultaneously." Goldberg's passion to make the national accounts a "liberating force in economic analysis"[40] pushed the system in three directions: measuring productivity in the economy, supplying the statistical needs of econometric modelling of the national economy, and plotting the intermediate transactions of the economy with input-output analysis. In all three areas Canadian statisticians and economists would excel.

There were prerequisites for his innovative surge. First, the quality of the raw data had to be assured. Statisticians are only as good as their data. If the accounts were to be increasingly integrated, then there had to be assurance that all the pieces not only fit together smoothly but also had been properly classified upon collection. Ever since the days of Robert Coats, the DBS had agonized over ensuring that its statistical series were constructed from uniform definitions of function and origin. Classification systems brought order to the statistical universe; they sorted and streamed data into usable channels. Commodities, industrial processes, occupations, and regions all had to be described and designated according to universal codes. In the face of Canada's growing industrial complexity during the war, a bright young labour economist, Neil McKellar, was set to work devising a new codification of industrial activities. It was laborious work; each commodity and activity had to be researched and tagged according to its chief component or purpose. By 1946 a new Standard Industrial Classification system was ready. Two years later, the Canadian system was harmonized with the new International Standard Industrial Classification of the United Nations Statistical Commission. All this data was harvested at the level of the individual "establishment," not the broader "industry." An enterprise might have plants scattered across the country and be involved in several lines of production, but an "establishment" was likely to be rooted in one place and usually conducted one process. Once the output of all the establishments in a particular line of business had been captured, it could be aggregated up into the output of an entire "industry."

Throughout the 1950s the system was fine-tuned by McKellar. A new classification of occupations was developed, as was a new classification of commodities for exports and imports. New geographical codes were developed for the whole of Canada so that economic data could be precisely keyed to place. Hand in hand with these changes were improvements in the bureau's ability to construct the sample groups from which it drew its data from Canadians. Was the shoe industry sample group, for instance, representative of the overall characteristics of that industry? Obviously, not every shoemaker in Canada could be surveyed, so the sample must reflect the larger reality of the industry. The Labour Force Survey, the national accounts' postwar cousin, was similarly finely groomed. Its goal of measuring employment through household activity rested on the selection of 25,000 households that reflected the overall social structure of the nation. Here too the DBS, spearheaded by the brilliant demographer Nathan Keyfitz, excelled. The quiet work of methodologists like Keyfitz and McKellar ensured Canada's national accountants that their work rested on the best data sampling techniques and classifications available.[41] "People talk about information systems as though these things come from nature," Goldberg once remarked. "And we all know what programmers say: 'garbage in, garbage out.' If you are to avoid putting garbage in, you must have classification systems which make sense, which are operational, which are applied consistently."[42]

The second qualitative breakthrough of the 1960s was the advent of the computer. Throughout the 1950s the Frieden calculating machines continued to clatter at Tunney's Pasture. A gender divide ran through the whole national accounts effort: male economists prepared the data for calculation, and female clerks then fed the data through the calculators. (Only in 1955 did the civil service abandon its stipulation that single women had to resign upon marriage.) It was slow, tedious work that required meticulous verification. Manual collation and manipulation of data clearly constrained the pace and sophistication of analysis undertaken by the National Accounts Division. All seasonal adjustment and constant dollar calculations, for instance, had to be painstakingly done by hand. This laborious manual working of numbers had woven itself into the culture of national accounting. Ledgers, pencils, and unwieldy calculating machines were the tools of the trade. This was the *craft* of national accounting. While it tended to breed conservatism in national accountants' attitude to any form of automation, manual calculation did instil a thorough appreciation of the architecture of the accounts in every national accountant's head. Computerization was therefore only hesitantly accepted at the DBS; recognition of the full potential of the computer for number crunching took a decade.

In the wake of the Second World War, electronic computation became the experimental darling of university labs and research corporations. Early computers were huge, hot, and pernickety. But by the early 1950s companies like IBM and Univac began offering more workable machines. From the statistician's point of view, the initial appeal of the computer was data storage. In 1955 the American Statistical Association hosted a conference in New York at which IBM and Univac machines were put through their paces. Goldberg was impressed. Back in Ottawa an Interdepartmental Electronics Committee was established. The DBS took a prominent role in this. "I am convinced that the time is approaching," the bureau's chief administrative officer wrote, "when we shall have electronic computers in the Bureau."[43] But, while staff were sent to New York for computer orientation courses, it was by no means clear for which statistical applications the computer was best suited. Which company offered the best machine? How reliable was the computer? How long would it take to make the staff computer literate?

The computer made its debut at the DBS in 1960 when an IBM 705 was bought to assist in taking the 1961 census. It quickly proved its worth by replacing the bureau's cumbersome card tabulation of census data. The federal government's initial inclination in this dawning age of electronic calculation was to run large mainframe computers – IBM 7040s and 360s – on a centralized basis. Individual departments booked time on the mainframe as their needs dictated. At the DBS the calculation of national economic accounts adopted this pattern. The word "database" surfaced. The computer offered a faster means of processing incoming data and storing it in a convenient, retrievable form for users both inside and outside the organization. It also allowed different data series to be readily linked and integrated – railway statistics, for instance, could be summoned alongside statistics of wheat production or energy costs. Sensing this potential, the Economic Council of Canada in 1965 hired a young American economist, Mike McCracken, to devise a workable magnetic tape database for the Canadian economy. Other government agencies like the National Energy Board and the Bank of Canada soon jumped onboard.

There was common agreement that the DBS's income and expenditure national accounts figures should be the linchpin of any database.[44] A series of inelegantly named computer languages – FORTRAN, MATOP, DATABANK MASSAGER – were experimentally applied to the data. John J. Deutsch, the chairman of the Economic Council of Canada, urged the DBS to hurry up its adoption of the computer age and dispatched an able economist, T.J. Vander Noot, to advise the DBS. At first, the computing procedures were almost glacial; punched data cards were daily sent by bus to the University of Montreal for processing on its mainframe, the results printed out, and then bused back to Ottawa. Out of all this, the Canadian Socio-Economic Information Management System (CANSIM) was born in 1969 as a "statistical public utility serving Canadian business, industry and education."[45] CANSIM made data retrievable in a neutral, nonprescriptive form; users could apply it to whatever analysis fitted their needs. Initially, CANSIM offered 7,000 statistical time series drawn from the Canadian economy. Soon, this was boosted to 24,000 series, to which fifty manipulation operations could be applied and delivered in the twinkling of a user's eye. The national accounts had joined the electronic age. The DBS was soon buying its own computers. The dowdy "brown books" of the late 1940s had become machine readable. The trick from now on would be, as Goldberg and methodologist Ivan Fellegi told a 1971 conference on the role of the computer in social and economic research, "to *keep ahead* of the information requirements of users." It would be, they concluded, a "visionary process."[46] For the National Accounts Division, this vision would include the welcome but daunting task of applying computers not just to the storage of data but also to their manipulation.

The availability of large, readily accessible databases enhanced the national accounts' relationship with the newest and most esoteric branch on the tree of economics: econometrics. If national accounting is about what *had* happened in the economy, econometrics is about what *could* happen in the economy. The great Norwegian economist Trygve Haavelmo labelled econometrics the "probabilistic approach" to the workings of the economy. Keynes had argued that the economy found its general equilibrium as a result of its major variables – consumption, income, and investment – working their influence. Econometricians, also writing in the 1930s, agreed but argued that economic performance was the outcome not of a few hefty relationships but of myriad interrelated variables. Dutch economist Jan Tinbergen likened the economy to a "cobweb" of relationships.[47] The econometrician's job was to build a model of these relationships, demonstrate them statistically, and then consciously alter their parameters to see how the model reacted. Some econometricians, like Jan Tinberger in the Netherlands, carried the approach to higher theoretical ground, adding mathematical procedures like linear programming – a technique of optimizing functions within an organization and showing how exogenous factors could enhance or diminish their performance – to the challenge of building dynamic models of public policy formation.

A central appeal of econometric modelling was its utility as an aid to decision making. "Knowledge is useful if it helps to make the best decisions," the Russian expatriate economist Jacob Marschak proclaimed in an early econometric text.[48] Norwegian econometrician Ragnar Frisch warned that econometrics could become so esoteric that it might have no "relevance to concrete realities" and become "playometrics."[49] The Dutch econometrician Tjalling Koopmans demonstrated such practicality in the Second World War when he designed a shipping schedule that demonstrated the optimal use of the Allies' beleaguered merchant fleet. After the war such permutations appealed to planners and finance ministers in the emerging welfare states of Europe and North America. What would be the effect of a subsidy here or a tax hike there? How would the altered state of one relationship in the model echo through the economy as a whole? What were the ripple effects of unemployment insurance or family allowances? As *Business Week* proclaimed: "Economics: The New Potentates Rule by Numbers."[50]

Econometricians became the postwar wizards of economics. Their art was wrapped in jargon, equations, and intensive analysis. Few outsiders really understood their esoteric trade. But their reputation soared. "If economics was the queen of the social sciences," Yale economist William Parker would write, "the queen of economics was 'theory' and its handmaiden was econometrics."[51] After the war, the University of Chicago became a hotbed of econometric research. There, the Cowles Commission for Research in Economics – funded by a wealthy American metallurgist – delved ever deeper into econometric theory and application. Headed by Lawrence Klein, a Nebraskan with a doctorate from the Massachusetts Institute of Technology, the Cowles Commission built a model of the United States economy and used it to predict that peace in 1945 would bring an economic expansion, not a return to depression.

Klein's work attracted many kudos. It also attracted some bright young Canadian economists like William Hood. Hood had grown up in Depression-era Nova Scotia and saw economics as a means of banishing bad times. After completing a master's degree under Vincent Bladen's tutelage at the University of Toronto, Hood did wartime service as a meteorologist. Predicting the weather seemed to whet Hood's appetite for prediction. After the war he succumbed to the allure of econometrics. It was, he believed, "an efficient way to view the economic world."[52] He liked its prescriptive power. Hood so impressed the Chicago people that he was asked to join Koopmans in editing a book on econometrics. Other Canadians followed. Rhodes Scholar Ian Stewart had his econometric epiphany at Cornell University, where the American national accounts were drilled into graduate students' minds as a prerequisite to econometrics. One "got" econometrics, Stewart recalls, a bit like people "get religion."[53] Suddenly, the world made sense.

Back in Canada econometrics gained a toehold. After the war C.D. Howe, Ottawa's powerful minister of reconstruction and then of trade and commerce, became a convert to applied economics. He saw it as a means of supporting the Liberal government's commitment to postwar economic stabilization and growth. In the summer of 1947 Howe gave the go-ahead to the department's chief economist, O.J. Firestone, to construct a short-term, macroeconomic model of the Canadian economy. The model would help the federal government to implement and track the income and employment policies announced in the 1945 white paper. Firestone invited Lawrence Klein to come to Ottawa, and

144 The Sum of the Satisfactions

for "three hot and busy but exciting months," economists in the Ministry of Trade and Commerce assembled data and took Klein's advice on structuring their model. When he departed in the fall, Klein left behind a little band of apostles. Men like Donald Daly, a Queen's University master's graduate who had just finished a thesis under W.A. Macintosh on unemployment, signed on. Tillman Merritt Brown arrived from the University of Toronto with his master's degree and vivid memories of Depression-era unemployment. The Trade and Commerce team, directed by Vic Macklin, was soon able to deliver a short-term forecast of Canadian economic performance to the minister of finance on the eve of every federal budget. This so-called "blue book" was Canada's first econometric fruit. It was all, Daly recalls, "great fun."[54]

The Canadian love affair with econometrics grew through the 1950s and 1960s. Econometric modelling had many variations. Big picture macroeconomic models attempted to project the twists and turns of the whole Canadian economy over the short, medium, and long term. Other models adopted a narrower focus, often intent on the performance of a particular industry or region. One distinguishing dimension of all these models was the difficulty of capturing the unusual openness of the Canadian economy to international trade. Another common denominator was the universal reliance on the DBS's national accounts data. In 1965 the bureau established an Econometric Research and Consultation Staff under economist Frank Denton to facilitate relations with this voracious new user of its numbers. Relations were particularly close with the newly created Economic Council of Canada, which was mandated to explore the medium-term prospects of the Canadian economy. (This tie was particularly cordial in light of the fact that the council's first chairman was John J. Deutsch, perhaps the oldest ally that the national accounts had in Ottawa. As Deutsch told his old friend Walter Duffett: "we wish to rely on your organization for the basic data we need for our analysis.")[55]

In the 1960s and early 1970s the econometric models came thick and fast. The Ministry of Trade and Commerce continued to anchor the federal budget with its annual "blue book" forecast but was soon joined by more sophisticated models. Under the direction of long-time national accountant Jack Sawyer, the University of Toronto's Institute of Policy Analysis unveiled its TRACE medium-term model. The Bank of Canada constructed its own RDX1 model, a quarterly forecast that contained 101 equations that could be manipulated. The Economic Council followed with its own medium-term model, CANDIDE. In 1972, CANDIDE's principal architect, Mike McCracken, launched Informetrica, a consultancy that offered modelling on a private client basis. Indeed, by the 1970s econometrics in Canada was becoming a crowded world. In 1974 the Conference Board, an Ottawa economic think tank, for instance, launched its AERIC model. These were heady years when Canadians embraced the predictive power of economics and econometricians toiled to fulfil that faith. Ian Stewart recalls the long hours and *esprit* that "wild econometricians" put into building their delicate worlds. The oil shocks and galloping inflation of the 1970s would tarnish this wizardry, but it could not undo the technocratic sense that man was now controlling, and not uncontrolled by, his economic fortunes.[56]

National accountants were willing accomplices in the rise of econometrics but not always total converts to its magic. After all, their talent and trust lay in analyzing the economic *past*, not the economic *future*. As Robert Crozier rather crankily put it: "the drift toward the algebraic expression of economic ideas is obviously associated with new work in the field of econometrics ... We are not nuclear physicists and most of what we know about economics can still be communicated in the form of lucidly written prose."[57] As if to prove the point, the DBS became a prime mover in a sprawling project to publish a compendium of historical statistics pertaining to Canada. Begun in 1958 at the urging of the Canadian Political Science Association, the project was spearheaded by economists Malcolm Urquhart of Queen's University and Ken Buckley of the University of Saskatchewan. The ubiquitous John J. Deutsch chaired the steering committee. When it appeared in 1965, *Historical Statistics of Canada* was a goldmine of historical data. DBS names – Goldberg, Blyth, Adler, Marshall – punctuated its list of contributors. The economic core of the volume was provided by the bureau's labour, balance of payments, and national accounts statistical series. Urquhart, himself an alumnus of the national accounting group at the DBS, oversaw the national accounts section and provided a plain language gloss of what the figures meant. The volume – a 700-page bargain at $15 – proved an abiding boon to the teaching of Canadian economic history and showed how engrained the national accounts had become in the national economic psyche.[58]

If national accountants were uneasy about projecting their numbers forward, they had no such qualms about further prying apart the existing economy to get at its intrinsic qualities. Two frontiers beckoned: productivity and the mechanics of intermediate transactions within the economy. Each represented another step away from the postwar preoccupation with the straightforward aggregation of national accounts.

Each represented a sophisticated attempt to get *within* the mechanics of the economy. Productivity studies sought to probe the fundamental efficiency of the economy: how much output did we get for the inputs that we made into the economy, or stated vulgarly, how much bang did we get for our economic buck? What was the quality of our growth? In a similar vein, analysis of intermediate transactions within the economy sought to *disaggregate* the whole, to show the constituent parts of every economic exchange. These parts could then be tracked on a matrix – an input-output table – and observed as they moved back and forth through the economy. To adopt a medical analogy, productivity was about nutrition, what the body extracted from the food put into it, and input-output analysis was about physiology, the functioning of the whole organism. National accounting sought to put an economic stethoscope to each of these internal processes.

Economists had long been aware that economic productivity was most easily expressed in terms of gross domestic product per unit of labour input, measured either in terms of the number of workers or the hours that they worked. In the decades after the Second World War, it was clear that GDP had surged dramatically and that the capital and labour inputs to this surge were significant. But how significant? The easiest manner of isolating labour's contribution was simply to divide an economy's output by the labour inputs. But, in fact, calculating productivity was a much more complex matter than one might naively assume. The nature of "output" was constantly changing; the quality of a product might improve. A farmer might better apply his capital by switching from a plough to a tractor, thereby dramatically altering the nature of his capital inputs. On the other side of the equation, the quality of the labour input might change as new technologies enhanced workers' capabilities or better education improved their skills. There was also the element of public choice – how many hours a national labour force *chose* to work. The problem was establishing symmetry, ensuring comparability. Productivity was thus seductively simple as a generality and maddeningly complex as an applied concept. By the 1960s, as interest in the nature of growth and prosperity grew, the productivity puzzle began to demand national accountants' attention.

The Americans had dabbled in labour productivity studies since the 1890s. After the Second World War the United States Bureau of Labor had focused on the manageable task of building productivity indexes for individual industries. America had committed itself to rebuilding Europe through the benevolence of the Marshall Plan; productivity studies offered a way of measuring Europe's rebound. In Ottawa economists like Gideon Rosenbluth urged the DBS to follow suit, but staff resources were tight. However, by the 1950s, the Canadian Manufacturers' Association and the Canadian Labour Congress were pressuring the DBS for such studies. "The demand for productivity statistics appears to be widespread," Goldberg told Mitchell Sharp, the assistant deputy minister of trade and commerce, "it is not confined to any particular interest group or segment of the population." The measurement of productivity was "no simple matter," Goldberg warned, but if the DBS undertook such research it would contribute to the long-run strengthening of "cost and efficiency consciousness" in Canadian business and labour. But, Goldberg ominously added: "There is no question that publication of productivity indexes may create public relations problems and we have to be prepared for that."[59]

Beginning in 1955 the DBS committed itself to a systematic program for measurement of productivity. Two goals were to be pursued: the creation of broad productivity indexes for the nonfarm business sector and the creation of indexes focused on individual industries, mainly in manufacturing. Hiring began and a National Productivity Council was established "to inspire Canadian industry to become more competitive, to promote labour-management cooperation and to disseminate information on productivity." But progress was slow. The field, Goldberg was forced to admit, was indeed full of "hazardous booby traps." It was almost impossible to construct consistent benchmarks for output – technologies, components, production runs, and applications all kept changing. "Professional wine tasters," Simon Goldberg once observed, "are asked to appraise the relative merits of different kinds of wine – they are not asked or expected to compare wines with scotch or soda or tea."[60] Goldberg liked to point out that whereas an ounce of refined gold was no different in 1962 than it had been in 1939, very few other products enjoyed such continuity. On the input side, how did you fold part-time and casual workers into broad productivity calculations that were usually based on full-time employment? Nonetheless, by the early 1960s, the first results were unveiled. One study showed that from 1949 to 1962, 45% of the increase in real GNP in Canada was due to growth in employment (i.e., more jobs all round) and that 55% was the result of increased output per worker.

But just as these results emerged, other economists suggested that the orthodox equation of ouput ÷ labour was too naive and that other variables – like the quality of education, the amount of research and development, energy costs, capital – needed to be factored into the calculation of productivity. "Multifactor productivity" was a more multi-

[margin annotations: "Finally gathered results." and "criticism of the methodology used"]

variate window on economic productivity, but it too was devilishly difficult to calculate. How did you weight the variables? Was energy more crucial than education? Economists like Larry Read and Thomas Rymes, veterans of the DBS's National Accounts Division, began elaborating the concept of multifactor productivity during the 1960s.[61] But precise calculation of productivity and public recognition of its importance remained stunted throughout the decade. Economic growth in North America had come relatively easily since the war, and rising productivity seemed to be on auto-pilot. As economist Richard Lipsey pointed out, "An apparently modest rate of increase in productivity of 2.0 percent per year leads to a doubling of output per hour of labor every 35 years. Productivity in Canada increased at a rate somewhat greater than this in every decade from 1900 to 1970."[62] But this crescendo peaked in the 1960s. Competition from surging economies like Japan and Germany with their new strategies for harnessing labour, capital, and technology began to challenge North America's productivity dominance. In response, national accountants could declare that they had at least crossed the conceptual doorstep of productivity measurement, even though as yet they had little practical advice to offer.

If productivity was only a faint blip on the radar screen of the Canadian national accounts, input-output analysis burned brightly in the 1960s. Ever since the Physiocrats in eighteenth-century France, economists had been conscious of the myriad reciprocal actions at work inside the economy.[63] One of their number, François Quesnay, talked about the "zigzag" action of an economy. But an entrenched belief in the sanctity of classical economics kept economists from trying to pull back the curtain from the internal operation of the economy. The economy was self-regulating, so what was the purpose of invading its inner sanctum? It took a devastating depression and a global war to topple this orthodoxy. The year 1936 is rightly regarded as the theoretical hinge in this reformation. Keynes's *General Theory* appeared that year. But lurking in the shadow of that great event is another seminal publication.

Wassily Leontief was a Russian émigré economist. He had grown up in prerevolutionary St Petersburg, where his father was an economist. Young Leontief followed in his father's footsteps, training in newly named Leningrad in the early years of the Soviet Union's command economy, before pursuing his studies in Germany. The Leontiefs were anticommunist Mensheviks who found themselves ill at ease in Bolshevik Russia. After a stint of consultancy in China, Leontief came to America, where he attached himself to the National Bureau of Economic Research and joined Harvard's Department of Economics. Leontief cut quite a figure: short and dapper, he loved opera, trout fishing in Vermont, and champagne at Cab Calloway's Cotton Club.

Leontief also left no doubt that he considered economics an empirical affair that must serve the practical needs of society. "I had seen too many economists trying to improve it," Leontief later said of the economy, "without trying to understand how it works."[64] He regarded the ravages of the Great Depression that he saw all about him in America as evidence of the bankruptcy of deductive economics. "Despite the remarkable increase in the volume of primary statistical data," he wrote in a groundbreaking 1936 article in the *Review of Economic Statistics*, "the proverbial boxes of the theoretical assumptions are in this respect as empty as ever." Like his compatriot Simon Kuznets, Leontief welcomed the awakening interest in national accounting but believed that national accountants must be armed with tools to allow them to interrogate the flows inside the economy. Every output within the economy, he reckoned, must ultimately become an input elsewhere in the economy. "It follows from the obvious nature of economic transactions that each revenue item," he wrote, "of an enterprise or household must reappear as an outlay item of some other enterprise or household." In the spirit of Quesnay's *tableau économique*, Leontief suggested that the economist's task was "to present the whole system of interconnected accounts in a single two-way table." The "empty boxes" would thus be filled with data that spoke to the real world, and "the vague generalizations of abstract theoretical statement will acquire concrete empirical significance." The economy could thereby be portrayed as "one huge accounting system."[65]

[handwritten margin note: Combination of all aspects into 1 large accounting system]

Leontief was proposing to construct a table – a matrix – in which the intermediate transactions that took place in an economy could be identified and recorded (e.g., the amount of rubber that a car manufacturer bought). Intermediate transactions were those things that happened to a good as it was transformed from raw materials to finished product – excavation, transportation, refining, assembling, marketing, and so on. Leontief argued that if all these individual actions could be differentiated and recorded, then the overall ebb and flow of the economy could be plotted in a matrix, or box, that set out in a minutely detailed picture the internal workings of the economy. In 1936 Leontief produced just such a matrix for the operation of the United States economy in 1919 – on which he plotted forty-one industrial sectors between which goods and services were produced and consumed. On one vector, steel production was, for instance, broken down into a maze of intermediate transactions – mining, rail transport, electricity, packaging, and so forth. On the other vector, these same inputs to steelmaking could be picked up in the outputs of the mining, transportation, and paper industries. Pinpointing all these transactions was a painstaking enterprise for the statistician, who was obliged to dig deep into the United States Census of Manufacturing and into trade journals to winnow out the precise value of each transaction. But once the matrix was complete, a very intimate picture of the internal functioning of the national economy was available. The production of any product could thereby be broken down, or *disaggregated*, into its coefficients; a ton of steel could be shown to be the product of so much iron ore, coal, labour, transportation, and so on.

Leontief then prescribed an active application for his matrix. Inspired by linear algebra, he suggested that by inverting the matrix, the flows within the economy could be traced in reverse so that the impact of, say, an increase in consumption in one industry could be traced back and its effect on all other industries monitored. This exercise had an immediate appeal to some American policymakers, who, imbued with the spirit of President Roosevelt's New Deal, were now of a mind to intervene in the once-sacrosanct workings of supply and demand. (Other Americans quickly formed ideological reservations about Leontief's machine – it smacked of Stalin's command economy.) From a corporate or government planner's point of view, if all the inputs and outputs that contributed to final demand in the economy could be identified in Leontief's input-output matrix, then input could be adjusted in order to observe its potential impact on output patterns. Leontief liked to employ the colourful epicurean metaphor of an input-output "recipe" by which the economy could be "cooked."

The outbreak of war heightened this appeal. Resources suddenly became scarce. Industries strained to meet their production goals. I/O analysis, as the input-output model now became tagged, offered a means of regulating final demand in the economy. How much consumption could the household sector be denied in order to free resources for military production? Furthermore, I/O analysis facilitated planning by allowing the projection of hypothetical levels of production into the matrix. Where would shortages occur? How big a surplus of production could be provoked? The United States Air Force employed an I/O table – nicknamed Project Scoop (Scientific Computation of Optimum Programs) – to systematize its procurement and training needs. Corporations like Western Electric developed similar models to help manage their resource inputs. For all its allure in a hothouse wartime economy, I/O analysis faced one severe limitation. Without

Wassily Leontief of Harvard University reveals his pleasure on learning that he has won the 1973 Nobel Prize in economics. Another Russian émigré to the United States, Leontief decried prevailing economic theory in the 1930s as "empty boxes" and then went on to design his own box – a matrix that disaggregated the production and consumption of the American economy into forty-one industrial sectors. By the 1950s Leontief's input-output table had become the best national accounting porthole on the dynamics of the economy. The advent of computers vastly extended the utility of input-output analysis. Leontief was a frequent visitor to Canada – both as a summer visitor to Quebec's Eastern Townships and as a statistical visitor to Tunney's Pasture. Courtesy of Corbis, U1783340.

electronic calculation, all the calculation of the initial table and subsequent inversions had to be done manually. Even the simplest inversion required days of labour on the Frieden calculators. Leontief's recipe needed long, slow cooking.

Peace saw interest in input-output analysis continue. Under Leontief's direction, Harvard established a research project on "interindustry" analysis. Richard Stone at Cambridge displayed similar interest. In Washington the Bureau of Labor Statistics set up an I/O unit to estimate postwar demand for steel. As the Cold War unfolded, American military and private sector "think tanks," like the RAND Corporation, continued to seek applications for Leontief's method. Throughout all this, Leontief kept up his crusade. In 1951 he told the readers of *Scientific American* that modern economics was not *modern* at all but "remains largely a deductive system resting upon a static set of premises, most of which were familiar to Mill and some of which date back to Adam Smith's *The Wealth of Nations*."[66] I/O analysis, he argued, would make the national accounts a "dynamic" tool of policy formulation. What excited Leontief most was the prospect that "the modern high-speed computing machine" might stretch the I/O table to encompass more industries while at the same time accelerating its manipulation. America was on the eve of a brave new world. "At the end of the current arms buildup there's the promise of a rich gift for American business: a new tool for research and policy-making," *Business Week* wrote of Leontief's "shiny new gadget."[67]

Ironically, the Cold War threw a barrier across Leontief's path. As American phobia about communism increased, so did the association of the I/O table with the planned economies of the Soviet block. The I/O approach's penchant for invading the inner workings of the economy invoked the mechanical workings of a planned economy and was therefore un-American. The Eisenhower administration stopped all public spending on input-output research. "It has been argued," Richard Caves of Harvard sadly pointed out, "that inter-industry analysis is wicked, and that its practitioners should desist for their own moral welfare because their product is fit only for consumption by totalitarian states."[68] Canadians had fewer inhibitions.

Goldberg was, as usual, the first to pick up the scent. I/O analysis had a double appeal to him. It held the promise of bringing the national accounts into more intimate contact with the economy – of unravelling the skein of intermediate transactions that constituted the daily economic pulse of the nation. It also promised to act as a powerful verifier of the consistency of national accounts statistics: every piece of input datum had to match up with its companion on the output side. If data could not be traced consistently through the whole table, then there were methodological problems with the data's collection and classification. I/O analysis thus had immense qualitative *and* quantitative potential. Early in 1952 Goldberg went to see Leontief in Boston and, over lunch, revealed his ambition of using the I/O table as "a powerful instrument for co-ordinating the Bureau's output of economic statistics." Leontief, Goldberg reported, found this "both sound and practical."[69]

Back in Ottawa, Goldberg launched pilot interindustry studies of six Canadian industries. It immediately became apparent that I/O work was exhausting and expensive. Economist Barbara Mercer reported that an "enormous amount of data" was required and that every aspect of production had to be broken down into its basest elements. Thus the bolts, screws, nuts, and every other component used in making, say, a piece of equipment had to be given a separate code so that they could be precisely allocated in terms of producer and user. The result, Mercer concluded, was "an expensive operation."[70] Undeterred, Goldberg pushed on and hired Jack Sawyer, a University of Chicago doctoral student with experience with the Cowles Commission. Sawyer proved both persuasive and productive. I/O analysis, he argued, offered "the bringing together of economic theory and statistics." It would illuminate Canada's industrial structure, cleanse the DBS's data of inconsistencies, and help to allocate resources in a national emergency.[71]

Goldberg was convinced and gave the go-ahead early in the 1950s for a Canadian I/O table that would capture the interindustry relationship of forty-two industries in the 1949 economy. Like Mercer, Sawyer and his team quickly found that "the greatest headache" was the meticulous breaking-down and categorization of each transaction passing between these industries. There was the additional problem of estimating the contribution of imported and exported material into Canadian production. Inventories also had to be factored into the model. By 1956 the table was ready. Never before had the inner workings of the Canadian economy been revealed in such detail. The chemical industry, for instance, had an output of $804 million. The I/O table showed that $43.8 million of this was consumed by the agricultural sector. Another $108 million went to construction. Households consumed $307 million. On the input side, chemical producers consumed $28.8 million of output from agriculture but, surprisingly for a growing industry, only $3.9 million in construction services. The industry paid $105 million in wages to households. Quesnay's eighteenth-century zigzag table had become a highly detailed portrait of a modern industrial economy.[72]

Despite its "experimental" status, the 1949 I/O table was considered a success. Sawyer added more industries to his square of interindustry relationships. Constant dollar values were built into the table to discount the erosion of inflation. Procedures for collecting data from Canadian industry were fine-tuned to get at the detail of each company's inputs and outputs. In 1961 work was initiated on the production of an annual I/O table for the Canadian economy. The Canadian public slowly became aware of this latest tool of macroeconomics. "DBS Working on New Guides to Help Economy Run Smoothly," a *Globe and Mail* headline announced. International acceptance of input-output analysis also accelerated. In 1957 the United States Congress had finally acknowledged that I/O tables were "an important aspect of the national accounts." Two years later the Office of Business Economics began work on an eighty-five-industry table for the American economy.[73] International conferences on input-output analysis began to convene, invariably presided over by Leontief like a grand patriarch. The United Nations' Department of Economic and Social Affairs took a keen interest and was soon publishing bibliographies and manuals on the "problems" of input-output analysis.[74] The quality and incisiveness of i/o data made the table a natural first cousin of econometric analysis. Together, they held the promise, in the words of *Business Week*, of "Lifting the Haze from the Future."[75]

A number of factors propelled Canada into the vanguard of i/o analysis in the 1960s. The early work on the 1949 table had set a Canadian template in place, an advantage that became apparent when computers arrived in the next decade. An inversion of the 42 x 42 industry matrix required about 74,000 manipulations, a task that took weeks by manual calculation but only minutes on a well-programmed computer. There was also a healthy cross-fertilization of i/o thinking from Canadian universities. Queen's University hosted a school for economic research each summer that served as a gathering place for DBS researchers and interested academics. Learned society meetings of economists and political scientists similarly cocked an ear to new developments in the world of national accounting. Of particular note in this respect were economists Gideon Rosenbluth of Queen's and Tadek Matuszewski of Laval. At the same time, the DBS recruited bright graduate students who avidly threw themselves into construction of the 1961 tables. Before leaving the DBS for the University of Toronto in 1960, Jack Sawyer hired Paul Pitts out of the Johns Hopkins graduate program in economics. Pitts was brilliant and, in collaboration with Matuszewski, was soon publishing in prestigious journals like *Econometrica* and the *Journal of the Royal Statistical Society*. Pitts was joined in 1962 by Terry Gigantes, a master's graduate from McGill with an uncanny knack for the twists and turns of linear algebra and a social democratic conviction that numbers could change the world.[76] There was a quirky intensity about the bureau's i/o team. Its members tended to live in a world of their own, fixated by the inner logic of their baroque statistical tables. Colleagues recall being invited to dinner parties at which Gigantes and Pitts spent the whole evening working out linear equations on napkins oblivious to all social niceties. Hovering above this intense coterie was the hyperactive Simon Goldberg, who in Sawyer's mind was "the inspiration of the work."[77]

Computers and stellar talent gave Canada's i/o program a powerful boost, but Canada's perennial sensitivity to its regions gave the effort its distinctiveness. This "old and vexed question," as one provincial deputy minister called it, had been a prime motivation behind the national accounts since the Depression. Since 1945 equalization payments from Ottawa had been calculated on the basis of the DBS's annual national income and expenditure tables. The 1960s accentuated Canada's sensitivity to region. Historians began describing the nation as a place of "limited identities."[78] As a 1967 DBS study noted, "the public has become conscious of this socially and geographically uneven economic growth and accepted responsibility for and a desire to turn the trend of economic retardation of these areas and people through government, business, labour and other social action."[79] The I/O method of probing the structure of the economy had an immediate appeal in this respect. Not only did it hold the promise of providing an intimate portrait of all the intermediate transactions within an economy, but with statistical surgery the model could be chopped down to focus exclusively on one particular region of the economy. This application was first evident in the work of Tadek Matuszewski, who attached his I/O research at the Université de Laval to the ambitions of Quebec's "Quiet Revolution." Quebec's new *maîtres chez nous* nationalism emphasized the retardation of Quebec's economic growth as a result of outside capital and management. I/O analysis offered a chance to hive the Quebec economy off from the national economy, thereby demonstrating its strengths and vulnerabilities. It also afforded planners, so much in vogue in the "new" Quebec, an opportunity to track interventions in the economy over time. The same application was evident in Belgium, where the Flemish provinces sought to demonstrate their stunted growth. Cities like Stockholm had likewise used I/O tables to isolate their municipal fortunes.

Input-output analysis had a similar appeal in Atlantic Canada, where there was a sense that the region had suffered a steady erosion of its economic underpinnings. The old "wood, wind and water" staples of the nineteenth-century maritime economy were in decline. The age of the Bluenose had waned. Even new industries like coal mining and steelmaking, introduced at the turn of the twentieth century to modernize the regional economy, lurched from crisis to crisis. Maritime manufacturing seemed to wither under central Canadian and foreign competition. The 1960s saw Ottawa respond to this decline through initiatives like regional economic expansion. But the region itself sought to take hold of its fate. In 1958 the Atlantic Provinces Economic Council (APEC) was established to probe the structure of the regional economy. As an early APEC study concluded: "A study of a regional economy involves a measurement of the vital processes which operate within the economy."[80] A statistical cross-cut of the maritime economy would facilitate workable developmental policies. It was hoped that better numbers would lead to better policy. So, beginning in 1962, the DBS agreed to lend its skills and data to an input-output study of the maritime economy sponsored by Ottawa and the Atlantic Development Board. "Inter-industry flow tables are essentially an accounting system," the contract stated, "which can be used to estimate the total effect of any given set of initial expenditures in a province on the output level of all economic activities in the province ... they can show the impact of federal government spending on the provincial economy; they can show the result of introducing new industries into the provincial economy."[81] This mandate provided an apt illustration of the technocratic instincts of the 1960s – better numbers would lead to better planning. Whether better planning would lead to more viable industries remained to be seen.

During the 1960s two crucial forces would propel the input-output study of the Atlantic Provinces to the forefront of global economic research. First, there was the creative personality of its principal researcher, Kari Levitt. Levitt was the daughter of the great Hungarian intellectual Karl Polanyi, a man who had first fled fascism in Europe in the 1930s and then McCarthyism in the United States in the 1950s to arrive in Canada as a kind of intellectual nomad. Polanyi's reputation rested on the argument in his best-known book, *The Great Transformation*, that capitalism was an adversarial economic system that was not culturally embedded in Western society and that the industrial revolution had estranged Western society from its more harmonious forms of communal relations. Daughter Kari grew up with the same questioning instinct. As a wartime statistics student at the London School of Economics, she read Keynes's *How to Pay for the War* and realized that numbers and politics might be combined "to put the world right." Looking back on the wreckage of the Depression, Levitt concluded that communism held the key to a better, more planned future. Arriving in Canada in 1947 Levitt first became a union researcher, then raised a family, and in 1958 finished a master's degree at the University of Toronto. Soviet repression of the 1956 Hungarian Revolution prompted her to make a clean break with the Communist Party, but her bent for social activism remained strong. She began doctoral studies at Toronto. In 1961 her supervisor, Burton Kierstead, pushed her in the direction of McGill, where he had long taught and where, she recalled, the economists were "solid NDP."[82]

Economics for a Better World

Canada's national accounts have always been an apolitical affair. They were undeniably born in the social and economic anguish of depression and war, but their production has always been beyond partisan political purpose. This constraint, however, has not stopped some national accountants from stepping beyond the neutral precinct of government statistical agencies to attach their numbers to causes that they see as just.

Even though so much of his input-output research was sponsored by the American military, Wassily Leontief believed passionately in disarmament. In the 1960s he used the I/O method to measure the implications of a reduction of American military spending in Vietnam on the national economy. Would disarmament provoke deep unemployment? Leontief suggested that a "compensating increase" in domestic spending would keep the economy on an even keel but might shift its regional balance.

In Canada, Gideon Rosenbluth, teaching economics at the University of British Columbia in the same decade, used I/O analysis to research his book *The Canadian Economy and Disarmament* (1967). With careful planning, Rosenbluth showed that the 4% of GNP that Canada spent on its military could be shifted into domestic social spending and thereby pay a "handsome dividend" to Canadians. Rosenbluth thanked many of his former DBS colleagues in his preface but never suggested that his findings reflected the agency's views.

Kari Levitt also wore her statistics on her sleeve. In 1970 she published a powerful essay on the incursion of foreign multinational corporations into Canada. *Silent Surrender* became an instant classic, a rallying call for those who saw a loss of national sovereignty in foreign ownership of the Canadian economy. The book drew heavily on the DBS balance of payments data but was in every way a personal statement. Levitt would later take her I/O expertise to countries like Trinidad in the Caribbean, where she modified the analysis to fit the heavy export dependence of these economies. Inspired by the thought of St Lucian economist Sir Arthur Lewis, Levitt then applied economic research to battle a "new mercantilism" that left Caribbean countries locked in dependency on the developed world.

Now a McGill professor, Levitt still needed a topic for her doctoral research, and here Leontief's input-output gospel won an immediate convert. If Western societies were to have planned economies, she reasoned, then the I/O table offered a "magic box" that allowed economists to look inside the economies that they were planning. The knack would be to apply Leontief's magic to the political ethos of regional development that had emerged in Canada since John Diefenbaker had talked of a "northern vision" and of bringing the West and the East into the economic union in the late 1950s. Levitt proved an adept academic entrepreneur. She built a coalition of interested parties around the proposition of putting the maritime region under the economic microscope. Academic economists were enlisted, as were federal granting agencies like the Social Science Research Council and the Canada Council. The Atlantic Provinces Economic Research Board lent its support. Finally, Levitt approached Simon Goldberg at the DBS, urging him to lend the agency's data and logistical assistance to the project. The cost looked daunting and the work problematic and painstaking, but Goldberg was "willing to gamble" on Levitt.[83] The DBS would provide space and raw data for Levitt's magic box. Very few doctoral theses ever take flight the way this one did. Indeed, it quickly ceased to be a one-person enterprise and would never come to examination as a piece of formal academic work. Instead, it became a team effort that would push Canada to the forefront of I/O analysis.[84]

The second, and ultimately decisive, element in Canada's embrace of I/O work was its determination to modify Leontief's conceptual framework. Other countries had been applying the original industry-to-industry I/O table to regional economies. But pioneering work by Tadek Matuszewski at Laval and the Quebec Bureau of Statistics indicated that the I/O table might provide a more realistic x-ray of the economy if it presented its data not on an interindustry basis but on an industry-by-*commodity* basis. The Leontief-like matrix that Levitt proposed would track all the intermediate transactions inside an economy in terms of which *commodities* each industry consumed or produced. Thus Leontief's symmetrical *square* industry-to-industry table would be superseded by an asymmetrical *rectangular* table that showed a set array of industries in relationship with a much larger array of commodities. A square box was thus stretched into a rectangle.

The DBS's own work on the 1961 I/O table of the national economy had been tending in this direction. Now Levitt and her team applied it rigorously to the four economies of Atlantic Canada. The hope was that the commodity-oriented rectangular tables would reveal the most

Kari Levitt in her McGill University office in the 1970s. Much of the intellectual power behind Canada's adoption of the input-output table as the most intricate tool of national accounting came from Quebec. Tadek Matuszewski of the Université Laval pioneered the method in Canada. He was quickly joined by economists from McGill University, most notably Kari Levitt. Levitt's brilliant application of I/O analysis to the Atlantic Canada economy in the late 1960s showed the utility of I/O analysis in understanding regional economies. Levitt would go on to make her name nationally as the author of the provocative 1970 study *Silent Surrender*, which detailed the effects of foreign investment on the Canadian economy. Courtesty of Kari Levitt, Montreal.

intimate detail of the Maritimes' economy. Hence every transaction within, say, the Cape Breton coal or steel industry would be laid bare in its fundamental economic strengths or vulnerabilities. This diagnosis would lay a foundation for intelligent planning. Levitt would later say that the project proceeded under "the inescapable impression that the expenditure of public funds without a coherent and relevant conceptual framework – or development strategy – is incapable of alleviating the relative underdevelopment of the Atlantic Region."[85] How politicians chose to devise and apply this strategy, Levitt also insisted, was their business; the statistician's role was to gather the data and build an apolitical matrix.

Levitt came to describe her work at Tunney's Pasture as "an adventure." The work was squeezed into an already busy academic life. The

summer hiatus in Canadian university life allowed the team to focus entirely on the Maritimes project. Weekdays blurred into evenings and
weekends. With computers still in their infancy, much of the work had
to be done manually. Data like the census of manufactures had to be
stripped down to extract just the right figures for each of the Atlantic
economies. Once the data were isolated, they were painstakingly entered onto a huge cardboard rectangular chart that Levitt spread
across two large tables. Researchers would literally crawl out onto the
table to pencil in figures pertaining to, say, the Prince Edward Island fishery – bait, hooks, wood for traps, gas for boats, and rubber gloves for
fisherman all took their constituent place under "fishing."

Like a godfather, Goldberg kept a paternal eye on the project, drop-
ping by even on weekends to inspect the cardboard matrix and lend
support. Goldberg also obliged by beefing up the bureau's I/O capability. In 1967 an Input-Output Statistics Division was added to the National Accounts branch at Tunney's. Like Levitt, Goldberg turned to his
old McGill alma mater for brain power. Two young Indo-Canadians,
Shaila Nijhowne and Kishori Lal, were hired to join Terry Gigantes.
Nijhowne and Lal each had a master's degree from McGill and came
imbued with what seemed to be an innate Indian genius for mathematics. Nijhowne's father had been a senior finance official in the Indian
government who had once introduced his daughter to Richard Stone in
New Delhi. Magnetically, Nijhowne was drawn to study economics at
Cambridge before eventually coming to Canada. Lal similarly arrived
in Canada imbued with a sense that numbers were a tool of national
development. Some in Canada thought him a "radical," but Canadians
had not grown up in partition-wracked Punjab or witnessed the birth
of the struggling Indian republic, where government was expected to
shape a new society. In Canada, Lal's social conscience and meticulous-
ness with numbers made him an ideal companion for the impatient –
Levitt called him "uninhibited" – Gigantes.[86] Altogether, they were a
self-possessed and, to the outsider, rather haughty group, obsessed with
a project that few could understand. As Paul Pitts suggested, they had
embarked on a project that "would be too ambitious at the present
time for many countries."[87]

In the summer of 1965 the first tentative I/O tables for the Atlantic
provincial economies as they existed in 1960 were run through their
paces at the DBS. Over the next winter, all the project's data was com-
puterized, drawing on the talents of Alison Morgan, a programmer
who Levitt recruited from Leontief's Harvard research team. By 1966
the project's 2000 pages of working papers describing methodology

Terry Gigantes as a dinner guest at Kishori Lal's Ottawa home, 1970s. Warm hospitality and Indian food made Lal's home a gathering place for input-output specialists. Gigantes, like Lal, had trained in the Department of Economics at McGill. Brilliant at linear algebra, Gigantes passionately believed that economic analysis could remedy the world's ills. He finished his statistical career at the OECD in Paris. Courtesy of Kishori Lal, Ottawa.

and hundreds of flow tables were delivered to the Atlantic Development Board. Pleased by what it saw, the board immediately asked that the tables be extended to 1965 and contracted the DBS to provide consultancy services for the application of the tables to developmental planning. Finally, in 1975, two thick volumes covering the entire project were published for public consumption. In her preface, Levitt suggested that she had provided a new "statistical toolkit" by which Canadians could understand their economic union.[88] Never before had a region of Canada seen its economy dissected in such close detail. Figures for household income, interprovincial trade, import and export content, government expenditure, and many other transactions were available on both an industry and commodity basis, all neatly sorted into the four provincial economies. At the same time, Levitt and her team had broken a new trail for international I/O analysis. By 1968 the United Nations would accept the rectangular I/O table as the template for its System of National Accounts. And by the early 1970s Leontief himself – always on the lookout for new "cooking recipes" – would take to describing the rectangular table as the "Canadian" table.[89]

The 1960s were golden years for Canada's national accounts. They became a "system." The addition of a balance of payments function had broadened the system's reach, an important extension for a country with an economy so open to the world. Work on financial flows and fixed capital formation had also extended the system's reach. Computers and databases had given the accounts greater speed and appeal to users. Econometrics emerged in Canada because national accountants first created the data. Initial steps had been taken toward better regional statistics. Increasing attention was given to the timely release of economic estimates and their subsequent revision. At the same time, the national accounts deepened their reach into the Canadian economy; productivity and input-output analysis had opened the way to a better quantitative understanding of the national economy. The accounts were now capable of both *aggregating* the economy and *disaggregating* it.

Throughout all this, a methodological campaign was waged. Simon Goldberg's abiding hymn was integration – the notion that all the national accounts data should be consistent and self-adjudicating. The shining virtue of I/O analysis was that it reinforced the central principle of balanced statistics in the national accounts – what went in on one side must be matched and justified on the other side. Without this attention to statistical purity, the system was not a system. In the words of the great American statistician Milton Gilbert: "It is only by having such an all-embracing framework that one can establish any order of priority in statistical collection. Otherwise the national 'program' of data-gathering tends to be like the program of a variety show; the first act is an acrobat, the second is an Irish tenor, the third is a tap dancer, and so on, with no connection between them. The parts of the program do not make up a whole drama or tell one story."[90] In the 1960s Canada's national accounts ceased to be a variety show. They had become, as Goldberg proudly suggested in 1967, a national "habit of mind."[91] The maturation of Canada's national accounts paralleled that of the United Nations' system. In 1968 the United Nations published a revamped guide to the System of National Accounts (SNA) that was embraced by all the market-oriented economies in its 130-nation membership. Titled *A System of National Accounts*,[92] it reflected much of what had been unfolding in Canada. Its I/O tables were rectangular. It portrayed the accounts as a means of both aggregation and disaggregation – "an aid to economic analysis and policy." The document was not universally binding. Developing nations, where statistical services were often rudimentary, were encouraged to use the document as a "suitable goal."[93] Even communist block countries, with their Marxist-based System of Material Product Balances, had been engaged in working out some form of commonality with the SNA. The SNA had thus also become an international habit of mind. The United Nations, for instance, calculated members' fees on the basis of GNP figures from their respective national accounts. National accountants had even formed their own club, the International Association for Research on Income and Wealth, which since 1949 had held conferences aimed at synchronizing the global keeping of national accounts. When the association began publishing its own journal, the *Review of Income and Wealth*, in 1966, Canadian names immediately appeared in the table of contents.

National accounting came in on the same tide of public esteem as did economics. "Economics," Leontief crowed in 1970, "rides the crest of intellectual respectability and popular acclaim." The citizens of North America and western Europe had placed their faith in a world framed, and often guided, by macroeconomic analysis. In Stockholm the Nobel Foundation agreed and in 1969 began awarding an annual prize in economics. In its first decade, the prize list was crowded with macroeconomists, national accountants, and econometricians: Tinbergen, Frisch, Samuelson, Kuznets, Hicks, Leontief, Koopmans, Meade, and Klein. Richard Stone would follow in 1984. The dismal science was not so dismal after all.

And on university campuses across the land, students crowded into lecture halls clutching copies of economics textbooks that they regarded as guidebooks to modern economic citizenship. "Today," Richard Lipsey of Queen's University wrote in the preface to his widely used economics textbook, "most economists agree that their subject is more than a stage for parading pet theories. Nor is economics just a container for collecting masses of unrelated institutional and statistical material. Economists are expanding the frontiers of knowledge about the economic environment and learning to understand and often to control it." Paul Samuelson agreed and gave prominence in his text to the role of national accounting as "the yardstick of an economy's performance." "The concept of national income," the newly minted Nobel laureate argued, "is indispensable preparation for tackling the great issues of unemployment, inflation, and growth."[94]

Across town from Tunney's Pasture, two former DBS national accountants, Larry Read and Thomas Rymes, had taken professorships in Carleton University's Department of Economics. Early in the 1960s they introduced national accounting to the department's syllabus. They insisted that no young Canadian economist would succeed without a solid understanding of the nation's national accounts. Simon Goldberg agreed and urged his junior staff to enrol. Goldberg also volunteered his own perspective as a guest lecturer. Other Ottawa mandarins and researchers followed suit. One of them was Thomas Shoyama, an economist at the Economic Council and future deputy-minister of finance. Shoyama told the students that the Canadian welfare state "simply will

An economist at the Massachusetts Institute of Technology, Paul Samuelson shows off his famous textbook *Economics* in 1970, the year he became a Nobel laureate in economics. The book is said to be the world's bestselling economics textbook, appearing in many languages. Samuelson collaborated with University of British Columbia economist Anthony Scott to prepare a Canadian edition of the book. There, Samuelson described national accounting as "this great invention of the 20th century – without which macroeconomics would be adrift in a sea of unorganized data."[95] Courtesy of Corbis, U1685067.

not work without information, data and the consequent apparatus to make decisions." He urged them to place their trust in the national accounts. Years later, Shoyama was sitting in Vancouver's airport when a man in a dark suit came up to him. He explained that he had been at that lecture a quarter-century before and that Shoyama's advice had steered him to a life of public service. He thought that Shoyama might like to know that he was now a deputy-minister.[96]

and Home Cooking

ıat is measurable and make measurable what
ırable.
ıllilei (1564–1642)

is the rallying cry of politicians everywhere.
ɔf happiness? … The Gross National Product
ırement of social justice, or human dignity,
ı attainment.
E. Trudeau, Vancouver speech, 1974

n't really measure prosperity, of course, for it
ɜ many of the things that make life worthwhile, such
ɹnsets and home cooking, and counts all manner of
ɒpleasant things, like the cost of hurricanes and wars.
  Fortune, 22 May 1978

[T]he Canadian system of national accounts is of a very
high order … Such a system takes years to build, and its
present excellence is a tribute to the work of statisticians
over the last two or more decades.
~ Sir Claus Moser, *Statistics Canada: Methodological
Review* (1980)

The earnest young member of Parliament in the corduroy jacket had a
question for Pierre Trudeau's government. Question period has never
been the Canadian House of Commons' finest hour. More often than
not, it degenerates into a set piece of Opposition questions bouncing off
a stone wall of government obfuscation. The New Democratic Party
member from Oshawa was nonetheless undeterred. Ed Broadbent had

a doctorate in political science and a social democrat's passion for justice. "Is the Government of Canada and the Dominion Bureau of Statistics giving consideration," he asked James Jerome, the parliamentary secretary to the president of the Privy Council, "to including in the computation of the Gross National Product the value of the housewife and of household domestic services?"[1] In other words, why did steel-making and executive pay packages register in the national accounts, while the daily labours of the nation's housewives remained statistically invisible? Couldn't some equivalent value at market prices be integrated into Canada's GNP for these services?

James Jerome was well briefed. No, he told Broadbent, domestic labour was outside the "standard national accounting conventions." Only labour that garnered a paycheque, that carried a dollar value, surfaced in the national accounts. And, he added, no thought was being given to bringing the housewife into the GNP.[2] Stymied as he was on that day in late 1970, Broadbent was not alone in questioning how Canadians regarded the calculation of their economic wellbeing. After a quarter-century of soaring postwar prosperity, Canadians in the early 1970s were beginning to look beyond the simple magnitude of their economic growth to ponder the *quality* of that growth. This was not just hippie philosophizing; it percolated throughout society. In 1968 Canadians had elected Pierre Trudeau as their "philosopher king" prime minister. Another aficionado of corduroy, Trudeau had promised a "just society." Exactly what this vision meant was unclear, but by 1972 Ivan Head, the prime minister's foreign policy guru, was writing in the prestigious journal *Foreign Affairs* that "the philosophy of unrestricted growth has been challenged" by the Trudeau government and that some sort of substitute for the GNP was needed. It would measure "net human benefit," thereby taking into account "such factors as environmental deterioration, community overcrowding and resource depletion." Trudeau himself began to weave these speculations into his own speeches. "'Prosperity' is the rallying cry of politicians everywhere," he declared in 1974. "But what of happiness? ... How often in our blindness do we reflect on the fact that those computers calculating the magical GNP regard with equal weight the manufacture of a motor vehicle and a fatal automobile accident ... If money is spent, the GNP is enhanced. The economy benefits ... We know in our hearts that this is false."[3]

Over at Tunney's Pasture, Canada's national accountants grew worried. Was the prime minister doubting the quality of their work or, more broadly, questioning the conceptual framework in which it was cast? Doubts about quality seemed unlikely. In 1972 Trudeau had appointed Sylvia Ostry as Canada's chief statistician. Ostry's appointment reflected Trudeau's faith in technocratic management. A McGill-trained labour economist, Ostry was intellectually precocious, a rare doctoral graduate in the federal civil service. Although she had joined the DBS in 1964, in many ways she was an outsider to its staid culture. She now became the first woman to reach deputy-minister status in the federal government. Ostry's predecessor, Walter Duffett, had built the DBS into an organization of 3,000 employees, whose expertise was showcased in the 1,300 regular publications that they produced. The Dominion Bureau of Statistics had adeptly stretched itself across the dramatically expanded statistical needs of Canada's welfare state. However, in appointing Ostry, Trudeau seemed to be indicating that he wanted *more* from his national statisticians. The main challenge, he told her, was "how best to ensure that the government receives and collects pertinent information on which to base its operational policy and planning decisions."[4]

A year earlier the Trudeau government had passed a new Statistics Act, one that had reinforced the centralized, fact-gathering reach of the organization and had rechristened the organization Statistics Canada. Canada now had a technocratic "chief statistician," not a stuffy, colonial-sounding "Dominion statistician." Ostry certainly arrived with reform on her mind. Statistics Canada, she quickly concluded, faced "a number of serious and complex problems" that were unlikely "to yield to quick and easy solution." Within days, she asked her directors general to join her in undertaking a "fundamental look at ourselves" in order to meet the public-policy-driven challenges of the 1970s. Everything from computerization to the confidentiality of data would be placed under the microscope in order to "strengthen the national statistical system."[5]

Ironically, one of the consequences of Ostry's arrival was the departure of Simon Goldberg. Ironic because Goldberg had spent fifteen years preaching the gospel of integration at the DBS. Inspired by the balancing quality of the national accounts – what went in as inputs must be balanced and verified by outputs – Goldberg had argued that the national accounts methodology could be used to bring discipline to the entire statistical system. But Goldberg had always been a methods man, consumed by the internal logic of the systems that he oversaw and often oblivious to the broader bureaucratic implications of his work. He was the insider's insider. Many saw him as the preordained successor to Walter Duffett. But Trudeau saw the situation differently, and, his ambitions undoubtedly bruised, Goldberg departed in 1972 to take charge of the United Nations' Statistics Division in New York. Method-ologically, he had been the guiding spirit of postwar Statistics Canada. Ostry saw integration more in organizational terms and would soon make root and branch changes in how Statistics Canada managed itself.

Organizational change worried the national accounts team far less than the implicit questioning of their art by observers like Broadbent and Trudeau. Since their Depression-era inception, the national ac-counts had been rooted in the belief that *production* was the cardinal determinant of national income. And production was invariably con-strued in a monetized manner. That which commanded a wage or a payment from society was the sole grist for the mill of political arith-metic. Money provided a universal denominator of economic activity, a proxy for the primary instincts of society at large. If society chose not to attribute a formal price to an activity, then it could not to be placed on the scales of the national accounts. The focus was on *exchange*. Economies worked because their participants pursued their self-interest in monetized terms. Ours was a civilization that voted with money. If excavating coal or stitching garments commanded wages in society and baking bread or nurturing children at home did not, the economist would focus on the monied activity. This approach was particularly un-derstandable for troubled economists – like Keynes, Kuznets, and Clark – trying to theorize their way out of the devastating Depression of the 1930s; demand had to be revitalized, and only those things that carried exchangeable value seemed capable of such manipulation. As they saw it, their urgent mandate was to stimulate the economy, not to reengi-neer the social values of society. The beauty of the System of National Accounts that materialized in the wake of the Depression and wartime agitation was that it provided a means of aggregating myriad existing statistical benchmarks into a hitherto unseen picture of the economy as a whole. Early national accountants habitually likened themselves to business accountants drawing up a balance sheet for a company, only theirs was to be a balance sheet for the entire economic society.

This preoccupation with what economists call the "boundary of pro-duction" – the limit of production calibrated by market value – has deep roots in Western culture. "It is not from the benevolence of the butch-er, the brewer, or the baker that we expect our dinner," Adam Smith famously wrote in *The Wealth of Nations*, "but from their regard to their own interest." Man, he noted, was imbued with "the propensity to truck, barter, and exchange one thing for another ... Every commod-ity, besides, is more frequently exchanged for, and thereby compared with, other commodities than with labour."[7] Thus pin making in a fac-

Canadian national accountants have carried their statistical expertise far and wide. Here, Simon Goldberg (middle), a twenty-three-year veteran of national accounting in Ottawa, chairs a meeting of the United Nations Statistical Commission in New York in 1979. Goldberg left Ottawa in 1972 to become director of the UN's Statistics Division. His assistant director, prominent American economist Nancy Ruggles, sits immediately to his right. Other Ottawa-trained national accountants have taken positions at the IMF, the OECD, and numerous universities. Goldberg once remarked that national accounting had become "a habit of mind"[6] across the globe. Courtesy of United Nations Archives, New York.

tory was economically significant, but tending the home hearth was not because it was never bartered or exchanged in the marketplace beyond the home. Such distinctions have, not surprisingly, become fodder for critiques by modern-day feminists. "If Adam Smith was fed by Mrs. Smith," economist Marilyn Waring has shrewdly noted, "he omitted to notice or to mention it. He did not, of course, pay her. What *her* interest was in feeding him, we can only guess, for Adam Smith saw no 'value' in what she did."[8]

The absence of the domestic economy in their calculations had long bothered national accountants. At a Royal Statistical Society meeting in 1934, a Dutch economist, for instance, tweaked Sir Josiah Stamp, Britain's grand old man of statistical economics: Stamp, the Dutchman pointed out, had failed to "consider the labour, of extreme importance to our welfare, performed by our housewives. That labour contributes certainly towards the family income, but plays no part in exchange, and payment for it, in material sense, is not given ... The whole is very much greater, but not quantitatively definable."[9] Throughout the late 1930s the preamble to early DBS reports attempting to assemble an estimate of gross national expenditures *"at market prices"* always included a statement that the "household economy" was "in no case to be appraised" as an addition to the *market* economy.[10] Market-driven prices alone were the denominator; they were the Esperanto of political arithmetic.

Attributing statistical weight to unremunerated activities in the gross national product, it was thought, would only bastardize the accounts' utility. What would the weight be? How could it be calculated? How would such outcomes be compared internationally or used by policymakers in the Ministry of Finance or by the Bank of Canada? An auto assembly worker received a negotiated wage that applied across the economic board, but a housewife baking bread might be viewed from varying economic perspectives. Would one estimate her contribution by comparing her effort to that of a waged baker? Or would one adopt an opportunity cost approach that appraised her effort in terms of what she *might* have done with her time in the waged economy? For example, should the domestic labour of, say, a woman lawyer who chose to stay home to bring up her children be calibrated at the wage of a nanny or nurse or at a lawyer's hourly rate? Interestingly, national accounts do make statistical stabs at the imputed value of rental income on owner-occupied homes and at the value of food grown and consumed on the farm. Such accommodations have allowed economists to smooth out the fluctuations in property and food costs so that the GNP does not twitch up and down as real estate and rental prices move through the business cycle.

In the 1940s, moreover, society at large was not demanding dramatic change in how gendered labour was regarded. The pressing goals of restoring prosperity and assuring victory outweighed such considerations. Thus, when a woman became a wartime riveter, her paycheque immediately entered the national accounts. But when Johnny came marching home and she returned to the hearth, her statistical weight was reduced to that of a consumer. Economists liked to trot out the joke, often attributed to Keynes, that if a man married his maid, the GNP would *drop* because domestic services once performed by a salaried maid would now be performed for "free."

The statistical invisibility of unpaid work in the home persisted throughout the postwar boom. At the same time, women began to stream into the formal economy. By 1970, 40% of Canadian women over fifteen years old were in the paid labour force. Astute economists suggested that this had a double impact on Canada's dramatic growth rate during these years. Not only did women swell the GNP by formally joining the ranks of those who brought home a paycheque, but by resigning traditional domestic duties, they opened up paid opportunities to other women who moved into the service economy as nannies, daycare workers, and cooks. However, for those who chose or were obliged to remain at home, the situation did not change. Their labour, statistically, counted for nothing. In 1960, when the National Council of Women wrote to the Diefenbaker government asking "for the inclusion of housework in the computation of the national economy," they were given the stock "boundary of production" response. "In the case of the bulk of housewives' services," the minister of trade and commerce, Gordon Churchill, politely told the Council, "there is no clear-cut market equivalent and thus no realistic way of determining what the value of these services actually is."[11]

The advent of second-wave feminism in the 1960s awakened the debate. Earlier feminism had demanded political equality; this new surge of feminism demanded economic equality. Within the formal economy, women argued for equal pay and the removal of glass ceilings in the professions. In Canada this initiative culminated in the 1967 appointment by the Pearson government of the first-ever Royal Commission on the Status of Women. The commission's subsequent 1970 report focused on improving social and political entitlements for women, ranging from daycare to abortion on demand. The report contained no recommendation on the statistical invisibility of unpaid work, but as Ed Broadbent's question in the House of Commons indicated, the wind was shifting. Canadians were beginning to ask questions about the quality of their economic existence, about the obliviousness of national accounting to a crucial aspect of Western civilization – unpaid work in the home done largely by women but at times by men – and to other not easily measured aspects of modern life, such as man's relation to "free goods" like water and air.

After three decades of concentrating on the mechanics of production within the economy, economists were now being buffeted in the direction of *welfare* economics, with its emphasis on increasing the equitability of capitalism. The ascendancy of macroeconomics since the 1930s had been marked by a reluctance on the part of economists to delve into the welfare implications of their calculations. But there was a dissident tradition. Classical economists like Alfred Marshall and Arthur Pigou had advocated that economists pay more attention to the welfare implications of their calculations. More recently, economists like Italian Vilfredo Pareto and Englishman John Hicks suggested that economics had an obligation to inform policymaking of the trade-offs that any economic decision entailed. Economics was not about cold, antiseptic calculation but about winners and losers, about progress at the expense of depleting resources. Pareto lent his name to one of the ubiquitous catch phrases of the 1960s – Pareto optimality. Could there be economic progress that rewarded all parties in a transaction – or at least allowed the winner to compensate the loser so that the winner still won but without leaving the loser in a zero-sum trap? National accounting had always presented "income" as a straightforward gain. There was never any attempt to demonstrate the cost of this gain in terms of resource depletion or impacts on the quality of life or the invisible contribution of unpaid work. The emphasis had been on growth, not on the mechanics of sustaining growth over the long haul. As John Hicks remarked in his 1939 classic *Value and Capital*, "income is the maximum amount an individual can consume during a period and remain as well off at the end of the period as at the beginning."[12]

Awareness of the Hicksian concept of income was at first confined to academic cloisters, but it soon had a more public echo. Throughout the 1960s the idea of "growth" became increasingly sullied. Even some of the grand old men of economics began to question its sanctity. "As a general formula, the desirability of as high and sustained a growth rate as is compatible with the costs that society is willing to bear is valid," Simon Kuznets wrote in the *New Republic* in 1962, "but in using it to judge economic problems and policies, distinctions must be kept in mind between quantity and quality of growth, between its costs and return, and between the short and the long run."[13] Economists attending the fiftieth anniversary conference of the National Bureau of Economic Research in 1971 were startled to hear two eminent macroeconomists, James Tobin and William Nordhaus, pose the question: "Is growth obsolete?" The two noted that "disillusioned critics indict both economic science and economic policy for blind obeisance to aggregate material 'progress,' and for neglect of its costly side effects. Growth, it is charged, distorts national priorities, worsens the distribution of income, and irreparably damages the environment." Instead of GNP, they proposed a "measure of economic welfare" (MEW), which would record growth's depletion of capital and natural resources as unavoidable components of sustained growth. The experimental MEW would even attempt to capture the economic weight of leisure. Economists had been too "blindly materialistic" in their previous calculations.[14]

The wider public soon picked up the theme. In 1968 Stanford University microbiologist Garrett Hardin sounded a clarion call for better stewardship of the physical world in his epochal *Science* magazine article, "The Tragedy of the Commons."[15] Economists, Hardin alleged, were prone to "nature-free equations."[16] There were, he argued, no technical solutions to the problems of growth, only behavioural shifts. Others noted the paradox that the national accounts treated activities, like mopping up an oil spill or waging a war, as an economic positive. Why should machinery bought to clean up pollution be treated as "growth"? Nobody doubted that North America's postwar suburban sprawl had added to the GNP, but why should the gas burned in the long commute to the urban core be treated as evidence of growth? Orthodox economists responded that there had always been "regrettable necessities" in any economy – to make steel, you had to make smoke – and that the national accountants had no business acting as judge and jury over what was "good" and "bad" in society.

A closely related problem was that the national accounts took no measure of resource depletion, that they treated the natural inputs to growth as infinitely available givens. In 1972 the blue-ribbon Club of Rome published *The Limits to Growth*, an impassioned look into resource depletion suggesting that the end was nearer than most people thought. The report had many flaws, principally its failure to recognize that resource depletion often stimulates rapid technological change, thereby alleviating the shortage. People nonetheless began to talk about living on "spaceship earth." "Anyone who believes exponential growth can go on forever in a finite world," economist Kenneth Boulding claimed, "is either a madman or an economist."[17] Even business, perhaps the GNP's most enthusiastic proponent since the war, began to voice some doubts. As *Fortune*, that most redoubtable of business magazines, noted: GNP "ignores many of the things that make life worthwhile, such as sunsets and home cooking, and counts all manner of unpleasant things, like the costs of hurricanes and wars."[18] *Time* concurred. Perhaps, it suggested, the time had come to measure the "nonmonetary penalties of industrial growth," such as "pollution and the nightmare of city congestion." America's national newsmagazine concluded with a backhand salute to the nation's housewives: the GNP, it argued, should reflect "the pleasure a husband derives when his wife cooks a gourmet meal instead of popping a TV dinner into the oven."[19]

By the reckoning of the so-called "new welfare economics," statistics must be more than yardsticks of aggregate output; they should be indicators of social improvement. Indeed, Broadbent's symptomatic question did provoke a bout of introversion at the DBS. Hans Adler, a seasoned national accountant who was now special adviser to Goldberg on integration, addressed the issue head on. There were many activities, he admitted, outside the grasp of the national accounts besides household work. Take, for instance, "do-it-yourself" work by suburban fathers on Saturday morning or the unpaid effort of a hospital volunteer. Such exclusions, Adler asserted, were not "intended to either ignore or belittle these services." Instead, their absence from the official numbers reflected methodological reservations on the statistician's part. It was "impossible to obtain a realistic estimate" of services that society chose to value in a nonmonetary manner. "At the moment," Adler concluded, "I cannot see how one can hope to fashion the many specific measurements which now exist and the many which no doubt will be created in the future into an overall index."[20]

Adler had put his finger on what was to be the abiding tension in the national accounts for the rest of the century. How was the national accounting system to be stretched to embrace new social and economic priorities in Western society while at the same time maintaining its methodological orthodoxy – the notion that the national accounts measure only the market value of transactions? The system had been born in the 1940s as a response to society's anxieties about depression, war, and economic stability in peace. It had been able to do this by rooting itself in hard, quantifiable data. Society wanted growth that ensured stability, and the national accounting system measured and paced this growth. Now society still wanted growth, but it also wanted new, more qualitative measures of this growth. Measuring factory shipments or government transfers was one thing, but attempting to calibrate the long-term degradation of the environment or the busy day of a housewife was quite a different challenge.

Adler was not alone in his qualms. The orthodox view was that the national accounts had been created to measure the raw locomotion of the economy and that they should continue to fulfil this mandate. Growth in and of itself was not morally wrong.[21] How society chose to generate this growth and apply it might have moral implications, but this was a matter with which politicians, not statisticians, had to deal. The income and expenditure figures at the heart of traditional GNP measure lent themselves to policy suasion and social management; they comprised "hard" data based on an uncontested common denominator – money. These new areas of concern involved more discretionary pressures and tremendous variability in public attitude. And while the price of a ton of steel was easily established in the market place, the "cost" of pollution, or sitting in a suburban traffic jam, or baking cookies in the family kitchen was a much more subjective matter.

Prominent economists elsewhere shared Adler's concern. Yale economist Arthur Okun urged his colleagues to resist the temptation to fold hard economic indices in with soft welfare indicators. "Producing a summary measure of social welfare," he warned, "is a job for a philosopher-king, and there is no room for a philosopher-king in the Federal Government." "The key to market-oriented activity is the presence of price tags," he insisted, and, however crucial they were to the support of our civilization, housewives had never sported price tags.[22] Over at the much respected Brookings Institute in Washington, Edward Denison, whose experience in national accounting went back to the pioneering days of the war, agreed. A single welfare index for the economy might seem "enormously convenient," but it would involve national accountants counting apples with oranges. Denson cautioned that "relations between environmental conditions and welfare are rarely linear, and nonlinear relationships are hard to establish. A little air pollution is harmless, more an annoyance, a great deal lethal."[23]

Despite the methodological sanctimony of the elders of national accounting, Adler sensed that the pressure for inclusion of some measure of welfare in the national accounts could not be ignored. The issue was not a "closed one." The public was changing its attitude to the nature of growth, and the national accounts should at least be seen to cock an ear to the concern. The system's legitimacy vitally depended on its connection with the public's perception of its utility. Classical economics had lost this connection with the public in the Dirty Thirties – a lesson that modern national accounting now had to heed in the 1970s. Thus, with a prime minister talking about measuring "net human benefit" and a nation demanding better stewardship of spaceship earth, Statistics Canada sought to alter its course. This shift pulled it in two directions. First, the national accounts would be made more socially inclusive. Groups, like stay-at-home moms, hitherto excluded from their calculation would be factored into the accounts. Not only would new heads and wallets now be counted, but an effort would be made to capture the interplay of social and economic factors in society. These yardsticks quickly came to be labelled "social indicators." Second, the statistical system would be adapted to capture environmental impacts of economic activity. These measurements would be called "environmental indicators." National accounting would thus be asked to broaden its scope from monitoring production to the more activist demands of *stewardship*.

It was all easier said than done. First, new skills had to be brought into the national accounting fold. National accountants had traditionally relied on a subtle blending of economics, logic, business accounting, and mathematics to work their art. But with pressure growing for inclusion of environmental and social indicators, skills beyond macroeconomic numeracy were required. Demographic insights would be needed to link social and economic activity. Engineering expertise would be needed to quantify environmental patterns, like depletion of natural resources and the deleterious impact of pollution. Second, national accounting would face a parallel challenge in building bridges to new partners, like feminist and environmental groups, in the framing and use of its statistics. The accounts had hitherto flowed along Keynesian streams to mainline monetary and fiscal branches of government like the Bank of Canada and the Ministry of Finance as well to the private sector labour and marketing experts.

But reworked boundaries of production meant that the accounts would now be increasingly relevant to federal ministries like Health and Welfare, Environment, and Energy, Mines and Resources. The expectations of such new users would have to be discerned and projects defined accordingly. Similar effort would have to be devoted to defining and gathering new types of data – data that would generally be "softer" than the hard economic data to which national accountants had hitherto been accustomed. How was air quality to be measured? Could leisure time or black-market or criminal economic activity be captured and quantified? Perhaps most daunting of all was the need to work through the conceptual underpinnings of an expanded set of national accounts. Could the system be recalibrated without eroding its intellectual integrity? Was there a danger of throwing the baby out with the bath water? Could the GNP live happily within the same statistical house as a "measure of economic welfare"?

This first flush of enthusiasm for realigning the national accounts initially focused on creating "social indicators." From the outset, the idea of simply scrapping the GNP was rejected. Instead, effort was devoted to working out a "judicious compromise" that allowed welfare considerations to inform the hitherto market-driven calculation of Canada's economic performance. The goal, still only vaguely understood, was to develop some sort of statistical weighting of social activities that had never before been priced and then to associate these numbers with the existing national accounts. Given its experimental nature, social indicator research was placed under the eye of the Office of the Senior Advisor on Integration, Simon Goldberg's old vehicle for pushing the statistical envelope. In 1971 one of Goldberg's last initiatives before departing for the United Nations was to oversee the creation of an Interdepartmental Committee on Levels of Living. Federal agencies in the early 1970s were hungry for statistical evidence of social trends. This evidence would help to rationalize decision making in a country that saw social engineering as the key to a just society.

After Goldberg's departure, Adler transformed this committee in 1973 into an Interdepartmental Committee on Social Indicators, a panel that encompassed fifteen federal agencies. Feelers were put out to other national statistical agencies to learn how they were striving to make their national accounts more socially inclusive. Most were groping for a solution. The Japanese Economic Planning Agency admitted that its effort to create a "net national welfare index" was encountering methodological problems. It was difficult, Tokyo reported, to set an objective valuation on nonmarket activity. A welfare-driven index "may not have so fine a conceptual framework as the present GNP."[24] Adler persisted. He visited Paris, where the Organisation for Economic Co-operation and Development (OECD) had established a working group on social indicators. Its members too were bogged down. Adler reported that "too many areas of the inquiry proposed by the social indicators group are still too new and conceptual and scientific problems remain to be solved." How, for instance, do you measure consumer satisfaction?[25]

Undaunted, Hans Adler assembled a Canadian social indicators team. From inside Statistics Canada, for instance, he enlisted Jenny Podoluk, an expert on household demographics and income distribution. She in turn brought Leroy Stone, a recent doctoral graduate in demographics from the University of Pennsylvania, to the project. Stone had expertise in a new social science tool called the System of Socio-Demographic Statistics (SSDS). The SSDS had been developed by Richard Stone for the United Nations' Statistics Division and held the promise of developing a set of statistical modules that measured social phenomena like housing and health and that could ultimately be related to the hard data of the national accounts.[26] Finally, Adler reached out for university brain power – long a practice of the National Accounts Division – to help flesh out the conceptual framework and to make the first, tentative stabs at estimating the economic impact of activities that had never before been placed in the national accounts' scale. Adler's principal recruit was Oli Hawrylyshyn, a Queen's University economist who set to work trying to transform the GNP into what he called "steward-ship accounting" that captured the environmental and social impacts of economic activity.

Late in 1974 Hawrylyshyn was able to publish an overview of "re-cent proposals for modifying and extending the measure of GNP."[27] Any transition to a measure of economic welfare that captured non-market activities as extensions of the GNP, Hawrylyshyn warned, must proceed cautiously. Every way that Hawrylyshyn turned, the statistical slope seemed slippery. It was easy enough to acknowledge that volun-teer work, leisure time, and do-it-yourself work ought to receive some economic weight, but how did you arrive at a measure of their indirect utility (i.e., a relaxed worker would perform better on the job – a wel-fare outcome) as opposed to its direct utility (i.e., Saturday chores would enhance home equity – a production outcome)? If, for instance, the household was now to be treated as a contributor to the gross na-tional product, then all intermediate costs associated with its internal working (e.g., clothes worn around the home, utility bills) must be de-ducted from its output as production costs.

The same devilish logic perplexed attempts to measure the benefit of services outside the home. Should the cost of policing the urban core, for instance, be considered real economic output when it may in fact be a deleterious outcome of the social deterioration of the urban environment under the pressure of economic growth? Despite all these predicaments, Hawrylyshyn persisted. "It is wrong to say that there cannot be natural weights for these components," Hawrylyshyn con-cluded, "because markets do not exist for them, as any scarce com-modity, be it shoelaces or water in Toronto, has an opportunity cost, a shadow cost. What is true is that there does not exist an adequate mechanism to manifest these prices ... The theory is not ready to yield empirical estimates."[28]

By 1978 Adler and Hawrylyshyn were ready to take a stab at meas-uring the as yet unmeasurable. They presented evidence of what the rel-ative economic value of "household work" was in Canada in 1961 and 1971. To do this, they surveyed a sample of two-parent families in Toronto and Halifax and gathered data on the time use of women in these families. Thus the amount of time that women spent cooking, tending children, cleaning, and performing other household functions was calculated and then multiplied by wage rates paid in the broader economy for the same functions. This was performed on both a cost-by-function basis (i.e., what a cleaner in the outside economy would earn for the same function) and on an opportunity-cost basis (i.e., what the woman might have earned if she had applied her talent to paid employment). The authors favoured the opportunity-cost approach because it gave "good approximation" of the aggregate in simple, popular terms. With this approach, they were able to calculate that household work amounted to $16 billion in 1961 and $38 billion in 1971. This suggested that household work was equivalent to 40% of Canada's GNP.

There were myriad conceptual problems with the work. How did one correlate home cooking with a waged cook in a restaurant? Was the homemaker, they wondered, to be compared with the head chef or the vegetable cutter? And any housewife knew that she seldom did just *one thing* at a time. So what wage do you impute to a "multi-tasked" homemaker? Nonetheless, the public was for the first time being provided with benchmarks that gave economic recognition to the nation's homemakers. Adler and Hawrylyshyn also suggested that the ratio of housework to GNP was not declining and therefore that any retrospective inclusion of housework as a welfare benchmark did not alter past patterns of growth in Canada.[29] Indeed, their research seemed to confirm that many women performed a "double day of labour": as women entered the formal workforce, the weight of their activities at home remained the same.

Such attempts at precise measurement were accompanied by looser statistics aimed at conveying some sense of the quality of Canadian life. In 1974, for instance, a thick compendium of social indicators, *Perspectives Canada*, was published by Statistics Canada. It presented a panoply of statistics that already existed on the social condition of Canadian life – housing, consumption, work, education – but it did not attempt to integrate these figures with the national accounts. Such social indicators, Sylvia Ostry suggested in her preface to the book, might be "perceived as barometers of social change," but there was "no consensus" as to their statistical comparability with the mainstream indicators of the national accounts.[30]

Behind the scenes at Statistics Canada, the faltering progress of social indicator research was more hotly debated. Leroy Stone complained that orthodox national accountants were cool to the idea of mixing their dollar-based figures with the softer outcomes of social indicator research. His SSDS system was "ahead of its time," and there were too few experts at the agency to push this frontier. There were also "vested interests" that resisted social indicators because they threatened the status quo. Stone concluded by urging Adler to deemphasize the "lofty discussions" of social indicators until demand was "crying out" for their integration into the national accounts.[31] The first flush of enthusiasm was fading, but attitudes had at least been shifted.

These developments echoed into the ranks of Canadian economists. Most economists recognized the social imperatives that were pushing for new inclusions in the national accounts, but at the same time they were acutely aware of the need to protect the original purpose of national accounting: the determination of national economic growth in market terms and the provision of reliable yardsticks of growth for international comparison. National accountants schooled since the war to provide the hard economic numbers that helped fine-tune the welfare state were now confronted by increasing demands that their numbers be stretched to embrace softer social and environmental activities hitherto unmeasured in the national accounts. It was a tension that would persist throughout the rest of the century. And as Richard Lipsey, one of Canada's most eminent economists, has noted, it was a tension that required a philosophic perspective.

Since emerging from the London School of Economics with a doctorate in 1957, Lipsey has seen five decades of economic debate and practice during his career. Textbook writer, professor on both sides of the Atlantic, and distinguished theorist of economic growth, Lipsey has always taken a nominalist approach to the subject of national accounting: "The key point is to decide what should and should not be included in any particular measure of national income." In his view, there is no essential, unilateral definition of national accounting: "What you include and exclude depends on why you want the measure." Early postwar national accountants, he notes, had no trouble answering this question. The accounts were assembled "to determine how fast an economy is growing and to compare the growth performance of different countries."[32] Such figures are defined by and devoted to the sole purpose of informing social and economic policy made by the state – everything from managing inflation to equalizing the economic condition of the provinces. Hence they measure only market conditions. They are, in short, the kind of hard numbers that a central bank governor or finance minister wishes to receive.

Problems arise, Lipsey points out, when national accounts figures are "used for a purpose for which they not originally designed." Lipsey, like many national accounts purists, has every sympathy for matters of the environment and the hearth. But since they are not measurable by clear empirical calibration, imputations for such phenomena "would introduce noise that is confusing and irrelevant to the exercise" and would thereby debase the original utility of national accounting. Central banks and finance ministries would lose faith in the numbers because the numbers would contain elements that detract from their original purpose. Lipsey drives home his point with two salient examples of unintended results of "diluting" the accounts with imputations that confounded their orthodox purpose. There was much talk in the 1970s of imputing economic value to leisure activities. Leisure, after all, restores vigour and perhaps thereby enhances productivity. The national accounts, it was suggested, should thus convey a measure of economic welfare from leisure. "But," Lipsey points out, "by valuing leisure, their index came up with the anomalous result that the terrible 1930s was a time of high welfare because all the unemployed were consuming so much high-value leisure!"[33] Similar unintended outcomes can arise out of imputing value to unpaid work in the home.

Assume that we gave in to the feminist call to include unpaid household work in national income. To see the problem, consider a typical Alberta resident who earns $60,000 a year and spends $20,000 relieving his wife of the duties that throughout all of history wives have had to manage: he employs a house cleaner, buys laundry and dry cleaning services, purchases such consumers' durables as a dish washer, a washing machine, a built-in vacuum cleaner, a deep freezer, and so forth. Contrast this with a Maritimer who earns $40,000 for doing more or less the same job as the Alberta resident. But he has to ask his wife to do that for which the Albertan pays. Now, if we give in to the demands that national income include unpaid household work, the two provincial incomes will be the same and the Maritime provinces will get zero equalization grants. So for purposes of determining equalization grants, what we need to know is the comparative *monetary incomes earned in the two provinces,* not the value of effort both paid and unpaid.[34]

Lipsey's point: devise a form of measurement suitable to the purpose intended and resist the temptation to graft new social imperatives onto established and workable systems. This would be the quintessential national accounting dilemma of the late twentieth century.

A similar debate emerged on the environmental front. Just as second-wave feminism helped to keep the issue of work in the home in the national consciousness, so too did the "limits to growth" awareness of the 1970s push the environment onto the national agenda. Unprecedented spikes in energy prices throughout the decade fired the debate. Abundant, cheap energy was no longer a given in Western societies. Pollution was no longer just unpleasant; it was dysfunctional. The joke circulated that GNP actually stood for "gross national pollution." Citizens clamoured for regulation. In 1971, for instance, a group of Vancouver activists founded Greenpeace as an instrument for chivvying polluters and governments alike. Politicians reacted. A federal Ministry of the Environment was created. Prime Minister Trudeau acknowledged that "economic growth is no longer a goal to be isolated from the general aims of mankind."[35] In 1969 the United States passed its National Environmental Policy Act, with its provision for "environmental impact assessment" of any major construction project.

Similar environmental initiatives followed in Canada. In 1975 Mr Justice Thomas Berger was asked to assess the environmental impact of the proposed Mackenzie Valley pipeline. He said no to any intrusion of the South's energy needs on the North. Some economists joined the public environmental crusade. South of the border, the prominent American economist Kenneth Boulding had warned as early as 1966 that the time had arrived for Western man to abandon the "cowboy economy," with its attitude of "illimitable plains and ... reckless, exploitative, romantic and violent behavior." Instead, Boulding called for a "spaceship" economy that measured not just consumption but also the balance of "exhaustible" and "reproducible" resources.[36]

But economists were ill-equipped to measure pollution. There was a yawning methodological gap between the hard identifiable cost of the production and consumption of a barrel of oil and the more subjective economic valuation of traffic-induced smog. Garbage and pollution did not fit neatly into the economist's tidy world of calculations. Exactly what dimension ought to be factored into the national accounts? The cost of pollution abatement? The social impact of environmental degradation? Or the drawing down of society's reservoir of natural wealth? "Practical knowledge, experience and measurement were necessary before anything very useful could be said about the society's ideal allocation of scarce inputs to waste disposal," University of British Columbia economist Anthony Scott has noted. "Realizing this, the economists said very little about pollution."[37] In Canada the situation was predictably compounded by the crosshatch of conflicting jurisdictions between Ottawa and the provinces.

Into this vacuum stepped Statistics Canada. Once again, Adler was in the hot seat. Adler's researchers faced *terra incognita*. One of them put his finger on the problem: "There has been no attempt ... to view the whole universe of environmental data as one system and to relate it directly to servicing the wide and divergent demands for these statistics, in other words, the development of a statistical system."[38] In July 1973 Statistics Canada therefore hosted a seminar where the development of common definitions, classifications, and concepts was discussed. In welcoming the delegates, Sylvia Ostry drew attention to the chasm between the mathematical methods of statisticians and the science-driven perspective of environmentalists. There was, she cautioned, a high risk of "stalemate."[39] A Statistics Canada paper presented at the seminar tried to demonstrate the potential of environmental statistics to quantify the flow of cadmium – who generated it, who used it, where it polluted – through the American economy in the 1960s.[40]

A direct result of the seminar was the creation of an Interdepartmental Committee on Environmental Statistics with a mandate to build a bridge between all the federal agencies with a stake in monitoring the economy. Consultants were hired. Outside environmental activists, like Pollution Probe, were interviewed. Several problems immediately materialized. Was research into quantifying environmental impacts to be rooted in available data, or should it begin with the invention of new data, new yardsticks to measure environmental outcomes? Similarly, was the goal simply to produce "raw data," or was it to produce "synthesized information" about the economy? Statisticians complained that outside demands for better environmental statistics were "poorly articulated." Monitoring the environment, one Statistics Canada senior manager bemoaned, had become a "beehive of activity" in the early 1970s and was "taking place in almost all areas and geographical locations, all accompanied by little apparent co-ordination or awareness of the activities of others." Where exactly was the market for environmental statistics in this "disorder"?[41]

The issue of methodology proved the biggest bugbear. Anthony Friend, one of Adler's researchers, was obliged to admit that "it is exceedingly difficult to achieve objective estimates of environmental damage cost benefits, the Achilles' heel being the conversion of subjective evaluations into monetary units."[42] This confusion over potential users and workable methods initially led Statistics Canada to the relatively simple exercise of compiling a compendium of all *existing* statistics that pertained to man's place in nature. This did not entail finding any common denominator that might allow some holistic index of man and his world to emerge. Thus in 1978 the agency published *Human Activity and the Environment: A Statistical Compendium*, a tightly-packed volume that brought under one cover all existing statistics pertaining to "the interactions between humans and other elements of the natural system."[43] In short order, it sold out its press run of 6,000 copies.

Throughout the late 1970s Adler's research group continued to look for a way to interrelate orthodox economic statistics and some sort of environmental indicator. Their work became increasingly esoteric and philosophical. Eventually, they drew on the work of French geometrist René Thom, who suggested that physical transformations in nature were best understood in terms of "stressors" that set up a dialectic chain of prompts and reactions between man and nature. Thus a stressor such as a spill of mercury into a river can be sequentially measured in terms of "environmental responses" (e.g., growing toxic concentrations and morbidity of aquatic life) and finally in terms of "collective and individual responses" (e.g., pollution clean-up and regulatory measures).[44]

Into the early 1980s another of Adler's researchers, David Rapport, attempted to convert the Stress-Response Environmental Statistical System (STRESS) into a workable empirical model. His test bed was a case study of the macroeconomic statistics on the uses of Lake Ontario and Lake Erie. The region was perhaps one of the most-studied ecosystems in North America. There were, for instance, data on the Great Lakes fishery that stretched back into the nineteenth century. The challenge would be to build these data into a taxonomy that integrated all available indices into an integrated index that reflected the region's overall ecological health. Stress indicators like waste levels, reduction of wetlands, and the introduction of exotic species were first calculated. Then response indicators like nutrient levels were estimated. Finally, collective and individual responses like attempts at pollution abatement were calculated. This taxonomy would, it was hoped, allow statisticians to gauge the impact of mercury poisoning on various lake-fish species.

It was fascinating and provocative research, but in the end it proved too esoteric to be of use to national accountants who were eager to feed hard statistical data into their national accounts worksheets. There were too many methodological problems with the STRESS approach. How, for instance, did you sort out the "pollutant loadings from diffuse sources"? Toronto's Humber River spilled a cocktail of pollutants into Lake Ontario, but just what share was attributable to road salt and what to waste from North Toronto manufacturing plants? Rapport candidly admitted that "ecosystem data is inherently variable" and that only "long-term intensive monitoring" would yield any useful sense of trends.[45]

It would be tempting to suggest that Statistics Canada had driven up a *cul de sac* in its 1970s research into the relationship of the economy and environment. Certainly, it had produced some esoteric research that seemed to have little potential for mainline national accounting.

But the agency had responded to public pressure for action on the environment and in so doing had revealed the complexity of the issue. It was now clear that there were no quick fixes. Consciousness had been raised. But where the next step lay was not yet evident. The onset of a recession in the early 1980s tended to cool public enthusiasm for a greener Canada. Moreover, Ottawa's imposition of the National Energy Policy in 1980 opened fissures in the nation over energy endowment and use: an environmental consensus between the energy-rich West and the energy-anxious East seemed remote.

In the interim an updated version of *Human Activity and the Environment* was published in 1986. In his preface to the book, Ivan Fellegi, who had just taken over as chief statistician, admitted that environmental data were "scattered," noting that such information "does not readily lend itself to integrated description or analysis." In short, the whole issue was "technically complex and ... often difficult to interpret."[46] Thus Western societies were slowly and often reluctantly creeping toward some kind of new understanding of their relationship with nature as statisticians around the world were left to ponder their role as handmaidens of this change. For much of the 1980s the path ahead was obscure in terms of political will and methodological ability. In many ways, the situation resembled that of the Dirty Thirties: an external awareness that the existing statistical system no longer captured the economy in a manner expected by most people was resisted due to an internal reluctance to embrace new and untried methods of measuring man in social and economic motion. Anxiety over global warming would reinvigorate the environmental debate in the 1990s, once again obliging Canada's national accountants to ponder the world beyond the comfortable boundaries of production, which had governed their work since the war. Should, for instance, the national accounts begin to measure the stock, or inventory, of natural resources available to man – the forests, minerals in the ground, water – and calculate their depletion against the growth made possible by their consumption?

Meanwhile, the intellectual callisthenics of social and environmental indicators tended to obscure the ongoing, mainline function of the national accounts: monitoring the national economy. An entire postwar generation had been habituated to the indices regularly churned out by national accountants to calibrate their economic prospects and problems. Indeed, a GNP that was calculated based on income and expenditure had become the ticker-tape of Western economic society and was unlikely to be dethroned as an indicator because new perspectives from the kitchen and the riverbank were beginning to capture the public's attention. Too much of the structure of the Canadian welfare state hinged on the quarterly appearance of the national income and expenditure accounts and on the telltale GNP figures that emerged from them. As Sylvia Ostry was quick to proclaim, the income and expenditure accounts were "indispensable in setting out underlying trends" of Canadian economic life.[47] Many might quibble about the nuances and boundaries of the national accounts, but few were prepared to abandon such insights altogether. As the Canadian futurologist John Kettle acknowledged: "The GNP is still going to be the basic way we test whether the economy is producing what people want, despite increasingly subtler ways of reporting the quality of life."[48]

In November 1965 Ottawa's Carleton University invited six prominent mandarins and economists to speak in celebration of the twentieth anniversary of the 1945 white paper on employment and income – the primordial document of the Canadian welfare state. They had been twenty prosperous and stable years. The speakers did not all agree that Keynes's ideas had run their pure theoretical course in Canada, but there was unanimity that the state now played a central role in shaping the employment and income of its citizens. A month later *Time* magazine echoed Milton Friedman's famous proclamation: "We are all Keynesians now."[49]

Not only were the national accounts delivering this crucial aggregate in current and constant dollars every quarter, but they were now also providing monthly real domestic product on an industry-by-industry basis, a figure that revealed the contribution of *individual* industries to the total change in real national output. This in turn made possible productivity analysis of Canadian labour and output on a sector-by-sector basis. The national accounts menu continued offering annual input-output tables, which allowed an intimate portrait of the flow of commodities *among* Canadian industries and provided benchmarks for the calculation of monthly GDP by industry. Balance of payments figures fleshed out Canada's trade situation, while financial flow accounts furnished an idea of who was borrowing and who was lending in the Canadian economy. Sister branches in Statistics Canada rounded out the monitoring of Canada's economy with monthly employment and inflation information. Furthermore, all of the above statistics were presented in frequently revised historical time series so that Canadians could see where they had been economically in real terms. The accounts were, in short, an instructive report card on Canada's economic condition – one that Canadian policy elites were not about to abandon lightly.

But, like a sophisticated sports car, the accounts required constant tinkering and fine-tuning. And the 1970s and 1980s brought constant maintenance headaches. The pressure for a major tune-up came from two sides: *externally* from users troubled by unprecedented malfunctioning of the Keynesian-inspired policies that had run so smoothly for nearly three decades; and *internally* from attempts to perfect the methodological working of the national accounting system. The first hints of trouble emerged in the 1960s. The war in Vietnam was overheating the American economy, thus driving up inflation and government spending. The energy crisis of the early 1970s pushed Western economies into recession while simultaneously accelerating inflation. Yet Keynesian orthodoxy was rooted in the belief that recession and inflation were mutually exclusive. Supply-side economists began suggesting that Keynesian monetary policy was smothering economic initiative with taxes and government deficits. Finance ministers and central bankers on both sides of the Atlantic wondered whether the Keynesian formula had lost its magic. Yes, there had been no repetition of the catastrophic depression of the 1930s. Keynesian stabilization policies had steadied the private sector. But now the danger seemed to come from short, sharp recessions that could be controlled by government but often at a price that contradicted Keynes's original intuitions. Government deficits might now coexist with high unemployment and inflation. Back at the 1965 Carleton conference on the Canadian welfare state, the ever-prescient John J. Deustch had seen it coming: "the problems of social and economic policy have proved to be much more complex than was thought during the first flush of the Keynesian revolution after the war. It has now been shown that the Keynesian doctrine has provided only a partial answer to the question of policy in the present-day world."[50]

The so-called "stagflation" of the 1970s placed unusual demands on national accounting, demands that the smooth sailing of the previous decades had never prompted. Inflation, for instance, created huge, windfall capital gains for those with fixed-interest liabilities. Lenders, on the other hand, saw their fixed income eroded by inflation. The national accounts were poorly positioned to capture such shifts in national wealth. Similarly, the accounts' in-bred dedication to aggregation of national income left them poorly placed to probe how individual sectors or regions of the economy performed under stagflation. There was a widespread sense that inflation was stifling productivity, giving rise to the demand that the accounts be redirected from macroeconomic reporting to *micro*economic investigation. The accounts, it was argued, should facilitate closely focused attempts to identify problems within the economy by supplying finely tuned data that allowed policymakers to drill down into the economy to determine how inflation or energy prices were eroding particular pillars of the economy.[51] Clearly, the comfortable reign of macroeconomics was coming to an end: welfare economics was now being called upon to elucidate the *quality* of Western life, and at the same time, microeconomics held out the promise of *disaggregation* as a means of probing small compartments within the economy. Macroeconomics was by no means dethroned, but economists now looked to microeconomics and welfare perspectives to fathom the economy. As the hesitant first steps toward measuring the environment and domestic labour had shown, any attempt to refit the mainstream functions of the national accounts confronted harrowing obstacles. New data streams, new classifications, and new quality checks could not be devised overnight. Microeconomic analysis could not be developed in isolation. It had to be made to "speak" to broader macroeconomic patterns.

But in the topsy-turvy 1970s the patience of policymakers and the general public very quickly wore thin. The good times were over. Anxiety over inflation and unemployment began to gnaw at the daily lives of millions of Canadians. In the 1950s and 1960s politicians looked to their national statisticians for guidance on the direction of growth; now in the 1970s numbers were more often than not needed to control a faltering economy. And since labour income was the largest component of the GNP, the national accounts began to be regarded as a portent of bad things by Canadians, who had become accustomed by postwar prosperity to thinking of the numbers from Tunney's Pasture as omens of good fortune. Take, for instance, this letter from a small Ontario manufacturer, which arrived on the desk of Prime Minister Trudeau in 1971: "I have been dutifully answering the enclosed stupid f**king questionnaire [from Statistics Canada] for months! And I'm tired of it. It might at least add one question. In big black print, you could ask, 'Do you have any suggestions that may assist in the creation of more jobs in your industry?'"[52]

By 1979 the assistant chief statistician, Guy Leclerc, ruefully admitted that "the recent years were not very healthy for the statistical system, which to a large extent, had been developed and tested when the situation was considerably more stable." The decade had, for instance, turned econometricians, with their complex models of the economy that fed off the national accounts, into forecasting gurus. The public hung on the forecasters' every word. Was inflation headed up or down?

How high was unemployment? "Increased analytical capabilities and sophistication among our users," Leclerc concluded, "is placing a sharp focus on the statistical output." The national accounts were facing "newer expectations and newer frustrations."[53] Bluntly put, the public expected faster, more accurate, and more incisive statistics from their national accountants.

The quality question had been around since the accounts first appeared in the 1940s. Users had two perennial complaints: the accounts' timeliness and their constant revision. The production of the annual and, after 1953, quarterly income and expenditure estimates of Canadian GNP had always been a trade-off between the statistician's desire for accuracy and the user's desire to get the estimate in his hands. A quarterly estimate of GNP allowed policymakers and business planners a quick heads-up on the condition of the economy. Were there signs of a recession? However, it took time to collect data. Surveys of manufacturing, profits, capital expenditure, and a myriad of other topics took time to administer. Some industries, like construction, were notoriously slow in getting their summary statistics together. Grooming the numbers then took time. Double-checking and publication also consumed time. All the while, users clamoured for the data. What use were figures that were released a year after the economic fact? Many pointed to the United States Department of Commerce, which speeded its data by using "flash" monthly estimates, hasty estimates based on a very preliminary reading of expenditure data just fifteen days after the end of the month. These figures, Tunney's Pasture liked to point out, were often off the mark and had to be dramatically revised over time. It was better to have solid data than quick data, they argued.

The timeliness question was most easily addressed. Beginning in the late 1960s, a concerted effort was undertaken to expedite the release of monthly and quarterly economic statistics. Procedures were tightened for data delivery and subsequent analysis. By the mid-1970s the wait for the all-important quarterly GNP had been reduced from a delay of 95 to 100 days after the reference quarter to a lag of only 55 to 60 days, thanks largely to the dogged efforts of Cyril Hodgins, a bright young economist who would go on to a distinguished academic career.[54] Speed of delivery was one thing, but the accuracy of the product posed more formidable concerns. The quarterly estimates were always massaged after their initial release as tardy data arrived and original inputs were adjusted and then consolidated into the annual GNP estimate. The credibility of the entire process hinged on the user's perception of the gap between the preliminary, quarterly estimate and the more polished annual "final" estimate. If the revision between first estimate and subsequent revisions seemed too large or unpredictable, users would begin voicing their concerns about the reliability of the quarterly estimates. The credibility of the whole GNP process hung on this gap's being within tolerable limits.

In 1965 Simon Goldberg, Hans Adler, and two of their brightest colleagues, Preetom Sunga and John Randall, published a "critical appraisal" of the Canadian quarterly national accounts since 1953 in the respected journal *Income and Wealth*. The third quarter estimate for 1958, they revealed, was based on 50% hard survey data of wages,

The Number Crunchers' Club

Professionals are a cliquish bunch. National accountants have proved no exception. Since its inception late in the Second World War, national accounting has drawn experts from around the world together to discuss problems and solutions. Honing the System of National Accounts, initially under the auspices of the United Nations, since the late 1940s has offered the grandest stage for such constructive consultation. But since 1947 national accountants have maintained their own professional association – the International Association for Research in Income and Wealth. Its first general conference was held in Cambridge, England (home of Richard Stone), in 1949. Since then, it has staged biennial conferences around the world, the most recent being at Cork, Ireland, in 2004 and at Joensuu, Finland, in 2006.

The association also publishes a journal, the *Review of Income and Wealth*. The *Review*'s pages capture the cutting-edge developments in national accounting. Contributors include many of the great names of international national accounting: Richard and Nancy Ruggles, André Vanoli, Phyllis Deane, and Jan Tinbergen, to name but a few. Canada's charter participation in national accounting is also remarkably evident. Simon Goldberg sat as chairman of the association in the 1970s, and Canadian statisticians, economists, and policymakers are a constant presence in the table of the journal's contents. In the 1970s alone, the journal boasted a stellar Canadian presence. Statistics Canada national accountants like Hans Adler, Jenny Podoluk, Kishori Lal, and Bower Carty were frequent contributors. Canadian academics like Jack Sawyer, David Dodge, Oli Hawrylyshyn, Thomas Rymes, Don Daly, O.J. Firestone, and Dan Usher swelled the Canadian contingent. For a country accustomed to playing a "middle power" role in the world, Canada has been a premier-league player in the world of national accounting.

profits, and rents, on 35% extrapolated out of production data (e.g., a shoe factory making this many boots must generate so many dollars), and on 15% from "tenuous assumptions or judgments" (i.e., our intuition suggests that this activity should generate about this amount). Their conclusion: "the first preliminary estimates of the quarterly accounts have portrayed faithfully the overall strengths and weaknesses of the economy." They detected only one instance in the whole period when a preliminary estimate indicated a trend for overall national economic performance to which the longer-term economy did not conform. They also pointed out that revising the GNP as tardy data were added in and the base year was periodically adjusted – or "rebased" – was a delicate, and time-consuming, process. Rome, they reminded critics of the accounts, was not built in a day – and revising the GNP would always require the patience of Job.[55]

But especially in the volatile economy of the early 1970s, users of GNP data tended to lose their patience easily. Unemployment was up, inflation was rising, and economic planning afforded little room for error. When, in 1969, the DBS released a historical revision of its GNP estimates for the years 1950 to 1961, the public immediately took note of the higher overall growth rate contained in the revision. New tax data, the 1961 census, and better corporate data from the system established by the Corporations and Labour Unions Returns Act had pushed the decade's average growth rate to 5.1% from 4.5%. The *Vancouver Province* voiced typical concern. Such upward post facto revisions did "damage" to economic planning in Canada. "If Canada is going to fumble around in an economic fog of its own making," the paper editorialized, "then one of the first priorities must be to shake out DBS ... the country can't afford misleading data."[56] Simon Goldberg was consternated and hurriedly explained to the minister of trade and commerce, Jean-Luc Pépin, that "estimates are as good as the information that is available at the time when they are made." Making estimates of the GNP would always be "a continuing process."[57] But the seed of doubt was sown.

A parallel erosion of trust in the utility of GNP estimates took place in the United States. There, the Department of Commerce's Bureau of Economic Analysis issued no fewer than four iterations of each quarter's GNP estimate. And under the pressure of the Vietnam War, this figure proved very bouncy and inflationary. For instance, the bureau's figures initially missed reporting a sharp build-up of inventories as companies responded to military demand and thereby low-balled growth. By the time the omission was caught, inflation had crept into the US economy, and the Johnson administration had an overheated economy on its hands. Distrust in the numbers persisted in the 1970s. *Fortune* magazine described the foibles of "tracking the ever-elusive gross national product." *Fortune* complained that "since the number is jerry-built from incomplete data, it's riddled with error: GNP is eternally being revised." Over the cumbersome American cycle of four estimates, the GNP in any particular quarter could vary as much as 4%. "What's a poor policymaker to do?" In response, America's senior statistician, George Jaszi, took the same line as Simon Goldberg: "The GNP statistics are a butter knife, not a scalpel." The problem was that in the 1970s the butter was not as thickly spread as it had been in the 1960s.[58]

Disquiet over the volatile GNP revision was reinforced by concern about just how accurate its companion unemployment figures were. Since 1945 Canada had used its monthly Labour Force Survey of 30,000 households to pioneer the estimation of unemployment in a mature industrial economy. The survey had proved brilliantly innovative, but by the late 1960s it had failed to adjust to structural and demographic shifts in Canada. For instance, it still sought to ascertain whether fourteen year olds were active in the labour force, a pre-welfare-state notion of employability. There were problems with seasonal adjustments; fewer Canadians now suffered job losses in wintertime. Did the Labour Force Survey really reflect women's new prominence in the workforce? The recession of the early 1970s brought these shortcomings to the fore. Many sensed that Canada was overestimating its unemployment. In 1971 the powerful Cabinet Committee on Planning and Priorities launched an inquiry into whether the unemployment figure given out by the DBS – then at 6.4% – was a "satisfactory measure of Canada's economic and political performance."[59] The deputy minister of finance, Simon Reisman, had no personal doubt "that there is a widespread unease concerning the extent and the quality of the information we now have about the labour force ... We need a sharper definition of unemployment."[60] This definition did emerge as the parameters and sample base of the Labour Force Survey were modernized. The base age of inclusion was, for instance, raised to fifteen. But, once again, a healthy public skepticism had sprouted around Canada's political arithmetic.

The Achilles' heel for the national accounts turned out to be not the number of unemployed but estimating the income of those who *did* work. Early in the decade senior bureaucrats and economic commentators complained that Statistics Canada's GNP revisions were larger than were acceptable to policymakers. Simon Reisman in the Ministry of Finance confided to Sylvia Ostry his fear that there was "a very real danger that the work of Statistics Canada in the realm of economic statistics will become discredited in the eyes of the users of the data in government and outside government." Why had GNP growth been estimated at 2.3% for the first quarter of 1971 and then been revised upward to 9.9% by June 1972?[61] Ostry responded that the Ministry of Finance had adopted a "one-dimensional perspective" on the revision process, one that tended to confuse how quarterly estimates were annualized into final figures. But, Ostry was obliged to admit, there *were* problems with the labour inputs to the national accounts. It had been "a difficult period for some years."[62] For the first time since its inception, Canada's System of National Accounts was facing a crisis of credibility. Users were questioning the accuracy of the statistics being placed before them, and without a foundation of trust, the system would cease to carry any weight in the national economic dialogue.

Other circumstances preconditioned the nature of the crisis that was about to unfold. First, there was pervasive nervousness in the corporate culture of Statistics Canada. The 1960s and 1970s had seen Canada's federal civil service enter the technocratic age. New departments, computerization, bilingualism, and a mood of what the French called *dirigisme* – an inclination to state-directed change – had engulfed Ottawa. The shifts all enhanced Ottawa's appetite for statistics. The agency's name was symptomatically changed to Statistics Canada. The trend had perhaps begun a decade earlier with the Glassco Royal Commission on Government Organization. The commission's 1962 report had been full of praise for the statistical work done at Tunney's Pasture but had come down strongly in favour of greater coordination and professionalization of Canada's statistical effort. The report called for better pay and resources for federal statisticians, but it also implicitly criticized the traditional, cloistered culture of the DBS. The agency seemed partitioned into efficient but largely autonomous divisions that failed to come together into an organizational whole. Subject-matter specialists, like the national accountants, often seemed to be divorced from the methodologists who worked up the all-important data that sustained the whole statistical apparatus. "Systematic integration" should be the order of the day. Without better management, there was a danger of "ossification."[63] Simon Goldberg's dedication to statistical integration in the late 1960s attempted to remedy this situation.

Sylvia Ostry's 1972 appointment as chief statistician was intended to herald a new technocratic dawn. Ostry almost immediately launched a study of ways to "strengthen" the national statistical system. The pronounced drift of these deliberations was toward more planning and oversight – more ways to connect the agency to its users and more ways to connect the various branches inside the agency to each other. Ostry created a new cadre of management at Statistics Canada: five assistant chief statisticians who would be inserted between the chief statistician and the directors general who had traditionally run the agency's operational bailiwicks. One of these new assistant chief statisticians would oversee the Economic Accounts and Integration Field, within which the national accounts were broken into a current reporting branch (i.e., GNP, balance of payments, and financial flows) and structural analysis branch (i.e., input-output analysis and productivity). Ostry then injected some new blood into these executive posts. She appointed Peter Kirkham to head the economic accounts. A mild-mannered professor from the University of Western Ontario, Kirkham had a doctorate in economics from Princeton but virtually no hands-on national accounting experience. He arrived in his new office just as a "perfect storm" was brewing in the world of Canadian national accounts – demands for the inclusion of household labour and the environment in the accounts were now accompanied by anxious queries from users like Simon Reisman at the Ministry of Finance.

To this day, statisticians at Tunney's Pasture debate the wisdom of the organizational changes of the 1970s. Too much managerial oversight, some allege. A breath of fresh air, others retort. Whatever the verdict, there was no denying that the changes of the early 1970s deeply disturbed the staid culture of the place. The creation of assistant chief statisticians seemed to introduce new hierarchy into an organization that had traditionally been flat and production-oriented. This seemed to centralize power in an agency that had long been loose and decentralized. To many minds, this meant the suffocation of statistical creativity. In the case of national accounts, it seemed to bode an end to the old, pioneering spirit that dated back to the days of George Luxton, when teamwork, not top-down direction, mattered most. Whatever the cause, the rank-and-file morale in national accounts hit a low ebb in the 1970s. It was as though the whole enterprise had succumbed to an existential crisis: the outside world questioned its worth, and senior management inside seemed unable to devise a new course.

Statistics Canada's corporate culture was further strained early in 1975 when, after only two and half years as chief statistician, Sylvia Ostry left to become the deputy minister of Consumer and Corporate Affairs. At her farewell, long-time business statistician Vince Berlinguette jovially, but also prophetically, suggested that in her short tenure Ostry had "learned that one of the Chief Statistician's jobs is not only to integrate statistics, but to stop them from disintegrating."[64] Peter Kirkham succeeded her. He was only thinly rooted in the organization's culture, a situation that he immediately exacerbated by adopting a passive, unassertive style of leadership. Griping from the lower decks soon materialized. "I would suggest that this organization is deep in statistical expertise at every level of work," one seasoned national accountant wrote Kirkham in a stinging eighteen-page memo, "but desperately poor in managerial resources. As a result, Statistics Canada has for some time now, continued to generate enormous amounts of sophisticated ideas on what we should be producing but at the same time, the machine to produce the output has virtually seized up as the gap between ideas and production widens." The place, he concluded, had become "an empty shell." To deepen the wound, the writer told Kirkham that he had "circulated this memorandum to a fairly large group of your staff."[65]

It quickly became apparent to insiders at Tunney's that there was indeed some fire behind the smoke. When Kirkham moved up to the chief statistician's chair, his role as assistant chief statistician for national accounting was filled by Guy Leclerc, a veteran business statistician. Leclerc had joined the DBS in 1957, following commerce studies at Laval in his native Quebec. Leclerc had won a reputation as a skilled statistician of Canadian business and finance, so much so that Goldberg hand-picked him to tackle the national accounts' timeliness problems in the early 1970s. Leclerc delivered, wrestling the delivery time down to fifty-five days. In doing so, he liked to say that he had quickly acquired an intimate understanding of the "plumbing" of the national accounts. Below Leclerc, Stewart Wells took over as director general of current national accounts. Wells was a Prince Edward Island boy whose lawyer father had worked for the Mackenzie King Liberals. "Stew" had spent his teen summers working on an Island farm, and even after he went up to McGill University to study economics, the grass roots remained beneath his feet. He imbibed the left-of-centre ethos of McGill's Department of Economics and, in the wake of Agatha Chapman, spent time as a researcher for labour unions in Montreal. A bit of university teaching and a stint with the Prices and Incomes Commission – a Trudeau creation designed to monitor the spiralling inflation of the 1970s – followed. His old McGill friend Terry Gigantes enticed him into national accounting at Statistics Canada in 1970. There, he formed a frank and productive relationship with Leclerc.

Wells grew worried that the labour income and consumer expenditure data being fed into the national accounts were deficient and were seriously eroding the quality of the division's GNP estimates. In April 1976 he spelled it all out to Leclerc in a long memo. In summary – to simplify a complex methodological problem – there had been a significant deterioration in the accuracy of data on Canada's retail trade collected by Statistics Canada. Old surveys of retail trade seemed to underreport consumer expenditure, and when new retail trade surveys came into practice in the early 1970s, they exposed the deficiency and necessitated large revisions in the national accounts. Over the period 1971–74 this deficiency amounted to nearly $7 billion and a sharp upward revision in the overall 1971–74 GNP estimate. At the same time, the Labour Division at Statistics Canada discovered that there was a persistent discrepancy between its calculation of labour income and the raw "control total" that could be taken from Revenue Canada's T-4 slips in the early 1970s. The problem was rooted in the 1972 transfer of responsibility for reporting the birth of new businesses to STC, from the Unemployment Insurance Commission (UIC) to National Revenue. In effect, with the change, some new businesses slipped through the data-gathering net. As a result, labour income – about 55% of the GNP – was underreported by the national accounts. Wells speculated that such dramatic revisions in consumer expenditure and labour income would ripple through to other economic indicators like the savings rate.[66] No wonder the *Vancouver Province* and Reisman, as the deputy minister of finance, were up in arms.

Things got worse. Somebody at Statistics Canada leaked Wells's memo to the *Globe and Mail*. Wells's forthright eloquence was eminently quotable. Wayne Cheveldayoff reported in the influential *Report on Business* that "some data sources" were having an "adverse effect" on GNP figures.[67] For a country locked in an unprecedented battle with inflation and unemployment, this was disturbing news. On Parliament Hill the Opposition Tories quickly picked up the scent and grilled the minister of Industry, Trade and Commerce, Jean Chrétien, about "what action" had been taken to correct the wonky performance of the annual GNP estimate. (Since 1965, the DBS/Statistics Canada had been accorded departmental status in the federal civil service. The agency was answerable directly to Parliament, and the chief statistician held his appointment "during good behaviour" and could be removed only "for cause." Since its inception in 1918, the bureau's interests had been attended to in Parliament by the minister of trade and commerce. Under the Clark government of 1979, the Treasury Board president oversaw the agency. The relationship was and remains rigidly apolitical.) Chrétien replied that it was "an extremely complex problem" and that because there were "very quick changes taking place in statistics," he could not give "an absolute answer at this time." A week later Chrétien supplied the Commons with a "technical rebuttal" to the leaked memo. The rebuttal described the GNP process in layman's terms and emphasized the slipperiness of making economic estimates. The economic data behind the estimate were "never one hundred percent accurate," and the economy itself was an "organism which is constantly growing and changing." Chrétien assured the House that Statistics Canada was engaged in negotiations with Revenue Canada to improve the reporting of UIC T-4 income and that the Retail Trade Survey was being streamlined.[68]

The Opposition and financial press seemed satisfied with Chrétien's action. The minister had clearly put pressure on Chief Statistician Kirkham, and changes were in train. Kirkham adopted the attitude that once these corrections were in place, the old status quo would reassert itself. His subsequent quiescence overlooked that with the statistical system, as in sport, the best defence is a strong offence. Men like Robert Coats and Herbert Marshall had instinctively known that statistics were only as good as their credibility in users' eyes. And once a hint of suspicion crept into this relationship, even spurious rumours might damage the statistics' public reception. The late 1970s were not a good time for passivity on the statistical front. The nation remained anxious as inflation stayed high, federal deficits grew, trade performance sagged, and unemployment proved resilient. To make matters worse, federal austerity in the wake of the economic downturn obliged Statistics Canada to introduce staff and program cutbacks for the first time since the Depression.

Not surprisingly, problems resurfaced in 1979. In January the C.D. Howe Institute, a private think tank, issued its policy review for 1978 and outlook for 1979. The report was highly critical of "complacency" in Canadian policy regarding inflation and unemployment. Weak economic performance was a reflection of weak policy. And this policy was in part due to poor statistical inputs. Statistics Canada was guilty of producing "misleading indicators." There was, for instance, a persistent gap between the household-oriented Labour Force Survey and the employer-oriented Large Employer Survey in calculating growth in manufacturing employment. Similarly, the Howe report argued that the constant and dramatic revision of the GNP had led the Trudeau government to adopt stimulative measures in mid-decade when subsequent revision of the national accounts revealed that the early decade economy was in fact *not* in perilous condition. The economy overheated, and inflation was nudged artificially upward.[69] Almost immediately, the *Globe and Mail* rejoined the critical chorus. Canada's "statistical weakness," an editorial alleged, lay in Statistics Canada's persistent underestimation of labour income in the 1970s and in the merry-go-round of GNP revision in the same years. The paper noted that after six years of complaints, the agency had yet to correct the discrepancies in its labour income calculation. How could good public policy be made out of such wobbly data? Management at Statistics Canada, the editorial concluded, had much for which to answer.

For prescient observers, the high-profile criticism being levelled at the national accounts threatened to undo a fundamental bond of the Keynesian revolution in Canada: that good policy emanated from good statistics. Ever since Colin Clark crunched his preliminary GNP numbers at Cambridge in the late 1930s and Winston Churchill established the Central Statistical Office in wartime London, reliable, apolitical economic statistics had provided the steady foundation of the modern welfare state. This tradition, which had been transplanted into Canada by the likes of Luxton and Deutsch, had stood the test of postwar policymaking admirably. Now, for the first time, it was under suspicion. National accountants like Guy Leclerc sensed the affront and resented the public airing of internal methodological problems. They also resented that the public controversy was being fed by internal discontent at the agency – "malcontents," Leclerc called them. Leclerc stood behind his "dedicated" staff: "Such people do not mind good and solid and well-founded professional criticisms but we may reach a point where we cannot sit here humbly and placidly and be the scapegoat for the ills of the Canadian economy … We do not produce perfect statistics, far from this; we have embarrassing revisions sometime[s], not all the time; the package of statistics we offer is certainly not a surprise to most Canadians – will anyone argue that there is very little inflation in this country, hardly any unemployment and a lot of growth?"[70]

The situation worsened in June 1979. The beleaguered Trudeau Liberals had called an election, and Canada's economic woes were foremost in the electorate's mind. Throughout the spring, Statistics Canada had reported that Canada's merchandise trade surplus had been growing. The dollar consequently appreciated. Then, just after the electorate had elected a Conservative minority government under Joe Clark, the agency revised the trade surplus downward. The dollar fell. "Now it comes out," the *Globe* snidely editorialized. The *Toronto Star* joined in: "It is an abomination." Statistics Canada seemed to be playing politics.[71] Leclerc defended his division's revision policy: users had insisted on more timely data, and this meant more frequent revisions down-stream as the data set became more complete. It was a question of "the lesser of two evils."[72] Wells defended the national accounts' apolitical mission: "The agency," he wrote to the *Globe*, "has a long tradition of political neutrality. Although you may think us dumb, you simply do not have the grounds for supposing us dishonest."[73]

Sinclair Stevens, the Treasury Board president in the fledgling Conservative government, announced that there would be an "investigation." The problem clearly had nothing to do with the new government, but the quality of the nation's economic statistics had everything to do with the new government's prospects. Throughout the autumn, the National Accounts Division prepared briefing notes on the situation for the new government. These frankly admitted that in six years since 1960 the GNP estimate had been revised by at least 1%. In an unfortunate coincidence, this admission came just as Statistics Canada announced that the expensive and time-consuming project that it had initiated in 1975 to rejig labour income data had to be abandoned for methodological reasons. Other remedies, Wells assured policymakers, were being expedited. There was some comfort in pointing out that American economic indicators were simultaneously under siege.[74] Nonetheless, the situation continued to fester. In October, Cheveldayoff told *Globe* readers that Statistics Canada was "still 2 years from better GNP data."[75]

The straw that broke the camel's back came in early November. The assistant director of the agency's Labour Division, Dr Boris Celovsky, became incensed at the conduct of a job competition for the division's directorship. He believed that two equally qualified colleagues had been unfairly passed over in the competition. As a consequence, he refused to be interviewed himself. Celovsky communicated his decision to Chief Statistician Kirkham in a biting memorandum that quickly veered from the case in hand to a rambling discussion of the "rather spotty" record of the agency as a whole over the last few years. All the problems with estimating labour income were trotted out, as were the frequent revisions of the GNP estimate. The revisions, Celovsky suggested, "might be called in the jargon 'macro-economic adjustments'" but were "more colloquially known as 'cooking' or 'fudging.'" Two days later, Frank Howard of the *Ottawa Citizen* published the letter in his regular and much-read column "The Bureaucrats."[76] Somebody had leaked the document. The same day, the issue surfaced in the Commons. In question period, Liberal Robert Andras buttonholed Sinclair Stevens and suggested that the "competence and integrity" of Statistics Canada were at stake. Andras alleged that the previous day Celovsky had been "grilled" by "security people" at Statistics Canada. The interrogation had excited Celovsky's heart condition to the point that he was now in intensive care in an Ottawa hospital. Andras then entered some of the ripest phrases of Celovsky's criticism – the damning use of "cooking" – into *Hansard*.[77]

The Clark government could not dissipate the high drama of the Celovsky affair. Stevens acknowledged the "crescendo of complaints and criticisms about the agency." He expressed his "utmost faith" in its work and tried to suggest that the problems were "inextricably bound up with human relationships and attitudes, not with the basic methodologies used by the agency." But too much of the nation's economic health hinged on public confidence in the work of Statistics Canada to let the issue fester any longer. "I have decided, therefore," Stevens told the Commons on 10 December, "to initiate a comprehensive but private examination of Statistics Canada's operations." He had reached this decision, he said, without consulting Canada's chief statistician. The results of the investigation would be made public, "subject only to the protection of innocent people." The goal was to "produce practical solutions that may be implemented expeditiously." Two studies would be commissioned: one by management consultants from Price Waterhouse Associates into the agency's management processes and the other by "a well-known international expert," who would address the technical and statistical production aspects of the agency.[78] Stevens later announced that Sir Claus Moser, one of Britain's most distinguished statisticians and president of the Royal Statistical Society, had accepted the challenge. The die was cast for Statistics Canada. Three days later, the numbers game came back to haunt the Clark government for the second time in the month. On 13 December the minority government fell on a motion of economic nonconfidence. The Tory Whip had miscalculated the vote.

Moser brought an immense reputation to his thorny assignment. A Jewish refugee from Hitler's Germany, he had cut a wide swath through English economics, statistics, and business. At various times, Moser had taught at the London School of Economics, headed the Central Statistical Office, been a director of the *Economist* and of merchant bankers N.M. Rothschild and Sons, and found time to become one of Britain's keenest opera lovers. In November 1979, just as the storm broke in Ottawa over Statistics Canada, Moser was delivering his presidential address to the Royal Statistical Society. His remarks revealed why he was so ideally suited to the challenge put before him by Sinclair Stevens. "In sum," Sir Claus sermonized, "I see the coming decade as the *quality decade* in government statistics in which every possible effort will be made to minimize and detect errors ... so that in due course all major series will be published with a quality label attached."[79] Stevens had also been insistent that the investigation into Statistics Canada's procedures be carried out *only* by non-Canadians. To this end, the four other members of the task force carried high statistical pedigrees. Richard Ruggles of Yale University was one of America's most distinguished theorists of national accounting, Dr Margaret Martin was the president of the American Statistical Association, and Dr Joel Popkin and Joseph Waksberg were one-time senior American statisticians now working as private consultants. Ruggles took on the specific challenge of examining Canada's System of National Accounts, which Moser saw as "the complex centre-piece of economic statistics both technically and organizationally." As a team, they worked hard and fast. They interviewed statisticians at Tunney's Pasture and then fanned out to meet with users, journalists, and academics. They read the press clippings from the fateful autumn before. All the while, a federal election dominated the nation's attention. By the time their report was ready in early March, the Trudeau Liberals were back in power.

Moser's findings made sweet reading at Tunney's Pasture. His findings on the state of Canada's national accounts leaned heavily on the wisdom of Richard Ruggles. There was criticism – but only after a glowing encomium. Ruggles believed that the Canadian national accounting system was "of a very high order." Internationally, it was "one of the most highly developed and integrated systems of information available" and "a tribute to the work of the last two or more decades." Ruggles detected no evidence of "deterioration in recent years." Canada's national accounts, he noted, were in the forefront of building computer databases like the Canadian Socio-Economic Information Management System (CANSIM), of linking social and economic indicators, and of attacking the problem of timeliness. With this in mind, Moser concluded that the criticisms made of the system in the press and in Parliament "were exaggerated and had little substance of fact," but, and here a more critical tone began to intrude, "they were symptomatic of the general feeling of unease and decline in confidence arising from organizational and budget difficulties."[80]

For Moser, the malaise of the late 1970s was organizational in origin. There had been "an excessive preoccupation with organization" at Statistics Canada, which had allowed attention to the crucial methodologies underlying its work to deteriorate. Moser was quick to acknowledge that there had been slippages in the quality of the processes that calculated the cost of living, labour income, and the GNP estimate. But these were attributable to managerial inattention and to the erosion of staff and programs by cutbacks. In the four years since 1976, for instance, the national accounts staff had slipped in number from 450 to 325. Morale was consequently low. There was an exodus of staff. And diminished attention had been given to methodological back-up and the perfection of new sampling and statistical integration. "It is all too easy to undermine the long-term build-up of a statistical system," he warned. And this is what had happened at Tunney's Pasture in the late 1970s. There had been a "perceived fall in reputation," and the agency had become "something of a political football."[81]

Two trends had to be reversed. The agency had to get back in closer touch with its users, both in government and in the private sector. Statisticians worked best when they were in communion with those who used their output. Moser strongly recommended the creation of a National Statistics Council to make this linkage, to give users a "voice" in the creation of the statistics on which they depended to make policy and manage markets. The other trend that needed to be emphatically reversed was the gradual starvation of the agency's resources. An organization could coast on its reputation only for so long before its skills and products began to look threadbare. This unravelling had become apparent to users and observers of the national accounts in the tumultuous late 1970s. The "core of the national accounts as an instrument for the integration of economic data" had been "eroded." The "methodological stock" had been dangerously run down. Things ceased to add up neatly. Data sets contradicted each other. Quicker estimates proved to be not necessarily better estimates. Experts left. (How painful it must have been for Simon Goldberg, now heading the United Nations' Statistics Division in New York to read Moser's diagnosis.) In short, Moser and his colleagues warned Ottawa that without better resources and better leadership, Statistics Canada might revert to being a "numbers factory" incapable of providing the society that it served with social and economic insight.[82]

"Ultimately," Moser wrapped up, "what matters most is the quality of leadership."[83] The Price Waterhouse consultants' study of Statistics Canada's organizational needs arrived at exactly the same conclusion at exactly the same time. The agency, their report urged, needed to pay much greater attention to the quality of its leadership. The chief statistician should have "proven executive management competence." There needed to be an assistant chief statistician dedicated to planning and development. A national statistical council would buttress such leadership with outside input. Let the managers manage the future, and let the statisticians analyze the present. Let each be professional in its own sphere. With this rubric in mind, Price Waterhouse suggested that national accounting should cling to a "management style" that resembled a "research laboratory," with the emphasis being on professional teamwork.[84]

Even before Moser delivered his prescription, change was afoot at Tunney's Pasture. In January 1980 Peter Kirkham resigned as chief statistician and took up a vice presidency at the Bank of Montreal. The deputy minister of Consumer and Corporate Affairs, Larry Fry, stepped into the chief statistician's office on a *pro tem* basis. Later that year Dr Martin Wilk was appointed to the post and brought with him the kind of corporate management skills that Moser had envisaged: a doctorate in statistics and hard-nosed executive experience with the American Telephone and Telegraph Corporation in the United States. The era of leaked memos seemed to have come to an end.

Historians often remark that a "decade" is an artificial compartment for historical purposes. But every once in a while an event or trend comes along that neatly fits into a decennial box. The Dirty Thirties certainly did. And for Canada's national accounts, the 1970s offer an unexpectedly tidy perimeter. The system had entered the decade as a relatively mature statistical apparatus, impressively evolved from its wartime Keynesian roots. Almost immediately, its basic precepts were challenged by critics eager to see its span stretched to encompass new social and economic activities – "sunsets and home cooking." The system had no sooner clumsily engaged this challenge when it suffered a systemic faltering. Methods and reality suddenly fell out of kilter. There was a crisis of confidence that for the first time corroded the credibility of how Canada did its economic arithmetic.

The decade ended with some serious soul-searching and with recognition of things done well in the past and holes to fill in the present. Guy Leclerc would tactfully describe the 1970s as "exciting times" for the national accounts, when the "creative tension" between old ways and new demands was at its keenest.[85] Stew Wells would more frankly tell his colleagues, family, and friends that these were "the worst years of my life."[86] But Wells, who would steer the accounts through much of the next two decades, survived, as did the system, which would work itself deeper into the heart of Canadian life. Almost symbolically reflecting this shift, a woman for the first time took on senior executive responsibilities in Canada's System of National Accounts. Barbara Clift, who had joined the DBS in 1958, was appointed director of the

Income and Expenditure Accounts in 1979, a responsibility that she would hold until 1988. (Clift would carry her national accounting talents abroad, bringing a Canadian perspective to national accounting work at the OECD and the United Nations and almost single-handedly designing a national accounts system for Uganda.) Early in the next decade, Stew Wells invited Richard Ruggles to come up from Yale to deliver a pep talk to the National Accounts Division's troops in Ottawa. "Looking back," he concluded his speech, "in view of all that has gone before, one cannot say that this is just the beginning, and hopefully it's not the end. We are in the middle of what is an interesting and exciting development – let's carry on."[87]

6 A Certain Flexibility

The economy is becoming harder to measure.
~ *Business Week*, 1994

[T]he memories of the Keynesian state are much clearer than the vision of what is to replace it.
~ Dian Cohen, CABE *News*, 1995

In effect, these indicators can serve as a continuous call to arms – an ongoing protection against environmental complacency.
~ Paul Martin, 2000

Lastly, practicality must be considered. The system incorporates a certain flexibility rather than the application of strictly fixed rules of the "all or nothing" type ... a pragmatic approach is to be preferred to a rejection on purist grounds.
~ OECD *Guidelines on Tourism Statistics*, 1991

It was the product of experts and acronyms – one that began as a 582-page draft and swelled to 711 pages of published text. There was no disguising the fact that the *System of National Accounts 1993* was a formidable document – its print dense and its narrative terse and legalistic. In their ungrammatical wisdom, the statisticians who had laboured for over a decade to craft this meticulous manual of national accounting had decided to drop the indefinite article from the system's name – in its last iteration in 1968 it had been "a" System of National Accounts (SNA). Now, it was bluntly styled "System of National Accounts," an appellation intended to convey its definitive, oracular quality. The book's pale-blue cover, however, reminded readers that something fundamental had transpired in the world of national accounting since 1968, when a volume of a mere 246 pages had been published. The system was no longer solely under the purview of the United Nations, as it had been since the United Nations Statistical Commission (UNSC) first convened in Geneva to discuss national accounting in 1947. The 1953 and 1968 SNA manuals had appeared under the UN's exclusive imprimatur. This latest volume, however, was the joint undertaking of five organizations: the United Nations, the International Monetary Fund (IMF), the Commission of the European Communities, the World Bank, and the Organisation for Economic Co-operation and Development (OECD). With this multilateral parentage, the new SNA was intended to build on the "proven strengths" of the established SNA while at the same time endeavouring to adapt to "new circumstances."[1]

In an age of intensifying globalization, *SNA 1993* was also designed "to be applicable to developed and developing economies alike," to be applied "almost universally." Its text was liberally punctuated with the word "harmonization." The 1968 SNA manual had acknowledged that "developing" nations could not be expected to meet the same national accounting standards as the "developed" world and had suggested that laggard nations might "adapt the full system to their own requirements" over time. No such latitude existed in 1993. Despite its ponderous length, the purpose of *SNA 1993* was to "clarify, simplify and harmonize" national accounting around the world.[2] As the French statistician André Vanoli noted, "the system that will dominate the work on national accounting at the beginning of the 21st century is stamped with the seal of universality."[3] Perhaps the most telling evidence of this newfound homogeneity was that since the late 1980s the Soviet Union – long a Marxist hold-out to market-driven national accounting – had begun to publish GDP figures. By 1993 the disintegration of the old Soviet Bloc was complete. Its Material Product System, which with Marxian determination had shunned any inclusion of the output of service industries in the output of the national economy, was also in the dustbin of history.

National accounting had become a truly transnational affair. Since 1993, for instance, the United Nations has annually been publishing its Human Development Report. The report allows the nation-to-nation comparison of living standards by calibrating such factors as literacy, life expectancy, and educational enrolment alongside GDP per capita.[4] The World Bank produces a similar world development indicators database, one that assembles 900 indicators encompassing everything from environmental impacts to political liberties. A lynchpin in each of these reports is the comparison of GDP per capita across borders, expressed either in US dollars or in purchasing power parities. National accounting has thus become an economic lingua franca. Statisticians in places as disparate as Canada, Russia, and Peru now all aspire to the same national accounting standards – standards that had first been glimpsed when George Luxton, Richard Stone, and Milton Gilbert had gathered in Washington in the fall of 1944 to draw up the postwar blueprint of national accounting. What had then been a tentative "tripartite" agreement in 1944 has thus become a universal accord.

Big Mac Currencies

Economic globalization has accentuated some of the oldest problems in economics. How do you compare GDP across international borders in a way that compensates for differing currency values? In a globally efficient economy, reason suggests that the same product (or basket of goods, as economists are wont to say) ought to cost the same. If it does not, your currency is likely over- or undervalued. The differential in the price across borders offers a very attractive way of telling whether a currency is over- or undervalued in its purchasing power. Out of this notion, economists have created a tool called the purchasing power parity (PPP): take a "basket" of standard commodities whose quality is the same across borders, convert its local asking price into American dollars, and then compare the outcomes. Thus economic analysis is refocused from market-driven exchange fluctuations to the actual local cost of a specific good or service against a universal standard. Within Canada, this suggested the possibility of measuring PPPs across provincial borders.

Sensing the intuitive appeal of this approach to economic comparability, the *Economist* in 1986 introduced its Big Mac currency report. The magazine took the standard-issue Big Mac hamburger (made to uniform standards in over 120 countries), obtained its local price, converted this into American dollars and then set out the spread of international purchasing power. Such "burgernomics" revealed that in 2001 a Big Mac cost $2.54 in the US, $2.14 in Canada, and a low of $1.20 in China. In Europe, on the other hand, a bite of a Big Mac took a much bigger bite out of your wallet.

Statistics Canada has used the PPP as a convenient way to investigate actual differences in price and output between Canada and its largest economic partner, the United States. The OECD and World Bank also employ the PPP as a more accurate means of demonstrating the actual gap between developed and developing countries. The World Bank's world development indicators depend heavily on the benchmark of gross national income expressed as PPPs, or "international dollars."

The revision had begun in 1979 when the UNSC directed leading experts like Richard Ruggles of Yale to discuss the inadequacies of the 1968 SNA. The experts reported in 1982 that a thorough revision was in order. With over 130 nations now submitting national accounts figures to the United Nations *Yearbook*, it was clear that the SNA was no longer a comfy club for the developed world. In 1985, therefore, the UNSC passed the national accounting torch to the Inter-Secretariat Working Group on National Accounts (creating yet another ungainly acronym, ISWGNA). This coordinating body would orchestrate the revision under the authority of a new umbrella of five organizations: the UN, OECD, World Bank, IMF, and European Commission.

National accounts were increasingly seen as the alphabet of the global economy. Eurostat, the statistical agency of the European Union, exemplified the new imperatives of global economic statistics. Since the 1950s western Europe had been on a course of economic integration. In 1970 the Commission of the European Communities began publishing integrated economic accounts for the whole union, basing its approach on the established SNA. Member nations of the EU were obliged by EU-wide regulation to conform to the standards of the European System of Integrated Economic Accounts (ESA): statistics were the necessary underlay of the allocation of the budget among member states and of the EU's dedication to regional equalization, much as they had been in postwar Canada. By the 1980s, with a common currency on the European horizon, there was every reason to ensure that European national accounts were tightly synchronized with those of the rest of the world.

The Inter-Secretariat Working Group entrusted the actual revision to a select group of experts, who were chosen on the basis of their expertise, not their nationality. The experts in turn called in specialists to address particular statistical problems. Between 1986 and 1992 the experts convened fourteen times, holing up in hotel conference rooms for as much as ten days while they worried through issues as disparate as the treatment of the booming service economy and the pressing need to capture the environment in their numbers. Canadians like Kishori Lal, Stewart Wells, Hans Adler, and Jacob Ryten contributed their expertise to these intense gatherings. In the end, some sixty-five experts from forty countries served as architects of the new SNA at meetings stretching from Moscow to Harare. At the intellectual heart of the exercise were statisticians like Peter Hill, an English academic seconded from the OECD's national accounting section; André Vanoli, France's leading national accountant; and the American Kevin O'Connor of the IMF's Statistics Department. In 1990 the final sewing-up of what had become

an unwieldy package of revisions and innovations was assigned to
Carol Carson, director of the Bureau of Economic Analysis in Washington, editor of the authoritative *Survey of Current Business*, and a historian of national accounting's evolution.[5]

A year later the 582-page draft was ready for the UNSC, which
unanimously recommended it to the UN Economic and Social Council
in the spring of 1993. The project had been, the volume acknowledged,
"a vast undertaking," one that gave the world an integrated system of
national accounts that captured economic performance at multiple levels
– from initial production, through financial flows, on through to the
calculation of national net worth. The SNA revision also gave the world
a powerful model of multilateral cooperation, the whole process marked
by "breadth and openness." As it had been when Richard Stone steered
statisticians though the SNA negotiations of the 1950s and 1960s, the
mood in the 1990s had been one of "persuasion and compromise" –
not arm-twisting and big power bullying. As André Vanoli frankly notes
in his history of these events, "such contexts always involve influence
struggles among persons or institutions. But there is no animosity what-
soever."[6] Vanoli credits statisticians like Carol Carson for acting as
"tension reducers in a multi-polar game."[7] National accounting had
thus become a quietly effective form of international diplomacy, one
that never captured the headlines but produced results that had implications for the economic citizenship of virtually every nation on the
face of the earth.

In the wake of approval of the new SNA in New York, every nation
turned to the challenge of harmonizing its own national accounts with
the new international rubric. Canada became the first OECD nation to
implement *SNA 1993*, albeit with modifications to accommodate Canadian sensibilities. Statistics Canada opted for a team approach, one by
which every innovation in the 1993 system would be synchronized in
the Canadian System of National Accounts (CSNA) by those statisticians most intimately involved in the aspect of the accounts affected by
a given innovation. Each implementation would be "owned" by the
statisticians who worked daily on the part of the system that an implementation affected. For all concerned, the onus was on practicality – on
making established ways fit with new standards. Indeed, Canadians'
greatest penchant as national accountants had always been their inveterate pragmatism, their desire to make the system cohesive and workable, while avoiding rigid statistical obsessions. When Kishori Lal,
director general in charge of the day-to-day operations of Canada's national accounts since 1984, proudly unveiled the revamped CSNA in

1997, he characteristically noted that Statistics Canada's "occasional departures from the 1993 SNA are primarily prompted by pragmatic considerations, such as our institutional structure, our statistical sources as well as the availability of resources and their cost-effective use." The Canadian instinct was to get the revised system up and running as quickly as possible. "Only a handful of countries are in the same league as Canada in producing the complete system of accounts recommended in the SNA," Lal patriotically announced.[8] Other nations would take longer to conform; the EU would follow in 2001, while the Americans have continued to move toward the new SNA in pragmatic steps over the last decade. In 2001 Tunney's Pasture revisited the implementation of *SNA 1993*, thereby further dovetailing Canadian national accounting practices with international guidelines.

A good example of Canada's pragmatic accommodation of the master SNA came in the area of financial services. The experts guiding the SNA's 1993 refurbishment had argued that the contribution to national production of the central bank should be measured in the same way as that of commercial banks. Lal and his team begged to differ. Canada's central bank in Ottawa was overwhelmingly dedicated to supporting the federal government's monetary operations. Only a small fraction of the Bank of Canada's activity – for instance, providing overnight credit cover to commercial banks – in any way conformed to the notion of commercial banking activity. Statistics Canada therefore asked the ISWGNA to reconsider its 1993 guideline for central banks. In 1996 the working group agreed that its standard might lead to "inappropriate results" and permitted Canada to continue valuing the output of its central bank in a fashion similar to a "non-market producer."[9] Many other nations quickly took advantage of the Canadian option, sensing that the Canadians had developed a national accounting practice that more closely conformed to the real world.

By 1997 the national accountants at Tunney's Pasture had made some 100 adjustments to synchronize their Canadian system of national accounting with the new international standard, a remarkably small number for such an all-encompassing system. The felicity of this marriage was in large part a reflection of the maturity of the existing Canadian architecture of national accounting. The Canadian system, as Lal pointed out, already possessed "the full slate of the sequence of interlocking accounts described and recommended in the 1993 SNA." It sat on the broad foundation of the quarterly income and expenditure accounts, which aggregated and balanced the basic income and consumption of the economy while at the same time showing the contribution of government, business, households inside the nation, and a rest-of-the-world sector that reflected interaction with economies beyond Canada's borders. Out of this grist, the GDP was milled.

The next analytical perspective on the economy was provided by the input-output tables, which broke national economic activity into complex matrices of "make" and "use" functions. Here, the emphasis was on *disaggregation*, on tracing the precise relation of commodities and industries in every productive transaction within the economy. Beyond these production accounts, the Canadian system provided financial flows analysis, which revealed the shifting pattern of financial assets and liabilities between the various sectors of the Canadian economy – who owed, who invested, and who saved. Providing the final tier of this architecture were the balance of payments accounts, which revealed Canada's trade and investment transactions beyond its borders. In addition to these operational accounts, the national accounts were also able to furnish a tally of national wealth – a national balance sheet of the net worth of all persons, corporations, and governments in Canada. National wealth was in fact the seminal product of Canadian national accounting, first estimated in the crisis of the First World War as a proxy for national stamina but left in abeyance for much of the rest of the century as the nation turned toward the Keynesian dynamics of calculating income and expenditure.

Canada's smooth adoption of the 1993 SNA also reflected the CSNA's resilience in rebounding from the crisis that had engulfed it in the late 1970s, when users had, for the first time in its history, come to question its reliability. The last two decades of the twentieth century would witness the ongoing repair and reinforcement of the system's core functions as well as recommitment to an expansion of the entire system to reflect a broader and more flexible approach to measuring economic society. These decades would see Canadian statisticians once again play their trump card in the game of economic statistics – the strong centralization of Canada's gathering and analysis of social and economic data. Ever since the days when Robert Coats had insisted that the Dominion Bureau of Statistics be created to act as a "central thinking office" to monitor the statistical pulse of the nation, Ottawa's grip on national numbers had never weakened. Centralization had afforded Canadian national accountants the commanding heights over the national economy since the founding efforts of John J. Deutsch, George Luxton, and Agatha Chapman in the 1940s. Centralization meant economies of scale in operation, consistency in methodology, and authority in analysis. It also meant that Canada could respond quickly and decisively to shifts in international economic theory and convention, be it the postwar embrace of Keynesianism or the ongoing revamping of the 1953, 1968, or 1993 SNA agreements. In all these lights, Canada was by the 1990s the envy of the statistical world. No other nation could boast so integrated a system of national economic accounts. This envied approach to gathering national statistics was perennially influenced by that most quintessentially creative of Canadian tensions – the pressure of the regions on Ottawa.

The application of national accounting to the postwar goal of regional equalization typified this harnessing of federal statistics to confederal ends. Numbers defined the "haves" and "have nots" within Canada's economic union. Regional imperatives thus kept Canada's national accountants on their toes, always attuned to the economic structure of the federation. The 1980s and 1990s would mimic this dialectic. On one flank, Ottawa used the national accounts to address the rising tide of a globalized economy – free trade in the hemisphere, tourism as a surging aspect of the world economy, concern over global warming. On another flank, the national accountants were obliged to respond to regional pressures within Canada: demands that the federation be rebalanced, that regions have their own "national" accounts, that particular industries and regions be probed by microeconomic investigation. This cross-current of centralizing and centrifugal forces obliged the CSNA to hone its methodological edge and keep close to its users' sensitivities. As the end of the century drew near, Canada's national accounts put the dark days of the late 1970s behind them and brought a lustre back to their reputation.

Even before the 1993 SNA was ratified, encouraging evidence emerged that Canada's national accounts had regained their creative edge. In 1991 the *Economist*, Britain's revered newsmagazine, published its "Good Statistics" guide. Exasperated by economic statistics that seemed "increasingly foggy, with balances of payments that do not balance and national accounts that do not add up," the magazine polled a panel of eminent statisticians to rank the national accounts of the ten largest OECD countries. Canada was the hands-down winner. The pundits gave Canada the highest rating for having the narrowest variance in the revision of its GDP, the very thing that had bedevilled its reputation at home in the late 1970s. At the same time, the panel ranked Canada last in the timeliness of the delivery of these same numbers, indicating that, in their opinion, accuracy clearly outweighed speed of delivery. Why was Canada a statistical winner, the *Economist* asked. Its answer: because Canada had a *centralized* statistical system that had always been well funded and was shielded from political inter-ference. By contrast, nations that spread their statistical efforts around various departments and levels of government had systems vulnerable to political interference and budget slashing. Systems like those of Canada, the Netherlands, Sweden, and Australia reaped the benefits of tight centralization. In 1993 the *Economist* repeated the survey, and once again Canada topped the list. "An advantage of centralized [sys-tems]," it argued, "is that they can shift resources quickly into new areas (e.g., from manufacturing to services), without begging govern-ment for more money."[10]

How did this excellence manifest itself? And what were its roots? Entering the 1980s, Statistics Canada's first urge had been to get closer to its users. Public questioning of the accuracy of the agency's statistics in the late 1970s indicated that there was a worrisome credibility gap between the makers of Canada's economic statistics and their users. In a world of high unemployment, inflation, and faltering Keynesian pre-scriptions, economic indicators flowing from the national accounts, from the Labour Force Survey, and from Statistics Canada's Prices Di-vision had a heightened impact on the public's economic psyche. But with the deputy minister of finance suggesting that national accounts and labour indicators were "exhibiting movements that border on the capricious" and the *Globe and Mail* suggesting that it was time to "raise questions about either the agency's competence or its integrity,"[11] the agency needed to get closer to its customers. In his 1980 review of the agency's methodological practices, Sir Claus Moser eagerly advo-cated the creation of a National Statistical Council composed of a "high level group of people interested in statistics and sympathetic" to the agency's problems. The council could serve as a sounding board and as "a protective forum" that would carry user expectations to Tunney's Pasture while at the same time explaining the agency's ways to the world that it served. "Recent criticisms," Moser concluded, "would not have been allowed to get so out of hand if there had been a National Statistical Council ready to speak up."[12]

In 1986 a National Statistics Council was duly created to build the bridge that Moser sensed was necessary. Under an outside chairman – Canadian studies guru Tom Symons – the council drew on the minds of its forty members to provide strategic guidance for the agency on what priorities and projects it should adopt. The national council was to be reinforced by an array of advisory committees that would bring outside professional wisdom to bear on targeted areas of Statistics Canada activity.

Significantly, the National Accounts Advisory Committee was up and running two years before the national council convened. The committee was stocked with outside experts, economists like Richard Lipsey of Simon Fraser University and Marcel Dagenais of the Université de Montréal. Lipsey was perhaps Canada's best-known economist; his bestselling university economics textbook had appeared in fourteen languages. Yale-educated Dagenais was a star of Quebec economics and editor of the *Revue canadienne de statistique*. Off-campus expertise was provided by economists like Mike McCracken and John Grant. McCracken had done pioneering econometric work for the Economic Council before establishing his own economic consulting firm, Informetrica. Grant was the much-quoted chief economist of Wood Gundy. Senior representatives from the Bank of Canada and the Ministry of Finance connected the committee with national accounts users downtown. National accounts alumni Simon Goldberg, now in his United Nations post in New York, was enlisted, soon to be joined by Carol Carson, director of the Bureau of Economic Analysis in Washington. (Sadly, a heart attack would claim Goldberg within a year.)

The chairmanship of the committee went to Ian Stewart, an economist trained at Queen's, Oxford (as a Rhodes Scholar), and Cornell. Stewart began his career as one of a group of what he would later label "wild econometricians" who had plunged into the macroeconomic model-building of the 1960s. When his enthusiasm for the "romance" of modelling the economy waned – too detached, he concluded, from the real and often unpredictably messy world of the man on the street – Stewart turned his talents to economic policymaking in Ottawa. In 1980 he was appointed the deputy minister of finance. Stewart was therefore ideally situated at the intersection of the public and private economies in Canada. From the outset, he made it clear that he considered the "hallowed" core of the national accounts to be "fundamental to economic judgment and decision-making" in Canada. When the newly elected Mulroney government made noises about cutting Statistics Canada's budget in 1984, Stewart and the committee quickly dispatched a resolution to Cabinet warning of any reduction of this "vital core" function of the national accounts.[13]

The advisory committee met twice a year to cast a critical mind over projects and reports set before it by staffers in the National Accounts Division. The meetings were feisty and frank. The experts generally liked what they heard. Since the accounts served as the anchor of the macroeconomic economy, they generally believed that there was "no need for a fundamental rethinking of the framework since the model produced valid results." Indeed, as interest in the economics profession shifted increasingly toward microeconomics and highly mathematized economics, the committee mounted sentry duty on the macroeconomic value of the accounts. At a 1988 meeting, for instance, Lipsey suggested that the "theorists" shunned reliance on the accounts because their "theories will be proved wrong" in the cold light of economic reality shed by the accounts. At the same time, the committee pushed the national accounts toward new frontiers: the environment, better regional statistics, and productivity studies. This was happy news for Stewart Wells, who in 1984 had assumed overall direction of the national accounts as assistant chief statistician. Heartened by such encouragement, Wells concluded that "we should soldier on."[14]

The national accounts acquired other boosters in the 1980s. In 1985 Martin Wilk stepped down as Canada's chief statistician. After the organizational agitations of the previous decade, Wilk had brought stability to the agency by tightening overheads and stressing the value of the agency's services to its users. Wilk's previous American corporate experience became evident in his insistence that Statistics Canada develop a coherent strategy for applying computers to the collection, analysis, and dissemination of statistics. Under Wilk's no-nonsense, bottom-line style of management, morale at Tunney's Pasture improved. So did public esteem for the agency. In 1983 the auditor general of Canada reported that he had found "a renewed sense of direction and purpose" at Statistics Canada, and two years later a Mulroney-government–instigated review of government programs concluded that Statistics Canada was "a tightly managed agency of government."[15]

The momentum developed by Wilk was perpetuated by the new chief statistician, Ivan Fellegi. With his appointment in 1985, Fellegi became Canada's first chief statistician to be bred entirely within the organization that he came to head. He had joined the agency in 1957 after fleeing his native Hungary. By day, Fellegi worked as a clerk – a "superclerk," he wryly came to describe himself – and by night he studied at Ottawa's Carleton University. In 1961 a Carleton doctorate in mathematics became his springboard to a career as a methodologist and social surveyor at the old Dominion Bureau of Statistics. (Some Hungarians seemed to excel in mathematics; George Jaszi, long-time director of the Bureau of Economic Analysis in Washington until 1986, was also born in Hungary.) Fellegi's expertise was rooted in a meticulous regard for the quality of data. He became internationally acknowledged as an authority in methodological problems as varied as interview bias and rolling survey samples. At the same time, Fellegi developed managerial instincts that served him well in the lean-and-mean 1980s and 1990s. By the time he took over from Wilk, he understood that Statistics Canada would thrive only if it delivered quality products that were relevant to users. "My job," he told the *Ottawa Citizen* in 1992, "is to keep my antennae out for issues and trends. I listen to business groups, governments, unions and education, justice and health communities. I have to know the most important issues facing this country not just this year but in five years."[16] The *Globe and Mail* agreed: Fellegi would preside over Statistics Canada's "dramatic transformation from a dusty numbers cruncher into an aggressive huckster of information."[17]

Ivan Fellegi was not, however, an economist. He had never done national accounts analysis. But for almost four decades he had been an observer as the small national accounts group at Tunney's Pasture grew in size and maturity. He had known Simon Goldberg. He understood the data inputs that fed the national accounts from the agency's wide net of surveying. Once established in the chief statistician's office, his genius would lie in providing the national accounts team with a stable organizational base, in keeping the fiscal wolf away from the door, and in constantly encouraging new application of the national accounts to the interests of civil society. Under this umbrella, the national accountants at Statistics Canada were left to pursue their creative purposes throughout the late 1980s and 1990s. In doing so, they attempted to travel both branches of a forked road. First and foremost, they dedicated themselves to bolstering and renovating the existing national accounts system. In hindsight, these might be styled the "old" national accountants. They were dedicated to the macroeconomic purposes of the postwar world. They operated within hermetic boundaries of production and were crucially important to the maintenance of economic stability within Canada's now well-developed welfare state. At the same time, national accountants increasingly turned their attention to the frontier of "new" national accounting, integrating society's use of the environment into the national accounting system, learning to measure nonmarket activities in the home and the volunteer sector, and capturing the statistical impact of activities like tourism that did not neatly fit into the box of standard national accounting.

These would be marvelous years for "old" national accounting. This was evident in the full blossoming of Canada's input-output (I/O) tables. In a great spurt of ingenuity in the 1960s, Canada had produced an internationally acclaimed input-output table that broke the national economy down into intricate "make" and "use" matrices, wherein just over 200 industries reciprocally produced and consumed over 600 commodities. These "rectangular" Canadian I/O tables reflected the operations of the economy in its most intimate detail. As a by-product, the table also obliged statisticians to winnow their data in a most meticulous fashion. The balancing quality of a table that tracked the inputs and outputs of every productive process – what went in must be observed coming out the other end – had attractive potential as a means of purging the statistical system of impure data, those that could not be validated by their reappearance elsewhere in the overall transaction. Put very crudely, sheet steel in the "make" matrix of the steel industry must be validated by an equal amount of sheet steel in the "use" matrix of the auto industry or any other industry that consumes sheet steel. If the numbers do not validate each other, something must be wrong with the data. The image of a finely balanced Swiss watch mechanism comes to mind.

This notion that the cleansing logic of I/O analysis could be pushed through the whole statistical system at Statistics Canada underlay the doctrine of *integration* during the early 1970s. Simon Goldberg was the great prophet of integration. "I would only add that the procedures," he wrote of I/O analysis, "are just as important for the producers of statistics because it provides a map of the cracks and gaps in the statistical system in quantitative perspective. This is what I mean when I say that the Input-Output table is a tool for statistical management, as well as analysis."[18] Integration became the mantra of the I/O experts in national accounts. Terry Gigantes took every opportunity to proclaim solemnly that statistical reconciliation based on the I/O model must be the "guiding philosophy which permeates all the actions and policies of the statistical office ... an all embracing one, encompassing the statistical system *as a whole*."[19]

It was heady stuff, but in the end it simply proved too much for a whole statistical system to swallow. There was an arrogance in the integration prescription – perhaps reflecting I/O analysis's roots in linear algebra – that offended other statisticians at Tunney's Pasture. It demanded too much change from a massive statistical system that had been built up over decades, one that possessed all sorts of engrained intuitions and rhythms that could not be changed in the twinkling of an eye. Given the esoteric nature of their art, national accountants did have a tendency to view themselves as a breed apart. This Keynesian aloofness sometimes bred resentment. Edward Bower Carty, the seasoned chief of the Balance of Payments Division, resented the bumptious I/O crowd: "It is important to remember that one must live in the house while one is remodeling it ... In the past the dismantling of functioning

processes before new fully functioning and tested processes were introduced placed the Bureau in a very exposed position." Furthermore, the
"skills required are rare and in short supply."[20] In the face of such skepticism, the momentum of integration not surprisingly petered out.
Goldberg left for New York in 1972. Gigantes departed for a post at
the OECD under Sylvia Ostry. And then, tragically, the most gifted of all
the I/O theorists, Paul Pitts, succumbed to his lifelong battle with depression and took his own life in 1978.[21]

For all their clock-like intricacy, Canada's I/O tables were by no
means perfect. Since 1971 Canada had produced annual I/O tables. But
their Achilles' heel was that they produced only *current* price measurements – that is, results that did not make allowance for the impact of
inflation over time by measuring in *constant* dollars. Since all the measurements produced upstream from the I/O tables by the income and expenditure accounts appeared in both current *and* constant dollars, there
was a missing link between the two systems of measuring national economic performance. Without constant dollar estimation, the I/O tables
could not be used to calibrate long-term growth rates or to elucidate
productivity in the Canadian economy. Their analysis was locked in the
present. Nor could the tables be used to cross-check income and expenditure account results at constant dollar rates. In other words, the interlocking relationship of Canada's sequence of national accounts was
breached and the utility of the I/O tables largely limited to current economic analysis.

When Kishori Lal became the director of the Input-Output Division
in 1974, he made this shortfall his first priority. Gigantes (who had by
then gone to work at the OECD in Paris) had made the first steps in this
direction; his 1972 historical revision of the national accounts had been
drawn from I/O estimates of personal expenditure based on a 1961 reference year. Lal pushed further forward. Unlike his predecessors with
their highfalutin fixation on statistical integration across the board, Lal
brought a strong practical bent to the assignment. Constant dollar I/O
analysis required the painstaking labour of establishing a deflator formula for every commodity used or produced by the system. Every commodity followed a slightly different rhythm of price and quality. Unique
conventions had to be developed to capture all these nuances within an
economy. For instance, the measurement of *quality* of service in a posh,
high-end department store is dramatically different from that in a self-
service, low-end department store. This differentiation was the finicki-
est type of economic analysis, but without it the I/O tables would have
diminished analytical utility.

Lal worked hard and fast, and within a year the first constant dollar tables were unveiled. They revealed the workings of the Canadian economy in the years 1961–66. By 1985 the deflation of the tables caught up with the constant dollar working of the income and expenditure accounts, so the I/O tables could now serve as benchmarks for the monthly GDP estimate *and* could be traced back on the same basis to 1961. In short, Canadians now had a fully rounded I/O report card on their national economy, issued 2¾ years after the reference year. Canada thus became the first country in the world to operate current and constant dollar I/O tables. The economic world took notice. The grand patriarch of I/O work, Nobel laureate Wassily Leontief, wrote that the deflated tables were "a beautifully executed piece of statistical work."[22] Simon Goldberg wrote from his post as the director of the UN's Statistical Office that "dynamic studies of the Canadian economy" were now possible and that other countries were scrambling to adopt the method.[23]

Having stretched the I/O tables back in time in constant prices, Lal and his staff then turned to the challenge of making the tables probe the regional diversity of the Canadian economy. The national accounts were by their very nature *national*. But the Canadian economy was a highly regionalized affair. Canada's provinces had strikingly different economic endowments and structures, with manufacturing concentrated in central Canada and resource production on the periphery. Interprovincial trade mimicked this patchwork. But the I/O tables' dedication to national "make" and "use" patterns did nothing to reveal these intricacies.

Throughout the 1960s the Dominion Bureau of Statistics (DBS) had been subjected to increasing pressure to furnish numbers that shed light on the provincial economies. Initially, Tunney's Pasture adopted a passive response to this pressure and watched as some provinces launched their own statistical enterprises. The Bureau de la statistique du Québec, for instance, became an innovative producer of economic numbers, acting in particular as an incubator of I/O analysis. But these scattered efforts did little to present the provincial economies in a national framework. In 1970, for instance, Newfoundland's premier, Joey Smallwood, complained that there was no national standard by which to compare provincial debt structures and called upon the "impartial authority" of the DBS to undertake this "difficult" task.[24] In 1967 the DBS had established a Regional Statistics Division, but the agency quickly discovered that large discrepancies in the provincial data sources blocked the methodological path. At the same time, Kari Levitt's groundbreaking application of the I/O method to dissecting the maritime provinces' economies indicated that there were other ways to get at the anatomy of the provincial economies.

In the 1980s Statistics Canada finally took up the challenge of regionalizing its economic numbers. The time was ripe for more focused economic data. Ottawa was relying heavily on its new Ministry of Regional Economic Expansion to pinpoint regional imbalances in the nation and alleviate them. "Mega-projects" were, for instance, in vogue nationally and therefore planners wanted to be able to calculate the precise impact of, say, an oil-sands plant on the region where it was situated while at the same time isolating its repercussions on other, more distant regions that might supply the sinews of production. How far and how intensely would the economic ripples of Fort McMurray's development be felt? I/O analysis could be used to isolate particular industries operating under peculiar pressures. Were certain industries and regions more susceptible than others to the "oil shocks" that had become part of the world economy in the 1970s? The companion branch of Statistics Canada's National Accounts Division – Structural Analysis under Rob Hoffman – co-opted I/O analysis to build a number of "impact models" that demonstrated, for instance, how Canada's international trade reacted to specific shocks. Similarly, I/O analysis was fitted to the particular needs of individual industries: Atomic Energy of Canada salesmen were able to show how a national nuclear energy program had powerful spin-off effects throughout the whole economy. Econometric consultants like Mike McCracken's Informetrica could equip themselves with much more precise data for the modelling work that they undertook for provincial clients. Such targeted I/O analysis had international parallels. At Harvard, for instance, Leontief and his researchers were using I/O analysis to pull apart the international arms trade and to project "limits to growth" scenarios of world agriculture and energy production and consumption.[25]

Back in Ottawa attention turned to the construction of a series of periodic interprovincial input-output tables – snapshots of the regionalized workings of the Canadian economy taken every five years. Once again, Lal's staff engaged in painstaking labour to groom the raw data so that crucial feedstock surveys of such activities as wholesale trade and manufacturing accurately captured the regional break-down of production and consumption across Canada. This process entailed some tricky reconceptualization. Hitherto, for instance, statisticians had to treat the Toronto head office of a large Canadian corporation as a proxy for its *national* economic significance. Even if 80% of the company's personnel worked in Alberta, that their paycheques were drawn on its Toronto head office made them "Ontario" workers. Now this company's activities had to be broken down and sorted into distinct provincial bailiwicks. Similarly, should a head office's overheads be allocated on a *pro rata* basis to each of its regional establishments? Federal government expenditures begged the same question. Was federal spending in any one province to be treated as the result of nonresident sector decisions or was the federal government to be treated as a resident spender in each province?

In the absence of much guidance on these methodological issues from SNA *1993*, Canada once again was obliged to feel its own way. Lal was fortunate to be able to entrust the sortie into regional economics statistics to Yusuf Siddiqi, a Pakistan-born economist who had worked in his native country's national accounts before coming to the DBS in 1965. After taking time off to do a master's degree in economics at the University of Toronto, Siddiqi returned to Ottawa and joined the I/O group in 1970. En route to ironing out all the methodological wrinkles, Lal's group created interregional I/O tables for 1974, 1979, and 1984 as modelling exercises. In 1990 Siddiqi produced a more sophisticated regional I/O table, but it too contained unresolved issues. The thorniest of these was making some kind of accurate provincial attribution of imports and exports as they flowed across Canadian provincial and international borders.[26] How did you pin down the provincial impact of a widget manufactured in Ontario but made of Alberta polystyrene and shipped to the American market by a Quebec trucking firm? And how did you measure trade flows across provincial boundaries when there were no customs offices to collect the information? Siddiqi and his colleagues unravelled these tangled issues, and in 1994 Statistics Canada was able to unveil a provincial I/O table for the reference year 1990, thereby giving the National Accounts Division a benchmark for its provincial accounts program.

As was so often the case in the evolution of national accounting, external events provided the final, decisive nudge toward perfecting what might be called subnational accounting in Canada. Two seemingly contrary developments broke over the nation in the early 1990s: an increasingly assertive mood of provincialism in federal-provincial affairs and Ottawa's determination to modernize the federal sales tax. These were years that strained the traditional bonds of Canadian unity. Quebec continued to assert its right to a "distinct identity," Alberta bridled at federal interference in the oil patch, and new political parties in the federal Parliament demanded a greater voice for the West and a secessionist option for Quebec. The Mulroney government's attempts to redefine the federal-provincial relationship – at Meech Lake and Charlottetown – foundered on the shoals of assertive provincialism. Whatever partisan or philosophical view one brought to these events, there was no avoiding the conclusion that decentralization seemed to be in the ascendancy in Canada. Symptomatic of this drift was the provinces' desire for a more tailored statistical portrait of their position in the economic union.

Against this fractious backdrop, Ottawa introduced the new Goods and Services Tax (GST) in 1991. It replaced the old Manufacturers' Sales Tax, which was levied at the manufacturer's gate and was said to penalize Canadian exporters who were often unable to pass the tax along to off-shore buyers because the price of their product was set by international markets. The GST was to be a fairer, more visible form of consumption tax; food, medical services, and education were, for instance, excluded from its application, or "zero-rated." The 7% tax would be levied only on the value added to a good or service by each participant in the production chain; a flow-through credit would cover each producer's GST payments made on materials consumed in their own operations. From an administrative point of view, the GST required adjustments in how national income and expenditure were calculated. There would be, for instance, an unavoidable lag between the time the accounts registered the GST as an accrual to the national income (i.e., when the purchaser paid the tax) and the later remittance of the tax by its collector. With this in mind, Statistics Canada warned that its first estimates of the tax's impact on the economy should be "interpreted with caution." National accountants simultaneously realized that the I/O table offered an ideal instrument for capturing the impact of the GST as it washed through the national economy. "From a national accounts perspective," two economists from the Income and Expenditure Division urged, "a thorough treatment of the GST requires a complete set of input-output relationships."[27]

Once again, external events nudged the National Accounts Division into action. The GST has never endeared itself to Canadians: it seemed a hefty, up-front swipe at their wallets, even if it did improve Canadian competitiveness and helped to erode the federal deficit. Retailers baulked at having to collect *two* sales taxes, one for Ottawa and another for their province. The Opposition Liberals fanned this discontent. As the 1993 federal election loomed, they unveiled their famous Red Book, with its promise that under a Liberal government the GST would "disappear." This promise was soon engulfed in rhetorical fog. The public wanted to believe that the dreaded tax would be summarily executed by the Grits. Opposition leader Jean Chrétien did little to correct this impression. "But the commitment we've made to the public," he told CTV News in early 1993, "is we want to get rid of the GST. I always said that the GST will go." But buried beneath the electoral rhetoric was an acknowledgment that the GST would be *replaced* "with a system that generates equivalent revenues" and was "fairer" to consumers and small business. As Liberal stalwart Sheila Copps put it, the $16 billion that the GST was estimated to produce every year couldn't "simply be kissed off."[28]

Victory at the polls brought the Liberals face-to-face with fiscal reality. The GST in fact contributed $18.4 billion to federal coffers in 1994. Replacing this revenue was easier said than done. As pressure grew for action, the Chrétien government mooted the idea of *harmonizing* federal and provincial sales taxes into a single, melded tax. An all-in-one tax would be less confusing for consumers and easier for retailers to collect. A harmonized tax would also end the patchwork of different tax rates that blanketed the nation. Politically, it would look like a different tax but would reap the same tax harvest. The Ministry of Finance began sounding out its provincial counterparts on the prospect of harmonization. But the issue had become too politicized for consensus. Conservative and New Democratic Party provincial governments felt no need to help the Liberals keep their Red Book promises. And the old bugbear of provincial autonomy provided most provinces with a ready excuse for denying Ottawa's pretensions, except in the three, Liberal-administered maritime provinces, where there was consensus.

On 23 October 1996 Ottawa and the provincial governments of Nova Scotia, New Brunswick, and Newfoundland signed an agreement to harmonize their respective sales taxes. The other provinces stood aloof and, in doing so, preserved the GST. Down east, however, a Harmonized Sales Tax (HST) of 15% would be introduced in April 1997. To clinch the deal, Ottawa assured its Atlantic partners that their tax revenue would not fall below a 1996 floor for the next five years. The combined tax collected would be duly apportioned between the four participants according to a formula driven by provincial economic statistics provided by Statistics Canada. As early as July 1996 Ivan Fellegi had assured the deputy minister of finance, David Dodge, that the agency could supply figures that would benchmark each province's allocation of sales tax. Fellegi promised Dodge that an enhanced provincial input-output table would offer a "complete and exhaustive" means of doing this, especially because its "balancing qualities" would capture all the intermediate transactions in each provincial economy.[29] Such numbers would support the HST by determining the relative share of HST generated in each province by consumer spending, residential construction, business, and the public sector itself.

The I/O tables, Fellegi told Dodge, would deliver provincial economic data "with acceptable accuracy, freedom from significant revision, and within what can be requested from business and households without creating serious problems."[30] Moreover, Statistics Canada could begin to deliver these data in a preliminary form within four months of the reference year and, as revised data became available, support a final, corrected payout. The only obstacle, Fellegi pointed out, was that the data sources that would be fed into these revamped provincial accounts would have to be "substantially and uniformly improved across all provinces and territories."[31] None of the HST partners balked at this proviso. The federal Treasury Board consequently increased Statistics Canada's annual operational budget by a hefty $42 million. Once again, the national accounts were being called upon to be the arbiter of what a fair share was in the Canadian economic union.

In December 1996 the work began in earnest. For a change, the agency came up with a fluid acronym for the project that lay ahead: PIPES, the Project to Improve Provincial Economic Statistics. Philip Smith, who had a doctorate in economics from Queen's University and had been director of the National Accounts and Environment Division since 1988, left his national accounts duties to take charge of the agency-wide effort. His challenge was to manage a formidable shift in how the national accounts reported provincial economic activity. First and foremost were the all-important goals of improving the quality and detail of provincial economic reporting and producing an annual provincial input-output table for all of Canada. These crucial HST goals depended on addressing the much broader challenge of renovating the data that would be fed into this provincialized system. Everything from the existing surveys of household expenditure to new surveys of construction, restaurant, taxi, and real estate activity, to name just a few, would have to be reformed and coordinated on an annual basis, ready to feed the HST formula for the 1997 reference year. Ironically, the whole exercise was reminiscent of Simon Goldberg's seemingly esoteric insistence on the integrative quality of I/O analysis. Now, however, there was a clear purpose in sight. "We need harmony and integration across our statistical program," Smith insisted. This entailed balancing a procrustean "'one size fits all' approach" against an "unreservedly differentiated, discordant program."[32] There must be a central harmony to Statistics Canada's economic numbers, but there must also be elasticity to allow numbers to be customized to specific economic functions.

In the course of the next three years, the PIPES team published over seventy technical studies aimed at streamlining and integrating the data sources that flowed into the national accounts. The centerpiece of the PIPES exercise lay in a concerted effort to integrate Statistics Canada's collection of information on the performance of the Canadian economy. In the past, the agency had conducted over 200 surveys of various segments of the Canadian business community. PIPES held out the vision of dramatically consolidating these into a single, tripartite survey of Canadian business. At its core was a more inclusive census of about 5,000 so-called "complex enterprises" in Canada, companies with activities in more than one business and/or in more than one province. In the slipstream of this "big business" data, a survey of about 60,000 "establishments" that operated under the auspices of these complex enterprises was taken. And to tap the broad foundation of the Canadian economy, data on about two million "simple enterprises," with operations in only one industry or province, were gathered by surveying or drawing on tax data.

The Unified Enterprise Survey thus facilitated the fine-combing of the Canadian economy, revealing precise detail of business activity ranging from the mom-and-pop corner store to the multi-industry conglomerate perched in a Bay Street tower. To complement this enhanced flow of business data, Statistics Canada's Business Register was similarly streamlined and made more inclusive – for example, not-for-profit companies and companies with no employees were added. GST registration numbers issued by Revenue Canada were coordinated with the Business Register. Other surveys in the Statistics Canada repertoire, like the Family Expenditure Survey, were revamped to conform to the new annualized and integrated pattern of the business surveys.

If the imperatives of decentralization propelled the PIPES project, the imperative of globalization lay behind a parallel effort to modernize the Standard Industrial Classification (SIC) system, which had been used since the late 1940s to categorize data fed into the national accounts. The multidigit SIC codes described economic activity in terms of establishments clustered around a common industrial core. Thus the codes enabled statisticians to construct a precise road map of the economy, one that captured the smallest machine shop at one end of the spectrum and a sprawling auto assembly plant at the other end. The codes also facilitated self-definition by the thousands of businesses that

were obliged to fill in the questionnaires. Subsequent revisions of the
SIC in 1960 and 1980 honed the slippery definition of exactly what
constituted an "establishment" and, in doing so, brought SIC-driven
data into ever closer alignment with the SNA.

Canada's embrace of continental free trade provoked a more thorough-
going reworking of the industrial classification system. Free trade with
the United States in 1989, followed by the signing of the North American Free Trade Agreement in 1994, drove home the necessity of a seam-
less system of industrial coding that would stretch uniformly over the
Canadian, American, and Mexican economies. At the same time, there
was a dawning realization that the SIC had to be expanded in order to
capture new forms of enterprise and new types of products, like soft-
ware, wireless communications, and specialized professional services
like interior decorating. Thus another acronym was born: NAICS, the
North American Industry Classification System, unveiled in 1996 as
the fruit of a joint Canadian, American, and Mexican negotiation.

Like the SIC, the NAICS had a hierarchical structure that encompassed all economic activities by dividing the economy into a pyramid
of 20 sectors atop 99 subsectors, then spreading out into 321 industry
groups and finally down to over 900 industries. The NAICS focused on
industrial processes. Thus a code 41 for the wholesale trade could be
telescoped to 413120 to encompass the wholesaling of dairy products.
At the same time, improvements were made to how industrial commodities were categorized with the unveiling of the North American
Products Classification System (NAPCS). With the NAPCS, a Ford auto
plant could now uniformly categorize all its inputs and outputs – a
Mexican-made carburetor, an American-made grille, and a Canadian-
made drive train – in one fluid transborder statistical system. At the
same time, the NAICS allowed statisticians to get at many of the new
processes of the service economy that had sprouted across the continent
in the 1990s. "Classifications serve as a lens through which to view the
data they classify," the chief statisticians of the three countries noted in
the accord that activated the NAICS in 1996. As PIPES had done for the
provincial economies of Canada, the NAICS had created "a single conceptual framework" for continental economic statistics.[33]

In 2000 PIPES bore fruit. The new provincial I/O tables became operational, fed with data from the Unified Enterprise Survey and speaking the language of the NAICS. The national accounts could therefore
now open a window on the economy of every province and the three
northern territories of Canada. Even little Nunavut was open for economic inspection. The dimensions of the overall I/O system were stag-

gering. The core national matrix matched 750 commodities with 300 industries. Now the matrix could be interrogated on a province-by-province basis. No other country in the world was capable of such regional dissection. It was all a far, far cry from the crude 41 x 41 matrix that Wassily Leontief had applied to the American economy a half-century earlier. Furthermore, it was only possible with the analytical power of the computer. Survey data now arrived by computer, were fed into the matrix by computer, and in virtually a twinkling of an electronic eye, emerged in a portrait of a provincial economy in motion.

The provincial I/O tables were immediately applied to the final division for the HST revenue of 1997. From now on, the provincial accounts would deliver a preliminary set of economic accounts for each province *four* months after the year closed. These preliminary accounts in April would show GDP by province, plus sources and disposition of personal income.[34] By November of the same year, the estimate would be revised. Then over the next three years, the estimates would be groomed to a final version as new data on the reference year became available and were fed into the table. And the HST agreement was far from the only outlet for this analysis. Provincial ministries of finance across the country now had a much more intimate picture of their economic turf. Businesses could now probe their markets and plan their expansions on a targeted provincial basis. Consultants, labour unions, and academics were also now able to get at the nitty-gritty of the Canadian economic union. It came as hardly a surprise when a group of Swedish national accountants, visiting Ottawa in search of some guidance on keeping track of their nation's economy, concluded that Canada had developed its national accounts to near-perfection. Canada was, they observed, "the country which appears to value official statistics the most."[35]

This honing of Canada's national accounts understandably went largely unnoticed on the streets of the nation. Constant dollar analysis and I/O tables were well beyond the ken of most Canadians. One change that the "average" citizen would have noticed was Canada's 1986 switch from gross *national* product to gross *domestic* product. It was a shift that virtually all the members of the United Nations' SNA "club" had or were undertaking. GDP gave a more realistic picture of Canada's economic situation because it captured the impact of *all* production taking place in Canada, regardless of who owned the assets. The old GNP captured all domestic production *plus* income made from Canadian investment offshore, *minus* income earned by foreign enterprises operating in Canada. Given the historically high levels of foreign

investment in Canada, GNP tended to underestimate national economic output by about 3%. Thus the 1986 switch appeared to make Canada a "richer" nation; in fact, it simply held a more realistic mirror up
to our economy. GDP better conveyed employment in the land and
thereby made for better productivity analysis. It also facilitated constant dollar measurement of the economy. The United States, where foreign ownership of the economy was much less, did not switch over to
GDP until 1991. With this switch, GDP completed its eclipsing of GNP
as the Keynesian icon of Western economic performance.

The switch to a GDP benchmark reflected a broader desire to keep
economic statistics realistically aligned with public sensibilities. The
1970s had seen two mild economic recessions that had shaken the public's faith in Keynesian predictability. Despite the proliferation of economic numbers placed before the public, there was a growing yearning
in the public mind for a more focused barometer of trends in the national economy. In Canada the Royal Bank, for instance, introduced its
"Trendicator," a basket of key economic indicators like housing starts
designed to isolate the general drift of economic conditions. But it was
American statisticians at places like the Federal Reserve and the University of Michigan who really pioneered the use of "leading indicators."
In 1981 Statistics Canada therefore introduced its own system of leading indicators to help the public to track emerging trends in the economy. Interest in leading and lagging indicators – yardsticks of economic
activity with strong predictive correlation – had existed since the 1920s,
when they were seen as a way to anticipate the business cycle. By the
1980s the quality of economic data allowed for the selection of ten
leading indicators of the Canadian economy, which would afford Canadians some idea of whether good times or bad times, or perhaps the
same times, lay ahead. Indicators included stock market performance,
the ratio of shipments to inventories of finished goods, and sales of fur-
niture and appliances. Given the crucial importance of the American
economy to Canada, the US's leading indicator was rolled into Canada's leading indicators. Some of the indicators could be traced back to
the early 1950s – all were measured on five-month rolling averages and
projected against the base year 1981. The composite leading index thus
joined the GDP, the unemployment rate, and the inflation rate in giving
Canadians straightforward yet reliable yardsticks by which to measure
their economic prospects.

To ensure that this vital information found a broad market, Statistics Canada revamped its delivery system for general economic reporting. The venerable *Canadian Statistical Review* had become a stolid,

and not widely read, monthly compendium of figures. In 1988 it was replaced by the street-savvy *Canadian Economic Observer* (CEO), a magazine-like treatment of economic themes that began each issue with an essay on current economic conditions. Thematic essays on Canadian economic trends followed. The CEO's editor, Philip Cross (another alumnus of Queen's University's Department of Economics) proved a feisty participant in the national economic dialogue. When, for instance, the Canadian economy faltered in the early 1990s, Cross warned economic commentators not to bandy the "R-word" – recession – about recklessly. Cross suggested that the orthodox definition of a recession – two consecutive quarters of decline in the real GDP – was too "arbitrary" a yardstick. Calling a recession on the basis of a narrow range of indicators was no longer supportable in an age of sophisticated, multivariate national accounting.[36] The CEO was thus not shy of controversy. In 1991, for instance, the magazine raised the ire of the Ministry of Finance by publishing an article arguing that the much-debated federal deficit was the product more of revenue shortfalls than of an explosive growth in government spending, a contention that Cross later admitted was "overdrawn."[37] The transmission of the agency's economic analysis to the world beyond Tunney's Pasture was intensified in 1995 when the *Daily*, the agency's voice to the world since 1932, went on-line. At 8:30 every morning, interested Canadians could greet the day with news of Statistics Canada's latest research. From the same computer, they could also tap into the database of the Canadian Socio-Economic Information Management System (CANSIM), draw down information on the latest GDP quarter, or discover how the balance of trade was faring.

The accounts found other ways to catch the nation's attention. The 1991 introduction of the GST had provoked a debate over whether the hefty bite the tax took at the cash register was stimulating tax evasion across the country. Talk of an underground economy excited ideological passions.[38] The Fraser Institute in Vancouver issued a report estimating that Canada's underground economy was equivalent to 22% of the measured economy. Economist Richard Lipsey worried that the *perception* of an illegal economy was "altering people's behaviour" and therefore warranted close empirical attention by the national accounts staff.[39] Statistics Canada took up the challenge. If one took into account only market-based production of goods and services that escaped detection in official estimates and excluded actual illegal transactions like those involving drugs and pornography, then the underground economy was "very unlikely to exceed 3% of measured GDP and is probably a lot less." It would take the introduction of nonmarket production like household work or volunteerism to boost the informal economy to any-where near a double-digit slice of the national economy. Canada did, therefore, seem to have some scofflaws, but they were not ruining its fiscal fabric.[40] Interestingly, the international SNA guidelines now quite routinely admitted imputations for activities such as the sex trade, which were no longer considered illegal in many countries and for which the wages of sin were easily calculable.

In 1994 national accounting marked its first half-century in Canada. In many ways, the "system" was a Keynesian dream come true. National accounting in the Western world had been developed around a notion of the state as an aggregation of homogeneous parts. The accounts sought to provide statistical illumination of how income was earned and spent in societies that valorized their wellbeing in monetized terms. The numbers fed policies that satisfied society's craving for stability and growth. In Canada the national accounts were the abiding handmaid-en of the welfare state. At the heart of this creativity lay a Canadian pragmatism that balanced theory and practicality. Above all, Canadian national accounts served Canadian needs – equalization being the most compelling example. But they did so without bastardizing the intellec-tual purpose of the whole enterprise of keeping a nation's books. Robert Parker, associate director of the Bureau of Economic Analysis in Washington, saluted the Canadian achievement in 1992: "Careful man-agement, limited detail, strict adherence to deadlines, and a willingness to acknowledge data deficiencies that cannot be remedied within the given time period allow the Canadians to publish timely, annual I/O tables."[41]

But by the 1980s the anxieties that had driven the welfare state's emergence in Canada were receding into the history books, and Cana-dians were beginning to look beyond aggregation as the sole end of society. Yet Canadian society enjoyed a comfortable complacency; a so-cial welfare safety net surrounded its members, and the state seemed to understand the art of tightening and loosening the net according to the tenor of the times. National accountants at Tunney's had proved very adept at measuring this net and thereby protecting its public credibili-ty. But it had all taken place within a Keynesian public policy frame-work dedicated to plotting economic equilibrium and aggregation. Stewart Wells, in charge of the national accounts field since 1984 and never far away from the activism of his days at McGill and in the la-bour movement, could sense the inertia creeping into the whole system. "The national accounting framework has not changed in twenty years," he frankly admitted to the National Accounts Advisory Com-mittee in 1988, "and there seems to be a tendency among national ac-countants not to push at frontiers."[42]

By the 1990s, however, there was mounting pressure to return to the frontier. On the ideological plane, there was a neoconservative (some would call it neoliberal) critique of the mechanics of the whole Keynesian approach. The stagflation of the 1970s had indicated that Keynesian macroeconomic policies did not always produce the desired effect of stability and growth. The countercyclical rhythm of surplus and deficit had been broken, and many Western states found themselves locked in deficit. Productivity had flagged – some said because the state had too intrusive a presence in the economy. While the ideologues battled, groups outside the traditional boundary of the national accounts mounted their own assaults on the legitimacy of the whole exercise. Many women wanted better inclusion in the system. Environmentalists demanded that the system measure society's depletion of the resources that fuelled economic expansion.

In a sense, this battle over the correct ideological orientation of Western society did not affect national accountants. Their role had always been apolitical: to provide whatever political arithmetic the state demanded. But the open conflict over the ultimate purpose of their statistical labour was intellectually disquieting. The hermetic seal of Keynesianism had been breached, yet nobody seemed to be able to suggest what might restore intellectual cohesion to the business of keeping a nation's books. Economic commentator Dian Cohen caught this mood in 1995: "What's more, our system of national accounts, a creation of the 1930s and 40s, is hopelessly outdated and gives a misleading picture of economic activity." The problem, she concluded, was that "the memories of the Keynesian state are much clearer than the vision of what is to replace it."[43] The same mood was beginning to creep over Tunney's Pasture. After a soul-searching discussion of the demand for environmental statistics, the advisory committee minutes recorded Stewart Wells in a pensive mood: "is situation re environment analogous to 1930s and Keynes? Can one think of environment to-day similar to that? Conceptual apparatus not so difficult to think of, but difficult perhaps for data to fill boxes." Toronto economist John Grant shared the perspective: "In a sense, we are waiting for a Keynes."[44]

But for national accountants, the late twentieth century would bring no new Keynes. Instead, the accounts would gradually, often painstakingly, take on new functions that did not neatly fit with the "hallowed" core accounts. The neat macroeconomic symmetry of a system based on aggregation would be modified in asymmetrical directions to provide calibration of phenomena outside the traditional boundary of monetized production. Air quality, work in the home, voluntary work, tourism, and even activities deemed illegal had to be brought into some sort of quantified relationship with the established system of measuring income and expenditure in society. At the same time, these problems were increasingly compounded by problems *within* the old corral of national accounting. A "new economy driven by service industries and yeasty growth of high technology" was emerging, an economy marked by the slow fade of traditional mainstays of the economy like manufacturing

Looking in the Rearview Mirror

Since their inception in the 1940s Canada's national accounts had been caught in a two-front battle. First and foremost, they had to report on recent economic performance. But such analysis would have been greatly enhanced if the historical perspective on economic behaviour could be reliably pushed back for comparative purposes. Many factors impeded such historical extension of the national accounts: skimpy data, insufficient expertise, stretched budgets, and the unbendable schedule of reporting on today's economy. Over time, many time series were pushed back to 1926, but past this year there was little attempt to retroactively apply modern notions of economic measurement. In a pre-income-tax era, it would, for instance, be difficult to calculate labour income. Economists like John J. Deutsch and O.J. Firestone made intelligent "guestimates" of pre-1926 GNP in Canada, but the methodology that they used was problematic.

It took fifteen years of concerted effort by Queen's University economics professor Malcolm "Mac" Urquhart to stretch Canada's national accounts back to Confederation. An Albertan, Urquhart did graduate work in Chicago before doing economic research while employed in the wartime bureaucracy, where he witnessed the birth of national accounting first-hand. In 1945 he carried this knowledge to Queen's, where he became an immensely popular teacher of economics. Unhappy that the 1965 volume *Historical Statistics of Canada* had no projection of Canada's pre-1926 GNP, Urquhart assembled a team in the 1970s to pull together a reliable macroeconomic portrait of the young nation's early economic growth. In 1993 *Gross National Product, Canada, 1870–1926: The Derivation of the Estimates* was finally published. Canadians now knew that the GNP stood at $382.5 million in 1867. They also could benchmark its slow growth in the late century, its dramatic expansion under Laurier, and its arrival in 1926 at a GNP of $5.3 billion.

and heavy industry. "The economy is becoming harder to measure," *Business Week* bemoaned. How, for instance, did you quantify capital in an "information economy"? Was a database capital? Was the intensive research and development behind the high tech revolution something that should be included in the national accounts as an abiding investment? How did you account for technology's ability to dramatically enhance the quality of a good (like a computer), while at the same time reducing its price? Observing all this, *Business Week* complained that "it is becoming clear that the real economy is vastly different from the one painted by the government's numbers ... The bum numbers are costing the country a bundle ... [and] leave economists fumbling with major policy questions."[45] Closer to home, Canadian economist Richard Lipsey urged his colleagues on the National Accounts Advisory Committee to shift their focus from "mere aggregation" to "innovation" – how growth is stimulated by technological innovation over time.[46]

This many-faced challenge would put a premium on Canadians' already well-demonstrated pragmatism. There was never a question of overturning the old national accounts. Too much of the structure and programs of the modern state depended on their perpetuation. As America's most distinguished national accountant, Richard Ruggles, warned the advisory committee: "laying out an idealized system *de novo* is a dangerous sport; in anything as complex and elaborate as a national accounting system it is not possible to foresee all of the ramifications which the adoption of specific treatments may have."[47]

Neither was the status quo an option. One needed only to recall the folly of classical economics' resistance to change in the Depression. The advisory committee was alert to the dangers of inertia. "Don't stand still," Mike McCracken warned, for "human capitalization and the environment need attention." Richard Lipsey agreed: it was "very important for STC [Statistics Canada] to lead not follow. If measurement brings home problems, there is a chance to alert people to environmental dangers."[48] Others worried that the baby might be thrown out with the bath water if the change was too precipitous. As Ruggles wisely noted: "if an attempt were made to cover all non-market production, it would swamp the actual transactions data in the national accounts."[49] Thus a line of contention was drawn between what Ian Stewart described as the "core protectors" and the "broadeners."[50] The resulting tension energized national accounting as it entered the new millennium. For some, the pace of change would be infuriatingly slow. For others, it conformed to the innate conservatism of statisticians, anchoring society with reliably long perspectives. But just as feminism had evolved into a "second wave" of development in the 1960s, there could be no denying that national accounting had entered its "second wave." It would strive to protect old gains while at the same time reaching out in new directions.

Tourism provoked the first glimpse of how new wine might be put in old bottles. Travel had been the meteoric service industry of the postwar world. Since the World Tourism Organization began charting the numbers in 1950, global tourism arrivals had burgeoned from 25.2 million to just over a half-billion annual tourist arrivals in 1992. Growth in tourism receipts had grown even more exponentially, topping US$315 billion in 1992. Only once, in energy-shocked 1982, did tourism numbers and receipts actually recede.[51] Tourism was an industry that infiltrated every nook and cranny of an economy, from chamber maids to aircraft manufacturers. But just who was a "tourist"? Business travellers or summer vacationers? What exactly was a tourist "trip"? How did you segregate the tourist from the macroeconomic picture? How did you isolate the tourist's impact on the national, regional, and local economies, especially since tourism was not an explicit category of demand in the national accounts? Statistics Canada, for instance, had long tracked tourist arrivals and trips abroad by Canadians, but as the industry expanded it became clear that there was no encompassing yardstick of its extent. Industrial classifications systems, like the NAICS, had no one industry called "tourism." "How do you measure something that has no shape?" became the common complaint.[52] The problem was that available data on tourism were fragmented over many jurisdictions, were partially qualitative and partially quantitative, and tended to focus on the "tourist" rather than on the industries that catered to the tourist. In short, the data did not fit neatly into or emerge smoothly from the national accounts.

By the 1980s demand for better tourism data began to coalesce. In 1983 the World Tourism Organization's General Assembly met in New Delhi and urged integration of tourism statistics into the SNA. As early as 1972 Ottawa had hosted a federal-provincial conference on the need for national tourism data as a means to bolster employment in the industry. Statistics Canada seemed the natural coordinator for such centralization.[53] But it took until 1984 for real action to materialize. By then, a broad coalition of industrial groups, like the Canadian Restaurant and Food Service Association, had found sufficient common cause with Canada's three levels of government to form a National Task Force on Tourism Data. Chief Statistician Martin Wilk chaired the group. From the outset, the task force was vexed by the methodological implications of measuring tourism. There was "no single data language" that conveniently wrapped numbers as disparate as "bed nights" and modes of transport.[54] How did you connect tourist demand (i.e., what the tourist wanted) with the supple side (i.e., what the industry did to cater to the tourist)?

Eventually, the task force came up with a workable, if rather loose, definition of the industry: tourism was "defined to include the direct supply of goods and services to facilitate business, pleasure and leisure activities away from the home environment."[55] Later, a distance of eighty kilometers away from home was stipulated in order to exclude a trip to the mall or the movies from the tourism net. Beyond this definition, the task force was stymied in trying to produce neatly dovetailed statistics for the industry. It was possible to identify the key sectors of the economy – like hotels, museums, taxis, and travel literature – within the national accounts, but it was impossible to correlate such hard data with softer data that reflected the *experience* of tourism. "The result," the task force reported in 1989, "has been, and continues to be, inadequate data for many purposes and, worse, incorrect comparisons and faulty judgments. When users of data do not know the various data are based on quite different definitions, only confusion can result."[56] In short, admitting such a hodge-podge of data into the national accounts would only pollute the integrity of the system.

The solution? Create a "satellite account" to the national accounts that would relate to the national accounts in some monetized ways but would also contain sufficient latitude to embrace "a much wider range of information." The satellite would serve as a "disciplined information system that has the potential to collect, order and interrelate the statistics describing all significant and measurable aspects of a specific subject matter."[57] At its core, it would contain orthodox national accounts statistics for the commodities and services consumed and supplied by tourism in the economy. Uncoupled from this hard statistical core would be other modules unrelated to the national accounts that captured other social, economic, and demographic aspects of tourism in Canada. The satellite account was a brilliant stroke: it cut the Gordian knot that plagued the relationship between the defenders of the "hallowed core" and the "broadeners." Statisticians in France, the world's biggest tourist destination, shared the credit for pioneering the idea of satellite accounts.[58] But it was at an Ottawa conference sponsored by Tourism Canada and the World Tourism Organization that the idea received its international seal of approval. That same year, the OECD in Paris issued a *Manual on Tourism Economic Accounts* that praised the pragmatism of the new device: "The system incorporates a certain flex-ibility rather than the application of strictly fixed rules of the 'all or nothing' type ... a pragmatic approach is to be preferred to a rejection on purist grounds."[59]

Freed of purist constraints, Canada's tourism satellite account was up and reporting by 1994. Statistics Canada boasted that it was "the first of its kind in Canada."[60] From this account, Canadians gained a more intimate picture of tourism's importance to their economy. The monetized core of the account revealed that almost 5% of total consumer expenditure in Canada was generated by personal tourism. Foreign spending on tourism services in Canada was equivalent to 4% of Cana-dian exports. Demographic data in the satellite showed that 467,000 Canadians had full-time employment in the tourism sector in 1988.[61] A set of national tourism indicators was also introduced to isolate the im-pact of tourism on particular sectors of the economy. In 1996 inter-provincial and territorial comparisons of tourism were introduced. These indicated, for instance, that the ratio of tourism GDP to total GDP was highest in the Yukon at 4.8%.[62] By almost every measure, tourism was surging in national economic importance. Better statistics were thus making Canadians more attuned to the economic and social impacts of tourism. "International visitors staying longer, spending more," the *Daily* typically reported.

The satellite account opened other methodological doors. It offered a way of acknowledging the unpaid domestic labour in a nation's econ-omy. Throughout the 1970s, national accountants had tinkered with methods for giving unpaid domestic work some statistical weight in their calculations. The problem was always finding the right formula for *imputing* value to what was done in the home "for free" or done outside the home as voluntary effort for the good of society. Yet for all the well-intentioned studies and academic conferences, any concrete move to implant such imputations in the actual national accounts al-ways ran up against resistance from the guardians of the "hallowed core." In the *Review of Income and Wealth*, Steven Landefeld and Stephanie McCulla of the US Bureau of Economic Analysis wrote of the worry "that broadening the accounts would essentially be trading off an incomplete, but useful, tool for a broader, but significantly less use-ful, tool."[63]

Second-wave feminism was not, however, ready to be deflected by methodological orthodoxy. The United Nations declared 1976-85 the Decade of Women to highlight the treatment of women in the world.

This vigilance was eloquently apparent in the writings of the New Zealand activist and politician Marilyn Waring. Her 1988 book, *Counting for Nothing: What Men Value and What Women Are Worth*, was a brilliant polemical attack on the gender bias of Keynesian national accounting. In a chapter cleverly called "A Calling to Account," Waring sought "to demystify, to empower, and frequently to enrage." She described the SNA as the product of "gentlemen estimators," who had constructed the whole system to serve their patriarchal economic ends. Waring lay siege to the boundaries of production behind which the system existed. How could the system come up with an imputed value for owner-occupied homes but shy away from women's labour within these homes? As far as the formal SNA economy was concerned, such women were "unoccupied" and unproductive.[64]

Waring reminded her readers that women working unpaid in the home or in the rural economy or in the developing world were "invisible" in the economic statistics published by the United Nations. Yet everyone's instinct pointed to the fact that society functioned largely because of this labour. "We women are visible and valuable to each other," she concluded, "and we must, now in our billions, proclaim that visibility and that worth. Our anger must be creatively directed for change."[65] The book became a global bestseller. It had facts. It had passion. And it soon had recruits. But it was also a polemic that tried to drag the SNA across a highly political line and make it the servant of welfare economics. This it had never been: national accounting was a mirror of society's received values and norms. The SNA was a mechanism for transactional economics. If society wanted to alter the nature of these transactions, so be it. But one could not fault the mirror for the imperfections of the beholder.

Purist indignation would, however, have been a foolish line to take at a time when Canadian society had set itself on a course of affirmative action in matters of gender. In 1993 Statistics Canada hosted an international conference "on the measurement and valuation of unpaid work" that signalled an end to almost fifteen years of debating the viability of measuring unpaid work.[66] On one front, the agency harnessed its social surveying to finding out more about domestic activities. The flagship General Social Survey began asking questions about how homemakers used their time. "Time use" statistics helped to determine how a woman (or a man) apportioned time between childrearing, cleaning, nurturing, and all her other "household duties." This provided a template that showed how a homemaker's time was employed over the long term. From this, a satellite account could be constructed by attributing a value to each activity. Two pricing approaches were employed: opportunity costs (i.e., what the person sacrificed in the open market by working at home) and replacement costs (i.e., what it would have cost to hire an outsider to perform the same function). The results were stunning: the "value of household work" amounted to almost 40% of the 1986 Canadian GDP, or $199 billion, if measured by the replacement cost method. When the opportunity cost method was utilized, the total fell to 31.5%, or $160 billion.[67]

The calculation of unpaid work in the household thus became an asymmetrical feature of the national accounts, housed in a satellite account at arm's length from the core accounts. As a 1995 report remarked, the era of ad hoc accounting was over. Canadians now had a benchmark by which to measure women's contribution to Canada's material wellbeing.[68] The numbers were not a product of pure national accounting, but they were helping to counteract the invisibility of which Marilyn Waring had so rightly complained.

The success of the tourism and unpaid work satellite accounts invited other initiatives. If the unpaid nurturing of the family was a mainstay value of Canadian society, so too was the voluntary instinct. Canadians had always displayed a willingness to reinforce society's fabric by donating their time and skills to causes that existed outside the formal economy. As Western societies became mature welfare states, attention became focused on the notion of "civil society" and what gave it cohesion. Since the 1970s an umbrella group called the Coalition of National Voluntary Organizations had been lobbying Ottawa to acknowledge the voluntary sector by measuring it in the census. By the 1990s there was growing recognition that a society's wellbeing rested on more than what its income and expenditure accounts revealed. It rested also on men and women organizing Boy Scout troops, on driving the aged to doctors' appointments, and on a vast array of nonprofit activities such as education and social services. Most of these existed as a result of voluntary labour or of transfers from government. Nobody doubted their vital contribution to society. But how was this to be measured? How did you calibrate the economic weight of a Tuesday evening Girl Guide leader with that of a full-time environmental activist? Did you combine nonprofit educational and social services, largely funded by government, with nonprofit groups that survived on volunteerism and sales of goods like composting bins or services like sheltering the homeless? What, in short, was a society's "social capital"?

In the face of such complexity, Statistics Canada opted for the same approach that it had taken to unpaid work: collect data on the extent and rhythms of the nonprofit and voluntary sector and *then* attempt to bring them into some relationship with the larger, formal economy. In 1987 a prototype National Volunteer Activity Survey was undertaken to try to capture the patterns of the sector. Like unpaid work, this initiative aroused broad interest among groups that wanted to demonstrate just how central these activities were to Canada's social capital. Federal government agencies like Heritage Canada and private advocates like the Canadian Centre for Philanthropy quickly lent their support. In 1997 a much more extensive National Survey of Giving, Volunteering and Participating was undertaken to pry apart the complexity of charitable giving, volunteering, and participatory behaviour in Canada. The survey revealed, for instance, that 31.4% of Canadians over age fifteen had volunteered in the nonprofit sector in the previous year.[69] Outside of Canada, the United Nations launched its own attempt to build a statistical corral for the nonprofit sector, commissioning Johns Hopkins University to spearhead the effort. In 2000 this critical mass prompted Ottawa to launch the Voluntary Sector Initiative as a public-private partnership. The goal would be to construct a satellite account for volunteerism that would put some quantitative value on the sector, thereby allowing policy in the area to be strengthened and monitored. Statistics Canada would coordinate the project. Once again, the national accounts were feeling their way to finding post-Keynesian relevance in society. In 1947 Richard Stone at Cambridge had sensed the need to fragment the system's early income and expenditure results into compartments that reflected how households, business, and government shared in the national economic pie. For this, he coined the term "social accounting." Now, as the century waned, "social accounting" was being asked to admit new charter members whose worth had hitherto escaped the statistical net.

The most obstreperous of these new elements was the environment. Just as the patriarchal economy had considered the domestic labour of women free, Western societies had long treated the environment as a "free good" exacting no price because its resources seemed so abundant and limitless. Pollution and energy shortfalls in the 1970s had raised unease about the folly of this complacency, but little progress had been made toward providing society with a statistical benchmark to measure man's degradation of the environment. Statistics Canada had tried, but the solutions offered proved too esoteric and disconnected from applied policy. The laws of physics and biology shared little with the dictates of economics. Moreover, unlike tourism and domestic labour, there was no cohesive interest group to discipline agitation for better environmental controls. The environment meant many things to many people. Budget cutbacks and economic recession in the early 1980s reduced environmental research at Tunney's Pasture to a trickle. By 1985 there was only a single statistician dedicated to the challenge of measuring the environment. To adopt a saying made popular by the American environmentalist Garrett Hardin, the environment was "usually no more than a ghost in the woodwork" in Canadian statistics.

But the wind began to shift. Statistical measurement is born out of social demand, and in the late 1970s, Western societies began to think greener thoughts. These were years when, in the words of the famous American bacteriologist René Dubois, the world began to "think globally, but act locally." Statistics Canada's environmental research in the 1970s had lacked obvious constituencies, a fact reflected in its free-floating focus. But the next decade saw a coalescing of government and special interest groups around the issue. In 1981 Environment Canada in Ottawa began consultation on a more structured approach to measuring man's impact on the environment. This led in 1986 to the publication of the first *State of the Environment Report in Canada*, a report card outlining man's impact – levels of cadmium and lead in the water, for instance – on the environment. A second version of the compendium report, *Human Activity and the Environment*, appeared at the same time. These events marked a reinvigoration of environmental research at Statistics Canada; an environment and natural resources section was brought to life in the structural analysis division of National Accounts. All this coincided with the greening of the Mulroney government. Environment minister Tom McMillan encouraged Environment Canada to sign an agreement with Statistics Canada to collaborate on a second state of the environment report. Uppermost in the initiative was the desire to provoke Canadians to think about the long-term cost of unchecked consumption of resources. Sustainability became the new lodestar. At Tunney's Pasture statisticians like Bruce Mitchell and Kirk Hamilton laboured to fill data gaps in areas such as waste generation and household environmental behaviour. Everything from the amount of phosphate that an average family used to the capital budgets dedicated to pollution clean-up had to be categorized and made measurable.

Canada was not alone in this shift. In 1983 the United Nations had asked Gro Harlem Brundtland, Norway's first woman prime minister, to head a World Commission on Environment and Development. Commissioned by the UN to set out "a global agenda for change," Brundt-land soon etched the imperatives of sustainable development into the world conscience. "What is required," the commission report urged in 1987, "is a new approach in which all nations aim at a type of development that integrates production with resource conservation and enhancement, and that links both to the provision for all of an adequate livelihood base and equitable access to resources." National accounting needed to be enlisted in this effort: "The process of economic development must be more soundly based upon the realities of the stock of capital that sustains it." The concept of *natural capital* – the environmental larder of land, air, water, and resources that sustained our way of life – was becoming central to measuring the environment. In effect, sustainable development required national accountants to supplement their habitual devotion to measuring the *consumption* of natural capital with an awareness of the hitherto unreported cost of the *depletion* of this natural endowment. Development became sustainable only when society understood the extent of the stock of resources at its disposal.[70]

In Ottawa, Prime Minister Brian Mulroney echoed this message in his 1990 *Green Plan for Canada*. Canadians, he pointed out, were "trustees of a unique, beautiful and productive northern land." The nation needed to adjust many habits in order to "go green." But we lacked the "tools" to exercise our "stewardship" over this natural patrimony. Mulroney called upon the national accounts to supply one of these tools: "a simple set of indicators so that the state of complex environmental systems can be presented concisely and understandably."[71] In 1993 Ottawa established a National Round Table on the Environment and the Economy, a panel of experts empowered to chivvy Canadians into better stewardship of their economy and their environment.

With such an encouraging hand extended toward it, Statistics Canada did not hesitate to act. First, the sign on the door was changed. The Income and Expenditure Accounts Division was relabelled the National Accounts and Environment Division. The division began work conceptualizing and implementing a satellite account for natural resources that could serve as the benchmark against which Canadians' demands on their environment might be measured. National accountants would present Canadians with "green aggregates," figures that demonstrated not only how their consumption generated growth but also how this took place at the expense of drawing down resources and generating pollution.

Once again, there were international echoes of Canada's gradual conversion to greener numbers. In New York the United Nations commissioned its Statistical Division to construct a "system of integrated environmental accounting." The UN effort ambitiously tried to integrate green numbers with aspects of the traditional national accounts, aiming, for instance, at a means to adjust fixed gross capital formation to reflect reductions in natural resource stocks. Progress in New York was, however, slow and methodologically difficult. Growing impatient, Ivan Fellegi and Jacob Ryten, Statistics Canada's leading men for economic survey methodology, suggested an alternative to cumbersome multilateralism: establish an ad hoc working group of experts to tackle issues head on. This approach had previously been applied to other sticky conceptual issues in national accounting: the Dutch city of Voorburg, for instance, had hosted discussions of how the new service economy should be treated in the SNA. Hence in 1994 the "London Group" on environmental statistics came into being. Philip Smith used this venue to explain Canada's more pragmatic approach to the problem: "the Canadian view," he told the London experts, "is that it will take many years of data development, research and professional discussion before meaningful, reliable and credible aggregates of this kind are possible from a statistical perspective."[72]

Despite his caution, Smith had a clear idea of what he wanted in his satellite account. First, there would be a natural resource stock account recording the size and composition of Canada's natural resources. Initial attention here focused on key assets like oil and timber, some renewable and others nonrenewable. There was even thought of creating such things as a wildlife account, which would track the nation's supply of moose and codfish (the latter, of course, a prophetic choice for the Atlantic fishery in the fateful 1990s). Second, a natural resource use account would track the manner in which these resources were consumed in the production of goods and services. Third, and totally novel for statisticians, an account would be created to quantify waste output. Where did pollution come from? What dysfunctional drag did it exert on growth? Lastly, an account would record current and capital spending on environmental protection. What did Canadians actually spend on catalytic converters and recycling boxes?

These seemed like simple goals, but they bedevilled the usual logic of statistics. National accounting instinctively sought to aggregate economic activity, but resources were consumed in a fragmented fashion in localities and under jurisdictions scattered from coast to coast. There were also qualitative issues. How did you put a monetary value on, say, varying types of coal? (Significantly, a young chemical engineer from Queen's University, Robert Smith, hired in the early 1990s after he had picked up a master's degree in environmental studies at York, would eventually be put in charge of the agency's revitalized environmental effort.) Or how did you factor in the march of extractive technology that might make resources, at present unrecoverable, worthy of future production?[73] Viewing these conundrums from his chief statistician's office, Ivan Fellegi conceded that statistics and the environment made for "a very difficult marriage."[74] But it was one that society was increasingly demanding. When Philip Smith left to tackle the PIPES project, his environmental shoes were filled by Claude Simard, a seasoned I/O practitioner.

So by 2000 there was to be no turning back. Statisticians had once again found themselves the handmaidens of social change. The pace of this change was for some excruciatingly slow. If statisticians were cautious in adapting their methods, Canadians as a whole were even slower in changing their environmental ways. The cataclysmic depression of the 1930s had produced a sufficient shock within society to stimulate the emergence of Keynesian national accounting. The ensuing war had accelerated this evolution and incubated national accounting with what seemed like reckless speed. Environmental degradation lacked this dramatic quality and therefore provoked only a fitful revolution. However much the smog hung stubbornly over Toronto and the polar icecap receded, a war-zone sense of urgency did not yet pervade environmental consciousness.

Could there be a new Keynes lurking in the environmental crisis? Could there be a new unifying principle for how man organized himself economically? Probably not. Too much rested on the economic infrastructure that the existing System of National Accounts reflected and sustained. Growth mattered. Change was most possible when there was momentum in society. The established stock and trade of national accounting – producing GDP, studying productivity – remained central to society's wellbeing. But the new millennium dawned with the creeping realization that the *quality* of growth and how it was measured had to change. "Progress" could no longer be what it had so comfortably and uncritically been for the past half-century. In 1995 *Atlantic* magazine published a trenchant article entitled "If the GDP Is Up, Why Is America Down?" The article's authors spoke for a San Francisco nonprofit think tank called Redefining Progress. How, they asked, could the economy be so buoyant when measured in conventional terms like the GDP if society at large battled anxiety about the quality of American life. Why were negative things like car crashes, floods, and pollution clean-up treated as positive growth by the national accounts? "The nation's central measure of well-being works like a calculating machine that adds but cannot subtract," they complained. "It treats everything that happens in the market as a gain for humanity." Were American economists living in "a statistical Potemkin village that hides the economy Americans are actually experiencing?"[75] North Americans wanted to assess their economic prospects not just in the here and now but over the horizon. Consumption today must not come at the expense of sustaining growth into the future. Hence the GDP must be augmented by a Genuine Progress Indicator (GPI), which would arrive at a measure of "progress" only after defensive expenditures like fighting crime and depleting natural resources had been netted out of its calculation. The GPI would also give weight to time spent in voluntary and leisure time. It would evaluate income distribution, educational attainment, and "human freedom."

The Genuine Progress Indicator had an immediate appeal. Some even talked of a Gross National Happiness Index. Others took to associating old-style national accounting with oil-coated sea birds and weapons salesmen, arguing that such outcomes were the natural offspring of the cult of "growth" promoted by the numbers. But many national accountants saw a fundamental misconception in such reasoning. National accounting was about measuring production, about annual *flows* in the economy, no matter what stimulated their generation. Catastrophes like hurricanes and oil spills were not about production but instead about the reduction of the *stock* of natural wealth. Just because the national accounts picked up the economic activity sparked by, say, cleaning up the environmental consequences of the *Exxon Valdez* disaster did not mean that the system valorized the abuse of the environment. The shock to wildlife and the physical environment created by such windfall losses to humanity should be captured in national balance sheet accounts where the depletion of natural capital or stock was increasingly being monitored.

National accounting found other ways to address the growing anxiety over the quality of our social and economic existence on the planet. In 1990 the United Nations began publishing a world development report that ranked countries according to such factors as their citizens' education, life expectancy, and economic wellbeing. The report would put "people back at the centre of the development process."[76] In Canada groups such as GPI Atlantic and the Pembina Institute in Alberta began developing genuine progress indices as "local pathways to global well-

"Ingenious insiders": University of British Columbia economist Anthony Scott has argued that the excellence of Canadian national accounting is rooted in the innovativeness of "ingenious insiders" at Statistics Canada. Pakistan-born Yusuf Siddiqi (left) and Indian-born Kishori Lal exemplify the pattern. Lal arrived at Tunney's Pasture in the late 1960s and helped to lay the foundation for Canada's famous rectangular input-output table. He would go on to become director general of the National Accounts Division. Siddiqi joined Lal's group in the 1970s and would mastermind the creation of an input-output model that could look inside the economies of individual provinces. Courtesy of Statistics Canada.

being."[77] As a statistical *system*, however, these indices left much to be desired. They sought to compare statistical apples and oranges: subjective values of "happiness" were being combined with objective economic and physical measures of performance. National accountants genetically distrusted such medleys. But as a means of raising consciousness about society's shifting expectations of economic progress, the GPI movement exerted legitimate pressure on the existing system of national accounts.

Keynes had based his worldview on maintaining economic equilibrium in the short term. The global environment now demanded that this equilibrium take on a more ecological and long-term perspective. Satellite accounts were a creative step in the right direction, but they were only a partial bridge to a new worldview. It was this challenge that Paul Martin, Canada's minister of finance, sensed in his 2000 federal budget. Canadians, he warned, "must come to grips with the fact that the current means of measuring progress are inadequate." Martin then announced that Ottawa would spend $700 million on new environmental technologies and practices, including a set of "environmental and sustainable development indicators." These, he concluded, "could well have a greater impact than any other single measure we could introduce."[78] The national accounts thus entered the new millennium with trepidation, at ease with their established duties but sensing that society now expected more.

Epilogue
Beyond Widgets

While the GDP and the rest of the national accounts may
seem to be arcane concepts, they are truly among the great
inventions of the twentieth century.
~ Paul Samuelson and William Nordhaus, *Economics*,
15th ed. (1995)

[T]he thick Bible that we pray with every day.
~ Philip Smith, interview, 2006

[N]ational accounting is far from being at cruising speed.
The problems to be solved are manifest and difficult.
~ André Vanoli, *A History of National Accounting* (2005)

[I]t's a lot easier counting how many widgets the nation
produces in a year than quantifying the creation and
marketing of knowledge.
~ *Business Week*, 13 February 2006

Ottawa, Valentine's Day, 2006, 7:00 A.M. Cold, slate-gray skies hang
over the nation's capital. On the radio, there is talk of that most dreaded of Ottawa weather – freezing rain. High on the twenty-first floor of
the R.H. Coats Building at Tunney's Pasture, Roger Jullion, director of
the crucial Income and Expenditure Division of Canada's national accounts, is ensconced in a warm boardroom. He is making pancakes on
an electric griddle. His assistant directors, Pat O'Hagan and Jim Tebrake,
are busy rounding out the breakfast preparations; juice, coffee, and
cutlery appear on a table normally reserved for statistics. It is employee appreciation day at Statistics Canada and Jullion, a 1973 recruit to
the national accounts team, has found a culinary way of showing his

staff of seventy that they are appreciated. But there is more to Jullion's pancakes than appreciation. Motivation is also on the director's mind – it is day one of the group's quarterly campaign to assemble an estimate of the nation's gross domestic product. "Production time," as Statistics Canada employees stoically refer to these intense periods of putting estimates together, has come. For the next fourteen days, only one thing will matter in the lives of these statisticians: getting the GDP estimate for Canada's economy in the last quarter of 2005 ready for release to the public on 28 February. Evenings and weekends will soon be offered up to the deadline god. There will be glitches with data bases and twists of public policy that skew the normal rhythm of GDP calculation. Jullion has seen it all many times before and has acquired the habit of laconically signing off on each glitch with the phrase "Fun with figures!"

To the average Canadian, or at least to the policymakers and planners who shape our daily economic life, Statistics Canada's quarterly release of a GDP estimate is the most familiar outcome of the whole national accounts process. When the estimate first appeared in the fall of 1953 – reporting on economic activity in the first and second quarters of that year – it equipped Canadians with a quintessential Keynesian tool of economic adjustment. For a mere 25 cents a copy, it allowed them to see where their economy had just been and, thereby, anticipate where it might now be heading. The "main purpose of the quarterly accounts," Simon Goldberg boasted, "is to facilitate making appraisals of emerging developments in the economy."[1] Armed with such knowledge, the mandarins overseeing the unfolding welfare state might decide to cool or stimulate the national economy by nudging the prime interest rate up or down. Businessmen might decide to curtail production runs or draw down inventory. And the mythical average citizen might decide that *this* was in fact the right year for a new car or a holiday in the Maritimes. In the lexicon of economic citizenship, the quarterly GDP estimate had become the most recognized term. By observing the GDP's barometric ups and downs, Canadians had learned to calibrate their economic citizenship, to measure their material wellbeing in a manner that no previous generation could. It provided illumination where only two generations ago in the 1930s economic darkness prevailed. Where once the nation stumbled along, a surer economic path now existed – the road behind was visible and the road ahead less daunting. Today, like the national accounts in general, the quarterly GDP continues to serve as "a form of alphabet" for our national economic dialogue.[2]

Building the GDP estimate is rather like gathering the harvest. Statistics are reaped from the myriad surveys that Statistics Canada undertakes – manufacturing, capital investment, government outlays, wages paid, personal spending – and then brought into the structure of national income. Outside agencies contribute other streams of data that extend the yield to reflect, for instance, taxation and Crown corporation operations. Jullion's staff separates this statistical harvest into four functional silos. The first – capital expenditures, inventories, and trade – captures what business spends on machinery and equipment, what is spent on residential and nonresidential construction, what is in inventories, and the pattern of Canada's trade flows across international borders. Another silo collects data on consumer expenditure and capital income: what Canadian consumers spend on goods and services, what corporations earn, and what investment income and financial services the nation generates. A third aggregation revolves around the estimation of labour income, as well as income and expenditure of governments, farmers, and other unincorporated businesses. Last, there is the collection of financial flow statistics, which reveal how money moves through the economy – who saves, where capital accumulates, and how money is intermediated through the economy.

Out of this last silo, statisticians are able to fashion an estimate of Canada's overall national wealth, which is always released in the wake of the GDP estimate. Drawing on this same statistical data, other members of Jullion's staff assemble numbers for the tourism satellite account and work out the purchasing power parities that allow Canadian economic performance to be cast in an international light. If one steps back from the dust and chaff of this harvest, one can detect the simple statistical framework first glimpsed by John Maynard Keynes in the 1930s. Gross national product, he argued, was the outcome of C (consumption) + I (investment) + G (government expenditure. Capture this statistically, and you capture the essential pulse of the economy.

It is, of course, not nearly that simple. The data have to be carefully groomed and vetted. Anomalies and impurities have to be winnowed out of the data. A constant eye has to be kept on the balancing nature of income and expenditure flows. What goes in as income must surface elsewhere as expenditure or investment. And once the grooming is done, each data stream in the overall national income and expenditure must be refreshed with data from the latest statistical harvest. These additions, or in the staffers' shorthand, "adds," are the real calisthenics of the quarterly estimate. Back in the precomputer 1950s, the adds made the quarterly campaign an absolutely brutal affair. Statisticians assembled the raw data and then handed it over to clerks who laboriously punched it onto huge ledger sheets with their Freiden calculating machines. For purposes of verification, two and sometimes three teams worked each addition, praying that after hours of laborious inputting their totals matched. Male statisticians prepared and verified the data; women clerks punched the keys. The noise of the clattering calculators was horrendous. The teams worked through the night. Cigarette smoke filled the air. People slept overnight at their desks. The deadline always mercilessly loomed.

Today, things are considerably different. The Friedens are long banished, replaced by the hum of computers. An add that took days to perform in the 1950s now can be executed in ten minutes on the computer. As a consequence, there is less overtime during the quarterly campaign. The whole operation now unfolds in smoke-free relative tranquility, broken only by questions about method and content asked over cubicle walls. Like the national economy itself, the data that have to be crammed into the estimate have expanded massively over the past half-century. But the computer can handle it. Moreover, each estimate is not just an exercise in attaching the last quarter's results to the existing income and expenditure series. It is also an active updating of the previous quarters as new data and revised data become available – the sometimes notorious bugbear of GDP revision. Thus construction of the estimate of the fourth quarter of 2005, an undertaking that began on 14 February, also provided a chance to revise the previous three quarters of that year and hence to provide an annual GDP summation. When the quarterly cycle begins again in May and Jullion's staff gear up for the first quarter of 2006, the fourth quarter of 2005 will get its first reworking. The previous sixteen quarters will also be revised.

For all its repetition, a freshness pervades each reaping of the GDP harvest. The process may seem mechanical, but it is in fact fraught with methodological dilemmas. This February there is worry, for instance, that Christmas retail spending in the fourth quarter has been diminished by the growing popularity of gift certificates. Canadians are less inclined to bestow tangible gifts and more inclined to give a credit note to a loved one. Actual sales in the stores decline in December and pick up in the usually arid retail month of January. In the interim, the gift certificates sit as liabilities on retailers' books. Or perhaps, economic observers might conclude, the depressed December retail sales are an inkling of an absolute downturn in consumer spending, a telltale of impending recession. Other dilemmas emerge. Had Hurricane Katrina's blow to New Orleans been felt in the timber mills of Canada? What effect could statisticians detect from the spike in energy prices in the fall of 2005? What about those $400 citizen dividend cheques that the Alberta government handed out in the fall? What about the rebates that Ontario paid to electricity users in 2005? Were these payments income subsidies to citizens or simple refund payments? A consensus emerges that they were refunds – money that was being returned to its rightful owners and was not therefore newly generated income to be reported in the national accounts. All of these quandaries had to be "worried through," as Jullion describes it, and their resolution worked into the impending estimate.[3] The quarterly GDP estimation is therefore an active intellectual process, a balancing act between the integrity of the "system" and the nuances of change.

And for all its maturity and computerization, there are still hints of the innovative spirit of George Luxton and Agatha Chapman up on the national accounts floors of the Coats Building. National accounting has never evolved into a prosaic, routine affair. Take, for instance, a young statistician named David Pringle. A Maritimer with a master's degree in economics from the University of Ottawa, Pringle has been a national accountant for five years. He jokes that he was never much good at mathematics in school. Yet his love of economics is evident. Above his desk, well-thumbed copies of Adam Smith's *The Wealth of Nations*, Keynes's *General Theory*, and J.R. Hicks's *The Social Framework* sit beside David Foot's bestseller *Boom, Bust and Echo*. It is Pringle's first time "flying solo" in preparing the financial flows component of the GDP estimate.

Pringle wears two hats in the financial flows section of the Income and Expenditure Division. During the quarterly GDP campaign, he integrates financial statistics from federal government business enterprises as diverse as Canada Post, Via Rail, and the Export Development Corporation into the estimate. For this, he assembles data from Statistics Canada's Public Institutions Division, the federal Ministry of Finance, and the Bank of Canada. As data arrive, he codes them, then sorts them into an Excel spread sheet to create a kind of temporary or quasi database ready for deployment into the existing financial flows framework in the national income and expenditure accounts. There's "a lot of learning by doing" in this job, Pringle admits. Luckily, he is surrounded by veteran national accountants. National accounting has never been a precise science – it's a subtle combination of hard fact, precedence, and a good dose of intuition. Pringle has discovered that those around him possess "a lot of oral history of how things are done." Michel Pascal, chief of the nearby Capital Expenditures, Inventories, and Trade Branch, has soldiered through over a hundred quarterly GDP estimates. David's immediate neighbour, Charles Wright, has twenty-six years' experience calculating the sum of Canada's accumulated non-financial assets – housing, machinery and equipment, land, and so forth. Pringle picks Wright's brain whenever the pieces of his own statistical jigsaw do not neatly fit into place. This partnership will persist after the GDP estimate is finalized, as Pringle's other hat entails calculating the national balance sheet – the source of the estimate of Canada's overall national wealth.

On Friday, three days into the estimate, Jullion gathers his staff in the boardroom for an update. The fourth add has just been completed and the printed result is circulated. The mood is jovial, and in the bilingual roundtable that follows problems are aired, worried through, and settled. Pringle reports that key data from the Public Institutions Division are late because various Crown agencies have been slow in reporting their financial situation. Bigger issues loom. Pringle's immediate boss, Joe Wilkinson, reports that a changeover in how the federal government reports its finances – from a cash to an accrual basis – is slowing his group's work. To make matters worse, mortgage data from Dun and Bradstreet are also tardy. There is further discussion of locomotive imports, gambling revenues, Christmas shopping, and soaring energy prices. Adjustments are made and other decisions postponed. "We feel," Jullion remarks, "we are bringing our own intuition to the figures, building these experienced judgments into the estimate. That's our value added to the whole process."[4] As the meeting concludes, Jullion announces that the next add, to be run on Sunday morning, should bring better quality and some clarity to the unresolved issues.

Early the next week there is another data discussion. The overall picture is crystallizing. Pringle's truant information has arrived. Work begins on drafting the letter that will be sent to the minister of industry on the morning of the actual release. The minister speaks for Statistics Canada on Parliament Hill. But he cannot be given prior, insider knowledge of the estimate; his relationship with Statistics Canada is an arm's-length, apolitical one. Instead, the only federal agencies to get an advanced inkling of the estimate are the Ministry of Finance, the Privy Council Office, and the Bank of Canada. They receive the estimate three "working hours" in advance of its actual publication and are thereby put in position to react to any public or political reaction that the estimate may trigger. As this formal deadline approaches, work begins on the text that will appear in the agency's on-line publication, the *Daily*, on the morning of 28 February. The translators and graphic artists arrive on the

The postmortem meeting the morning after the release of the quarterly GDP, March 2007. National accountants, central bankers, federal officials, and economic consultants discuss the implications of the just-released GDP figures, probably the best-known indicator of Canada's economic health. Speaker phones pull in opinion from Bay Street and provincial capitals. Income and Expenditure Accounts director Roger Jullion (lower left) briefs the meeting on the fourth quarter of 2006 – an annualized GDP growth rate of 1.4%, the slowest in three years in Canada. Karen Wilson (beside Jullion), the current director general of National Accounts, awaits questions from users of the estimate. Across the table, the director of the Balance of Payments Division, Art Ridgeway (on the left), stands by for questions on Canada's trade and international investment position. Income and Expenditure assistant director Pat O'Hagan (beside Ridgeway) provides fine detail of the GDP estimate. Courtesy of Statistics Canada.

scene. Preparations begin to upload the latest quarterly results into Statistics Canada's database for the Canadian Socio-Economic Information Management System (CANSIM). Late on Friday afternoon the agency's policy committee is briefed, and the final draft of the ministerial letter is approved. All is ready. On Monday afternoon, officials at the Department of Finance and the Bank of Canada will get their briefing and designated information officers in the division will get their briefing on the estimate in anticipation of journalistic and public inquiries.

Exactly two weeks after Jullion made his pancakes, at 7:00 on the morning of 28 February, the journalists begin arriving for the GDP lock-up at Tunney's Pasture. At exactly 8:30 A.M. the *Daily* posts the results of two arduous weeks' work: the Canadian GDP grew by 0.6% in the fourth quarter of 2005 and by 2.9% for the year as a whole. This represents a slight slowing of growth from the 0.9% of the third quarter. But the bottom line is that Canadians are continuing to enjoy prosperous times: investment and exports are up, nonresidential construction and equipment purchases have increased, industrial production is up, and capital investment is up. The only discouraging sign is a surge in imports, which has tended to check internal economic expansion. As always, the tone of the press release is restrained and nonjudgmental. "Another solid gain in labour income and corporate profits" is about as celebratory as the text gets.[5] Within an hour, the wire services are carrying the story. The CBC chooses to emphasize import-softened growth in December, the last month of the quarter. Across the country, bank economists and academics begin to put their spin on the data. Will the Bank of Canada, many speculate, have to cool demand with a hike in its prime lending rate?

The following morning Jullion and his managers return to the boardroom on the twenty-first floor for a scheduled postmortem with prominent users of their data. Conference phones link the assembled economists and bureaucrats with Bay Street and the Quebec Ministry of Finance. The questions range from focused to speculative. Do the manufacturing figures reveal a trend away from gas-guzzling sport-utility vehicles and toward crossover surrogates? Is Statistics Canada considering supplementing old-fashioned GDP with a "command GDP" indicator, a system that takes a country's terms of trade into its estimate of growth? The Canadian dollar's recent surge in value has brought the idea of command GDP into vogue. The *Globe and Mail* has suggested that such a device would dramatically boost the GDP of a country like Canada with its soaring loonie.[6] Karen Wilson, director general of the entire Canadian System of National Accounts since 2001, is sitting in on the meeting and fields the question. She says that Statistics Canada is looking into the idea but worries that "talking heads" in the media may misinterpret such a currency-oriented yardstick. A caller from Toronto chips in a warning that countries that rely on currency-based economic analysis leave the door open to "Dutch disease," whereby high currency value promotes cheap imports that rot local ability to manufacture. Jullion then provides his own commentary on what the figures reveal; he is talking to experts who want finer detail and a bit more candid insight. Did Hurricane Katrina pump up demand for Canadian lumber in the United States? There is no evidence as yet, Jullion replies. He is careful with his words. He is reluctant to call crossover sport-utility vehicles "trendy"; his numbers count cars, not fads. But there is no mistaking that the overall tone of Jullion's message is upbeat. Canada is on an economic roll. Final domestic demand was "going gangbusters" throughout the year. The outsiders like what they hear and an hour and a half later are on their way back to the economic trenches of the nation. Two weeks after it began, the quarterly GDP cycle is over. Down the corridor, David Pringle puts on his other hat and begins thinking about the national balance sheet.

The GDP is the most prominent feature of a cascade of information that flows from the national accounts into the economic consciousness of the nation. However, there are other tributaries. Just the day before the GDP release, Art Ridgeway and his team in the Balance of Payments Division had made their scheduled report on Canada's all-important trade and international financial situation.[7] "Current account surplus hits record $30.2 B," the *Ottawa Citizen* reports. It is the largest surplus on record. "There's a lot of cash floating around," Ridgeway tells the postmortem meeting two days later. Economist Warren Lovely of the Canadian Imperial Bank of Commerce says that Canadians can start thinking of their currency as a "petro-currency."[8] On Saint Patrick's Day, Pringle and his colleagues release their quarterly national balance sheet accounts, a calculation of the sum of all the nonfinancial assets – such as land, capital goods, and real estate – plus all financial assets and liabilities. This is the grown-up offspring of the ballpark figure that Sir George Foster asked R.H. Coats to supply at the height of the First World War. Coats's back-of-an-envelope estimation came to $16.2 billion. In the fourth quarter of 2005, Canada's net worth has bulged to $4.5 trillion. "The official result," the *Globe and Mail* editorializes, "is that every single Canadian, whether gurgling in the crib or hunched over this year's tax returns, is worth $137,000."[9] The figure reveals nothing about how this wealth is *distributed*, but it does satisfy a primal craving to know what the nation is "worth," especially when it can be broken down into such benchmarks as household net worth.[10]

The national accounts thus echoed through Canadian national discourse in familiar ways as 2006 unfolded. Their political arithmetic was evident in other national conversations. Late in January, for instance, Canadians went to the polls in an unusual winter election. Economic concerns echoed from the hustings. Throughout the previous fall, for instance, there had been much talk of Canada's productivity record, a debate informed by the research of the national accounts' Micro-Economic Analysis Division. Could Canada maintain its beleaguered manufacturing sector in the face of competitors like India and China, where labour was cheap? Did we spend enough on research and development? The answers were not easy; productivity was a slippery concept for most Canadians to comprehend, particularly when it was expanded beyond its traditional labour-output polarity into multifactored analysis. "We are looking for a way to describe it that is not phoney and doesn't frighten people," the minister of industry, David Emerson, had told the *Globe* in October.[11] When the election broke, there was much citing of productivity data that seemed to contradict the evident prosperity of the Canadian economy. A rising dollar and a world hungry for natural resources, many argued, did not disguise the underlying structural weakness of the economy. Productivity expert and National Accounts Advisory Committee member Richard Lipsey was among them: "We are staggering along. We are going in the right direction but we have not got there yet."[12] In many ways, productivity remained an experts' debate – the *Globe* would label it the "forgotten issue" of the campaign – but there was no doubt that, at least for the economic pundits and business and labour leaders, the national accounts were feeding another crucial national debate.

There were other echoes of national accounting in the election. The phrase "human capital" often surfaced in the campaign rhetoric. Although GDP measured the nation's economic pulse, it said nothing about the intangible "wealth" bestowed on Canadians by factors outside the traditional marketplace. Canada, the argument went, should be considered something that was more than the sum of its market economy. Such a measure ought to capture the worth of a society beyond the aggregate of price tags generated by its markets; it should also begin to weigh depletion of future resources and the *quality* of life in a consuming society. For instance, the Green Party – finally a viable alternative on the national political stage – championed the development of a "wellbeing index" that would benchmark the quality of life in Canada by combining measures of economic performance with social phenomena like poverty and volunteerism.[13] The Greens no longer considered themselves a one-tune environmental party; they now centred the environment in a broad political agenda. Once again, the national accounts were being reminded that society was inching toward a new expectation of their mandate.

The accounts provided the feedstock for another issue troubling the national political dialogue, an issue long familiar to Canadians – equalization of the fiscal capacity of the provinces. Like any other decade in Canada's history, the 1990s witnessed shifts in the rewards and responsibilities of federation. The steady rise in energy prices brought increased prosperity to Alberta and, for the first time, had driven growth in Newfoundland and Nova Scotia. At the same time, the sagging fortunes of other resource industries like pulp and paper and the painful adjustment costs exacted on central Canadian manufacturing by globalization eroded the economic base – and tax revenues – of one-time stalwarts of equalization like Ontario. Equalization, born in 1945 and formalized in 1957, had always operated in the interest of diminishing the gap between "have" and "have-not" provinces in Canada. The goal of equalization – putting a floor of minimum services beneath every Canadian's feet – was beyond reproach as a core Canadian value.

Instead, the political hot potato was the formula by which redistribution was calculated. Based on the fiscal capacity of Canada's five "middle-income," as the formula states, provinces (i.e., Quebec, Ontario, Saskatchewan, Manitoba, and British Columbia), the formula was an arcane affair understood by few beyond number crunchers in the Ministry of Finance. But its political repercussions in provinces like Ontario, where public spending on social services and education had fallen below the national average, fanned discontent. Pointing to Statistics Canada's provincial income and expenditure tables, Ontario's Liberal premier, Dalton McGuinty, alleged in 2004 that his province suffered a $23 billion shortfall between what it paid into federal coffers and the services that it received from the federal government.[14] McGuinty used the number as evidence of Ontario's bruised sensibilities within Confederation. "The folks in Tim Horton's" coffee shops, he argued, should know what they were getting out of Confederation. Although Ottawa and other provinces disputed McGuinty's analysis, the issue persisted. It surfaced in the 2006 federal election as the need to correct Canada's "fiscal imbalance." Eager to find a political compromise, the newly elected prime minister, Stephen Harper, engaged in consultations to rejig the equalization formula. Should oil and gas royalties be counted as regular provincial revenues? *Plus ça change*, many political commentators remarked as they watched this latest rebalancing of the political union that is Canada. Throughout all this, nobody naysayed the numbers that fed the debate. Canadians might argue ferociously about political choices, but they never doubted the numbers that informed their ultimate decisions.

At Tunney's Pasture, Philip Smith, who in 2001 became Statistics Canada's assistant chief statistician for National Accounts and Analytical Studies, took quiet pride in this largely unsung national achievement. He light-heartedly referred to the thick international manual for the System of National Accounts (SNA) that constantly sat on his desk as "the thick Bible that we pray with every day."[15] Kishori Lal, who in retirement still made regular appearances to counsel upcoming national accountants in the refinement of their art, smilingly talked of "our SNA religion."[16] Up on the twenty-sixth floor of the R.H. Coats Building, Chief Statistician Ivan Fellegi had similar reverence for the numbers that his people produced. Canadian governments, he said, have displayed a "deep desire to get on the inside of a problem with numbers." Canada's national pragmatism rests on a tradition of "evidence-based decision making." And, he added emphatically, Canadians expected numbers that were not tainted by political calculation, a fact that was "understood in the bone by senior Ottawa bureaucrats."[17]

This statistical objectivity was appreciated from afar. Canadian Lucie Laliberté, a seasoned balance of payments expert who left Statistics Canada for a senior post with the International Monetary Fund (IMF) in 2000, looked back admiringly on her Ottawa years from her Washington office: "The numbers in Canada come from the bottom up, not from the top down." The numbers were never "cooked."[18] Foreign observers were also quick to identify another cardinal advantage of Canadian national accounting: its tight centralization. However much the pendulum of Canadian federalism had swung back and forth over the decades between Ottawa and the provinces, Robert Coats's vision of centralized national statistics had remained unchallenged.

By contrast, even in the great federal republic to Canada's south, the taking of the national statistical pulse remained fragmented. The Bureau of Economic Analysis in the US Commerce Department watched the structure of the American economy, while the Bureau of Labor Statistics in the US Labor Department monitored the job situation. The United States Bureau of the Census took the third role in this statistical ballet, collecting industrial production data and conducting the census. A delicate statistical diplomacy therefore always prevailed in Washington. In Ottawa, however, a big box approach to statistics had long prevailed. National accounts, employment, and inflation numbers were all generated under one roof. The *Daily* and the *Canadian Economic Observer* covered the whole statistical spectrum of the Canadian economy. As one-time director of the Bureau of Economic Analysis in Washington and long-time coordinator of the SNA revision process, Carol Carson had watched Canadian national accountants at work for decades. Centralization, she believed, allowed Canadian statisticians to "think whole pictures." And because they could "think big," Canadian national accountants afforded themselves flexibility in their art, an ability to be "practical" and "pragmatic," a knack for balancing the demands of real-world economics and the "esoteric beauty" of national accounting theory.[19]

In the sixty years since George Luxton made the first "rough stabs" at calculating Canada's national income, Statistics Canada has risen to world leadership in maintaining national accounts. Luxton's mantle has most recently been worn by Philip Smith (right), assistant chief statistician for National Accounts and Analytical Studies (2001–07). Smith, with a doctorate in economics from Queen's University, succeeded McGill-trained Stewart Wells (left). The Queen's-McGill connection has deep roots in the making of Canada's national accounts. Men like Wells and Smith have been the behind-the-scenes mandarins who have provided the numbers that help Canadians to inform their economic citizenship. Courtesy of Statistics Canada.

This strategic privilege explained why Canadians were pioneers in the input-output analysis that dissected the inner rhythms of their federalism and in satellite accounts that brought statistical coherence to such phenomena as tourism. This practical bent was still very much in evidence at Tunney's Pasture as Canada's national accounts entered the new millennium. The rapid emergence of the so-called information technology (IT) economy in the 1990s provides a persuasive example of this nimbleness. Real GDP, for instance, has traditionally been calculated by measuring changes in the *value* of production and then correcting them against changes over time in the *price* of the product involved. Once a deflated or constant value for the product in question is established, the real change in production becomes evident. Statistics Canada's GDP rested on prices calibrated using base years that periodically were "rebased" forward in time – 1961, 1971, 1981, 1986, and 1992. This was called the Laspeyres method. The IT economy introduced a quirkiness into this calculation: the price of many technology products tended to *fall* fairly rapidly over time, while their capacity increased dramatically.[20]

Most Canadians will recall that their first home computer cost an arm and a leg in the mid-1980s and did comparatively little. Today, the average home computer costs much less and does much more. Digital cameras provide another persuasive example of what economists like to call "hedonic regression." As the pixel capacity of cameras has grown over the last decade, the price of digital cameras has plunged.[21] As a result, any calculation of, say, 2006 real GDP based on 1992 base prices would tend to overweight growth by not taking into account the marked shift in relative price of many products at the heart of the "new economy." To reduce this bias, Statistics Canada in 2001 switched its GDP calculation to a chain Fisher index system. Devised by Yale economist Irving Fisher, the chain Fisher system created an index that blended current and base prices, then shifted it forward – like the yardsticks in a football game – with every quarter measured. The index hop-scotches forward with every measurement, thereby reducing bias in the growth calculation and bringing Canadian GDP into line with its American counterpart, which has also adopted the Fisher approach.

The "new economy" called forth other innovations in the Canadian national accounts. Computers and the evermore precise collection of economic data – "microdata" – acted as the handmaidens of microeconomic analysis in the late twentieth century. Such precise data have allowed national accountants to wander from their long dedication to macroeconomics – aggregate economic outcomes – to more closely focused explorations of economic performance. Microeconomists invoke the telling image of "drilling down" into the economy to interrogate its inner rhythms. Statistics Canada responded to this opportunity by establishing a Micro-Economic Analysis Division in the early 1990s, bringing in Queen's University economist John Baldwin to head the research.

Baldwin built a team that was ideally situated to explore the fine detail of how the new economy was breaking over Canada. The ensuing *Canadian Economy in Transition* series applied microeconomic analysis to the changing dynamics of the nation's industrial structure. A 2003 study, for instance, laid out the "emerging geography of new economy industries in the 1990s." How had the yeasty growth of high technology shifted the core of Canadian manufacturing? What regions had gained? The results were dramatic. The information and communications technologies (ICT) sector – a bundle of nineteen manufacturing and service industries – had spurted in employment by 70% in the decade. By 2001, 4.1% of all paid workers in Canada were in the ICT sector, and 74% of them worked in enterprises that did not exist in 1990. Science-based industry had grown fastest in Alberta. The ICT sector was also a predominantly urban phenomenon, employing 9.1% of workers in Ottawa-Hull, for instance. The national accounts had thus acquired an additional zoom lens, one that enabled policymakers to move beyond the big picture and to home in on the productivity, employment, investment, and regional implications of macro change in the economy.[22]

Canada has thus built a System of National Accounts that over a half-century has dexterously stretched, rather like Saran Wrap, over the country's changing economic needs. The country has constructed a system of useful economic information that has informed its policymaking and Canadians' general sense of citizenship. In doing so, Canada has lived up to the ambition of the United Nations' "fundamental principles of official statistics," that of creating statistics that are "an indispensable element in the information system of a democratic society." As McGill economist E.F. Beach told the Glassco Royal Commission in 1961: "The Bureau appears as a kind of conscience of the country."[23]

In this, the nation has drawn powerful inspiration from economic thinkers beyond its borders – Kuznets, Keynes, Stone, Leontief, to mention the great masters. Canada has also brought its own theoretical perspective to the process. Simon Goldberg understood the imperatives of statistical integration, a talent that propelled him to the head of the United Nations' Statistical Division as the culmination of his career. Canadians continue to pioneer the theoretical frontier of national accounting. Erwin Diewert of the University of British Columbia has done groundbreaking work in explaining the biases inherent in index numbers, which are crucial to cost of living analysis. In 1995, for instance, Diewert was invited to give evidence to the US Senate on bias in the US consumer price index. He was the only non-American to be called. In the words of several of his admiring colleagues, Diewert's "career has been a personal quest to develop tools for economic modeling and econometrics that meet the needs of applied analysis for real world economics problems."[24] Other Canadians share the theoretical limelight with Diewert. Richard Lipsey at Simon Fraser University has led Canadians to many economic frontiers, most recently by suggesting that they need to pay much more attention to technology's powerful

Field Day, 2006: Canada's national accountants picnic on the shores of the Ottawa River. "There is no more effective quietus to economic quackery and misguided pressures," R.H. Coats wrote in 1941, "than statistical fact."[26] The task continues. Courtesy of Statistics Canada.

and transformative effects on long-term growth. "Dr. Lipsey," the *Globe and Mail* has suggested, "has a knack for devising theories that incorporate the usual math, Greek letters, charts and graphs, but also include a heavy dose of reality."[25] Canadians can also take pride in the lifetime work of another west coaster, Anthony Scott of the University of British Columbia, who since his pioneering doctoral research at the London School of Economics in the 1950s has reminded economists that resource depletion is as important as resource consumption in the economic equation.

But, as Anthony Scott admits, it has been the "ingenious insiders" at Tunney's Pasture who have really given Canadian national accounting its distinctive flair. From the "rough stabs" of George Luxton and Agatha Chapman down to the intricacies of modern I/O tables and quarterly GDP estimates, Canadian national accountants have displayed a canny knack for finding the middle ground between high theory and practical application. From her office in Washington, Lucie Laliberté sums up the instincts instilled during her twenty-five years at Tunney's Pasture: "Measure what you can measure, and then make intelligent adjustments."[27]

National accountants the world over are still making rough stabs. There is a restless quality to national accounting. The distinguished French statistician André Vanoli has been central to the unfolding of national accounting for decades and senses its protean quality: at the end of his nearly 500-page history of the craft, he concludes that "national accounting is far from being at cruising speed."[28] Nobody knows this better than Karen Wilson, the current director general of Statistics Canada's National Accounts Division. Wilson manages the day-to-day operation of the accounts, a job she took over in 2001, following the professional footsteps of Stewart Wells and Kishori Lal. She is the first woman to hold the post. In the early years of Canada's national accounts, women statisticians, perhaps sensing that they were aspiring to make their mark in a male world, tended to forsake marriage, instead "marrying" their work.[29] Wilson is by contrast a working mother who has balanced the demands of obtaining economics degrees from Waterloo and Carleton while raising two children at home with her duties as a civil servant. (She recounts realizing that her day job was beginning to permeate her home life when she overheard her five year old offer her three year old a "billion dollars" in return for surrendering a toy.)[30]

As director general, Wilson has to keep her eye on both the "old" and the "new" national accounts. In February 2006, for instance, just as Jullion and his staff began piecing together their quarterly GDP estimate, Wilson boarded a plane for Frankfurt, Germany. There, she donned her hat as a member of the Advisory Experts Group (AEG), the blue-ribbon panel of statisticians empowered by the multilateral Inter-Secretariat Working Group on National Accounts to prepare the next revision of the SNA. The members of the AEG are chosen for their expertise, not their nationality. Frankfurt was to be the last intensive session of fine-tuning before a package of recommended changes to the SNA was to be presented to the five partners overseeing the SNA – the UN, Organisation for Economic Co-operation and Development (OECD), World Bank, IMF, and Commission of the European Communities – in 2007. Thus, for eight intense days, Wilson and her fellow experts were cloistered in a meeting room at the European Central Bank. Experts from countries with less developed statistical systems were invited to share in the deliberation; the AEG must always keep an eye on the broad applicability of their revisions. In all, twenty-seven experts filled the room. As she had in the 1993 revision, American Carol Carson was acting as the project manager of what is being called the 2008 SNA; hers is the challenge of nudging often disparate expert opinion into consensus.

From their European perch, Wilson and her colleagues were acutely aware that the world expects changes in the SNA. Waves of economic change have rolled through the economies of the developed world since the last SNA revision in 1993. The old smokestack economy in Europe and North America has been eroded by freer trade. Whole industries have been repositioned on the world map by globalization. A so-called "new economy" that thrives on services and intangible goods like knowledge and technological know-how has surged into existence. It has also provoked dilemmas for national accountants. Is a computer database packed with marketing data actually "worth" anything in GDP terms? Is the value of the Nike brand name – symbolized by the famous swoosh logo – simply an intermediate expense that reflects the cost of obtaining a patent or is the research behind its development a

---

Googling the Economy

There was a time when the national accounts were taught as foundation knowledge to all young economists. Beginning in the 1950s, a chapter on the national accounts was the obligatory starting point in most macroeconomic textbooks. Since then the national accounts have slowly faded out of university teaching and have increasingly been relegated to the sidelines of textbooks. The accounts have, in effect, become a "given" in our economic consciousness, assumed knowledge available at the click of a computer key. This fate perhaps salutes their success in informing our economic citizenship. But many "old-time" national accountants decry this decline, arguing that young economists must understand the macroeconomic architecture of the economy before they can really comprehend their craft. Economics, they go on to argue, has become too driven by theory, too "mathematized," and too reliant on computer modelling.

Statistics Canada has nonetheless gone to considerable lengths to reach out to Canadians with its national accounts message in new electronic ways. Interested Canadians can go to "The Canadian Economy Online" at http://canadianeconomy.gc.ca for an excellent introduction to the Canadian economy. Through the agency's home site at http://www.statcan.ca, readers can access a "National Economic Accounts" module for a glossary of terms and methodologies as well as news on latest research and data. The same site also provides access to the *Daily* and access to a catalogue of Statistics Canada publications. The *Canadian Economic Observer* may be accessed at http://www.statcan.ca/english/ads/11-010-XPB/index.htm.

capital asset worth millions? Globalization has also galvanically altered how money flows between economies; new financial instruments carry money around the world in ways that established balance of payments barely recognize. For example, is a cash withdrawal off a Canadian debit card at an automated teller machine in the Punjab a tourist expenditure or a cash transfer from an Indo-Canadian in Toronto to a relative in India? And the old, usually bilateral flow of remittances between companies operating across borders has now become a tangled (many allege deliberately so) skein of financial arrangements between enterprises that are more transnational than national. Economists politely label these arrangements "special purpose entities": the public sees them as offshore enterprises that seem to escape national surveillance. For national accountants, the question is whether all the twists and turns of globalization and the new economy can be fitted into the existing national accounting box.

In 1936 Wassily Leontief castigated the prevailing economic orthodoxy for the "empty boxes" of its theory. Keynes had earlier assailed the "obstinate adherence to ancient rules of thumb" that had paralyzed Western economies in the Depression. As the new century dawned, Karen Wilson and the Advisory Expert Group faced another challenge. Did the SNA capture the recent seismic shifts in the world economy? Were these shifts permanent or ephemeral? Could the boundaries of production be shifted toward measuring intangible economic activity without destroying the workability of established national accounting? Even as it met in Frankfurt, the AEG was reminded of these imperative questions. *Business Week* told its readers that "the U.S. is well down the road to becoming a knowledge economy, one driven by ideas and innovation" and that "it's a lot easier counting how many widgets the nation produces in a year than quantifying the creation and marketing of knowledge."[31]

If, the magazine argued, the Bureau of Economic Analysis in Washington took account of these "missing pieces" – investment in education, research and development, the export of expertise – in its "gloomy numbers show," then the American economy might appear "stronger" than the national accounts suggested.[32] Even the *Economist* entered the debate: "It's high time that economists looked at more than just GDP." Citing a recent OECD report, the venerable British magazine argued that the time had arrived for the GDP to take into account noneconomic factors such as "leisure time, income inequality and the quality of the environment." If, for instance, the French penchant for long summer holidays and American workaholism were weighed as factors contributing to or detracting from an individual's wellbeing, then European "economic" performance might not seem to lag behind that of the United States. Similarly, if adjustment were made for the range of national income distributions, then countries like France and Britain might in fact be more "successful" than the United States. Without these adjustments to modern sensibilities, the *Economist* complained, orthodox GDP-style calculations in fact stood for "grossly distorted picture."[33]

Facing such esteemed criticism, the AEG continued its work. Radical reworking of the SNA was not an option. The existing accounts buttressed too many public policies and attitudes. Instead, the task was to stretch or, in Carol Carson's words, "tweak" the 1993 SNA to accommodate change. Indeed, the goal of the group has become not the creation of a 2008 SNA but more the working up of a first revision of the 1993 SNA. A menu of forty-four substantive issues has been drawn up for consideration, some involving a substantial repositioning of the boundary of production – the defining qualification for measurement in the SNA – and others involving the fine-tuning of existing standards.[34] In Frankfurt a consensus on probable change was beginning to take shape. Many of the changes had been worked up and groomed by small subgroups of experts. These groups were named for the cities around the globe where they first convened. Not all were dedicated to national accounting problems, but all addressed statistical impasses. The "Canberra II" group, of which Karen Wilson had been a member, focused on the question of whether the intangible capital – ideas, databases, research and development – that is so central to the dynamism of the new economy should now be treated as a lasting capital asset in the national accounts. Hitherto, such capital had been treated as an intermediate cost of producing something.

Once a city group reports the diagnosis of a particular issue to the Inter-Secretariat Working Group in New York, its proposals are posted on the website of the United Nations' Statistical Division, thereby allowing UN members to review the proposal and to comment on their willingness to adopt it. Each nation's reaction is then posted on the division's website. It is a creeping process of consensus building. But as Carol Carson, the ringmaster of the whole process, suggests with some pride, it allows for "real intellectual reciprocity," and since the onus is on ensuring the workability of each proposed change, it tends to draw on statisticians' professionalism rather than exciting stubborn national resistance.

Moreover, within the dialogue, nations with established national accounting systems are able to work out their innate conservative resistance to change and, in worrying the issue through, to elucidate its rationale for UN members with less developed national accounting systems. If an issue is too unwieldy and encounters resistance, it is reserved for future reconsideration, usually by a subgroup of experts. Carson points, for instance, to the rise of satellite accounts in the 1990s as a good example of how the AEG has eased change into the mainstream of national accounting. Tourism statistics were given coherence and utility in freestanding satellite accounts without debasing the core integrity of the accounts. They acted as a "testing ground" for statistics that spoke to an increasingly important global industry. Statisticians got "to have their cake and eat it too" with satellite accounts, she wryly observes.[35]

Thus the periodic revisions to the System of National Accounts since its first iteration in 1947 – when just a handful of developed nations were corralled into agreement by Britain's Richard Stone – has developed into a model of multilateral collaboration that in its quiet, deliberative way has pushed the frontier of national accounting forward in method and inclusion for over a half-century. Few other international conventions can boast as much.

For Carson, there were moments at the Frankfurt meeting when she felt "almost lyrical" about the progress of the AEG since 1993.[36] Once again, the new economy provides two telling examples of this pattern of revamping the SNA. The meteoric rise of "high-tech" companies in the 1990s created acute employment problems given the challenges in recruiting and retaining competent workers. One solution was to offer employee stock options (ESOs) – that is, the right of employees to purchase stock in the company at a fixed price at some later date once they have proved their loyalty and utility to the company. While ESOs were not invented by the high-tech revolution, they surged in popularity because of it. From the perspective of the national accounts, ESOs had the effect of introducing a new, somewhat hidden production cost. The 1993 SNA made no mention of ESOs. But, as the new century dawned, national accountants became aware that ESOs represented a huge new form of wealth in society. How should they be evaluated? And when? Did ESOs become actual wealth or compensation when the right was issued at the time of initial employment, or when the right was actually vested in the employee's name some years later, or when the right was actually exercised (i.e., sold)?

This dilemma was acutely felt in Canada, where the Silicon Revolution had taken full flight. In reaction, the federal budget in 2000 amended the Income Tax Act to tax capital gains on ESOs when they were exercised while allowing their holders to apply for a deferral of the tax impact of the benefit. Even though the high-tech bubble burst in 2001, statisticians continued to grapple with the issue. Careful consideration by Eurostat and then the AEG groomed the issue to the point that the 2008 revision of the SNA will contain the recommendation that ESOs be registered in the national accounts as labour compensation valued at the time they are vested in the employee's name. "The United States strongly supports the initiatives to improve the accounting for employee stock options," Washington informed the United Nations. "There have been important changes in the economic environment in this area, and improving the national accounting treatment is important to the national account users." South Africa, by way of contrast, also supported the change, but added, perhaps predictably: "As yet we do not have the statistics on employee stock options but will start with the collection of related information in the forthcoming round of economic surveys."[37]

The new economy has insinuated itself into the revised SNA in other ways. The new economy is fuelled by ideas, which have never been treated in economic accounting with the same weight as hard, cold assets like machinery and real estate. But intensive research and development lie at the heart of the new economy. As any observer intuitively senses, the knowledge economy's most precious asset is its intellectual capital. But the national accounts treat money spent on generating ideas – research and development – as a straightforward intermediate expense, a transitory cost of doing business. Growth today comes as much from knowledge as it does from building factories. In the words of Robert Solow, the Nobel-winning theorist of growth, "you see the computer everywhere except in the productivity data."[38] More impatient observers of the economy have begun to suggest that there is unmeasured "dark matter" – the intangible worth of Microsoft or Boeing research, for instance – that makes the American economy stronger than the traditional national account numbers might indicate.[39]

Experts the world round have wrestled with the challenge of giving better economic weight to knowledge. The issue is thorny. The solution might be to recategorize research and development as capital in the national accounts – to bring it within the conventional asset boundary and treat it like any other hard asset in the economy. But where and when would that boundary be drawn? Much research and development is highly esoteric and leads nowhere in practical terms. How long would an idea have to be applied before it could be considered a lasting aspect of production? Is the Plato scholar toiling away in ancient texts an addition to productive national knowledge? The question of research and development is as conceptually slippery as it gets for national accountants. Steve Landefeld, who heads the Bureau of Economic Analysis in Washington, admits that he feels "discomfort" over how exactly the knowledge economy can be consistently measured and brought into his national income statistics. What weight should statisticians give to all the capital flows that underlie the intensive research propelling the development of a drug like Prozac? How do you give weight in the national accounts to the capital stock of good, old-fashioned American know-how? How do you give economic weight to the technical inspirations of a Thomas Edison or a Steve Jobs? Nonetheless, the Bureau of Economic Analysis is determined to construct a "new architecture"[40] for its accounts and has been actively building a research and development satellite account. This spirit is now reflected in the Frankfurt consensus of the AEG: research and development will henceforth be considered part of a nation's capital formation. In classic national accounts fashion, the boundary of production will be moved, this time to capture the economic impact of an intangible asset.

The Frankfurt consensus contains other boundary shifts and fine-tuning. Defence capital expenditures, once considered simply a part of government's current expenditure, have been moved to capital formation in the post-Cold War world. In future, any military expenditure with a useful life of more than a year will be treated as capital expenditure. Catastrophic events like hurricanes and terrorist attacks have provoked an adjustment in how insurance industry production is measured. The attack on New York on 11 September 2001, for instance, produced a paradoxical outcome for the insurance industry. Insurance production or output was traditionally calculated by deducting claims from premiums collected. But the abnormal severity of the attack on the World Trade Centre shocked this calculation, yielding a negative output for the insurance industry because claims temporarily swamped premiums. In reality, insurance premium pay-outs were actually putting money back into the American economy as New York scrambled to repair the huge hole that had been punched in its human and physical foundation. In the future, catastrophic events hitting the industry will be "smoothed out" by applying a twenty-year average to the year of the aberration, thereby removing the volatility from macroeconomic performance.

Thus the AEG holds its mirror up to the events of a changing world. With his acerbic wit, John Maynard Keynes famously observed in *The General Theory* that "practical men, who believe themselves to be exempt from any intellectual influences, are usually the slaves of some defunct economist."[41] Since the crisis of the Depression, national accountants have time and again displayed their practical bent. In doing so, however, they have never been slaves to defunct authority. They have always moved the boundaries of their thinking and their measurement as times dictated, always after cautious deliberation but always in a way that has kept them connected to the societies that they serve. Although the national accounts may appear to be a maze of "arcane concepts," as American economists Paul Samuelson and William Nordhaus have remarked, they are "truly among the great inventions of the twentieth century."[42] Indeed, national accounting was one of the great intellectual adventures of that century. For the first time since primitive barter societies existed, civilized people were able to look *inside* the economy that supported their existence, measure it, and then proceed to build a better life on the basis of the information.

And Canadians have long been primary beneficiaries of this new insight. Since the dark days of the Second World War, when John J. Deutsch and George Luxton first tried to pry the lid off Canada's national income, Canadians have proved remarkably adept at understanding how national income flows through their society and at applying this knowledge to the construction of a better society. Karen Wilson believes that the Canadian achievement in national accounting is "unique and amazing." Other nations have approximated the Canadian model of a strongly centralized and integrated set of national accounts, but not one has equalled the breadth and thoroughness of the Canadian system. The British, Australians, and Dutch all share with Canada a similar correlation between good economic statistics and a relatively stable and affluent society. But only Canada boasts a System of National Accounts that carries economic data so tightly from its gathering in the homes, factories, and fields of the nation right on through to its delivery in analyzed form to the citizens and policymakers of the nation. Canadians are today one website away from a set of national economic accounts that captures their economic existence through the full spectrum of income and expenditure, balance of payments, income-output tables, monthly GDP estimates, productivity studies, and national balance sheets. The national accounts offer every Canadian and Canadian society at large the opportunity to perform what the English moral philosopher Jeremy Bentham described as the "calculus of felicity," a calculation of the material benefits of existence.[43]

And what of the twenty-first century? The national accounts have never purported, as Deutsch made clear back in 1941, to capture the entire "sum of the satisfactions" in Canadian society. The accounts have succeeded in measuring the monied transactions that take place within Canada and, on occasion, in imputing hard statistical value to soft activities that sometimes impinge on Canadians' economic life. But since the 1970s there has been constant pressure on the accounts to cross the frontier into welfare economics – to stretch their scope and method to embrace the "social capital" of Canadian society and the "natural capital" that makes Canadians' way of life sustainable.[44] "The national accounts," Philip Smith frankly admits, "offer a solid, time-tested framework and information base for understanding and managing market-derived income and produced wealth, but they do not presently encompass natural, human and social capital."[45]

For two decades Statistics Canada has with increasing urgency been trying to devise this yardstick and to put it into use as a new benchmark of society's development. Measuring man's use, and degradation, of the environment has steadily risen in the Canadian consciousness. But the "environment" is an amorphous concept, one that has very often defied the national accountant's desire for precise measurement. Calibrating humanity's use of the natural world involves many variables; it is never a simple reciprocity of user and resource. Any body of water, for instance, has multiple users – urban water works, transportation companies, irrigating farmers, power companies, pleasure seekers, fishermen, and not the least, aquatic life. Each of these brings a different notion of sustainability to the estimation of water's quality and abundance. Still, there has been progress. Together with Environment Canada and Health Canada, Statistics Canada now publishes a water quality indicator – based on samples taken from 345 water sampling sites across the country – that provides a mathematical tool for reporting ambient water quality. Water can now be ranked from "poor" to "excellent" in terms of its ability to sustain aquatic life. Similar work is under way on the measurement of greenhouse gas emissions in Canada and of how Canadian households consume energy and nonrenewable resources.[46]

Framing all this effort is the strategic challenge of trying to quantify Canada's natural capital. How long will our forests last? How fertile is our soil? How can we use such figures to add a depletion dimension

to our economic calculations? There is now a growing recognition –
one supported with federal money and interdepartmental support – that
sustainable development in Canada will hinge on knowing the inventory of natural wealth that remains to be harvested for man's use. This
task is daunting. Robert Smith, who heads the expanding Environmental Accounts and Statistics Branch of the "new" national accounts, acknowledges that the data are not as yet "very robust." There is "no
road map" by which to plot these "unique and complex" matters.
Smith's wish for Canada is that environmental accounting will one day
become "part of the fabric of life" in Canada. There are promising
signs. There are stirrings elsewhere in the world. Statistics Canada, for
instance, has signed a five-year agreement with China to facilitate its
development of environmental statistics. Sixteen of the world's twenty-
five most polluted cities, Smith notes, are in China.[47] Standards for environmental accounting are being developed; the five charter members
behind the SNA 1993 produced guidelines in 2003 for "integrated environmental and economic accounting" that will shape the future building of national accounts.[48] On the other hand, the United States has yet
to even begin the arduous task of finding a niche for environmental
measurement in its national accounts.[49]

If Canadians are inching closer to a better appreciation of their natural wealth, so too are they expanding their knowledge of their social
capital. Statistics Canada, for instance, has investigated the role of nonprofit and volunteering in Canadian society, using a satellite account to
construct a statistical picture of activities that are never reflected in paycheques but that provide a crucial glue for the social cohesion of Canadian society – "doing good." A 2004 study revealed that if one were to
impute a replacement cost value to nonprofit and volunteer work and
activities – such as donations in kind and voluntary labour in social
services – the Canadian GDP would be expanded by 8.6%, or $61.8 bil-
lion in 1999.[50] At the same time, the Unpaid Work Analysis Branch of
the national accounts continues to track labour and social phenomena
that have traditionally never surfaced in the income and expenditure
accounts. The Baby Boom's impending mass retirement is demanding
statistical attention in Canada. A recent study has suggested that the
nation's aging population will travel an increasing number of paths in
its transition to retirement.[51] Work has begun on constructing a pension
satellite account that will attempt to articulate the potential stock and
flows of pension funds that will be available to support the Baby Boom
in its golden years.

Canadians are therefore beginning to glimpse the new statistical face of hitherto intangible aspects of their society. They are also beginning to comprehend Canada in a new environmental light, one that stresses depletion as much as it stresses consumption. So far, however, these are only fleeting glimpses that in no way approximate the kind of pervasive totality that the old national accounts have supplied for the past half-century. This, no doubt, reflects the fact that Canadians are still not entirely sure where the new national accounts should lead them. Indeed, as long as they continue to agonize over their collective responsibility to the environment and over the sustainability of their social capital, there can be no encompassing statistical system to capture a national consensus that has yet to define itself.

It bears reflection that the old national accounts were born out of the absolute desperation of the Depression and the Second World War. In 1945 Canada embraced national accounting because it had exhausted the old alternatives. There could be no going back to the staggering unemployment of the Depression. There was at the same time near universal agreement that economic stability and sustained employment should be the abiding goals of society. And national accountants obliged this sentiment with numbers that built sound policy and social equity. Canada is a better country for their effort. Their numbers have never allowed Canadians to capture the entire sum of their satisfactions, but they have always been sufficient to reveal the dynamic core of Canada's economic society.

After all, national accounting can respond only to society's wishes. It cannot *lead* society. In the Depression theorists like Kuznets, Keynes, and Leontief responded to Western societies' hankering for a new way to manage their economic affairs. Practitioners like George Luxton, Agatha Chapman, and Simon Goldberg then carried the theory into practice. The transition was never easy. Two weeks before his sudden death in January 1945, young George Luxton obliged an invitation from the Canadian Youth Commission to speak on the topic "Wanted: Jobs after the War." "During the depression," he told his Ottawa audience, "attempts were made to reassert the position of the national government; efforts were made to capture a new national outlook; but it was a period of constant frustration."[52] Within months of his death, however, the numbers that Luxton had worked up on national income over at the Dominion Bureau of Statistics served to break down this frustration and open the way for a stable and prosperous postwar Canadian society.

As the twenty-first century unfolds, it remains to be seen whether the earth's deteriorating environment or the dramatic fraying of the social fabric will in some way coalesce to provoke a crisis of similar magnitude to that of the Depression and the traumatic war that followed it. If it does, history suggests that the national accounts will find a way to supply the appropriate numbers – to give societies another "new national outlook." Challenge, as always, lies ahead.

Notes

ACKNOWLEDGMENTS

1 André Vanoli, *A History of National Accounting* (Amsterdam: IOS Press, 2005), 490.

INTRODUCTION

1 CBC Business News, 21 April 2005; *National Post*, 9 June 2005; *The Epoch Times*, 25–31 March 2005; *Globe and Mail*, 16 March 2005; *Globe and Mail*, 24 December 2004.
2 Dominion Bureau of Statistics, *Annual Report* (Ottawa: King's Printer, 1919), 8.
3 "The Work of the Dominion Bureau of Statistics," CKCO radio address, January 1947, in Library and Archives Canada (LAC), Dominion Bureau of Statistics and Statistics Canada Collection, RG 31, vol. 1421.
4 Darrell Huff, *How to Lie with Statistics* (New York: Norton, 1993), 3, 100.
5 Sir Claus Moser, "Statistics and Public Policy," *Journal of the Royal Statistical Society* 143 (1980): 1–31 at 1.
6 Speech on radio station CKCO, Ottawa, January 1947.
7 Sir Francis Galton, *Natural Inheritance* (London: Macmillan and Son, 1889), 62–3.
8 Arthur L. Bowley, "The Improvement of Official Statistics," *Journal of the Royal Statistical Society*, part 3, September 1908, 478.
9 Robert Hamilton Coats, *First Annual Report of the Dominion Statistician* (Ottawa: King's Printer, 1919), 8, 51.
10 J.M. Keynes, *How to Pay for the War: A Radical Plan for the Chancellor of the Exchequer* (New York: Harcourt, Brace, 1940), 13. Keynes had originally published these thoughts in the *Times* of London in the fall of 1939.
11 Paul A. Samuelson and William D. Nordhaus, *Economics*, 15th ed. (New York: McGraw-Hill, 1995), 402.

12 David C. Colander and Harry Landreth, eds, *The Coming of Keynesianism to America: Conversations with the Founders of Keynesian Economics* (London and Brookfield: Edward Elgar, 1996), Galbraith interview, 141.

13 The prize is actually called the Bank of Sweden Prize in Economic Sciences in Memory of Alfred Nobel. Citations for all laureates are listed at http://www.nobelprize.org.

14 See http://unstats.un.org/unsd/1993/introduction.asp.

15 See the United Nations Statistical Commission, "Fundamental Principles of Official Statistics," http://www.instats.un.org/unsd/methods/htm.

16 Walter Lippman, quoted in John J. Deutsch, *Canadian Economic Policy since the War* (Montreal: Canadian Trade Committee, 1966), 132–3.

17 Marilyn Waring, *If Women Counted: A New Feminist Economics* (New York: HarperCollins, 1990), xvii, 2–3.

18 William Nordhaus and James Tobin, "Is Growth Obsolete?" in *Economic Growth: Fiftieth Anniversary Colloquium V*, 1–80 (New York and London: National Bureau of Economic Research and Columbia University Press, 1972).

19 Kenneth R. Boulding, "The Economics of the Coming Spaceship Earth," in Robert Costanza, Charles Perrings, and Cutler Cleveland, eds, *The Development of Ecological Economics*, 3-12 (Cheltenham and Brookfield: Elgar Reference Collection, 1997), 12.

20 Richard Lipsey, *An Introduction to Positive Economics* (London: Wiedenfeld and Nicholson, 1963), 360, original emphasis; Lipsey interview, 2006.

21 See http://www.unstats.un.org/unsd/statcom/commission.htm.

22 *Economist*, 11 September 1993, 65.

23 John Baldwin interview, 2005.

24 Richard Ruggles, quoted in Sir Claus Moser et al., *Statistics Canada: Methodological Review*, March 1980, Statistics Canada (STC) 2589E.

25 *Economist*, 11 September 1993, 65.

26 Statens Offentliga Utredningar, *Development and Improvement of Economic Statistics* (Stockholm: Swedish Government Reports, 2003), 18.

27 Philip Smith, "Rethinking the System of National Accounts: What Is Needed for the 21st Century?" unpublished paper, 1 October 2002, STC.

28 Simon Reisman interview, 2005.

29 Carol Carson interview, 2006.

30 Sir Francis Galton, quoted in Huff, *How to Lie*, 3.

CHAPTER ONE

1 See Ernest Scott, *Australia during the War* (Sydney: Angus and Robertson, 1938), 309–11.

2 J.C. Stamp, "The Wealth and Income of the Chief Powers," *Journal of the*

Royal Statistical Society 82 (July 1919): 441–89 at 442; J.C. Stamp, "Methods Used in Different Countries for Estimating National Income," *Journal of the Royal Statistical Society,* part 3 (1934): 423–66.

3 R.H. Coats, "Beginnings of Canadian Statistics," *Canadian Historical Review* 27, no. 2 (June 1946): 109–30 at 120–1.

4 R.H. Coats, "The Place of Statistics in National Administration," *Transactions of the Royal Society of Canada,* sec. 2 (1929): 81–93 at 81.

5 R.H. Coats, *Wholesale Prices in Canada, 1890–1909: Special Report* (Ottawa: King's Printer, 1910), 490.

6 R.H. Coats, *The Rise in Prices and the Cost of Living in Canada, 1900–1914: A Statistical Explanation of Economic Causes* (Ottawa: King's Printer, 1915), 28.

7 See R.H. Coats et al., *Report of Departmental Commission on the Official Statistics of Canada* (Ottawa: King's Printer, 1912), "Preface"; copy in Library and Archives Canada (LAC), RG 31, vol. 1420.

8 Ibid., "Preface."

9 Sir George Foster to R.H. Coats, 7 July 1915, LAC, RG 31, acc. 89–90/133, box 8, file 834.

10 See R.H. Coats, "The Wealth of Canada and Other Nations," *Journal of the Canadian Bankers' Association* (October 1919): 80-6. Coats was in fact modifying Josiah Stamp's earlier estimation of Canadian wealth, which had appeared in the same journal in January 1916.

11 R.H. Coats to Sydney Fisher, 7 December 1915; R.H. Coats to Sir George Foster, 15 December 1915; both in LAC, RG 31, acc. 89–90/133, box 10, file 877.

12 W. Stewart Wallace, ed., *Memoirs of the Rt. Hon. Sir George Foster* (Toronto: Macmillan, 1933), 166.

13 Dominion Bureau of Statistics, *Annual Report* (Ottawa: King's Printer, 1919), "Preface."

14 *Financial Post,* October 1935.

15 R.H. Coats to A.E. Sproul, 22 May 1919, LAC, RG 31, acc. 89–90/133, box 10; *Sun* (New York), 27 May 1919.

16 See, for instance, *Toronto Globe,* 22 May 1925.

17 *Report on the National Wealth of Canada and Its Provinces as in 1929,* Dominion Bureau of Statistics (DBS) publication 11-D-20 (1931), 1.

18 Richard Fitz Nigel, "Preface," in *Dialogue Concerning the Exchequer,* trans. of *Dialogus de Saccario* by Charles Johnson (Oxford: Clarendon, 1983).

19 See, for instance, Leonard J. Savage, *The Foundations of Statistics* (Chicago: University of Chicago Press, 1954); and Mary Poovey, *A History of the Modern Fact: Problems of Knowledge in the Sciences of Wealth and Society* (Chicago: University of Chicago Press, 1998).

20 J. Spedding, R. Ellis, and D. Heath, eds, *Works of Francis Bacon* (London: Longman, 1870), 51.

21 Thomas Hobbes, *Leviathan* (Cambridge: Cambridge University Press, 1991), 35.

22 David Salsburg, *The Lady Tasting Tea: How Statistics Revolutionized Science in the Twentieth Century* (New York: W.H. Freeman, 2001), ix.

23 See John W. Kendrick, "The Historical Development of National-Income Accounts," *History of Political Economy* 2 (1970): 284–315; George Jaszi, "The Concept of National Income and National Product with Special Reference to Government Transactions" (PhD thesis, Harvard University, 1946); Angus Maddison, "Measuring and Interpreting World Economic Performance, 1500–2001," *Review of Income and Wealth*, ser. 51 (March 2005): 1–35; and Paul Studenski, *The Income of Nations: Theory, Measurement, and Analysis, Past and Present: A Study in Applied Economics and Statistics* (New York: New York University Press, 1958).

24 William Petty, *Political Anatomy of Ireland* (written 1672, published 1691).

25 William Petty, quoted by Alessandro Roncaglia, entry on William Petty, in J. Eatwell, M. Milgate, and P. Newman, eds, *The New Palgrave: A Dictionary of Economics* (London: Macmillan, 1988), 854.

26 Studenski, *Income of Nations*, 27.

27 Crawford Goodwin, *Canadian Economic Thought: The Political Economy of a Developing Nation, 1714–1914* (Durham: Duke University Press, 2000), 188.

28 S.F. Wise, "Robert Fleming Gourlay," in Francis G. Halpenny, ed., *The Dictionary of Canadian Biography*, vol. 9, 330–6 (Toronto: University of Toronto Press, 1976); Robert Gourlay, *Statistical Account of Upper Canada*, abridged and introduced by S.R. Mealing (Toronto, McClelland and Stewart, 1974).

29 See David A. Worton, *The Dominion Bureau of Statistics: A History of Canada's Central Statistical Office and Its Antecedents, 1841–1972* (Montreal and Kingston: McGill-Queen's University Press, 1998), ch. 1.

30 See ibid., ch. 2.

31 Richard Cartwright, quoted in Goodwin, *Canadian Economic Thought*, 66–7.

32 Ibid.

33 *Mechanical and Manufacturing Industries of Canada by Groups: Special Report on the Census Returns* (Ottawa: Queen's Printer, 1895), 4.

34 *Census and Statistics Bulletin II: Manufactures of Canada* (Ottawa: King's Printer, 1907), ix.

35 Canada, *Mechanical and Manufacturing Industries of Canada* (Ottawa: Queen's Printer, 1895), 5.

36 *Survey of Production in Canada, 1920 and Later* (Ottawa: Dominion Bureau of Statistics, 1923), 2.

37 Coats to Sydney Fisher, 7 December 1915, LAC, RG 31, acc. 89–90/133.

38 D.A. MacGibbon, *An Introduction to Economics* (Toronto: Macmillan, 1937), 21.

39 Alfred Marshall, quoted in Studenski, *Income of Nations*, 4, 20.

40 Alfred Marshall, *Industry and Trade* (London: Macmillan, 1923), 6.

41 R.H. Coats, *Memorandum on the Organization and Work of the Dominion Bureau of Statistics with Special Reference to Future Development* (Ottawa: King's Printer, 1921), 3.

42 *Scan*, Statistics Canada's employee magazine, May 1975.

43 Coats to L.C. Moore, private secretary to the prime minister, 23 January 1923, LAC, RG 31, acc. 89–90/133, box 5.

44 R.H. Coats to Eric Adams, 19 May 1933, LAC, RG 31, acc. 89–90/133, box 10.

45 *Annual Report of the Royal Bank of Canada* (1928), 8.

46 W.C. Clark, "Business Research and Business Statistics," *Journal of the Canadian Bankers' Association* (January 1921): 206–16 at 211.

47 See W.I. King, *Wealth and Income of the People of the United States* (New York: Macmillan, 1915); and Frederick Macaulay and Oswald Knauth, *Income in the United States: Its Amount and Distribution, 1909–1919* (New York, NBER, 1922).

48 R.H. Coats to Lt.-Col. Henry Willis-O'Connor, 13 January 1931, LAC, RG 31, acc. 89–90/133, box 5.

49 I am grateful to Dr H.B. Neatby for this vignette.

50 Andrew Mellon, quoted in Richard Norton Smith, *An Uncommon Man: The Triumph of Herbert Hoover* (New York: Simon and Schuster, 1989), 118–19.

51 See, for instance, R.H. Coats to L.C. Moore, private secretary to the prime minister, 23 January 1923, LAC, RG 31, acc. 89–90, box 6.

52 *Report of the Royal Commission on Price Spreads* (Ottawa: King's Printer, 1935), 9.

53 F. Maclure Sclanders to R.H. Coats, 27 November 1937, LAC, RG 31, vol. 1410.

54 H.G.L. Strange to R.H. Coats, 4 December 1937; R.H. Coats to H.G.L. Strange, 6 December 1937; both in LAC, RG 31, vol. 1410.

55 See LAC, RG 31, vol. 1408, file 1466.

56 *Report of the Royal Commission on Dominion-Provincial Relations: Book II – Recommendations* (Ottawa: King's Printer, 1940), 9–10.

57 *Report ... Price Spreads*, 137, 273.

58 Evidence of Tim Buck, Royal Commission on Dominion-Provincial Relations, LAC, RG 33, reel C6991, 9726.

59 Ibid., 3847–9.

60 J.M. Keynes, quoted in Louis W. Pauly, *The League of Nations and the*

Foreshadowing of the International Monetary Fund (Princeton: Department of Economics, 1996), 24.

61 J.M. Keynes, *How to Pay for the War* (New York: Harcourt, Brace, 1940), 13.

62 Simon Kuznets, quoted in *Current Biography* (1972): 266.

63 Wassily Leontief, "Quantitative Input: Output Relations in the Economic System of the United States," *Review of Economic Statistics* 18, no. 1 (August 1936): 105–16 at 105.

64 See Robert Skidelsky, *John Maynard Keynes*, vol. 3, *Fighting for Britain, 1937–1946* (London: Macmillan, 2000).

65 *Times* (London), 13 September 1939.

66 Colin Clark, *National Income, 1924–1931* (London: Macmillan, 1932), vi.

67 Simon Kuznets, quoted in *Current Biography* (1972): 266.

68 See Carol Carson, "The History of the United States National Income and Product Accounts: The Development of an Analytical Tool," *Review of Income and Wealth*, no. 2 (June 1975): 153–81.

69 See J.W. Duncan and W.C. Sheldon, *Revolution in United States Government Statistics, 1926–1976* (Washington, DC: United States Department of Commerce, 1978).

70 *The National Income of Canada*, DBS publication 13-D-56 (1934), "Preface."

71 See Bank of Nova Scotia, *Monthly Review*, November 1935, December 1935, May 1937, and July 1938.

72 D.C. MacGregor, J.B. Rutherford, G.E. Britnell, and J.J. Deutsch, *National Income: A Study Prepared for the Royal Commission on Dominion-Provincial Relations* (Ottawa: King's Printer, 1939), 11.

73 Alex Skelton to D.C. MacGregor, 23 March 1938, LAC, RG 33, ser. 23, vol. 54.

74 See Doug Owram, "The 'New Millenialists': Economics in the 1930s," in *The Government Generation: Canadian Intellectuals and the State, 1900–1945*, 193–220 (Toronto: University of Toronto Press, 1986).

75 D.C. MacGregor to Alex Skelton, n.d., LAC, RG 31, acc. 89–90, box 10.

76 MacGregor, Rutherford, Britnell, and Deutsch, *National Income*, 10.

77 D.C. MacGregor, "The Position of Statistics in the Universities," LAC, RG 31, vol. 1418, Miscellaneous file, part 1.

78 D.C. MacGregor, "The Position of Statistics in the Universities," "External Forces Governing the Development of the Bureau," "Personnel," and "Limitations of the Work of the DBS from the Standpoint of Economic Research," all in LAC, RG 31, vol. 1418, Miscellaneous file, part 1.

79 MacGregor, Rutherford, Britnell, and Deutsch, *National Income*, 9.

80 Ibid.

81 *Report ... Book II – Recommendations*, 9–10, 84–5.

82 R.H. Coats to Alex Skelton, 18 February 1939, Bank of Canada Archives, file 3B-342.

83 R.B. Bryce, Memo of conversation with Mr. Bangs of the Dominion Bureau of Statistics, 19 March 1942, LAC, RG 19, vol. 445, file 111-1R.

84 R.H. Coats to Harold Innis, 26 September 1940, University of Toronto Archives, Innis Papers, box 1.

85 Sydney B. Smith, *National Income: Scope of Inquiry and Method of Approach* (Ottawa: King's Printer, 1939).

86 S. Cudmore to A.L. Neal, 26 October 1939, LAC, RG 31, vol. 1420.

87 John J. Deutsch, "War Finance and the Canadian Economy, 1914–20," *Canadian Journal of Economics and Political Science* 6, no. 4 (November 1940): 525–37 at 537.

88 Keynes, *How to Pay*, 13.

CHAPTER TWO

1 *Ottawa Citizen*, 9 April 1942; W.L.M. King diary, 9 April 1942, Library and Archives Canada (LAC), http://collectionscanada.gc.

2 W.L.M. King diary, 24 February 1944, LAC, http://collectionscanada.ca/king/053201/05320112e.html.

3 See J.L. Granatstein, *The Ottawa Men: The Civil Service Mandarins, 1935–1957* (Toronto: Oxford University Press, 1982).

4 R.B. Bryce, "Draft Notes on National Income for Dr. Clark in Reference to Meeting on April 9," 8 April 1942, Bank of Canada Archives, file 3B-342.

5 R.B. Bryce, "Notes on Meeting on National Income Statistics, Thursday, April 9, 1942," n.d., Bank of Canada Archives, file 3B-342.

6 Ibid.

7 Ibid.

8 W.C. Clark to J.L. Ilsley, 13 April 1942, LAC, RG 19, vol. 3440.

9 John J. Deutsch, "War Finance and the Canadian Economy, 1914–20," *Canadian Journal of Economics and Political Science* 6, no. 4 (November 1940): 525–37 at 537. Other academics lent their expertise to retrospective analysis of the First World War. See, for instance, J.A. Corry, "The Growth of Government Activities in Canada, 1914–1921," *Annual Report of the Canadian Historical Association* (1940): 63–73; and F.A. Knox, "Canadian War Finance and the Balance of Payments, 1914–18," *Canadian Journal of Economics and Political Science* 6, no. 2 (May 1940): 226–57.

10 See J.L. Granatstein, *Canada's War: The Politics of the Mackenzie King Government, 1939–1945* (Toronto: Oxford University Press, 1975).

11 S. Cudmore to A.L. Neal, 26 October 1939, and Minutes of the National

Income Committee, 14 November 1939, LAC, RG 31, vol. 1420; Sydney B. Smith, *National Income: Scope of Enquiry and Method of Approach* (Ottawa: King's Printer, 1939).

12 Canada, *The National Income of Canada: 1919–1938* (Ottawa: Dominion Bureau of Statistics, 1941), "Preface."

13 A.L. Neal, "Part I: National Income of Canada," April 1941, LAC, RG 31, acc. 1989–90/133, box 9, file 876.

14 J.J. Deutsch, "Some Comments on the Dominion Bureau of Statistics Report on National Income, 1919–1938, Part I," 28 April 1941, Bank of Canada Archives, file 3B-342.

15 Ibid.

16 R.B. Bryce to S.B. Smith, 13 February 1941, Bank of Canada Archives, file 3B-342.

17 D.C. MacGregor to S. Cudmore, 8 April 1941, LAC, RG 19, vol. 445, file 111-1R.

18 R.H. Coats to Harold Innis, 30 October 1941, University of Toronto Archives, Innis Papers, box 1.

19 R.H. Coats to W.C. Clark, 24 January 1942, Cudmore note attached, LAC, RG 19, vol. 445, file 111-1R.

20 R.B. Bryce, "Memo of Conversation with Mr. Bangs of the Bureau of Statistics," 19 March 1942, LAC, RG 19, vol. 445, file 111-1R.

21 R.B. Bryce, "Memorandum for Dr. Clark Re: Dr. Coats' Letter on National Income," n.d., Bank of Canada Archives, file 3B-342.

22 See W.K. Hancock and M.M. Gowing, *British War Economy* (London: Her Majesty's Stationery Office, 1949).

23 Colin Clark, *The National Income, 1924–1931* (London: Macmillan, 1932), vi, original emphasis. See also Colin Clark, *National Income and Outlay* (London: Macmillan, 1937); and Colin Clark, with J.G. Crawford, *The National Income of Australia* (London and Sydney: Angus and Robertson, 1938).

24 J.M. Keynes, *The General Theory of Employment, Interest and Money* (London: Macmillan, 1936), "Preface."

25 J.M. Keynes, *How to Pay for the War: A Radical Plan for the Chancellor of the Exchequer* (London: Macmillan, 1940), 4.

26 See Robert Skidelsky, *John Maynard Keynes*, vol. 3, *Fighting for Britain, 1937–1946* (London: Macmillan, 2000), 69–71.

27 Hancock and Gowing, *British War*, 222.

28 H. Hashem Pesaran and G.C. Harcourt, "Life and Work of John Richard Nicholas Stone, 1913–1991," *Economic Journal* 110 (February 2000): 146–65 at 163.

29 Skidelsky, *John Maynard Keynes*, vol. 3, ch. 3.

30 See James Meade and Richard Stone, "The Construction of Tables of National Income, Expenditure, Savings and Investment," *Economic Journal* 51 (June–September 1941): 216–33; and Richard Stone, James Meade, and David Champerdowne, "The Precision of National Income Estimates," *Review of Economic Studies* 9, no. 2 (1942): 111–25.

31 Joseph W. Duncan and William C. Shelton, *Revolution in United States Government Statistics, 1926–1976* (Washington, DC: United States Department of Commerce, 1978), 87; Milton Gilbert, "War Expenditures and National Production," *Survey of Current Business* (March 1942): 9–16 at 12.

32 John Kenneth Galbraith, "The Job before Us," *Fortune*, January 1944, 83. See also David C. Colander and Harry Landreth, eds, *The Coming of Keynesianism to America: Conversations with the Founders of Keynesian Economics* (London and Brookfield: Edward Elgar, 1996), Galbraith interview, 186.

33 John Kenneth Galbraith, "Germany Was Badly Run," *Fortune*, December 1945, 62.

34 J.K. Galbraith, "Germany Was Badly Run," *Fortune*, December 1945, 173–78, 196–200.

35 On Bryce's intellectual gestation, see Colander and Landreth, eds, *Coming of Keynesianism*, 2–8, 39–48; T.K. Rymes, *Keynes' Lectures, 1932–35* (Ann Arbor: University of Michigan Press, 1989); Granatstein, *Ottawa Men*, 256ff; Enid Barnett, *The Keynesian Arithmetic in Wartime: Development of the National Accounts, 1939–1945* (Kingston: Harbinger House, 1998); Don Patinkin and J. Clark Leith, eds, *Keynes, Cambridge and the General Theory: The Process of Criticism and Discussion Connected with the Development of the General Theory* (Toronto: University of Toronto Press, 1978), 39–42 and appendix 1.

36 J.M. Keynes to R.B. Bryce, 11 April 1942, LAC, RG 19, vol. 3444.

37 L. Rasminsky to G. Towers, 4 November 1942, Queen's University Archives, W.C. Clark Papers, box 10.

38 Deutsch, "Some Comments."

39 John J. Deutsch, "The National Income: An Explanation," *Canadian Banker*, July 1941, 412–23.

40 Mabel Timlin, *Keynesian Economics* (Toronto: University of Toronto Press, 1942). See also Shirley Spafford, *No Ordinary Academics: Economics and Political Science at the University of Saskatchewan, 1910–1960* (Toronto: University of Toronto Press, 2000).

41 See D.C. MacGregor, "Manufacturers' Expenses, Net Production, and Rigid Costs in Canada," *Review of Economic Statistics* 27, no. 2 (May 1945): 60–73.

42 *Report of the Royal Commission on Dominion-Provincial Relations – Book II Recommendations* (Ottawa: King's Printer, 1940), 140.

43 W.C. Clark to J.L. Ilsley, 13 April 1942, LAC RG 19, vol. 3440.

44 Kenneth Wilson, "Canada's Unsolved Problem – How Big is Our National Income?" *Financial Post*, 17 April 1943.

45 R.B. Bryce to V. Bladen, 25 July 1942, LAC, RG 19, vol. 445.

46 See Ian Drummond, *Political Economy at the University of Toronto: A History of the Department, 1888–1982* (Toronto: University of Toronto Press, 1983).

47 W.C. Clark to D. Gordon, 23 September 1942, LAC, RG 19, vol. 3440.

48 See Granatstein, *Ottawa Men*.

49 S. Leacock to G. Luxton, 23 November 1935, in possession of Jean Cooper, Ottawa.

50 R.B. Bryce to L. Richer (Dalhousie University), 30 May 1940, LAC, RG 19, vol. 3444. Two weeks later Bryce's assistant, W.A. Macintosh, a Queen's economist, told Clifford Clark that Luxton was "keen and energetic, with a slight appearance of exuberance about him"; see W.A. Macintosh to W.C. Clark, 15 June 1940, LAC, RG 19, vol. 3580.

51 George Luxton, "National Income Tables as Tools for Fiscal Analysis," 23 February 1942, LAC, RG 19, vol. 3580.

52 George Luxton, "Canada: Estimated National Income and Expenditure, 1939–1942/43," n.d., Bank of Canada Archives, file 3B-342.

53 Ibid.

54 George Luxton, "Money Flow Concepts and the Logic of Social Accounting," 17 February 1944, Bank of Canada Archives, file 3B-342.

55 R.B. Bryce to W.C. Clark, 12 April 1943, LAC, RG 19, vol. 3440.

56 See, for instance, George Luxton, "Post-war Employment and National Income under Full Employment, Post-demobilization Conditions," 29 June 1943, Queen's University Archives, John J. Deutsch Papers, box 87. Luxton thanks Agatha Chapman and Malcolm Urquhart for their help in writing this paper.

57 S. Cudmore to Hector MacKinnon, minister of trade and commerce, 15 and 17 February 1944; S. Cudmore, "Functions of the Interdepartmental Advisory Committee on Statistics," n.d.; and S. Cudmore, "Statistical Preparations for Dealing with Post-war Problems," n.d.; all in LAC, RG 31, vol. 1416, file 1550.

58 R.B. Bryce to D.C. MacGregor, 28 July 1944, LAC, RG 19, file 111-1R-0.

CHAPTER THREE

1 See Donald Moggridge, ed., *The Collected Writings of John Maynard Keynes*, vol. 26, *Activities, 1941–1946: Shaping the Post-War World: Bretton Woods and Reparations* (London: Macmillan, 1980), 113; and Robert Skidelsky, *John Maynard Keynes*, vol. 3, *Fighting for Britain, 1937–1946* (London:

Macmillan, 2000), 358. With only eighteen people at Keynes's dinner party, it seems unlikely that a junior mandarin like Luxton would have been present.

2 J.E. Meade and Richard Stone, *National Income and Expenditure* (London: Oxford University Press, 1944), 3.

3 Richard Stone, "Function and Criteria of a System of Social Accounting," *Income and Wealth*, ser. 1 (1951): 1–74.

4 Edward F. Denson, "Report on Tripartite Discussions of National Income Measurement," *Studies in Income and Wealth* 10 (1947): 3–22 at 3.

5 "Richard Stone – Autobiography," http://www.nobelprize.org/nobel_prizes/economics. Stone won in 1984.

6 Denison, "Report on Tripartite Discussions," 7. A staff member at the National Income Unit in Washington, Denison held a doctorate in economics from Brown University and had served with John Kenneth Galbraith and Richard Ruggles on the US Strategic Bombing Survey. He would become a prolific writer on national accounting.

7 Richard Stone, quoted in M. Hashem Pesaran and G.C. Harcourt, "Life and Work of John Richard Nicholas Stone, 1913–1991," *Economic Journal*, no. 110 (February 2000): F146-F165 at F149.

8 See Richard Ruggles, "The United States National Income Accounts, 1947–1977: Their Conceptual Basis and Evolution," in Murray F. Foss, ed., *The U.S. National Income and Product Accounts: Selected Topics*, 15–49 (Chicago: University of Chicago Press, 1983).

9 Agatha Chapman, Walter Duffett, Malcolm Urquhart, and George Luxton, "Suggested Content of National Income and Expenditure," n.d., Bank of Canada Archives, file 3B-342.

10 Agatha Chapman alumni file, University of Toronto Archives, file A73-0026/056; *Varsity* student newspaper, 28 November 1928.

11 Stephen Leacock, "What Is Left of Adam Smith?" *Canadian Journal of Economics and Political Science* 1, no. 1 (February 1935): 41–51 at 50.

12 "SCM Association of McGill University: Report of the General Secretary for the Year 1931–32," McGill University Archives, RG 2, box 0049, file 00618.

13 "SCM Association of McGill University: Report of the General Secretary for the Year 1936," McGill University Archives, RG 2, box 0049, file 00619.

14 Student Christian Movement files 1938–39, McGill University Archives, RG 2, box 0049, file 00620.

15 Betty Kobayashi Issenman, Dr Grant Lathe, Ruth Plumpton (Luxton's daughter), and Muriel Duckworth interviews, 2005.

16 Ruth Plumpton interview, 2005.

17 "Russia Today," *Financial Post*, 17 November and 1, 8, 15, and 29 December 1934.

18 See, for instance, J.W. Popkin, *The First Century: A History of the Investment*

Department Sun Life Assurance Company of Canada, 1871–1973 (Montreal: n.p., n.d.), 47. Popkin's dates are incorrect.

19 M. Hashem Pesaran, "The ET Interview: Professor Sir Richard Stone," *Econometric Theory* 7 (1991): 85–123 at 87.

20 Thomas Shoyama interview, 2004.

21 Robert Crozier, *Looking Backward: A Memoir* (Nepean, ON: n.p., 1998), 10; Robert Crozier interview, 2005.

22 Pesaran, "ET Interview," 88.

23 Gideon Rosenbluth interview, 2004.

24 John Kenneth Galbraith, quoted in James Tobin, "Hansen and Public Policy," *Quarterly Journal of Economics* 90, no. 1 (February 1976): 32–7 at 32; Walter Salant, "Alvin Hansen and the Fiscal Policy Seminar," *Quarterly Journal of Economics* 90, no. 1 (February 1976): 14–23.

25 See Library and Archives Canada (LAC), R8274, Eric Adams Papers, boxes 2, 9, 10.

26 George Luxton, speech text, Queen's University Archives, John J. Deutsch Papers, box 87, file 857. See also LAC, MG 28 I 11, Papers of the Canadian Youth Commission.

27 Queen's University Archives, F.A. Knox Papers, box 1 – 1944/5 diary.

28 Alex Skelton, Luxton obituary, *Canadian Journal of Economics and Political Science* 11, no. 4 (November 1945): 478–9.

29 Herbert Marshall, "Memorandum re: Bureau of Statistics Reorganization," 24 January 1946, LAC, RG 31, vol. 1424.

30 J.T. Marshall, "Memorandum on Reorganization of Central Staff," [c. early 1945], LAC, RG 31, vol. 1424.

31 See Judith Alexander, "Our Ancestors in Their Successive Generations," *Canadian Journal of Economics* 28, no. 1 (February 1995): 205–24; and R.W. Dimand, M.A. Dimand, and E.L. Forget, eds, *A Biographical Dictionary of Women Economists* (Cheltenham: Edward Elgar, 2000). Chapman is listed in the latter.

32 C.M. Isbister to G. Luxton, 23 March 1942, LAC, RG 19, vol. 3444; Dr Claude Isbister interview, 2004.

33 A.L. Chapman and C.M. Isbister, "National Accounts for Canada – Income and Expenditure," *Canadian Banker*, no. 53 (February 1946): 102–9.

34 Ibid., 102.

35 Ministry of Reconstruction, *Employment and Income with Special Reference to the Initial Period of Reconstruction* (Ottawa: King's Printer, 1945), 1.

36 W.L.M. King, Address to Committee [of the Dominion-Provincial Conference], 26 November 1945, LAC, RG 47, vol. 80.

37 See Wilfrid Eggleston, *The Road to Nationhood: A Chronicle of Dominion-Provincial Relations* (Westport, CT: Greenwood, 1972).

38 Claude Isbister, quoted in *Net National Income at Factor Cost and Gross National Expenditure at Market Cost in Canada*, DBS publication 13-D-58 (1945); *National Accounts Income and Expenditure, 1938–1945*, DBS publication 13–201 (1945). On 9 November the Dominion statistician, Herbert Marshall, had written to Robert Bryce, "we are doing our utmost to improve our 'national income' figures so that they will have the greatest possible degree of currency"; see LAC, RG 19, vol. 445, file 111-1R.

39 "Remarks Made at the Dominion-Provincial Conference on Provincial Statistics by G.D. Iliffe," November 1947, LAC, RG 19, vol. 3709.

40 W.C. Clark to H. Marshall, 27 December 1948, LAC, RG 31, acc. 89–90/133, box 5.

41 Herbert Marshall, "Speech to Conference of Business Newspaper Editors," 22 February 1946, LAC, RG 31, vol. 1421.

42 Ibid.

43 Kathleen James to Members of the National Income Study Group, 10 April, 1947 LAC, RG 31, acc. 89–90/133, box 6.

44 Memo by Herbert Marshall, 24 June 1953, LAC, RG 31, vol. 1490.

45 J.W. Edmonds, "New Yardsticks of Canada's National Output Clears the Way for Reconstruction Planning," *Financial Post*, 1 December 1945.

46 *Ottawa Evening Citizen*, 13 February 1953.

47 All user correspondence in LAC, RG 31, acc. 89–90/133, box 6, file 405.

48 Requests spanning 1947–52 in LAC, RG 31, acc. 89–90/133, box 6, file 405.

49 Herbert Marshall, "Statistics in the United Nations World: The Work of the UN Statistical Commission," c. 1948, LAC, RG 31, vol. 1432.

50 United Nations, *Measurement of National Income and the Construction of Social Accounts* (Geneva: United Nations, 1947).

51 See Igor Gouzenko, *This Was My Choice* (Toronto: Dent and Sons, 1948).

52 There is a considerable literature on the wider history of the Gouzenko affair. See, for instance, Reg Whitaker and Gary Marcuse, *Cold War Canada: The Making of a National Insecurity State, 1945–1957* (Toronto: University of Toronto Press, 1994); and R. Bothwell and J.L. Granatstein, eds, *The Gouzenko Transcripts* (Ottawa: Deneau, 1982).

53 See note 52 above.

54 Eric Adams, "Raids and Seizures – notes," LAC, R8274, Eric Adams Papers, box 16, file 12.

55 Eric Adams, "Bounders in the Boudoir," LAC, R8274, Eric Adams Papers, box 16, file 12: Raids and Seizures. See also "Rex vs E.G. Adams," LAC, MG 30 A94, vol. 45, Maxwell Cohen Papers.

56 *The Report of the Royal Commission to investigate the facts relating to and the circumstances surrounding the communication, by public officials and other persons in positions of trust, of secret and confidential information to*

agents of a foreign power, transcripts of evidence, testimony of Kathleen Willsher, 25 February 1946, LAC microfilm T-1368, 760.

57 June Callwood, *Emma* (Toronto: Stoddart, 1984), 108.

58 *The Report of the Royal Commission to investigate the facts relating to and the circumstances surrounding the communication, by public officials and other persons in positions of trust, of secret and confidential information to agents of a foreign power* (Ottawa: King's Printer, 1946), sec. 3, 14.

59 *Toronto Star*, 16 July 1945.

60 "Agatha Chapman – notes," LAC, R8274, Eric Adams Papers, box 16, file 32.

61 Gideon Rosenbluth interview, 2004.

62 *Montreal Star*, 18 July 1946.

63 Ibid.

64 *Montreal Star*, 19 August 1946.

65 *Montreal Star*, 18 July 1946.

66 *Globe and Mail*, 21 August 1946.

67 *Ottawa Evening Journal*, 27 November 1946; *Globe and Mail*, 28 November 1946.

68 Memorandum on Reorganization of Central Staff by J.T. Marshall, n.d., LAC, RG 31, vol. 1424.

69 "Agatha Chapman – notes," LAC, R8274, Eric Adams Papers, box 16, file 32.

70 Interview with Robert Crozier, 2005.

71 "Agatha Chapman – notes," LAC, R8274, Eric Adams Papers, box 16, file 32.

72 C.M. Isbister to "Dick" Stone, 15 February 1947, LAC, RG 31, acc. 89–90/133, box 6.

73 Minutes of the Committee of Management, Department of Applied Economics, meeting of 18 February 1947, Cambridge University Archives.

74 *Toronto Star*, 24 March 1947.

75 Agatha Chapman, with assistance from Rose Knight, *Wages and Salaries in the United Kingdom, 1920–1938* (Cambridge: Cambridge University Press, 1953).

76 *Montreal Gazette*, 19 October 1963. For a strikingly similar story on the American side of the border, see Landon R.Y. Storrs, "Red Scare Politics and the Suppression of Popular Front Feminism: The Loyalty Investigation of Mary Dublin Keyserling," *Journal of American History* 90, no. 2 (September 2003): 491–524.

77 Simon Kuznets, "Suggestions for an Inquiry into the Economic Growth of Nations," in *Problems in the Study of Economic Growth*, 3–22 (New York: NBER, 1949), 3.

78 Crozier, *Looking Backward*, 14–15.

79 Robert Crozier to Gordon Betcherman, editor, *Canadian Business Economics*,

18 November 1997. The journal subsequently asked Crozier to contribute an article on the birth of the Canadian System of National Accounts; see Robert Crozier, "The Development and Evolution of the National Accounts: 'This Great Invention of the 20th Century," *Canadian Business Economics*, November 1998.

80 David Slater interview, 2004.

81 Thomas Rymes interview, 2004.

82 Hans Adler interview, 2004.

83 Ibid.

84 See J.L. Granatstein, *The Ottawa Men: The Civil Service Mandarins, 1935–1957* (Toronto: Oxford University Press, 1982), 134–9; and Irving Abella and Harold Troper, *None Is Too Many: Canada and the Jews of Europe, 1933–1948* (Toronto: Lester, Orpen Dennys, 1982).

85 Gideon Rosenbluth and Hans Adler interviews, 2004.

86 *Scan*, Statistics Canada's employee magazine, May 1986.

87 Simon Goldberg, "The National Accounts: Whither Now?" *Canadian Journal of Economics and Political Science* 22, no. 1 (February 1956): 73–91 at 91.

88 *National Accounts Income and Expenditure, 1938–1945*, appendix, DBS publication 13-201 (1945); L.M. Read interview, 2004.

89 Jenny Podoluk, *Survey of Incomes in the Legal Profession in Canada, 1946, 1947 and 1948*, DBS publication 13-D-63 (1950).

90 *National Accounts Income and Expenditure, 1926–1956*, DBS publication 13–504A (1958); V.R. Berlinguette, "Measurement of Real Output," *Canadian Journal of Economics and Political Science* 20, no. 1 (February 1954): 59–75.

91 *Seasonally Adjusted Economic Indicators, 1947–1955*, DBS publication 61–503 (1957), 11.

92 United Nations, *A System of National Accounts and Supporting Documents* (New York: United Nations Statistical Office, 1953), 1.

93 H. Marshall to C.D. Howe, 12 September 1949, LAC, RG 31, vol. 1430.

94 Simon Goldberg, "Paper on National Accounts for Dominion-Provincial Statisticians' Conference, January 1953," LAC, RG 31, vol. 1425.

95 J.B. Bergevin, DBS *Pasture-ized News*, vol. 1, April 1953, n.p.

96 Lorne Rowebottom interview, 2004.

CHAPTER FOUR

1 *Debates of the House of Commons*, 5 April 1955, 2728–33.

2 Ibid.

3 Ibid.

4 Order in Council, P.C. 1955–909, 17 June 1955.

5 William Hood and Anthony Scott, *Output, Labour and Capital in the Canadian Economy* (Ottawa: Queen's Printer, 1957), 330.

6 David Slater, *Consumption in Canada* (Ottawa: Queen's Printer, 1957), 4.

7 Royal Commission on Canada's Economic Prospects, *Final Report* (Ottawa: Queen's Printer, 1957), 324–30, quotation at page 15. See also Stephen Azzi, *Walter Gordon and the Rise of Canadian Nationalism* (Montreal and Kingston: McGill-Queen's University Press, 1999), 51.

8 Anthony Scott interview, 2004.

9 Royal Commission on Canada's Economic Prospects, *Final Report*, 95.

10 Walter Gordon, *Final report: Royal Commission on Canada's Economic Prospects* (Ottawa: Queen's Printer, 1957), 474; Simon Goldberg, 1955 speech, in Library and Archives Canada (LAC), RG 31, vol. 1425.

11 F.H. Leacy to Walter Duffett, 14 April 1960, LAC, RG 31, vol. 1490; *Debates of the House of Commons*, 12 April 1960, 3144ff.

12 Doug Hartle, *Canadian Annual Review for 1960* (Toronto: University of Toronto Press, 1961), 236–7.

13 *Canadian Statistical Review*, June 1957. See also Philip Cross, "Tracking the Business Cycle: Monthly Analysis of the Economy at Statistics Canada, 1926–2001" *Canadian Economic Observer* (December 2001): 3.1–3.20.

14 John J. Deutsch, "Canadian Economic Policy, 1945–65: A Summing Up," in *Canadian Economic Policy since the War*, 123–31 (Montreal: Canadian Trade Committee, 1966), 131.

15 Hans Adler, "Conference of European Statisticians' Working Group on the National Accounts and Balances in Geneva," 24 November 1967, LAC, RG 31, vol. 1504.

16 Simon Goldberg, "The Function of Integration in a Statistical Office," 30 May 1962 speech, in LAC, RG 31, vol. 1458.

17 S.A. Goldberg and F.H. Leacy, "The National Accounts: Whither Now?" *Canadian Journal of Economics and Political Science* 22, no. 1 (February 1956): 73–91 at 75.

18 Jacob Viner, *Canada's Balance of International Indebtedness, 1900–1913* (Cambridge, MA: Harvard University Press, 1924).

19 Dominion Bureau of Statistics, *The Canadian Balance of International Payments: A Study in Methods and Results* (Ottawa: King's Printer, 1939), 18.

20 H. Marshall, F.A. Southart, and K. Taylor, *Canadian-American Industry* (New Haven and Toronto: Yale University Press and Ryerson Press, 1936).

21 Harry Johnson, *The Canadian Quandary: Economic Problems and Policies* (Toronto: McClelland and Stewart, 1977), 12.

22 C.D. Blyth, "Canada and the Outside World: As Seen through the Canadian Balance of Payments," Montreal, 1954, Bower Carty Papers, Statistics Canada (STC) Library.

23 Irving Brecher and S.S. Reisman, *Canada-United States Economic Relations* (Ottawa: Queen's Printer, 1957), 2–4.

24 Johnson, *Canadian Quandary*, 12.

25 *Debates of the House of Commons*, 14 December 1951, 1957.

26 See Dominion Bureau of Statistics, International Trade Division, *Quarterly Estimates of the Canadian Balance of International Payments*, STC 67–001; and *The Canadian Balance of International Payments in the Post-War Years, 1946–1952*, STC 67–502.

27 Interviews with A.E. Safarian and Franklin B.Y. Chow, 2004.

28 Bower Carty, *The Canadian Balance of International Payments and International Investment Position: A Description of Sources and Methods*, STC 67–506E; Thomas Rymes interview, 2004.

29 William Hood, *Financing Economic Activity in Canada* (Ottawa: Queen's Printer, 1958), 464–5.

30 See L.M. Read, "The Development of National Transactions Accounts: Canada's Version of or Substitute for Money Flows Accounts," *Canadian Journal of Economics and Political Science* 23, no. 1 (February 1957): 3–56.

31 Bower Carty, in "Some Recent Developments in the Dominion Bureau of Statistics," Montreal, 1969, STC 1374, 22; [no author] "The Canadian Financial Accounts," *Canadian Statistical Review*, STC 11–003E, November 1966.

32 Anthony Scott, "Canada's Reproducible Wealth," in Raymond Goldsmith and Christopher Saunders, eds, *The Measurement of National Wealth*, 193–216 (London: Bowes and Bowes, 1959), 214; and Hood and Scott, *Output, Labour and Capital*.

33 Thomas Rymes interview, 2004; and fixed capital formation files in LAC, RG 31, vols 1466, 1508.

34 [No author], "The Measurement of the Stock of Fixed Capital by Industry in Canada: A Progress Report," *Canadian Statistical Review*, STC 11–003E, July 1964; and Robert R. Solow, "Technical Change and the Aggregate Production Function," *Review of Economics and Statistics*, August 1957.

35 Edward F. Denison, *The Sources of Economic Growth in the United States and the Alternatives before Us* (New York: Committee for Economic Development, 1962), 1–2.

36 Dorothy Walters, *Canadian Income Levels and Growth: An International Perspective* (Ottawa: Economic Council of Canada, 1968), 1–2.

37 See Commission on International Development, *Partners in Development* (New York: Praeger, 1969).

38 Tom Kent to Walter Duffett, 3 November 1969, LAC, RG 31, vol. 1546.

39 Simon Goldberg, "The Demand for Official Statistics and Their Utilization in Canada with Special Reference to the Role of the National Accounts," presented to International Statistical Institute conference, Canberra, Australia, September 1967, STC 3430, "Introduction."

40 Dominion Bureau of Statistics, *Brief to the Special Committee on Science Policy*, Senate of Canada, December 1968, STC 3643, "Preface."

41 See Herbert Marshall, "History of the National Accounts," 7–12, LAC, RG 31, vol. 1488; and [no author], "The Standard Industrial Classification and the Standard Commodity Classification," *Canadian Statistical Review*, June 1961.

42 Simon Goldberg, Notes on New York meeting of the Conference on Research in Income and Wealth, June 1965, LAC, RG 31, vol. 1472.

43 Simon Goldberg to J.T. Marshall, 19 March 1956, LAC, RG 31, vol. 1414.

44 See Dennis Featherstone, "Data Banks and DATABANK: An Introduction," LAC, RG 31, vol. 1450.

45 Canada, *Introduction to the Canadian Socio-Economic Information Management System (CANSIM)* (Ottawa: Queen's Printer, 1969), v.

46 Simon Goldberg and Ivan Fellegi, "The Computer and Government Statistics," Cuernavaca, Mexico, October 1971, LAC, RG 31, vol. 1578; Mary Lennox and T.J. Vander Noot, "Introduction to the Canadian Socio-Economic Information Management System (CANSIM)," STC 12–530A.

47 "Tinbergen" entry, in John Eatwell, Murray Milgate, and Peter Newman, eds, *The New Palgrave: A Dictionary of Economics*, 652–4 (London: Macmillan, 1987).

48 William Hood and Tjalling Koopmans, *Studies in Econometric Method* (New York: John Wiley and Sons, 1953), 1.

49 "Frisch" entry, in Eatwell, Milgate, and Newman, eds, *New Palgrave*, 428–30.

50 *Business Week*, 6 January 1963.

51 William N. Parker, "An Historical Introduction," in William N. Parker, ed., *Economic History and the Modern Economist*, 1–10 (London: Basil Blackwell, 1986), 6.

52 William Hood interview, 2005.

53 Ian Stewart interview, 2005.

54 Interviews with William Hood, Ian Stewart, and Donald Daly, 2005; T. Merritt Brown, *Specification and Uses of Econometric Models* (Toronto: Macmillan, 1970); Ronald Bodkin, Lawrence Klein, and Kanta Marwah, *A History of Macroeconomic Model-Building* (Aldershot: Edward Elgar, 1991).

55 J.J. Deutsch to W. Duffett, 26 June 1964, LAC, RG 31, vol. 1539.

56 See Bodkin, Klein, and Marwah, *A History*, ch. 9; Mervin Daub, *Canadian Economic Forecasting: In a World Where All's Unsure* (Montreal and Kingston: McGill-Queen's University Press, 1987), chs 3 and 4; and "A History of Business Economics in Canada," special issue *Canadian Business Economics* 5, nos 2–3 (Winter/Spring 1997).

57 R.B. Crozier to S. Goldberg, 4 April 1965, LAC, RG 31, vol. 1449.

58 M.C. Urquhart and K.A. Buckley, *Historical Statistics of Canada* (Toronto: Macmillan, 1965).

59 Simon Goldberg to M.W. Sharp, 21 August 1954, LAC, RG 31, vol. 1471.

60 Simon Goldberg, "The Nature of Productivity Studies," 12 July 1962, LAC, RG 31, vol. 1448.

61 See L.M. Read, "The Measurement of Total Factor Productivity," June 1961, STC 2020E; and T.K. Rymes and Alexandra Cas, *On Concepts and Measures of Multifactor Productivity in Canada, 1961–1980* (Cambridge, UK: Cambridge University Press, 1991).

62 Richard Lipsey, Douglas Purvis, and Peter Steiner, *Economics* (New York: Harper and Row, 1988), 209.

63 François Quesnay, quoted in Almarin Phillips, "The Tableau Économique as a Simple Leontief Model," *Quarterly Journal of Economics* 69 (February 1955): 137–44 at 139.

64 Christian de Bresson, "Some Highlights in the Life of Wassily Leontief – an Interview with Estelle and Wassily Leontief," in Erik Dietzenbacher and Michael Lahr, eds, *Wassily Leontief and Input-Output Economics*, 135–47 (Cambridge, UK: Cambridge University Press, 2004), 141.

65 Wassily Leontief, "Quantitative Input and Output Relations in the Economic System of the United States," *Review of Economic Statistics* 18, no. 1 (August 1936): 105–16 at 105–6.

66 Wassily Leontief, "Input-Output Economics," *Scientific American*, October 1951.

67 "Pushbutton Planning," *Business Week*, 15 December 1951.

68 Richard Caves, "The Inter-Industry Structure of the Canadian Economy," *Canadian Journal of Economics and Political Science* 23, no. 3 (August 1957): 313–29 at 329.

69 Simon Goldberg to H. Marshall, 4 January 1952, LAC, RG 31, vol. 1498.

70 Barbara Mercer, DBS Economics Seminar, 28 November 1952, LAC, RG 31, vol. 1472.

71 J.A. (Jack) Sawyer, "Why Construct an Input-Output Table?" 14 August 1953, LAC, RG 13, vol. 1498.

72 *The Inter-industry Flow of Goods and Services, Canada, 1949*, DBS publication 13–510 (1956); John A. Sawyer, "The Measurement of Inter-Industry Relationships in Canada," *Canadian Journal of Economics and Political Science* 21, no. 4 (November 1955): 480–97.

73 *Globe and Mail*, 10 December 1963.

74 United Nations, Department of Economic and Social Affairs, *Studies in Methods: Problems of Input-Output Tables and Analysis*, ser. F, no. 14 (New York: United Nations, 1966).

75 *Business Week*, 17 December 1966.

76 Richard Nielsen, "Lives Lived," *Globe and Mail*, 3 February 1998.

77 Jack Sawyer interview, 2005.

78 See J.M.S. Careless, "'Limited Identities' in Canada," *Canadian Historical Review* 50 (March 1969): 1–10.

79 Michael Szabo, "Regional Statistics Program in the DBS," December 1967, LAC, RG 31, vol. 1541.

80 Arthur C. Parks, *The Economy of the Atlantic Provinces, 1940–1957* (Halifax: APEC, 1959), 90.

81 File on "Atlantic Provinces Economic Council – 1960s," LAC, RG 31, vol. 1535.

82 Kari Levitt interview, 2005.

83 Ibid.

84 Atlantic Provinces Economic Council contract with the DBS, 1964, LAC, RG 31, vol. 1535.

85 Kari Levitt, *Input-Output Study of the Atlantic Provinces, 1965*, vol. 1, *Social Accounting Matrix and Models* (Ottawa: Information Canada, 1975), 11.

86 Kari Levitt interview, 2005.

87 Paul Pitts, "Comments of the DBS Input-Output Staff on the Recent Publication by the Economic and Social Council of the United Nations," 29 March 1965, LAC, RG 31, vol. 1448.

88 Levitt, *Input-Output*, vol. 1, *Social Accounting*, "Introduction."

89 Anne P. Carter and Wassily W. Leontief, "Goals for the Input-Output Data System in the Seventies," *Survey of Current Business* 57, no. 7 (July 1971): 28–32 at 30.

90 Milton Gilbert, "Discussion of Measurement of National Income," *Econometrica* 17, supplement (July 1949): 256, quoted in Sawyer, "Measurement," 480–1.

91 Simon Goldberg, "The Demand for Official Statistics and their Utilization in Canada with Special Reference to the Role of the National Accounts," September 1967, STC 3430, 12.

92 *System of National Accounts*, ser. F, no. 2 (New York: United Nations Staistical Office, 1968).

93 Ibid., "Preface."

94 Lipsey, Purvis, and Steiner, *Economics*, xix; Paul Samuelson and Anthony Scott, *Economics*, 3rd Canadian ed. (Toronto: McGraw-Hill, 1970), 224.

95 Paul A. Samuelson and William Nordhaus, *Economics*, 15th ed. (Chicago: University of Chicago Press, 1995), 402.

96 Interviews with Thomas Rymes, Larry Read, and Thomas Shoyama, 2004.

CHAPTER FIVE

1 *Debates of the House of Commons*, 25 November 1970, 1457.

2 Ibid.

3 Ivan Head, "The Foreign Policy of the New Canada," *Foreign Affairs* 50, no. 2 (January 1972): 237–52 at 242; and Ivan Head to R.J. Desramaux, 7 May 1974, and Guy Leclerc to P. Kirkham and R.J. Desramaux, 8 May 1974, both in Library and Archives Canada (LAC), RG 31, vol. 1610.

4 P.E. Trudeau to S. Ostry, 1 June 1972, LAC, RG 31, vol. 1610.

5 P.E. Trudeau to S. Ostry, 1 June 1972, and S. Ostry to P.E. Trudeau, 15 July 1972, both in LAC, RG 31, vol. 1610; S. Ostry to all directors, 15 June 1972, LAC, RG 31, vol. 1593.

6 Simon Goldberg, "The Demand for Official Statistics," 1967 speech, LAC, RG 31, vol. 1416.

7 Adam Smith, *An Inquiry into the Nature and Causes of the Wealth of Nations* (New York: Bobbs-Merrill, 1961), 15.

8 Marilyn Waring, *Counting for Nothing: What Men Value and What Women are Worth* (London: Allen and Unwin, 1988), 19, original emphasis.

9 Professor C.A. Verrijn-Stuart, in discussion of Stamp's paper "Methods Used in Different Countries for Estimating National Income," *Journal of the Royal Statistical Society* (1934): 455–66 at 457.

10 Emphasis added.

11 Jean Klinck to Donald Fleming, 21 March 1960; and Gordon Churchill to Jean Klinck, 5 April 1960; both in LAC, RG 31, vol. 1523.

12 J.R. Hicks, *Value and Capital* (Oxford: Clarendon Press, 1939), "Preface."

13 Simon Kuznets, "How to Judge Quality," *New Republic*, 20 October 1961, 29.

14 William Nordhaus and James Tobin, "Is Growth Obsolete?" in *Economic Growth: Fiftieth Anniversary Colloquium* (New York: NBER, 1974), 4.

15 Garrett Hardin, "The Tragedy of the Commons," *Science*, no. 162 (1968): 1243–8. One could argue that academic economists like Anthony Scott and H. Scott Gordon in Canada had long before identified the problem of depleting common property, but it took Hardin to carry this consciousness into the public realm.

16 Garrett Hardin, "The Tragedy of the Commons," *Science*, no. 162 (1968): 1243–8.

17 Kenneth Boulding, "The Economics of the Coming Spaceship Earth," in Henry Jarret, ed., *Environmental Quality in a Growing Economy: Essays from the Sixth REF Forum*, 3–14 (Baltimore: Johns Hopkins Press, 1986), 3.

18 "Tracking the Ever-Elusive Gross National Product," *Fortune*, 22 May 1978, 100.

19 "A Gauge of Well-being," *Time*, 9 April 1973, 75.

20 Hans Adler, "Service of Housewives in the National Accounts," 24 December 1970, LAC, RG 31, vol. 1485.

21 See Benjamin M. Friedman, *The Moral Consequences of Economic Growth* (New York: Knopf, 2005).

22 Arthur Okun, "Social Welfare Has No Price Tag," *Survey of Current Business*, July 1971, 129.

23 Edward Denson, "Welfare Measurement and the GNP," *Survey of Current Business*, January 1971, 13–15.

24 Shuntaro Shishido to S. Goldberg, 25 May 1971, LAC, RG 31, vol. 1613.

25 Hans Adler, quoted in OECD Working Group on Social Indicators, working notes, LAC, RG 31, vol. 1599.

26 Leroy Stone, "What Is SSDS?" c. November 1971, LAC, RG 31, vol. 1588.

27 Oli Hawrylyshyn, *A Review of Recent Proposals for Modifying and Extending the Measure of GNP* (Ottawa: Statistics Canada, 1974), STC 11-558, 7.

28 Ibid., 51, original emphasis. See also Hans Adler, "Selected Problems of Welfare and Production in the National Accounts," *Review of Income and Wealth* (June 1982): 121–32.

29 Hans Adler and Oli Hawrylyshyn, "Estimates of the Value of Household Work, Canada, 1961 and 1971," *Review of Income and Wealth* (December 1978): 333–55.

30 *Perspectives Canada: A Compendium of Social Statistics* (Statistics Canada: Ottawa, 1974), "Preface," Statistics Canada (STC) 11-507E.

31 Leroy Stone to Hans Adler, 5 May 1972, LAC, RG 31, vol. 1588; Hans Adler interview, 2004.

32 Richard Lipsey interview, 2006.

33 Ibid.

34 Ibid.

35 Pierre Elliott Trudeau, quoted in Guy Leclerc to D. Kirkham and R.J. Desramaux, 8 May 1974, LAC, RG 31, vol. 1608.

36 Boulding, "Economics of the Coming Spaceship Earth," 3, 14.

37 Anthony Scott, "Economists, Environmental Policies and Federalism," in Patrick Grady and Andrew Sharpe, eds, *The State of Economics in Canada: Festschrift in Honour of David Slater*, 405–49 (Montreal and Kingston: McGill-Queen's University Press, 2001), 411. See also Anthony Scott, "National Wealth and Natural Wealth," *Canadian Journal of Economics and Political Science* 22, no. 3 (August 1956): 373–8. For a pioneering attempt to apply the material flows used in national accounting to environmental accounting, see Peter Victor, *Pollution: The Economy and the Environment* (Toronto: University of Toronto Press, 1972).

38 A.M. Friend to H. Adler, 7 March 1973, LAC, RG 31, vol. 1606.

39 Sylvia Ostry, "Data Needs in the Environment Seminar," 23 July 1973, LAC, RG 31, vol. 1606.

40 A.M. Friend, "Development of Environmental Statistics," n.d., LAC, RG 31, vol. 1606.

41 Peter Kirkham to Sylvia Ostry, 14 March 1974, LAC, RG 31, vol. 1606.

42 Anthony Friend, "Conceptual Frameworks and a Unified Approach to Environmental Statistics," *Canadian Statistical Review*, October 1981, vi.

43 Statistics Canada, *Human Activity and the Environment: A Statistical Compendium* (Ottawa: Statistics Canada, 1978), "Preface," STC 11–509.

44 David Rapport and Anthony Friend, *Towards a Comprehensive Framework for Environmental Statistics: A Stress-Response Approach* (Ottawa: Statistics Canada, 1979), 34, STC 11–510.

45 David Rapport, "The Stress-Response Environmental Statistics System and Its Applicability to the Laurentian Lower Great Lakes," *Statistical Journal of the United Nations*, 1983, 377–405, quotations at page 377.

46 Ivan Fellegi, "Preface," in *Human Activity and the Environment: A Statistical Compendium*, (Ottawa: Statistics Canada, 1986), "Preface," STC 11–509E.

47 S. Ostry to S. Reisman, 8 March 1973, STC Trouble file, vol. 1.

48 John Kettle, quoted in Guy Leclerc, "Strengthening of National Economic Accounts: A Canadian Viewpoint," paper presented to the Inter-American Statistical Institute, September 1979, 6, STC 0019.

49 *Time*, 31 December 1965.

50 John J. Deutsch, "Canadian Economic Policy, 1945–65: A Summing Up," in *Canadian Economic Policy since the War*, 123–34 (Montreal: Canadian Trade Committee, 1966), 131.

51 See Richard Ruggles, "The Role of the National Accounts in the Statistical System," in Nancy D. Ruggles and Richard Ruggles, eds, *National Accounting and Economic Policy: The United States and UN Systems*, 70–90 (Cheltenham: Edward Elgar, 1999).

52 Ontario manufacturer to P.E. Trudeau, 14 May 1971, LAC, RG 31, vol. 1579. Statistics Canada was, of course, not in the business of asking for policy advice in its surveys.

53 Leclerc, "Strengthening," 8.

54 See Cyril Hodgins, "Advanced Preliminary Estimates of the Quarterly National Accounts: An Exploration of Methodology," LAC, RG 31, vol. 1484; and Leclerc, "Strengthening."

55 S.A. Goldberg, H.J. Adler, J.D. Randall, and P.S. Sunga, "The Canadian Quarterly National Accounts: A Critical Appraisal," *Review of Income and Wealth*, ser. 11 (1965), reprinted in Preetom S. Sunga, *System of National Accounts: Collected Articles of Preetom S. Sunga*, 7–72 (Ottawa: Statistics Canada, 1991), 22.

56   *Vancouver Province*, 5 September 1969.

57   S. Goldberg to J.L. Pepin, 18 September 1969, LAC, RG 31, vol. 1541.

58   George Jaszi, quoted in *Fortune*, 22 May 1979, 100–4.

59   "Record of Cabinet Decision – Meeting of October 14, 1971 'Economic Measures,'" LAC, RG 31, vol. 1589.

60   S. Reisman to A.W. Johnson, 24 August 1972, LAC, RG 31, vol. 1594. See Peter Hicks, "The Meaning, Uses and Limitation of the Unemployment Statistics," *Canadian Statistical Review*, July 1972.

61   S. Reisman to S. Ostry, 23 February 1973, STC Trouble file, vol. 2; Reisman interview, 2005.

62   S. Ostry to S. Reisman, 8 March 1973, STC Trouble file, vol. 1.

63   *Report 12: Economic and Statistical Services, Report of the Royal Commission on Government Organization* (Ottawa: Queen's Printer, 1962–63), 38.

64   Dinner remarks – V.R. Berlinguette, 11 February 1975, LAC, RG 31, vol. 1594.

65   Frank Curry to Peter Kirkham, 18 August 1975, "Statistics Canada, 1975: How Did It Reach Its Present Sad State of Affairs," Bower Carty Papers, STC Library.

66   S. Wells to G. Leclerc, 15 April 1976, STC Trouble file, vol. 1.

67   Wayne Cheveldayoff, "Some Data Sources Reported Having Adverse Effect on GNP Figures," *Globe and Mail*, 22 October 1976, B1.

68   *Debates of the House of Commons*, 8, 15, and 16 November 1976, 832, 974–80, 1039–40.

69   C.D. Howe Research Institute, *Policy Review and Outlook, 1979: Anticipating the Unexpected* (Montreal: C.D. Howe, 1979), 16–21. See also Wayne Cheveldayoff, "Statistics Canada: Big on Numbers, But Its Reliability in Question," *Globe and Mail*, 23 December 1978.

70   G. Leclerc to P. Kirkham, draft, 8 January 1979, STC Trouble file, vol. 1.

71   *Globe and Mail*, 6 June 1979; *Toronto Star*, 7 June 1979.

72   G. Leclerc notes, 1979, STC Trouble file, vol. 2.

73   Stewart Wells to *Globe and Mail*, 6 June 1979, STC Trouble file, vol. 1.

74   See, for instance, *Fortune*, 22 May 1978, 100; and *Economist*, 9 February 1980.

75   Wayne Cheveldayoff, "Statscan Still 2 Years from Better GNP Data," *Globe and Mail*, 6 October 1979.

76   *Ottawa Citizen*, 8 November 1979.

77   *Debates of the House of Commons*, 9 November 1979, 1140–41.

78   Ibid., 10 December 1979, 2182–88.

79   Sir Claus Moser, "Statistics and Public Policy," part 1, *Journal of the Royal Statistical Society* 143 (1980): 1–31 at 13, original emphasis.

80   Sir Claus Moser et al., *Statistics Canada: Methodological Review*, March 1980, ch. 1, para. 18, p. 4, STC 2589E.

81 Ibid., ch. 1, para. 53, p. 10.

82 Ibid., ch. 1, para. 87, p. 18.

83 Ibid., ch. 1, para. 84, p. 16.

84 Price Waterhouse Associates, *Statistics Canada: Organizational Study*, February 1980, 16, STC 2552E.

85 Guy Leclerc interview, 2006.

86 Stewart Wells interview, 2005.

87 Ruggles, "Role of the National Accounts," 90.

CHAPTER SIX

1 *System of National Accounts 1993* (Brussels/Luxembourg, New York, Paris, and Washington: Eurostat, IMF, OECD, UN, and World Bank, 1993), "Foreword" and "Preface."

2 Ibid., "Preface."

3 André Vanoli, *A History of National Accounting* (Amsterdam: IOS Press, 2005), 124.

4 See http://hdr.undp.org/en/francais

5 See Carol Carson, "The History of the United States National Income and Product Accounts: The Development of an Analytical Tool," *Review of Income and Wealth*, ser. 2 (June 1975): 153–81.

6 Vanoli, *A History*, 141.

7 Ibid., 142.

8 Kishori Lal, "Certain Problems in the Implementation of the International System of National Accounts 1993: A Case Study of Canada," *Review of Income and Wealth*, ser. 45 (June 1999): 157–77 at 176.

9 K. Lal, "Remaining Differences between the 1997 Canadian System of National Accounts and the 1993 International System of National Accounts," in *Collected Articles of Kishori Lal: System of National Accounts, 1967–2003*, 141–63 (Ottawa: Statistics Canada, 2003), 151–2.

10 *Economist*, 7 September 1991 and 11 September 1993. The 1993 survey also pointed out that the Canadian national accounts were costly and labour intensive on a national per capita basis.

11 *Globe and Mail*, 6 June (quotation) and 6 October 1979.

12 Sir Claus Moser et al., *Statistics Canada: Methodological Review*, March 1980, 14, Statistics Canada (STC) 2589E.

13 Ian Stewart to Hon. Harvie Andre, 6 December 1984, Minutes of the National Accounts Advisory Committee (hereafter NAAC), 5–6 December 1984; Ian Stewart interview, 2005.

14 NAAC, 28 March 1988.

15 Canada, *Report of the Auditor General* (Ottawa: Supply and Services Canada,

1983), 487; Canada, *Management of Government: Major Surveys – A Study Team Report to the Task Force on Program Review* (Ottawa: Supply and Services Canada, 1986), 66.

16 *Ottawa Citizen*, 24 October 1992.

17 *Globe and Mail*, 18 August 1993.

18 S. Goldberg to S. Wells, 31 January 1985, NAAC, January 1985.

19 Terry Gigantes, quoted in "Final Draft of the Task Force on the Canadian System of National Accounts," 27 September 1972, Library and Archives Canada (LAC), RG 31, vol. 1606, original emphasis.

20 E. Bower Carty to J.M. Léger, 3 January 1975, LAC, RG 31, vol. 1602.

21 See John Sawyer, "Paul R. Pitts, 1934–1979," *Canadian Journal of Economics* 11 (February-November 1978): 719.

22 W. Leontief to K. Lal, 28 March 1977, STC, Lal Collection. Kishori Lal and Yusuf Siddiqi interviews, 2006.

23 S. Goldberg to K. Lal, 16 January 1978, STC, Lal Collection.

24 Joey Smallwood to Walter Duffett, 29 January 1970, LAC, RG 31, vol. 1541.

25 See, for instance, W. Leontief, A.P. Carter, and P.A. Petri, *The Future of the World Economy: A United Nations Study* (New York: Oxford University Press, 1977).

26 See Y.M. Siddiqi and M. Salem, "Regionalization of Commodity-by-Industry Input-Output Accounts: The Canadian Case," STC Input-Output Division, Technical Series No. 87-E, 1995.

27 D. Clancy and P. Smith, "The Treatment of the GST in the Income and Expenditure Accounts," STC Income and Expenditure Accounts Division, Technical Series No. 13, 1991, 16.

28 CTV News, 22 January 1993.

29 Ivan Fellegi to David Dodge, 19 July 1996, NAAC, 12–13 September 1996.

30 Fellegi to David Dodge, 19 July 1996; memo, "Developing Statistics Required for the Provisional Allocation of a Harmonized gst Collection"; both in NAAC, 12–13 September 1996.

31 Ibid.

32 P. Smith, "The Central Goal of PIPES," 17 November 1997, PIPES, Technical Series No. 13, 2.

33 *North American Industry Classification System: Canada 1997* (Ottawa: Statistics Canada, 1998), "Preface," STC 12-501-XPE.

34 See *Provincial Economic Accounts* (Ottawa: Statistics Canada, annual), STC 13-213-PPB.

35 Statens Offentliga Utredningar, *Development and Improvement of Economic Statistics* (Stockholm: Statens Offentliga Utredningar, 2003), 17.

36 Memo on Recessions, NAAC, 25–6 January 1993.

37 H. Mimoto and P. Cross, "The Growth of the Federal Debt," *Canadian Economic Observer*, June 1991 STC 11-010-XPB; also editor's note in August 1991 issue.

38 See, for instance, "Underground Economy Runs Deep," *Vancouver Sun*, 24 June 1993; and "Cheaters: How Dodging Taxes Feeds a Growing Underground Economy," *Maclean's*, 5 November 1993.

39 R. Lipsey to S. Wells, 30 September 1993, NAAC, 16–17 November 1993.

40 Philip Smith, "Assessing the Size of the Underground Economy: The Statistics Canada Perspective," Vancouver presentation, 21–2 April 1994, 22, NAAC, 16–17 September 1993. See also Gylliane Gervais, "The Size of the Underground Economy in Canada" (Ottawa: Statistics Canada) STC 13-603E, no. 2.

41 "Trip Report: Canadian Input-Output Program," attached to Robert Parker to Kishori Lal, 6 August 1992, STC, Lal Collection.

42 NAAC, 28–9 March 1988.

43 Dian Cohen, "The Economic Crisis: A Crisis in the Theory of the State," CABE *News*, Winter 1995, 8–9.

44 NAAC, 15–16 September 1988.

45 "The Real Truth about the Economy: Are Government Statistics So Much Pulp Fiction?" *Business Week*, 7 November 1994.

46 NAAC, 10–11 April 1995.

47 Richard Ruggles, "Possible Future Directions for National Accounts," 3, NAAC, 30 April 1984. See also Richard Ruggles, "The Role of the National Accounts in the Statistical System," in Nancy D. Ruggles and Richard Ruggles, eds, *National Accounting and Economic Policy: The United States and UN Systems*, 70–90 (Cheltenham: Edward Elgar, 1999).

48 NAAC, 28–9 March 1988.

49 Ruggles, "Possible Future," 6.

50 Ian Stewart interview, 2005.

51 See World Tourism Organization, *Yearbook of Tourism Statistics* (Madrid: World Tourism Organization, 1999).

52 National Task Force on Tourism Data, *Newsletter* 1, no. 2 (1986); Shaila Nijhowne interview, 2005.

53 See Federal-Provincial Conference on Tourism, 1972–75, LAC, RG 31, vol. 1606.

54 Statistics Canada, *National Task Force on Tourism Data: Final Report* (Ottawa: Ministry of Supply and Services Canada, 1989), 8.

55 Statistics Canada, *Final Draft Report: National Task Force on Tourism Data* (Ottawa: Ministry of Supply and Services Canada, 1986), 8–12, quotation at 7.

56 Statistics Canada, *National Task Force on Tourism Data*, 11.

57 Ibid., 16.

58 See Vanoli, *A History*, 102, 182–7.

59 OECD, *Tourism Committee: Manual on Tourism Economic Accounts* (Paris: OECD, 1991), 21.

60 J. Lapierre and D. Hayes, "The Tourism Satellite Account," STC National Accounts and Environment Division, Technical Series No. 31, 1994, xxxiv.

61 Ibid.

62 See C. Barber-Dueck and D. Kotsovos, *The Provincial and Territorial Tourism Satellite Accounts for Canada*, STC 13-F0063XPE, 2002.

63 J. Steven Landefeld and Stephanie H. McCulla, "Accounting for Nonmarket Household Production within a National Accounts Framework," *Review of Income and Wealth*, ser. 46, no. 3 (September 2000): 289–307 at 291.

64 Marilyn Waring, *Counting for Nothing: What Men Value and What Women Are Worth* (Wellington, New Zealand: Allen and Unwin, 1988), 264.

65 Ibid.

66 Statistics Canada, *Households' Unpaid Work: Measurement and Valuation*, "Preface," Studies in National Accounting, STC 13-603E.

67 Statistics Canada, *The Value of Household Work in Canada, 1986*, Technical Series No. 19, STC 13–001, 1992. See also United Nations, *Methods of Measuring Women's Economic Activity: Technical Report* (New York: United Nations, 1993).

68 Statistics Canada, *Households' Unpaid Work*, 64.

69 Statistics Canada, *Caring Canadians, Involved Canadians: Highlights from the 1997 National Survey of Giving, Volunteering and Participating*, 10–11, STC 71-542XPE.

70 World Commission on Environment and Development, *Our Common Future* (Oxford and New York: Oxford University Press, 1987), 37–8, 52.

71 Canada, *Canada's Green Plan for a Healthy Environment* (Ottawa: Environment Canada, 1990), 142.

72 Statistics Canada, *The Canadian National Accounts Environmental Component: A Status Report*, 7, STC, National Accounts and Environment Division (NAED), Technical Report No. 30, 1994.

73 See, for instance, André Vanoli, "Reflections on Environmental Accounting Issues," *Review of Income and Wealth*, ser. 41, no. 2 (June 1995): 113–56; and Anthony Scott, "Economists, Environmental Policies and Federalism," in Patrick Grady and Andrew Sharpe, eds, *The State of Economics in Canada: Festschrift in Honour of David Slater*, 405–49 (Montreal and Kingston: McGill-Queen's University Press, 2001).

74 Ivan Fellegi interview, 2006.

75 Clifford Cobb, Ted Halstead, and Jonathan Rowe, "If the GDP Is Up, Why Is America Down?" *Atlantic*, October 1995, 60.

76 See http://hdr.undp.org/en/francais

77 See http://www.pembina.org (quotation) and http://www.pembina.org.

78 As quoted in "NRTEE Indicators Overview Paper Stakeholder Workshop,"
   28 March 2001, 1, NAAC, 25 June 2001.

EPILOGUE

1 S.A. Goldberg, H.J. Adler, J.D. Randall, and P.S. Sunga, "The Canadian
  Quarterly National Accounts: A Critical Appraisal," *Review of Income and
  Wealth*, ser. 11 (1965), reprinted in Preetom S. Sunga, *System of National
  Accounts: Collected Articles of Preetom S. Sunga*, 7–72 (Ottawa: Statistics
  Canada, 1991).
2 A phrase coined by German economists Dieter Brummerhoff and Utz-Peter
  Reich, quoted in T.K. Rymes and Harry H. Postner, "On the Teaching of
  National Accounts and Economics," paper presented to the Canadian Economics Association, 2 June 2000, Vancouver.
3 Roger Jullion interview, 2006.
4 Ibid.
5 *Daily*, 28 February 2006, http://www.statcan.ca/Daily/English. See also
  Statistics Canada, *Canadian Economic Accounts Quarterly Review*, Statistics
  Canada (STC) 13-010-XIE. These and other regular GDP data are available at
  http://www.statcan.ca and through Statistics Canada's CANSIM database.
6 *Globe and Mail*, 1 March 2006.
7 See Statistics Canada, *Canada's International Investment Position*, STC
  67-202.
8 *Ottawa Citizen*, 28 February 2006.
9 *Globe and Mail*, 18 March 2006.
10 See Statistics Canada, *National Balance Sheet Accounts, Quarterly Estimates*,
   STC 13-214-XIE.
11 *Globe and Mail*, 3 October 2005.
12 *Globe and Mail*, 2 January 2006.
13 Ibid.
14 See Statistics Canada, *Provincial Economic Accounts*, STC 13-213-PPB, table
   7.
15 Philip Smith interview, 2006.
16 Kishori Lal interview, 2006.
17 Ivan Fellegi interview, 2006.
18 Lucie Laliberté interview, 2006.
19 Carol Carson interview, 2006.
20 Statisticians have developed a sophisticated mechanism – the chain index –
   to allow for the ongoing economic valuation of goods that fall in price while
   increasing in capacity; see http://www.statcan.ca/english/concepts/chainfisher/
   methodology.htm.

21 See Kari Manninen, "Hedonic Price Indexes for Digital Cameras," *Survey of Current Business*, February 2005, 22–7.

22 See Desmond Beckstead, Mark Brown, Guy Gellatly, and Catherine Seaborn, "A Decade of Growth: Emerging Geography of New Economy Industries in the 1990s," 2003, STC 11-622-MIE No. 003.

23 "Report on the Bureau of Statistics: Economic Analysis and Statistics," November 1961, Library and Archives Canada (LAC), RG 31, vol. 1535.

24 Richard Harris, David Laidler, and Alice Nakamura, "A Biographical Sketch of Walter Erwin Diewert," *Canadian Journal of Economics* 29 (April 1996): 678–95 at 678.

25 *Globe and Mail*, 6 June 2006.

26 Canada, *Annual Report of the Dominion Statistician* (Ottawa: King's Printer, 1941).

27 Lucie Laliberté interview, 2006.

28 André Vanoli, *A History of National Accounting* (Amsterdam: IOS Press, 2005), 485.

29 Some aspiring women economists, however, began to buck the trend. For instance, "The last time I saw you in Ottawa," Betty Robinson MacLeod, a Royal Bank economist, wrote triumphantly to Simon Goldberg on 8 May 1956, "you predicted I would get married and be lost to the world of economists and statisticians – and you were right in the first half of your prediction at any rate"; in LAC, RG 31, vol. 1490.

30 Karen Wilson interview, 2006.

31 *Business Week*, 13 February 2006.

32 Michael Mandel, "Why the Economy Is a Lot Stronger Than You Think," *Business Week*, 13 February 2006, 63–4.

33 *Economist*, 11 and 18 February 2006.

34 These issues are all listed, accompanied by a status report on their progress and the reaction of UN member nations to each proposed outcome, at http://unstats.un.org/unsd/sna1993/issues.asp.

35 Carol Carson interview, 2006.

36 Ibid.

37 See "1993 SNA Update Issues," http://unstats.un.org/unsd/sna1993/issues.asp.

38 Robert Solow, quoted in Carol Corrado, Charles Hulten, and Daniel Sichel, "Measuring Capital and Technology: An Expanded Framework," in Carol Corrado, John Haltiwanger, and Danile Sichel, eds, *Measuring Capital in the New Economy*, 11–45 (Chicago: University of Chicago Press, 2005).

39 Ricardo Hausmann and Federica Sturzenegger, "'Dark Matter' Makes the US Deficit Disappear," *Financial Times*, 8 December 2005.

40 Dale W. Jorgenson, J. Steven Landefeld, and William D. Nordhaus, eds,
    A New Architecture for the U.S. National Accounts (Chicago: University
    of Chicago Press, 2006).

41 J.M. Keynes, *The General Theory of Employment, Income and Money* (New
    York: Harcourt, Brace, and World, 1936), 383.

42 Paul A. Samuelson and William D. Nordhaus, *Economics*, 15th ed. (New
    York: McGraw-Hill, 1995), 402.

43 Jeremy Bentham, *Fragment of Government* (1776).

44 See World Bank, *Where Is the Wealth of Nations? Measuring Capital in the
    21st Century* (Washington, DC: World Bank, 2006).

45 Philip Smith, "Rethinking the System of National Accounts: What Is Needed
    for the 21st Century?" 2, STC speech text, June 2002.

46 See Statistics Canada, *Concepts, Sources and Methods of the Canadian
    System of Environmental and Resource Accounts*, 1997 STC 16-505-GPE.

47 Robert Smith interview, 2006.

48 See United Nations, Commission of the European Communities, IMF, OECD,
    and World Bank, *Integrated Environmental and Economic Accounting 2003*,
    UN document, ser. F, no. 61, rev. 1, 2003.

49 See, for instance, William D. Nordhaus and Edward C. Kokkelenberg, eds,
    *Nature's Numbers: Expanding the National Economic Accounts to Include
    the Environment* (Washington, DC: National Academic Press, 1999).

50 See Statistics Canada, *Satellite Account of Nonprofit Institutions and Volun-
    teering*, STC 13-015-XIE.

51 See Leroy O. Stone, ed., *New Frontiers of Research on Retirement*, 2006 STC
    75-511-XPE.

52 George Luxton, "Wanted: Jobs after the War," 11 December 1944, John J.
    Deutsch Papers, Queen's University Archives.

Index

Stevens, Sinclair, 199
Stewart, Ian, 214, 233
Stone, Leroy, 177, 179
Stone, Richard, 8, 64, 66–7, 71, 76,
   78, 80, 84–6, 90, 100, 102,
   110–11, 113, 118, 122, 160, 163,
   207, 209, 239, 261
Strategic Bombing Survey, 68
Stress-Response Environmental
   Statistical System, 184
Studenski, Paul, 41
Student Christian Movement, 89–90,
   92
Sun Life Assurance Company, 71,
   79–80, 82, 88, 91, 95, 128
Sunga, Preetom, 190
Survey of Current Business, 67
Symons, Tom, 213
System of National Accounts, 1968,
   162
System of National Accounts, 1993,
   8–9, 205–6, 211, 221
System of Socio-Demographic
   Statistics (ssds), 177–9

tableaux economiques, 25, 149
Talon, Jean, 28
Tarshis, Lorie, 70, 77
Taylor, Kenneth, 131
Tebrake, Jim, 247
Thom, René, 184
Timlin, Mabel, 73–4, 78, 94, 114
Tinbergen, Jan, 142, 163, 190
Tobin, James, 10, 68, 92, 172
tourism, 131, 234–6
Towers, Graham, 54, 71–2, 77–8,
   85, 108

Trudeau, Pierre E., 165–7, 182, 188,
   195, 197, 201
Tupper, Charles, 87

underground economy, 229–30
unemployment insurance, 75
United Nations' Statistical Division,
   9, 12, 118, 168
unpaid work, 238–9, 272
Urquhart, Malcolm "Mac," 82, 87,
   93, 145, 232
Usher, Dan, 190

Vander Noot, T.J., 141
Vanoli, André, xi, 190, 208–9, 263
Victor, Peter, 296n37
Viner, Jacob, 131

Walters, Dorothy, 137
Waring, Marilyn, 10, 169, 237
Wartime Prices and Trade Board, 57,
   85, 129
Wells, Stewart, 195–6, 203–4, 208,
   215, 230, 259
Willsher, Mary Kathleen, 105–6
Wilgress, Dana, 55
Wilk, Martin, 203, 215–16, 243
Wilkinson, Joe, 252
Wilson, Karen, 253–4, 263–6, 270
World Tourism Organization, 234–5
Wood, Kingsley, 67
World Trade Centre: 11 September
   2001 attacks, 269
Wright, Charles, 252

Young, Arthur, 26–7